Plate 1   Default stationery pad icons

1 bit	4 bit	8 bit

Plate 2   Default part-editor icons

1 bit	4 bit	8 bit

Plate 3   Default part-viewer icons

1 bit	4 bit	8 bit

Plate 4   Custom icons

Document

        1 bit   4 bit   8 bit

Stationery

        1 bit   4 bit   8 bit

Part editor

            1 bit   4 bit   8 bit

Part viewer

            1 bit   4 bit   8 bit

Plate 5   Selected appearance of icons

Icon   Highlighted   Selected   Background
            icon   border   selection

Apple
PRESS

OpenDoc Programmer's Guide

For the Mac OS

Addison-Wesley Publishing Company

Reading, Massachusetts   Menlo Park, California   New York
Don Mills, Ontario   Wokingham, England   Amsterdam   Bonn
Sydney   Singapore   Tokyo   Madrid   San Juan
Paris   Seoul   Milan   Mexico City   Taipei

ISBN 0-201-47954-0
1 2 3 4 5 6 7 8 9-MA-0099989796
First Printing, December 1995

Library of Congress Cataloging-in-Publication Data

Apple Computer, Inc.
    OpenDoc programmer's guide for the Mac OS
        p.   cm.
    Includes index.
    ISBN 0-201-47954-0
    1. Cross-platform software development.   2. Macintosh (Computer)—
Programming.   I. Title.
QA76.76.D47A67   1996
005.7—dc20
                                                                    95-46579
                                                                    CIP

Contents

Figures and Tables

Chapter 12   Basic Interface Elements   509

Chapter 13   Guidelines for Part Display   553

Chapter 14   Guidelines for Content Manipulation   581

About This Book

OpenDoc is a set of shared libraries that you can use to build editors and viewers for compound documents, as well as other component software. This book, the *OpenDoc Programmer's Guide for the Mac OS*, describes how to use those libraries to develop OpenDoc part editors for the Mac OS platform on Macintosh and Mac-compatible computers.

This book is a companion to the *OpenDoc Class Reference for the Mac OS*, which provides reference documentation to the classes, methods, types, constants, and exceptions defined by OpenDoc. The *Programmer's Guide* provides an architectural overview, synthesizes design concepts, and gives specific programming recommendations to illuminate and make more accessible the large amount of information documented in the *Class Reference*. The *OpenDoc Class Reference for the Mac OS* is included on the CD-ROM that accompanies this book.

This book does not provide code samples. For detailed tutorial instructions and code listings taken from functioning Mac OS part editors, see the *OpenDoc Cookbook for the Mac OS*. Code samples from the *OpenDoc Cookbook for the Mac OS* and from other sources are included on the CD-ROM that accompanies this book.

What to Read

This is the first book to read if you intend to develop a part editor. It contains three parts: overview information, programming instructions, and human interface guidelines.

Part 1, "Basics," contains two chapters that you should read before reading any other parts of the book.

- Chapter 1, "Introduction to OpenDoc," provides a high-level overview of OpenDoc, from both the user's and programmer's point of view.

- Chapter 2, "Development Overview," briefly presents the OpenDoc class library and gives general strategies for part-editor development.

Part 2, "Programming," consists of nine chapters that describe the OpenDoc programming interface and give detailed programming suggestions. Read the chapters in any order, as you need the specific information they contain.

- Chapter 3, "Frames and Facets," describes how your part uses frames and facets to lay itself out correctly, to interact with its containing part, and to embed other parts within itself.

- Chapter 4, "Drawing," describes how your part uses canvases, frames, facets, shapes, and transforms to draw and print its contents correctly.

- Chapter 5, "User Events," describes how your part responds to user manipulation, including how it activates itself and how it responds to mouse events and other types of user events.

- Chapter 6, "Windows and Menus," describes how your part can set up and manipulate the elements of its user interface, such as windows, dialog boxes, controls, and menus.

- Chapter 7, "Storage," presents OpenDoc storage concepts and describes how your part stores its data.

- Chapter 8, "Data Transfer," describes how your part can use the clipboard, drag and drop, and linking facilities of OpenDoc.

- Chapter 9, "Semantic Events and Scripting," describes how your part can use OpenDoc to respond to and send scripting commands.

- Chapter 10, "Extending OpenDoc," describes how your part can extend its capabilities through the OpenDoc extension mechanism and how it can use the existing extensions provided with OpenDoc.

- Chapter 11, "OpenDoc Runtime Features," describes the general runtime environment within which your part editor executes. It describes how to create and release objects, discusses binding, illustrates the runtime relationships among OpenDoc objects, and describes the OpenDoc document shell, the part of OpenDoc that represents the process in which your part editor runs.

Part 3, "Human Interface Guidelines," consists of three chapters that describe both the visual interface and the interactions your part should provide for users.

- Chapter 12, "Basic Interface Elements," describes the recommended appearances for basic interface elements such as icons, pointers, and borders.

- Chapter 13, "Guidelines for Part Display," describes how to display your parts, including where to place windows, how to indicate complex selections, when to activate your part, and how to provide multiple views of your part's content.

- Chapter 14, "Guidelines for Content Manipulation," describes how to interact with the user to modify the contents of your part, including adding and resizing frames, creating sequenced frames, undoing commands, and transferring data through the clipboard, drag and drop, or linking.

Three appendixes give summary information:

- Appendix A, "Embedding Checklist," summarizes the tasks your part must perform to be a container part—that is, to be able to embed other parts within itself.

- Appendix B, "HI Checklist," summarizes the considerations to keep in mind during development to make sure that your part presents a correct and consistent user interface.

- Appendix C, "Installing OpenDoc Software and Parts," shows how and where to install the results of your development efforts—part editors, stationery documents, extensions, shell plug-ins, and help files—onto the user's machine.

The glossary at the end of this book applies to all of the OpenDoc developer documentation. The glossary includes terms used in the *Class Reference* and the *Cookbook* as well as in this book.

Conventions Used in This Book

This book uses various conventions to present certain types of information.

Special Fonts

All code listings, reserved words, and the names of data structures, constants, fields, parameters, and functions are shown in Letter Gothic (`this is Letter Gothic`).

Types of Notes

There are several types of notes used in this book.

Note
A note formatted like this contains information that is interesting but possibly not essential to an understanding of the main text. The title may be more descriptive than "Note," for example, "Runtime relationships." (An example appears on page 44.) ◆

IMPORTANT
A note like this contains information that is especially important. (An example appears on page 282.) ▲

Mac-Specific Information

OpenDoc is a cross-platform technology, and most of its concepts and features are platform-independent. Thus, even though this book is specifically designed for Mac OS developers, the information is organized and presented in as platform-neutral a manner as possible.

In most sections of this book, aspects of a topic that are specific to Mac OS are called out as such. That way, you can get at least a general idea of how platform-specific your code must be, and therefore how simple or complex it may be to convert it to another platform.

Note on Code Presentation

In an attempt to be as language-neutral as possible, this book presents very little code. Prototypes for the methods of `ODPart`, where presented, are in the System Object Model (SOM) Interface Definition Language (IDL). As an example of what IDL prototypes look like, here is the prototype for the `AddProperty` method of `ODStorageUnit`:

```
ODStorageUnit AddProperty(in ODPropertyName propertyName);
```

Note the directional attribute ("in") that precedes the type designation of the single parameter.

The few short listings of implementation code are in C++. In implementation listings, note that every call to a method of a SOM-based class (as all OpenDoc classes are) includes an extra parameter, the environment parameter, that does not appear in the method's IDL prototype. Here is an example (in C++) of a call to the `AddProperty` method:

```
su->AddProperty(ev, kODPropContents);
```

The OpenDoc Class Reference CD-ROM

This book is accompanied by the *OpenDoc Class Reference CD-ROM*, a CD-ROM disc that contains the complete text of the *OpenDoc Class Reference for the Mac OS*. The *OpenDoc Class Reference for the Mac OS* is the complete reference to the OpenDoc programming interface. It documents all classes, methods, types, and constants defined by OpenDoc for use by part-editor developers.

The *OpenDoc Class Reference CD-ROM* includes two electronic versions of the *Class Reference* plus additional useful programming information. The CD-ROM contains these items, among others:

- The complete *OpenDoc Class Reference for the Mac OS* in QuickView format— the same format used by the *Macintosh Programmer's Toolbox Assistant*. In this format, you can use full-text searching capabilities and ubiquitous hypertext jumps to find reference information quickly. You can even search for information and retrieve method templates from within development environments that can communicate with QuickView.

21

- The complete *OpenDoc Class Reference for the Mac OS* in Adobe™ Acrobat™ format. This format provides a fully formatted book with page-numbered table of contents, index, and cross-references. You can print all or portions of the book, and you can also view it online. When viewing online, you can use the indexed search facilities of Adobe Acrobat Reader 2.1 for fast lookup of any information in the book.

- Source code for SamplePart, the sample part editor developed by the OpenDoc team. SamplePart is documented fully in the *OpenDoc Cookbook for the Mac OS*.

- Additional source code for other part-editor samples.

- The complete set of OpenDoc recipes created by the OpenDoc development team. Recipes are short, informal documents that illustrate specific points about OpenDoc programming and typically include brief fragments of sample code.

The *OpenDoc Class Reference CD-ROM* also includes an Adobe Acrobat version of this book (the *Programmer's Guide)*, plus relevant articles from *develop* magazine and other useful documentation.

Developer Products and Support

APDA

APDA is Apple's worldwide source for over three hundred development tools, technical resources, training products, and information for anyone interested in developing applications on Apple platforms. Customers receive the quarterly APDA Tools Catalog featuring all current versions of Apple development tools and the most popular third-party development tools. Ordering is easy; there are no membership fees, and application forms are not required for most of our products. APDA offers convenient payment and shipping options, including site licensing.

To order products or to request a complimentary copy of the APDA Tools Catalog, contact

APDA
Apple Computer, Inc.
P.O. Box 319
Buffalo, NY 14207-0319

Telephone	800-282-2732 (United States)
	800-637-0029 (Canada)
	716-871-6555 (International)
Fax	716-871-6511
AppleLink	APDA
America Online	APDAorder
CompuServe	76666,2405
Internet	APDA@applelink.apple.com

If you provide commercial products and services, call 408-974-4897 for information on the developer support programs available from Apple.

CI Labs

Component Integration Laboratories, Inc. (CI Labs) is a nonprofit association dedicated to promoting the adoption of OpenDoc as a vendor-neutral industry standard for software integration and component software.

CI Labs supports several levels of participation through different membership categories. If you are interested in shaping the future direction of component software, or if you simply need to be kept abreast of the latest developments, you can become a member. The CI Labs association is growing rapidly as understanding and support of OpenDoc increase, and we look forward to hearing from you.

Component Integration Laboratories, Inc.
PO Box 61747
Sunnyvale, CA 94088-1747

Telephone	(408) 864-0300
Fax	(408) 864-0380
Internet	CILABS@CILABS.ORG
World Wide Web	http://www.cilabs.org

Basics

Introduction to OpenDoc

Contents

OpenDoc is a revolutionary technology that brings a new class of applications and documents to the Windows™, Mac OS, OS/2, UNIX®, and other personal-computer platforms. With OpenDoc, hardware and software developers can deliver new software technologies to individual users, better server integration to corporate users, and enhanced multimedia content to all users.

OpenDoc enables the creation of a new kind of software. This cooperative component software supports compound documents, can be customized, can be used collaboratively across networks, and is available on multiple platforms. In doing so, OpenDoc fundamentally changes the nature of software development for personal computers.

This chapter starts with a review of the reasons why OpenDoc was created, followed by an overview of OpenDoc concepts: how OpenDoc documents are structured, how OpenDoc software handles events and user interaction, how to extend OpenDoc's capabilities, and how to ensure cross-platform compatibility for your OpenDoc software. Each of these topics is developed more fully in subsequent chapters.

Why OpenDoc?

Customer demand for increasingly sophisticated and integrated software solutions has led to large and sometimes unwieldy application packages, feature-laden but difficult to maintain and modify. Developing, maintaining, and upgrading these large, cumbersome applications can require a vast organization; the programs are difficult to create, they are expensive to maintain, and they can take years to revise.

Upgrading or fixing bugs in one component of such an application requires the developer to release—and the customer to buy—a completely new version of the entire package. Some developers have added extension mechanisms to their packages to allow addition or replacement of certain components, but the extensions are proprietary, incompatible with other applications, and applicable only to certain parts of the package.

Because of the barriers put up by the current application architecture, users are often frustrated in attempting to perform common tasks.

■ Users often cannot assemble complex documents from multiple sources because of the many error-prone, manual operations required.

■ Users usually cannot edit different kinds of content within a single document. Most applications support only one or a few different kinds of content, such as a single format for text and a single format for graphics. Furthermore, the editing procedures for a given kind of content are different across applications, complicating data transfer among applications.

■ Business users are forced to choose between the reliability of shrink-wrapped software and the extra features of custom solutions designed for their needs. To increase reliability while maintaining and adding custom features, businesses need simple and standardized designs and procedures.

■ Business users, whose hardware is often heterogeneous, demand cross-platform versions of their application packages. At the same time, application developers wish to leverage their development investment by delivering their software on multiple platforms. But the conflicting requirements and user-interface conventions of different platforms make cross-platform software difficult to develop and confusing to use.

■ Users may not be able to use an editor or tool provided by an individual developer or small development team because the editor may be incompatible with the users' current application package, and the developer may have insufficient resources to develop an entire integrated package.

■ Computers often frustrate users' efforts to collaborate with others. Users cannot share documents across applications, recover changes to shared documents, or, with rare exceptions, manipulate the contents of one document from within another.

OpenDoc addresses these issues by defining a new kind of application, one with advantages to both users and developers in the increasingly competitive software markets of today and the future. OpenDoc replaces the architecture of monolithic **conventional applications,** in which a single software package is responsible for all of its documents' contents, with one of **components,** in which each software module edits its own content, no matter what document that content may be in. See Figure 1-1.

Figure 1-1   Monolithic application versus components

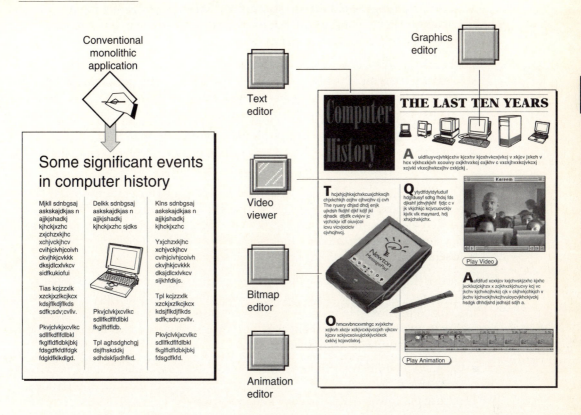

OpenDoc allows developers, large or small, to take a modular approach to development and maintenance. Its component-software architecture makes the design, development, testing, and marketing of integrated software packages far easier and more reliable. Developers can make incremental improvements to products without a complete revision cycle and can get those improvements to users far more rapidly than is possible today.

For programmers, this is a radical shift in approach, although its implementation is not difficult. For users, this is only a minor shift in working style; its main effect is to remove the barriers to constructing and using complex documents imposed by conventional monolithic application architecture. It gives them what they are used to, plus more.

OpenDoc components allow users to assemble custom **compound documents** out of diverse types of data. They also support cross-platform sharing of information. They resolve user frustrations with conventional applications by removing the barriers listed earlier.

- OpenDoc makes it easy for users to assemble any kind of content in any kind of document. OpenDoc documents will accept all kinds of media for which components exist, now and in the future.

- OpenDoc makes it easy for users to edit any kind of data, in place, in any document. Users can readily transfer that data to any other document and edit it there just as easily. Users can focus on document content and take advantage of the context provided by the surrounding document.

- OpenDoc allows businesses to customize their software solutions by assembling components into shrink-wrapped packages, thereby obtaining needed features, increasing reliability, and saving on training costs. In-house developers can then enhance the packages by developing components that integrate smoothly with the off-the-shelf software.

Some developers bundle components together into packages that are similar to conventional monolithic applications; others sell individual components for specialized purposes, to users or to other developers for bundling. Users can purchase packages and use them as is, or they can modify a package by adding or replacing individual components.

- OpenDoc documents are potentially transferable across platforms. OpenDoc components are easy to port and easy to integrate with existing applications on any platform.

- OpenDoc lowers market barriers to wide, cross-platform distribution for small developers. Any component can be designed to work in any OpenDoc document on any platform. Small development teams can create individual components with the knowledge that they will integrate smoothly with existing packages created by larger developers.

- OpenDoc promotes collaboration, allowing users simultaneously or separately to build documents as a team, on a single machine or across networks. Documents are not owned by single applications, and changes are recoverable through a draft history that is available for every document. Pervasive scripting support, rich data-transfer capabilities, and an extension mechanism allow users to manipulate their own and other documents in powerful ways.

While providing these advantages, OpenDoc exists harmoniously with existing monolithic applications; the user need not abandon conventional applications in order to start using OpenDoc. Furthermore, it is relatively easy for a developer, as a first step toward adopting OpenDoc, to modify a conventional application so that it works with OpenDoc components.

Table 1-1 summarizes some of the principal advantages of the OpenDoc approach to software, for both users and developers.

Table 1-1   OpenDoc advantages

	For users	For software engineering	For software marketing	For small development teams
Modularity	Can easily add or replace document parts	Can easily test and upgrade components; can reuse components	Can assemble packages with great flexibility	Can create components that work seamlessly with all others
Small size	Less memory and disk space needed	Easier to design, code, debug, and test	Easier, cheaper distribution	Faster development, easier distribution of a component
Multiple platforms	Documents may travel across platforms; users select familiar editors on each	Development effort on one platform can be leveraged to others	Opportunities for increased market share	Application of limited resources can be used across different platforms
Scriptability/ extensibility	Greater control over behavior of document parts	Increased ability for communication among parts	Better coordination among components in a package	Increased ability to communicate with other components

What OpenDoc Is

OpenDoc is a set of shared libraries designed to facilitate the easy construction of compound, customizable, collaborative, and cross-platform documents. To do this, OpenDoc replaces today's *application-centered* user model with a *document-centered* one. The user focuses on constructing a document or performing an individual task, rather than using any particular application. The software that manipulates a document is hidden, and users feel that they are manipulating the parts of the document without having to launch or switch applications.

This document-centered model does not mean that OpenDoc supports only those kinds of data found in paper documents; an OpenDoc document can contain data as diverse as navigable movies, sounds, animation, and database information such as networked calendars or virtual folders as well as traditional spreadsheets, graphics, and text. OpenDoc is an ideal architecture for multimedia documents. In OpenDoc, each new kind of medium—video, sound, animation, simulation, and so on—can be represented as a part of any document. Thus, an OpenDoc document is automatically able to contain future kinds of media, even kinds not yet envisioned, without any modification.

Although OpenDoc lends itself directly to complex and sophisticated layout, its usefulness is by no means restricted to page-layout applications or even compound documents. The scripting and extension mechanisms allow for communication among parts of a document for any imaginable purpose. Tools such as spelling checkers, when created as components, can access the contents of any parts in a document that support them; database-access components can feed information to any parts of a document; larger programs such as high-end printing applications can use specialized components to manipulate the data of all parts of a document for purposes such as proof printing and color matching.

The rest of this chapter summarizes the main features of OpenDoc, for both users and developers; the rest of this book explains in more detail how to develop software that provides those features.

Parts

OpenDoc uses a few simple ideas to create a structure that integrates a wide range of capabilities. The basic elements are *documents,* their *parts,* their *frames,* and the *part-editor* code that manipulates them. Those elements, represented in a set of object-oriented class libraries, define a number of object classes. The classes provide interoperability protocols that allow independently developed software components to cooperate in producing a single document for the end user. Through the class libraries, these cooperating components share user-interface resources, negotiate document layout onscreen and on printing devices, share storage containers, and create data links to one another.

This section describes what part editors, parts, and frames are and how parts are categorized, drawn, and stored in documents. It also describes the two different kinds of part editors, and points out that you can develop other kinds of OpenDoc components as well.

Documents, Parts, and Embedding

Documents, not applications, are at the center of OpenDoc. Individual documents are not tied to individual applications. In creating OpenDoc documents, collections of software components called **part editors** replace the conventional monolithic applications in common use today. Each part editor is responsible only for manipulating data of one or more specific kinds in a document.

The user does not directly launch or execute part editors, however. The user works with **document parts** (or just **parts**), the pieces of a document that, when executing, include both the document data and the part-editor code that manipulates it. See Figure 1-2.

Figure 1-2   Parts in an OpenDoc document

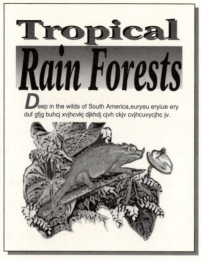
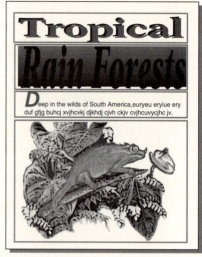

A page as it normally appears   A page with part boundaries shown

A part can exist as document on its own, or it can be **embedded** in other parts, allowing the user to create documents of arbitrary complexity.

Parts and the User

In general, a user can perform all the tasks of an application by manipulating a part instead of separately launching or executing its controlling software. For example, a user can create and use a spreadsheet part that looks and acts just like a spreadsheet created by a spreadsheet application. However, there are four main differences between a document consisting of parts and a document created by a conventional application:

■ An OpenDoc document is built and manipulated differently. OpenDoc users can assemble a document out of parts of any kind—using their graphics part editor of choice, for example, to embed illustrations within a word-processor document. Developers can write or assemble such groups of part editors for sale as integrated packages, or users can purchase individual part editors separately.

■ New parts of any kind can be added to an OpenDoc document. The user can purchase additional part editors—for example, a charting utility to accompany a spreadsheet—and immediately use them, for example, to embed charts into existing documents.

■ In editing, copying, or pasting a part, the user need not be aware of the code that is executing. In fact, the user cannot directly launch a part editor at all. The user manipulates the part data itself, within the context of the document. (It is not necessary to open the part into a separate window for editing.) The document containing that part is opened and closed independently of the part's part editor.

■ The user can replace part editors. If the editor for a specific kind of part in a document is not available, or if the user prefers to use a different part editor—for example, to replace one charting utility with another—the user can specify that the new editor be used with all parts created under the previous editor. Thus, the user has the freedom to work with all of the editors of a package or replace any of them with others that the user prefers.

Part Editors

A part editor has fewer responsibilities than a conventional application. Each part editor must

■ display its part, both onscreen and when printing

■ edit its part, by changing the state of the part in response to events caused by user actions

■ store its part, both persistently and at runtime

At runtime, a part is the equivalent of an object-oriented programmatic object in that it encapsulates both state and behavior. The part data provides the state information, and the part editor provides the behavior; when bound together, they form an editable object. As with any programmatic object, only the state is stored when the object is stored. Also, multiple instantiations of an object do not mean multiple copies of the editor code; one part editor in memory serves as the code portion for any number of separate parts that it edits.

OpenDoc dynamically links part editors to their parts at runtime, choosing an editor based on the kinds of data that a part contains. Dynamic linking is necessary for a smooth user experience because any sort of part might appear in any document at any time.

Other Software Components

A user can apply several kinds of OpenDoc components to compound documents. A part editor, as noted earlier, is a full-featured OpenDoc component; it allows the creation, editing, and viewing of document parts of a particular kind. Part editors are the functional replacements for conventional applications; they represent the developer's primary investment. Like applications, part editors are sold or licensed and are legally protected from unauthorized copying and distribution. On the Mac OS platform, a part editor's name, copyright statement, and credits can appear in an "About…" dialog box accessible through the Apple menu.

A **part viewer** is a special variety of part editor that can display and print a part of a particular kind but cannot be used to create or even edit such a part. To enhance the portability of OpenDoc compound documents across machines and across platforms, developers are expected to create and freely distribute part viewers without restriction, for all kinds of parts that they support. A part viewer is really just a part editor with its editing and part-creation capability removed; the developer can create both from the same code base.

Wide availability of a particular part viewer encourages purchase and use of its equivalent part editor, because users will know that other users will be able to view parts created with that editor. (In some cases it is possible to view a part even when neither its editor nor viewer is present; see the discussion of translation in the section "Part Data Types" on page 41.)

The OpenDoc architecture also allows for the development of software components that, unlike part editors, are not directly involved in storing, editing, and displaying document parts. Special components called **services,** for example, could provide software services to parts or documents. Spelling checkers or database-access tools, when developed as services, could increase the capabilities of part editors. Users could apply them to a single part, to all the parts of a document, or even across separate documents.

Version 1.0 of OpenDoc provides complete support for part editors and part viewers. Future releases may explicitly support services and other types of component software as well.

Frames and Embedding

Parts in an OpenDoc document are hierarchically arranged. The logical structure of a document, which underlies its visual presentation, consists of the embedding relationships among its parts and their frames.

Parts are displayed in **frames,** bounded areas that display a part's contents. Frames are commonly rectangular, but may be any shape. The **display frame** of one part—the frame within which the part is viewed—can itself be embedded within the content of another part. Figure 1-3 shows such a relationship: the inner frame is an **embedded frame** of the outer part, the inner part is an **embedded part** of the outer part, and the outer part is the **containing part** of the inner part.

Figure 1-3   A containing part and an embedded part

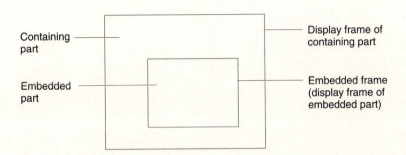

Containing part

Embedded part

Display frame of containing part

Embedded frame (display frame of embedded part)

An embedded part is logically contained in its containing part, just as its frame is visually embedded in the containing part's frame. The containing part, however, largely ignores the characteristics of its embedded parts. The containing part treats its embedded frames as regular elements of its own content; it moves, selects, deletes, or otherwise manipulates them, without regard to what they display. The embedded part itself takes care of all drawing and event handling within an embedded frame.

Every document has a single part at its top level, the **root part,** in which all other parts of the document are directly or indirectly embedded. The root part controls the basic layout structure of the document (such as text or graphics) and the document's overall printing behavior. Figure 1-4 shows an example of the relationships of the root part and two embedded parts:

■ Part 1, a text part, is the root part.

■ Part 2, a graphics part, is embedded in part 1.

■ Part 3, another text part, is embedded in part 2.

Each embedded part is displayed within its frame, which is embedded at some location in the containing part's content. (See Figure 1-11 on page 55 for an explanation of the visual characteristics of the frame borders.)

Figure 1-4   Parts and frames in a document

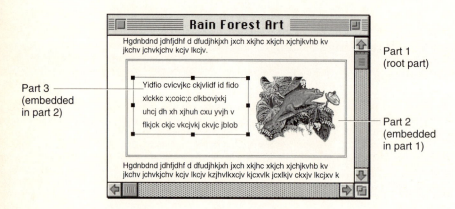

Because it can contain embedded frames displaying any kind of content, the document is not a monolithic block of data under the control of a single application. It is instead composed of many smaller blocks of content controlled by many smaller software components. In large part, OpenDoc exists to provide the protocols that keep the components from getting in each other's way at runtime and to keep documents editable and uncorrupted.

All parts can be embedded in other parts, and every part must be able to function as the root part of a document. However, not all parts must have the ability to embed other parts; simple or specialized utilities such as clocks or sound players may have no reason to contain other parts. Such parts are called **noncontainer parts** (or *monolithic parts*); they can be embedded in any part, but they cannot embed other parts within themselves. Parts that can embed as well as be embedded are called **container parts.** It is somewhat simpler to write an editor for a noncontainer part than for a container part, although container parts provide a far more general and flexible user experience. Unless embedding makes absolutely no sense for your purposes, you should create part editors that support embedding.

Parts can have more than one display frame
A part embedded in a document is not restricted to
appearing in a single frame. Parts can have multiple
frames, displaying either duplicate views or different
aspects of the same part. See "Presentation" on page 48 for
more information. ◆

Part Data Types

Fundamental to the idea of a compound document is that it can hold different
types of data. Each part editor can manipulate only its own data, called its
intrinsic content. For a simple bitmap-drawing part, for example, the elements
of its intrinsic content may be bitmaps; for a simple text part, they may be
characters, words, and paragraphs. If a part contains an embedded part, that
embedded content is manipulated by its own part editor. No part editor is
asked to manipulate the content elements of any part whose data it does not
understand.

OpenDoc supports both specific and general classifications of data type, so that
it may associate parts with specific part editors as well as well as with general
classes of part editors when appropriate.

Part Kind

Different parts in a document hold data of different purpose and different
format, understandable to different part editors. For meaningful drawing and
editing to occur, OpenDoc must be able to associate a part editor only with data
that the editor can properly manipulate.

OpenDoc uses the concept of **part kind,** a typing scheme analogous to file type,
to determine what part editor to associate with a given part in a document.
Because OpenDoc documents are not associated with any single application, a
file type is insufficient in this case; each part within a document needs its own
"type," or in this case, part kind.

Part kinds are specified as **ISO strings,** null-terminated 7-bit ASCII strings. A
part kind specifies the exact data format manipulated by an editor; it may have
a name similar to the editor name, such as "SurfDraw" or "SurfBase III",
although names more descriptive of the creator and the specific data format
itself, such as "SurfCorp:Movie:QuickTime", are preferable. (The user of such a
part would see a different but related string describing the part kind, which in
this case might be "SurfTime movie".)

Part-editor developers define the part kinds of their own editors. A single editor can manipulate more than one part kind, if it is designed to so, and a single part can be stored with multiple representations of its data, each of a different part kind. All parts created by an editor initially have its part kind (or kinds), although that can change; see "Changing Part Editors" on page 44.

Part Category

The concept of part kind does not address the similarities among many data formats. For example, data stored as plain ASCII or Unicode text could conceivably be manipulated by any of a number of part editors. Likewise, video data stored according to a standard might be manipulated by many different video editors. Furthermore, text that closely resembles ASCII or Unicode, and stored video that adheres in all but a few details to a particular standard, might nevertheless be editable or displayable to some extent by many text editors or video editors.

It might be unduly confining to restrict the editing or display of a part of a given kind to the exact part editor that actually created it. Unless the user has every part editor that created a document, the user cannot edit or even view all parts of it. Instead, OpenDoc facilitates the substitution of part editors by defining **part category,** a general description of the kind of data manipulated by a part editor. When users speak of a "text part" or a "graphics part," they are using an informal designation of part category.

Like part kinds, part categories are specified as ISO strings. Part categories have broad designations, such as "plain text", "styled text", "bitmap", or "database". Part-editor developers work with **Component Integration Laboratories (CI Labs),** a consortium created to coordinate cross-platform OpenDoc development, to define the list of part categories recognized by OpenDoc. See "Cross-Platform Consistency and CI Labs" on page 71 for more information on CI Labs. See Table 11-2 on page 477 for a list of defined part categories.

Each part editor specifies the part categories that it can manipulate. For each defined part category (such as "plain text") the user can then specify a **default editor** (such as "SurfWriter 3.0") to use as a default with any part in that category whose **preferred editor**—the part editor that created it or last edited it—is missing.

Embedding Versus Incorporating

When the user pastes data into a document, the pasted data can either be incorporated into the intrinsic content of the destination part (the part receiving the data), or it can become a separate embedded part. As Figure 1-5 shows, the destination part—the part receiving the data—decides whether to embed or incorporate the data. It bases the decision on how closely the part kind and category of the pasted data match the part kind and category of the destination content.

Figure 1-5   Embedding versus incorporating pasted data

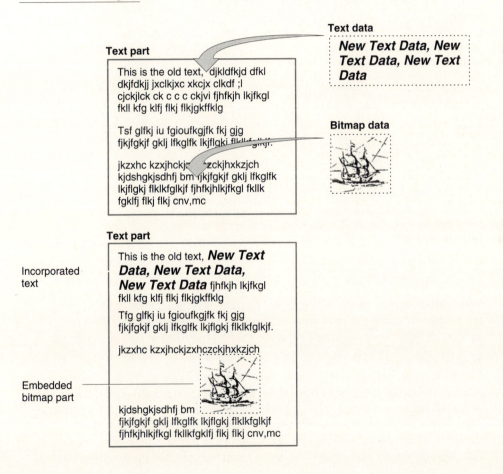

This is how the decision is made:

■ If the part kinds of pasted data and destination match, the data should be incorporated; the SurfWriter text shown in Figure 1-5, for example, is pasted into the intrinsic data of the SurfWriter (text) part.

■ If the part categories are different, the pasted data should be embedded; the SurfPaint bitmap shown in Figure 1-5, for example, is embedded in the SurfWriter text part.

■ If the part categories are the same but the part kinds are different (a possibility not shown in Figure 1-5), the destination part should, if possible, convert the data to its own kind and then incorporate it. Of course, if the destination part cannot read the part kind of the pasted data, it should embed it as a separate part.

In all of these cases, it is the destination part that decides whether to embed or to incorporate. The user can guide that decision by manually forcing a paste to be an incorporation or an embedding; see "Handling the Paste As Dialog Box" on page 337 for more information.

Note
For the data being pasted, *part kind* and *part category* refer to the kind and category of the outermost, or enclosing, data. There may be any number of parts embedded within that data, of various kinds and categories. Those parts are always transferred as embedded parts, regardless of whether the outermost data is itself incorporated or embedded. ◆

Changing Part Editors

When a part editor stores or retrieves the data of its part, it can only manipulate it using the part kind or kinds that the editor understands and prefers. Furthermore, different systems may have different sets of available part editors. Therefore, the editor assigned to a part can change over the part's lifetime.

For example, the user might open a document (or paste data) containing a part of a kind for which the user does not have the original part editor. In that case, OpenDoc substitutes the user's default editor for that part kind or part category (if the default editor can read any of the part's existing part kinds). If the default editor cannot read the part, OpenDoc searches for an editor that can. Once OpenDoc locates and assigns a new editor to the part and the user saves changes, the new editor then becomes the part's preferred editor, and it subsequently stores the part's data using its own part kinds. See the section "Binding" on page 474 for more detailed information on this process.

Lack of a part editor never prevents a user from opening a document. If no editor on the user's system can read any of the part kinds in a part, the part contents remain unviewable and uneditable, and its preferred part editor and part kinds do not change. Nevertheless, OpenDoc still displays an icon representing the part within the area of the part's frame, and the user may be given the option of translating the data into an editable format, as described next.

Translation

Changing the part editor for a part often means changing data formats and therefore may involve loss of information or may not be directly possible. For example, any text editor may be able to display and edit plain ASCII text without loss, but a sophisticated word processor may be able to read another word processor's data only imperfectly, if at all.

Nevertheless, the user can in some cases choose to employ a part editor with a part that the editor cannot directly manipulate. In such a case, OpenDoc or a part editor performs the necessary **translation** to convert the part into a format usable by the editor. Translation is possible only if the appropriate **translator,** or filter, is available on the user's machine to perform the translation between part kinds. The **fidelity,** or quality, of the translation depends on the sophistication of the translators. Translators are platform-specific utilities that are independent of OpenDoc; OpenDoc simply provides an object wrapper for a given platform's translation facilities.

OpenDoc provides support for translation when a document is first opened, during data transfers such as drag and drop, through semantic events, and at any time the user chooses.

Displaying Parts

In preparing a compound document for viewing, two issues are of prime importance: managing the competition for space among the parts of the document, and making provisions for each part to draw itself.

OpenDoc provides a platform-independent interface for part editors, although the interface does not include any drawing commands or detailed graphics structures. OpenDoc provides an environment for managing the geometric relationships among frames, and it defines object wrappers for accessing platform-specific graphic and imaging structures.

Drawing Structures

Each part in an OpenDoc document is responsible for drawing its own content only (including, at certain times, the borders of the frames embedded within it). Thus, a part does *not* draw the interiors of its embedded frames, because they display the content of other parts (which must draw themselves). Drawing a document, therefore, is a cooperative effort for which no part editor is completely responsible; each part editor is notified by OpenDoc when it must draw its own part.

Drawing in OpenDoc relies on three fundamental graphics-system-specific structures, for which OpenDoc provides these related objects:

- **Canvas,** a description of a drawing environment. In the QuickDraw graphics system on the Mac OS, for example, this object is a wrapper for a graphics port (`GrafPort`). A **dynamic canvas,** like a screen display, can potentially be changed through scrolling or paging; a **static canvas,** like a printer page, cannot be changed once it has been rendered. OpenDoc allows for different behavior when drawing onto dynamic and static canvases.

- **Shape,** an object that describes a geometric shape. In the QuickDraw graphics system on the Mac OS, this can represent a region or a polygon; in QuickDraw GX, it is equivalent to a shape object.

- **Transform,** a structure that describes a standard set of 2-dimensional transformations, such as offset, scaling, or rotation. It is equivalent to a mapping in the QuickDraw GX graphics system on the Mac OS.

When a part actually draws itself within a frame, it uses an object closely related to the frame. A **facet** is an object that is the visible representation of a frame (or a portion of a frame) on a canvas. A frame typically has a single facet, but for offscreen buffering, split views of a part, or special graphic effects, it may have more than one.

In general, frames control the geometric relationships of the content that they display, whereas facets control the geometric relationships of frames to their containing frame or window. The facet is associated with a specific canvas, and both frames and facets have associated shapes and transforms. Figure 1-6 summarizes some of the basic relationships among frames, facets, shapes, transforms, and canvas in drawing; for more detail see "Transforms and Shapes" on page 135.

Figure 1-6   Frames and facets in drawing

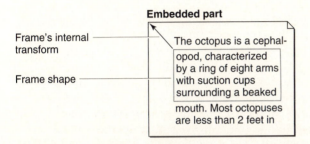

Embedded part

Frame's internal transform

Frame shape

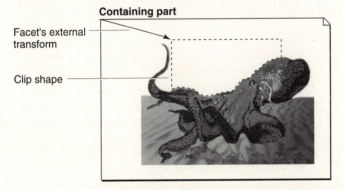

Containing part

Facet's external transform

Clip shape

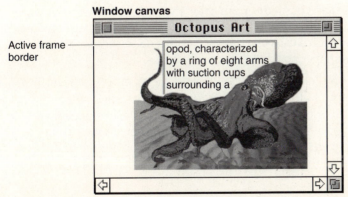

Window canvas

Active frame border

The top of Figure 1-6 shows the content area of an embedded part as a page with text on it. The portion of the part that is available for drawing is the portion within the **frame shape,** assigned to the part by its containing part. (A part may have more than one frame, but only one is shown here.) The frame's **internal transform** positions the frame over the part content. (Another shape, the **used shape,** defines the portion of the frame shape that is actually drawn to; in this case, the used shape equals the frame shape.)

The center of Figure 1-6 shows the facet associated with this embedded part's frame. (A frame may have more than one facet, but only one is shown here.) The **clip shape** of the facet defines where drawing can occur, in relation to the content of the containing part. In this case, the containing part is the root part in a document window, but it could be an embedded part displayed in its own frame. The clip shape is typically similar to the frame shape, except that, as shown in Figure 1-6, it may have additional clipping to account for other embedded parts or for elements of the containing part that overlap it. The facet's **external transform** positions the facet within the containing part's frame and facet. (Another shape, the **active shape,** defines the portion of the facet within which the embedded part responds to events; in this case, the active shape equals the frame shape.)

The bottom of Figure 1-6 shows the result of drawing both parts on the window's canvas. The portion of the embedded part defined by the frame is drawn in the area defined by the facet. If this embedded part is the **active part,** meaning that the user can edit its contents, OpenDoc draws the **active frame border** around it; the shape of that border equals the facet's active shape.

Presentation

There are many ways that a part editor can draw the contents of a part. A word processor can draw its data as plain text, styled text, or complete page layouts; a spreadsheet can draw its data as text, tables, graphs, or charts; a 3D drawing program can draw its shapes as wireframe polyhedrons, filled polyhedrons, or surface-rendered shapes with specified lighting parameters.

For any kind of program, individual frames of a single part can display different portions or different views of its data. For example, in a page-layout part, one frame of a page could display the header or footer, another could display the text of the page, and yet another could show the outline of the document. For a 3D graphics part, different frames could show different views (top, front, side) of the same object. For any kind of program, an auxiliary palette, tool bar, or other set of controls might be placed in a separate frame and be considered an alternative "view" of the part to which it applies.

OpenDoc calls such different part-display aspects part **presentations** and imposes no restrictions on them. Figure 1-7 shows some examples of different presentations for individual parts in a document. There are only three embedded parts, but two of them have several display frames, each with a different presentation.

Figure 1-7   Several presentations for three parts in a document

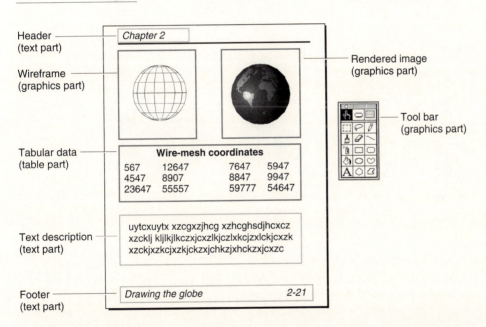

Your part editor determines the presentations that its parts can have, and it stores a presentation designation (for your own drawing functions to make use of) in each of your part's frames. You can store other display-related information as the **part info** data of a frame. Each frame and each facet have the capability to store part info data that you can access; in that data, you can store any useful private information relating the display of your part in that frame or facet. Only you use the part info data of your frames and facets.

View Type

OpenDoc does not specify presentation types, but it nevertheless defines some aspects of part display. Each frame has a **view type,** a designation of the fundamental display form of the part in that frame. Basically, view type controls whether a part is to be displayed in icon form or with its contents visible.

In most situations in most documents, each part displays its contents, or some portion of its contents, within its frame. However, a part can also display itself as one of several kinds of icons; see Figure 1-8 for examples. Each basic display form (large icon, small icon, thumbnail, or frame) is a separate view type; your part editor stores a designation of the part's view type in each of your part's display frames. A single part can have different view types in different frames.

Figure 1-8   View types for a part

Large icon   Small icon   Thumbnail   Frame

On the desktop and in file directories (folders on the Mac OS), parts are individual closed documents and by default have an icon view type. When such a document opens, the part gives its frame a frame view type, and its contents (including embedded parts) then become visible. Nevertheless, open documents can have embedded parts displayed as icons. Keep in mind that a part with an icon view type is not necessarily closed or inactive. A sound part, for example, might have nothing but an icon view type, even when playing its sound.

Each containing part specifies, by setting a value in its embedded part's frame, the view type it prefers the embedded part to have. Your container parts can specify the view type for each embedded frame they create; when embedded, your parts should initially display themselves in the view type expected by their containing parts. See, for example, "View Type" on page 159 and "View Type" on page 512 for more information and guidelines.

Document Windows and Part Windows

Compound documents are displayed in windows. A **document window** is a window that holds a single OpenDoc document; that document can contain a single part or many parts. Document windows in OpenDoc are essentially the same as the windows that display a conventional application's documents.

An architectural cornerstone of OpenDoc is that it provides **in-place editing** of all parts in a compound document. Users can manipulate the content of any part, no matter how deeply embedded, directly within the frame that displays the part. Opening a part into a window of its own is not a prerequisite for editing.

Nevertheless, a user might wish to view more of a part than is displayed within a frame. Even if a frame is resizable and supports scrolling of its contents, the user may find it more convenient to view and edit that frame's part separately, in its own window. To support this convenience, OpenDoc allows users to open a separate window, called a **part window,** which looks similar to a document window. See Figure 1-9 for an example.

Figure 1-9   An embedded frame opened into a part window

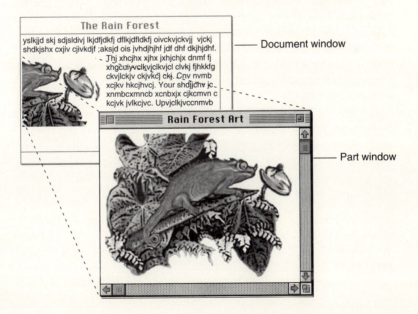

Document window

Part window

Like document windows, part windows can themselves contain embedded parts. But because your part is the root part in any part windows that your part editor creates, you may take a more active role in window handling than you do for your part when it is an embedded part in a document window. See "Creating and Using Windows" on page 225 for information on handling part windows; see "Viewing Embedded Parts in Part Windows" on page 573 for guidelines for part-window placement.

Frame Negotiation

In a compound document with embedded parts, the embedding hierarchy and the frame locations determine the geometric relationships among parts. Each part controls the positions, sizes, and shapes of the frames embedded within it. If an embedded part needs to change the size of its frame or add another frame, it must negotiate for that change with its containing part. This **frame negotiation** allows an embedded part to communicate its needs to its containing part; however, the containing part has ultimate control over the sizes and shapes of its embedded frames.

Figure 1-10 shows a simple example of frame negotiation. A user edits an embedded part, adding enough data so that the content no longer fits in the embedded part's current frame size. The embedded part requests a larger frame size from the containing part. The containing part can either grant the request or return a different frame size from that requested. In this example, the containing part cannot accommodate the full size of the requested frame and so returns a frame size to the embedded part that is larger than the previous frame size but not as large as the requested one.

Figure 1-10   Frame negotiation

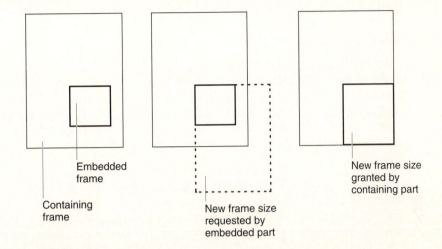

The frame-negotiation process is described in more detail in "Frame Negotiation" on page 116.

Event Handling

Most part editors interact with the user primarily by responding to user events. **User events** are messages sent or posted by the operating system in response to user actions, activation or deactivation of a part or window, or messages from other event sources. Based on information in a user event, a part editor might redraw its part, open or close windows, perform editing operations, transfer data, or perform any sort of menu command or other operation.

OpenDoc has several built-in event-handling features that help your part editor function properly within a compound document. For example, instead of polling for events, as a typical application does, your part editor acts when notified by OpenDoc that an event has occurred.

This section notes some of OpenDoc's event-handling features; for more information on user events, see Chapter 5, "User Events."

The Document Shell and the Dispatcher

Part editors respond differently to user events than conventional applications do. Part editors do not receive events directly; OpenDoc receives them and dispatches them to the proper part.

Because they are not complete applications, and because they must function cooperatively, part editors run in an environment that itself handles some of the tasks that conventional applications typically perform. That environment is called the OpenDoc **document shell;** it is a shared library that handles certain application-level tasks and provides a shared address space for each OpenDoc document, within which part editors manipulate document content.

Whenever an OpenDoc document is opened, OpenDoc creates an instance of the document shell. The shell creates global objects and uses them to open the document. OpenDoc then loads the part editors for all parts that appear in the document window; the part editors read in the data of their own parts. The shell receives both user events and scripting-related events (see "Scripting Support" on page 68). The shell uses the OpenDoc **dispatcher** to dispatch those events to the proper part editors, based on event location and ownership of shared resources such as menus.

The document shell is described in the section "The Document Shell" on page 500. How the dispatcher sends events to parts is described in the section "How User Events Are Handled" on page 190.

Handling User Commands

As a result of user actions or commands, OpenDoc interacts with part editors to perform these common application activities: part activation, menu handling, and undo. In general, the document shell receives events and passes the appropriate information to the proper part.

Activation and Selection

In response to user actions, individual parts in a document become active and thus editable. A part is active if it possesses the **selection focus;** the user can select and modify its contents in this state. The active part may also possess the menu and keystroke focus; see "Focus Transfer" on page 207 for more information on foci.

Parts activate themselves in OpenDoc, and the individual parts in a document must cooperate to transfer the selection focus among each other as appropriate. Note that when a part is not in the active (editable) state, it need not be idle; multiple parts within an OpenDoc document can perform different tasks at the same time.

Switching among OpenDoc documents, and among individual parts within a document, can involve a much less intrusive context switch than switching from one conventional application to another. Users are less likely to be irritated, because the wait before they can edit a newly activated part is less likely to be perceptible.

The active state is different from the selected state. When a part is **selected**, its *frame* is made available for manipulation. Because embedded frames are considered to be content elements of their containing part, they can be selected and then moved, adjusted, cut, or copied just like text, graphic objects, or any other content elements. Thus, whereas an active part is manipulated by its own part editor, a selected part is manipulated—as a frame—by its containing part. Figure 1-11 shows the visual differences among the inactive, selected, and active states of an embedded part.

Figure 1-11   Inactive, active, and selected states of an embedded part

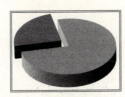
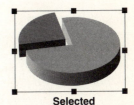

Inactive   **Active**   **Selected**

An **inactive** part, one that is not being edited, need not have a visible frame border. A selected part's frame border is drawn by the containing part; its shape typically corresponds to the frame shape, and its appearance should follow guidelines for selected frames specified in the section "Selected Frame Border" on page 526. An active part's frame border is drawn by OpenDoc; its shape corresponds to the active shape of the embedded part's facet, and its appearance is fixed for each platform.

When a part becomes active, more than its own frame border changes.
Figure 1-12 illustrates some of the visual changes to a window caused by
part activation.

Figure 1-12   Inactive and active states of a graphics part

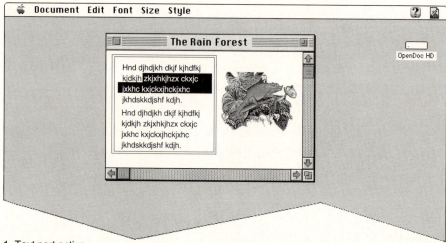

1. Text part active

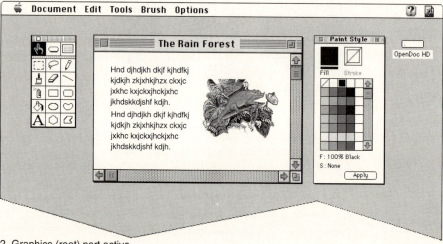

2. Graphics (root) part active

Figure 1-14   The Mac OS Document and Edit menus

Most of the items in the Document menu are handled by the document shell; see "The Document Shell and the Document Menu" on page 503 and "The Document Menu" on page 248 for more information. Most of the items in the Edit menu are handled by the currently active part; see "The Edit Menu" on page 252 for more information.

Your part editor can add menus of its own, and it can modify—within limits and according to certain rules—the standard OpenDoc menus. See "Menus" on page 537 for more specifics.

Undo

Applications on many platforms provide a form of **undo,** which allows a user to reverse the effects of a recently executed command. OpenDoc provides better support for undo than do most current platforms, in at least two ways:

- The undo action can cross document boundaries. This is important because a single drag-and-drop action can affect more than one part or document.

- OpenDoc allows multiple sequential undo actions. The user can undo multiple sequential commands, rather than only one.

OpenDoc support for undo is described in more detail in Chapter 5, "User Events."

Storage and Data Transfer

All the data of all parts in a document, plus all information about frames and embedding, is stored in a single document file. OpenDoc does not require the user to manually manage the various file formats that make up a compound document; OpenDoc manages and holds all the pieces. Thus, storage is easier for developers, and exchanging documents is easier for users.

OpenDoc uses the same data-storage concepts for data transfer (clipboard, drag and drop, and linking) that it uses for document storage.

Storage Basics

The OpenDoc storage system manages persistent storage for parts. It is a high-level persistent storage mechanism that allows multiple part editors to share a single document file effectively. The storage system is implemented on top of the native storage facilities for each platform that supports OpenDoc.

Storage in OpenDoc is based on a system of structured elements, each of which can contain many data streams. The system effectively gives each part its own storage stream, as shown in Figure 1-15. This design maintains maximum compatibility with the many existing application storage systems that assume stream-based I/O.

The core of the OpenDoc storage system is the **storage unit,** an element that can contain one or more data streams. The data of each part in a document is kept in at least one storage unit, distinct from the data of other parts. Storage units can also include references to other storage units, and OpenDoc uses chains of such references to store the embedding relationships of the parts within a document. Storage units and the other elements of structured storage of OpenDoc are described further in Chapter 7, "Storage."

Figure 1-15   Multiple data streams in a single OpenDoc document

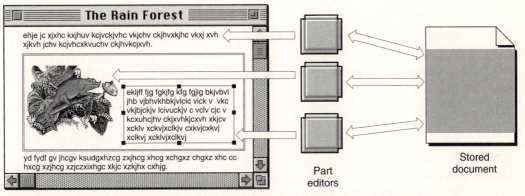

Displayed document

Document Drafts

OpenDoc documents have a history that can be preserved and inspected
through the mechanism of drafts. A **draft** is a captured record of the state of
a document at a given time; the user decides when to save the current state of
a document as a new draft and when to delete older drafts. All drafts are stored
together in the same document, with no redundantly stored data.

The OpenDoc draft mechanism helps in the creation of shared documents.
When several users share a document, each in turn can save the current state of
the document as a draft and then make any desired changes. Users can always
look back through the drafts of the document they and the others have created.
Also, if translation occurs during the process of sharing documents, the user
can possibly consult an older draft to recapture formatting information that

might have been lost in translation. Figure 1-16 shows an example of the dialog box through which the user can manipulate drafts.

Figure 1-16   The Drafts dialog box

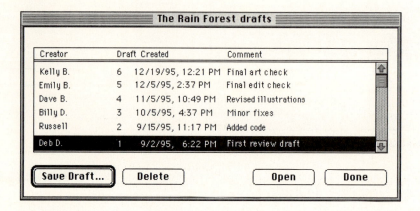

Parts also interact with their drafts to create the objects needed for embedding other parts and to create links to data sources. See "Drafts" on page 285 for more information.

Stationery

OpenDoc gives the user additional aids for constructing compound documents. One of these aids, central to the user's ability to create new kinds of parts, is stationery.

Stationery pads are specialized parts or documents whose only purpose is to serve as templates for the creation of other parts. A stationery part is never opened; when the user attempts to open a stationery part, a copy of that part is created and opened instead. Users can create stationery with specific formatting and content to create letterheads, forms, or other templates. Stationery parts can be embedded in documents, or they can exist as stand-alone documents themselves.

Figure 1-17 shows an icon for a stationery document on the desktop. The user drags the stationery icon and drops it onto the document, at which time a copy of the stationery part is embedded in the document and opened into a frame, displaying the part's initial contents.

Figure 1-17   Dragging a stationery part from the desktop into a window

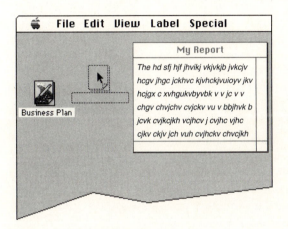 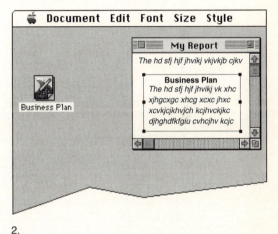

1.   2.

It is typically through stationery that users first gain access to your part editor. When you develop and ship a part editor, you also provide one or more stationery documents. To create a part using your part editor, the user does not launch the editor; instead, the user double-clicks on your stationery document or drags it into an open document window.

Data Transfer

OpenDoc includes several built-in data-transfer features that allow users to create and edit OpenDoc documents more easily than is usual with conventional applications. Users can put any kind of media into a document with simple commands, and OpenDoc helps your part editor respond to those commands.

In OpenDoc data transfer, the **source** is the part (or the portion of its content) that provides the data being transferred, and the **destination** is the part (or the location in its content) that receives the transferred data.

When source data in one format is transferred to a destination whose data is written in another format, translation may be necessary; see "Translation" on page 45. Translation usually involves loss of data, and it is less necessary if part editors provide standard content formats, as promoted by CI Labs; see "Cross-Platform Consistency and CI Labs" on page 71.

Clipboard

Clipboard data transfer allows for easy exchange of information among documents, using menu commands familiar to most users. OpenDoc supports clipboard transfer of any kind of data, including multipart compound data, into any document.

Clipboard transfer is a two-stage process. The user first selects some portion of the content of the source part (possibly including embedded parts) and places a copy of that content onto the clipboard buffer by executing the Cut or Copy command. At any subsequent time, the user can copy the clipboard data to the destination (back into the same part, into another part in the same document, or into another document) by executing the Paste command.

As noted in the section "Embedding Versus Incorporating" on page 43, OpenDoc allows for an intelligent form of pasting in data transfer, anticipating user expectations about the result of a pasting operation when the destination holds a different kind of data from the source. Subject to user override, the destination part can decide whether to embed the data as a separate part or incorporate it as content data into itself.

Clipboard transfer is discussed in detail in the section "Handling Pasted or Dropped Data" on page 336.

Drag and Drop

Drag-and-drop data transfer is similar to clipboard transfer, except that it involves direct user manipulation of the data being transferred, rather than the intermediate use of the clipboard. OpenDoc supports drag and drop within documents, across documents, and to the desktop. Users can even drop non-OpenDoc data into OpenDoc parts.

Figure 1-18 shows the use of drag and drop to transfer a piece of information from a spreadsheet part to a text part within a document. As with clipboard transfer, OpenDoc uses intelligent pasting in drag and drop; the spreadsheet part includes a plain-text version of the selection being dragged, so that the destination part (the text part) can directly incorporate it at the location of the drop.

Figure 1-18   Using drag and drop within a document

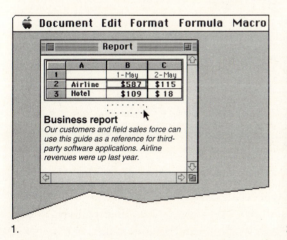
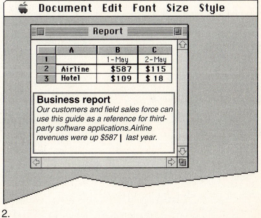

Drag and drop works equally well between separate documents. In terms of the user experience, the data-transfer facilities of OpenDoc actually blur the distinction between a part and a document. If the user drags a closed document (represented as an icon on the desktop) into an open document window, a copy of the transferred document either becomes an embedded part in the window's document or is incorporated into the intrinsic content of the document's root part. Likewise, if the user selects the frame of an embedded part in an open document window and drags that part to the desktop, a copy of that part immediately becomes a separate, closed document represented by icon, as shown in Figure 1-19.

Figure 1-19   Dragging a part to the desktop

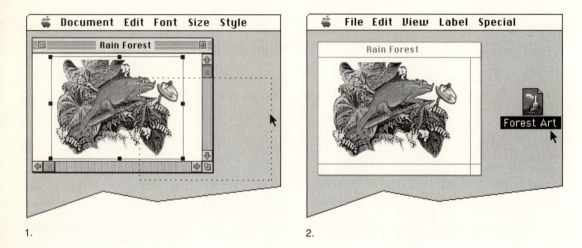

1.   2.

Drag and drop is discussed in detail in the section "Drag and Drop" on page 361.

Linking

Linking allows the user to view, within a part's frame, data that is a live (updatable) copy of data in a different location—in the same frame, in a different frame, in a different part, or even in a different document. When the data in the source location changes, OpenDoc notifies the destination part— either automatically or manually, depending on user preference—and facilitates updating the destination copy.

Linked data can include embedded parts, and the source of a link can be in the same part as its destination, in a different part in the same document, or in an entirely different document. Figure 1-20 shows a simple example of linking between two parts in a document. In this example, whenever the user changes the values in the linked spreadsheet cells, the bar graph adjusts its display accordingly.

Figure 1-20   Linking spreadsheet data to a bar chart

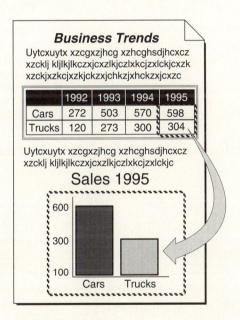

Users create a link when pasting data, using a dialog box to link the source of the data to its destination. (See Figure 8-3 on page 337 for an example of the dialog box.) This simple user interface to linking makes the use of links more attractive to users than some other systems do.

Linking is discussed in detail in the section "Linking" on page 372.

Extensibility

The OpenDoc architecture is designed to be extended. Using built-in features, you can enhance the capabilities of and communications among your parts in a compound document, and you can even develop component software that goes well beyond the standard OpenDoc model of parts and compound documents.

The main point of departure for enhancing OpenDoc is the extension mechanism, a general method for adding programming interfaces to objects. Additional mechanisms are the focus-module and dispatch-module interfaces, which allow you to add new kinds of focus and new kinds of event handling to your part editors.

OpenDoc already includes several instances of extensions, one of which is its support for scripting. This section introduces the features of the scripting extension and then summarizes how you can add other extensions for other purposes.

Scripting Support

A major feature available with OpenDoc is the ability to make parts scriptable, allowing users to customize their applications to handle user-specific tasks. Working in a compound-document environment with scriptable parts, sophisticated users can use standard document-editing procedures to add application-like functionality to parts. Likewise, programmers can create complex client applications and present them in the form of compound documents.

The scripting model supported by OpenDoc is called *content-centered scripting,* or scripting based on a content model. For a part to be scriptable, its part editor must have a **content model,** which lists the **content objects** and operations that the part makes available for scripting. OpenDoc provides a way to deliver scripting messages, or **semantic events,** from a scripting system to a part editor, which responds to the events. OpenDoc supports any scripting system based on the **Open Scripting Architecture (OSA).** AppleScript, Frontier, and QuicKeys on the Mac OS platform are examples of OSA-based scripting systems. The Mac OS implementation of the Open Scripting Architecture is described in *Inside Macintosh: Interapplication Communication.*

Your part editor can provide increasing levels of scripting support, including *scriptability*, *recordability*, and *customizability*. They are described in Chapter 9, "Semantic Events and Scripting."

Scripts can be attached to parts, and a user-interface control such as a button might consist of nothing more than a part that executes a script when activated. Script editors also can send semantic events to parts. Figure 1-21 shows an example of a script editor sending a semantic event based on a scripting command ("Set chartType of part "sales chart" to type3DPie") to a document. The root part's semantic interface decodes the *object specifier* in the event (part "sales chart") and determines the content object to which the object specifier applies (in this case an embedded part). The embedded part then performs the specified operation.

The scripting support in OpenDoc is an enhancement of OpenDoc's basic capabilities and is one of several extensions provided with OpenDoc. It is recommended, but not required, that all part editors support scripting.

Figure 1-21   Sending a semantic event to an embedded part

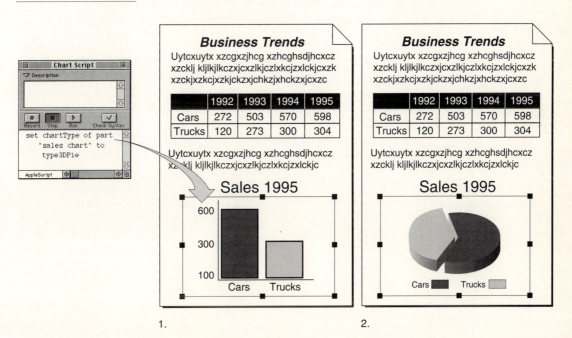

1.   2.

Other Extensions

The basic architecture of OpenDoc is primarily geared toward mediating the geometric interrelationships among parts, their sharing of user events, and their sharing of storage. Direct communication among parts for purposes other than frame negotiation is mostly beyond the basic intent of OpenDoc. If separate parts in a document (or across documents) need to share information, or if one part needs to manipulate the contents or behavior of another part, you need to extend the capabilities of OpenDoc in some way.

OpenDoc allows you to add these kinds of capabilities to part editors through its extension mechanism. A part editor can create an associated **extension** object that implements an additional interface to that editor's parts. Other part editors can then access and call that interface.

The OpenDoc support for scripting is an example of an extension interface, as noted in the previous section. Other extension interfaces can, however, provide faster interaction and lower-level communication between parts than is possible by passing semantic events. A word processor, for example, might construct an extension interface to give related part editors or other tools access to its text. A developer of a large software solutions package might use extensions to provide greater integration among its software components.

Figure 1-22 shows some possible examples of communication through OpenDoc extensions. The figure shows a text part and a graphics part that share a tool palette (a third part). The palette displays the appropriate tools for the currently active part and, when the user makes a tool selection, communicates the information back to the active part. A spelling checker provides its service to all parts in the document and accesses their text through their extensions. Furthermore, the text part and graphics part in this figure communicate directly through an extension mechanism; the text part updates the graphics part with the current figure number and caption.

Figure 1-22   Parts communicating through extensions

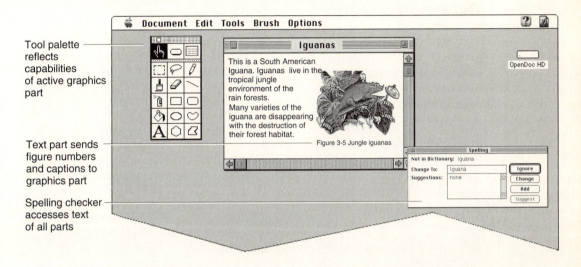

Tool palette reflects capabilities of active graphics part

Text part sends figure numbers and captions to graphics part

Spelling checker accesses text of all parts

In addition to the scripting extension, OpenDoc includes existing extensions and other kinds of enhancements that allow you to extend the OpenDoc Part Info dialog box, extend the capabilities of the OpenDoc document shell, or provide for additional kinds of user events or foci. Use of the OpenDoc extension mechanism is discussed further in Chapter 10, "Extending OpenDoc."

Cross-Platform Consistency and CI Labs

OpenDoc was designed from the beginning to be a cross-platform architecture. The programming interface to OpenDoc is general enough to be readily implemented on many platforms, adapting well to different user-interface designs and different runtime models. Although OpenDoc does not provide a complete programming interface—it does not, for example, replace the graphics system or drawing commands for any platform—it provides consistent structure within which such system-specific interfaces can be used. As a result, users on all platforms obtain a uniform experience in embedding and manipulating all kinds of media.

Part of this uniformity is built into OpenDoc, and part comes from additional platform-independent user-interface guidelines that part-editor developers must follow. Because platform-neutral user-interface guidelines and programming standards are so important, and because data integrity and data-transfer protocols are so critical in cross-platform settings, OpenDoc is affiliated with an organization devoted to solving these issues in a vendor-independent fashion.

Component Integration Laboratories, Inc. (CI Labs), is a nonprofit association dedicated to promoting the adoption of OpenDoc as a vendor-neutral industry standard for software integration and component software. CI Labs is composed of a number of platform and application vendors with a common interest in solving OpenDoc issues and promoting interoperability.

Organizations and individuals who want to participate in the move to a component-software model are invited to join CI Labs. CI Labs supports several levels of participation through different membership categories. Specific membership benefits vary by category, but all members influence the future direction of OpenDoc technology.

We encourage you to add your name to one of our electronic mail information lists at CILABS.ORG, download files from our server at FTP.CILABS.ORG, or look up our Web page (http://www.cilabs.org). If for some reason you are unable to get files from our server, we can send you an information packet. For details on membership levels and how you can become a member, please provide the following information to CILABS@CILABS.ORG or use our U.S. mail address:

Name
Company name
Title
Street address
City
State/Province
Zip code/Postal code/Country
Telephone number
Fax number
e-mail address

Send to

Component Integration Laboratories, Inc.
P.O. Box 61747
Sunnyvale, CA 94088-1747

Telephone	(408) 864-0300
Fax	(408) 864-0380
Internet	CILABS@CILABS.ORG
World Wide Web	http://www.cilabs.org

Development Overview

Contents

Creating OpenDoc software is not difficult, but it represents a shift in approach from conventional application development. OpenDoc part editors are in general smaller than applications, they do not have direct access to some operating-system services such as event dispatching, they do not own their documents, and they must work in close cooperation with other part editors. The cross-platform design of OpenDoc means that some aspects of part development may seem foreign, but it also means that writing part editors for multiple platforms is far easier than doing so for conventional applications.

OpenDoc is an object-oriented system, but a part editor can be written easily in procedural code and still fit into the OpenDoc class structure. Existing applications can also be retrofitted easily to work in the OpenDoc environment. OpenDoc is extensible, and many of its components are replaceable, allowing for innovation by developers at both the system and application levels.

This chapter introduces the OpenDoc class library and presents a high-level summary of several approaches to developing an OpenDoc part editor. For additional discussions of general development-related issues, see also Chapter 11, "OpenDoc Runtime Features."

The OpenDoc Class Library

OpenDoc is a set of shared libraries with a largely platform-independent, object-oriented programming interface. This section introduces the classes implemented in the OpenDoc libraries and the design goals behind them.

The interfaces to all of OpenDoc's classes are specified in the **Interface Definition Language (IDL),** a programming-language-neutral syntax for creating interfaces. IDL is part of the **System Object Model (SOM),** a specification for object binding at runtime. IDL interfaces are typically compiled separately from implementation code, using a SOM compiler. See the section "Developing With SOMobjects and IDL" on page 83 for more information.

Because OpenDoc uses IDL and SOM, part editors and other OpenDoc objects that have been created with different compilers or in completely different programming languages can nevertheless communicate properly with each other. Furthermore, they can be independently revised and extended and still work together.

For more complete information on the OpenDoc class library, including detailed descriptions of all public OpenDoc classes and methods, see the *OpenDoc Class Reference.*

A Set of Classes, Not a Framework

OpenDoc is a set of classes whose objects cooperate in the creation and manipulation of compound documents. It is designed to be as platform neutral as possible. The object-oriented library structure, in which object fields are private, facilitates the replacement of existing code in a modular manner. Also, by using abstract classes and methods, OpenDoc defines a structure for part editors while specifying as little as possible about their internal functioning.

The OpenDoc class library is not an object-oriented application framework in the full sense of the word. That is, even though the design of OpenDoc allows you to create a part editor, it does so at a lower level, and without forcing as much adherence to interface and implementation as is typical for an application framework.

You can create a part editor just as effectively in either way, however: directly through the OpenDoc library interfaces, or indirectly through the interfaces of a framework such as the **OpenDoc Development Framework (ODF),** a part-editor framework that allows you to develop simultaneously for both the Mac OS and Windows platforms. The main difference is that, if you use a part-editor framework, you need implement less code yourself, and it is easier to ensure consistency in the final product.

The principal classes in the OpenDoc class hierarchy are shown in Figure 2-1. All classes are derived from the superclass `ODObject`, itself a subclass of `somObject`, the fundamental SOM superclass (not shown). The figure shows these categories of classes:

- Names in bold represent abstract superclasses that your part editor is likely to subclass.

- Names in italics represent classes whose objects your part typically creates for its own use. You create these objects by calling methods described in the section "Factory Methods" on page 463.

- Names in plain text represent classes whose objects you part editor calls but typically never has to create; they are created for you by OpenDoc.

Figure 2-1   The OpenDoc class hierarchy (principal classes)

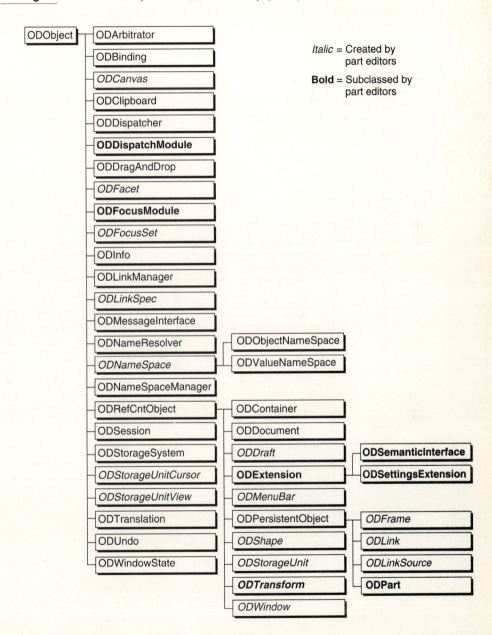

Italic = Created by
         part editors

Bold = Subclassed by
        part editors

Runtime relationships

For an illustrated discussion of the relationships of
the principal OpenDoc objects in terms of runtime
references among them, see the section "Runtime
Object Relationships" on page 487. ◆

Classes shown in Figure 2-2 are support classes, consisting mostly of iterators
and simple sets. They are all direct subclasses of ODObject. (A separate set of
specialized OpenDoc support classes, used solely for scripting, is shown in
Figure 9-2 on page 415.)

Figure 2-2   OpenDoc class hierarchy (support classes)

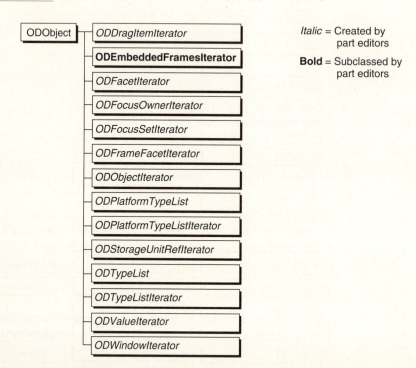

Compared to some application frameworks, there is little inheritance in the
hierarchy represented in Figure 2-1 and Figure 2-2; OpenDoc instead makes
extensive use of object delegation, in which objects unrelated by inheritance

cooperate to perform a task. This relatively flat inheritance structure preserves the language-neutral flavor of OpenDoc and improves ease of maintenance and replaceability.

The OpenDoc classes can be divided into three groups, based on how a part editor might make use of them:

- the class (ODPart), which you must subclass and implement to create your part editor

- the bulk of the implemented OpenDoc classes, whose objects are created either by your part editor or by OpenDoc, that your part editor calls to perform its tasks

- the classes that you can subclass and implement to extend OpenDoc

The following sections summarize these groups of classes.

Classes You Must Subclass

The OpenDoc classes listed in this section are abstract superclasses that you are intended to subclass if you wish to implement their capabilities.

The Class ODPart

The class ODPart is central to OpenDoc; it is the one class that you must subclass to create a part editor. ODPart represents the programming interface that your part editor presents to OpenDoc and to other parts.

ODPart is an abstract superclass with approximately 60 defined methods. When you subclass ODPart, you must override all of its methods plus a few inherited methods; however, you need to provide meaningful implementations only for those methods that represent capabilities actually supported by your part editor. The rest can be stub implementations.

There is one additional class that you must subclass and implement if your part is a container part. You must provide an iterator class (a subclass of the abstract superclass ODEmbeddedFramesIterator) to allow callers to access all of the frames directly embedded in your part.

Classes for Extending OpenDoc

OpenDoc provides these classes specifically for enhancing its features:

- The class `ODExtension` is the abstract superclass from which extensions to OpenDoc are defined; OpenDoc allows you to add new methods to existing classes by associating objects of class `ODExtension` with the specific class that they extend. The classes `ODSemanticInterface` and `ODSettingsExtension` are examples of currently existing subclasses of `ODExtension`.

- The class `ODSemanticInterface`, when subclassed, represents the interface through which a part receives semantic events, thus allowing it to be scriptable.

- The class `ODSettingsExtension`, when subclassed, represents an object with which your part editor can create and display a Settings dialog box for your part editor.

- The class `ODDispatchModule` is used to dispatch certain types of events (such as keystroke events) to part editors. You can provide for dispatching of new types of events or messages to your part editor by subclassing `ODDispatchModule`.

- The class `ODFocusModule` is used to describe a particular type of focus (such as the selection focus). You can provide new types of focus for your part editor by subclassing `ODFocusModule`.

- The class `ODTransform` represents a graphical transformation matrix used for drawing. You can subclass it to extend the kinds of transformations it can perform. This class is somewhat different from the other classes in this category, because it can be used as is; for this reason, the class also appears in the next section.

Classes You Can Use

The OpenDoc classes listed in this section implement most of the OpenDoc features that your part editor uses. By using or creating objects of these classes, your part can function within an OpenDoc document and can embed other parts.

Abstract Superclasses

These classes are never directly instantiated. The classes `ODPart` and `ODEmbeddedFramesIterator`, mentioned in the previous section, are abstract superclasses. Other abstract superclasses are mentioned in the section "Classes for Extending OpenDoc" on page 80.

The abstract superclasses in the following list are special; they define the basic inheritance architecture of OpenDoc. Not only would you not instantiate these classes, but you would probably never directly subclass them. When developing a part editor, you would use (or further subclass) one of their existing subclasses.

- `ODObject`. This is the abstract superclass for most of the principal OpenDoc classes. All subclasses of `ODObject` define objects that are extensible.

- `ODRefCntObject`. This is the abstract superclass for reference-counted objects—objects that maintain a count of how many other objects refer to them, so that OpenDoc can manage memory use efficiently.

- `ODPersistentObject`. This is the abstract superclass for persistent objects—objects whose state can be stored persistently.

Implemented Classes

These classes are implemented in ways unique to each platform that supports OpenDoc. Some represent objects that are created only by OpenDoc, whereas others represent objects that your part editor may need to create.

- The session object. The class `ODSession` represents the user's opening of and access to a single OpenDoc document.

- The binding object. The class `ODBinding` represents the object that performs the binding of part editors to the parts in a document.

- Storage classes. The primary classes of objects associated with document storage are the class `ODStorageSystem` and the set of classes (`ODContainer`, `ODDocument`, `ODDraft`, and `ODStorageUnit`) that constitute a **container suite.** The container-suite objects all work closely together and are implemented differently for each platform or file system.

- Data-interchange classes. The classes `ODLink`, `ODLinkManager`, `ODLinkSource`, `ODLinkSpec`, `ODDragAndDrop`, and `ODClipboard` all relate to transfer of data from one location to another. These objects do not represent documents, but they nevertheless use storage units to hold the data they transfer.

- Drawing-related classes. The imaging classes `ODCanvas`, `ODShape`, and `ODTransform` represent imaging structures in a given graphics system. The classes `ODWindowState` and `ODWindow` represent windows on a given platform. The layout classes `ODFrame` and `ODFacet` represent the frame and facet structures that define the layout of embedded parts.

- Event-handling classes. The classes `ODArbitrator` and `ODDispatcher` control what kinds of user events are sent to which part editors during execution. The classes `ODMenuBar` and `ODUndo` give part editors access to the menu bar and to previous states of themselves, respectively.

- Semantic-event classes. Besides the abstract class `ODSemanticInterface` (which must be subclassed), the classes `ODNameResolver` and `ODMessageInterface` are associated with sending or receiving semantic events (scripting messages), and connecting to a scripting system. (Figure 2-1 does not show the entire object hierarchy involved with semantic events and scripting; see Figure 9-1 on page 414 for a more complete picture.)

Service Classes

These classes exist mainly as services for other classes to use:

- The `ODStorageUnitCursor` and `ODStorageUnitView` classes facilitate access to specific values in specific storage units.

- The `ODFocusSet` class provides convenient grouping of foci (access to shared resources such as the keyboard or menu bar) for activation and event handling.

- The `ODNameSpaceManager` and `ODNameSpace` classes provide convenient storage for attribute/value pairs. The classes `ODObjectNameSpace` and `ODValueNameSpace`, subclasses of `ODNameSpace`, provide name spaces for OpenDoc objects and for data, respectively.

- The `ODInfo` class provides the Part Info dialog box, which your part displays in response to a user selection from the Edit menu.

- The `ODTranslation` class provides platform-specific translation between data formats.

- The object descriptor classes (shown in Figure 9-2 on page 415) provide scripting support in the form of an object-oriented encapsulation of Apple event descriptor structures.

- Many classes have associated iterator classes and list classes that are used for counting through all related instances of the class.

Writing OpenDoc Software

This section briefly summarizes some high-level aspects of the design and implementation of a part editor. It discusses

- issues related to developing with the System Object Model that underlies all OpenDoc classes

- protocols that your part can participate in to accomplish its tasks

- several development scenarios for creating OpenDoc software

Developing With SOMobjects and IDL

OpenDoc is implemented as a shared library consisting of a set of classes constructed using SOMobjects™ for the Mac OS, the implementation of the System Object Model (SOM) for the Mac OS platform. The interfaces to SOM classes must be written in the SOM Interface Definition Language (IDL) and compiled by the SOM compiler, usually separately from the implementations of the classes.

The implementation of OpenDoc objects as SOM objects has several advantages to the use of OpenDoc as a shared library:

- SOM objects are dynamically bound. Dynamic binding is essential to the nature of OpenDoc, in which new parts can be added to existing documents at any time.

- All SOM objects, whether their implementations were compiled under different compilers in the same programming language or in different languages, communicate consistently and pass parameters consistently.

- Unlike with other object-oriented architectures, the modification and recompilation of a SOM class do not necessarily require the subsequent recompilation of all of its subclasses and clients.

Because OpenDoc consists of SOM classes, the class `ODPart` is naturally a SOM class. If you want your part editor—which is a subclass of `ODPart` plus any other classes that you define—to also consist of SOM classes, then you must write your interfaces in IDL, separate from your implementations, and you must compile them with the SOM compiler. The result of the compilation is a set of header and stub implementation source files, in one of the procedural or object-oriented programming languages, such as C or C++, supported by the SOM compiler. You complete your development by writing your implementations into the stub implementation files and compiling them, along with the headers, using a standard compiler for your programming language.

If you write your part-editor interfaces in IDL, you will notice that the IDL syntax is very similar to that of C and C++. It includes essentially the same character set, whitespace rules, comment styles, preprocessing capabilities, identifier-naming rules, and rules for literals. But there are a few differences in source-code appearance to note when declaring or calling methods of SOM-based objects:

- In IDL method declarations (function definitions), each parameter declaration is preceded by a *directional attribute* ("in", "out", or "inout") that notes whether the parameter is used as an input, or as a result, or as both. See, for example, the declaration for the ODPart::FacetAdded method on page 108.

- The C++ interface to any method of a SOM object includes an extra initial parameter, the **environment parameter** (ev), used by all SOM methods to pass exceptions. See "SOM Exception Handling" on page 460 for more information.

- The C interface to any SOM method includes another extra parameter, before the environment parameter, specifying the object to which the method call is directed.

Advantages of making all your classes SOM classes include a greater ability to develop portions of your part editor (or set of editors) using different programming languages and compilers, and a lesser need for recompilation of all of your code when you change portions of it. These advantages may be compelling only if your libraries are very large, however, because they must be balanced against the disadvantages of working in both IDL and a separate programming language.

You are not required to make your part-editor classes SOM classes. If you are developing in C++, for example, you can use C++ classes instead. The generally preferred procedure is to create only one SOM class, a subclass of ODPart whose interface contains nothing but your public methods (overrides of the methods of ODPart and its superclasses). That SOM class delegates all of its method calls to a C++ wrapper class, which contains the functionality for the public methods as well as any private fields and methods. Additional classes can be subclasses of your C++ wrapper class.

Advantages of developing in C++ with a single wrapper object include a lesser need to work with interfaces in two languages (IDL and C++), a smaller memory and calling overhead for your objects, and the availability of C++ features (such as templates) that are not supported by SOM.

SOM class ID and editor ID

A **SOM class ID** is an ISO string whose format is *"module::className"*. A part editor's **editor ID** is a SOM class ID that uniquely defines the editor; you need to specify your editor ID in your editor's IDL interfaces. For example, the editor ID for AcmeGraph 1.0 might be "Acme::AcmeGraph". Editor IDs are used for binding; see "Information Used for Binding" on page 474 for more information. ◆

For more information on SOM and using the SOM compiler on the Mac OS platform, see the *OpenDoc Cookbook for the Mac OS.* For a more detailed description of the Interface Definition Language and instructions on programming with SOM, see, for example, *SOMObjects Developer Toolkit Users Guide* and *SOMObjects Developer Toolkit Programmers Reference Manual* from IBM.

OpenDoc Protocols

OpenDoc imposes very few restrictions on how your part editor does its job. The inner workings of your editor's core data engine are of little concern to OpenDoc. The engine should be able to free storage when requested, it should adequately handle cases where the part can be only partially read into memory, and it should handle any multiprocessing issues that arise. Other than that, it simply needs to provide an interface to OpenDoc and use the OpenDoc interface to accomplish OpenDoc-related tasks.

The programming interfaces that your part editor uses (and provides) to perform specific tasks are called **protocols**. The methods of `ODPart`, for example, participate in approximately 12 protocols, such as part activation and undo. This section briefly describes the protocols; Table 2-1 on page 90 lists the methods of `ODPart` that you have to override to participate in each protocol.

Which Protocols to Participate In

To implement the simplest possible part, you need to participate in only some OpenDoc protocols, and you need to override only some methods of `ODPart`. As a minimum, your part editor must be able to

- draw its part
- retrieve its part's data
- handle events sent to its part
- store its part's data, if it permits editing

Unless it creates extremely simple parts, your part editor must also provide some sort of command interface to the user. It must then be able to

- activate its part
- handle menus
- handle windows, dialog boxes, and palettes

If you wish your parts to be able to contain other parts, your part editor must be able to

- embed frames and manipulate them
- create facets for visible frames
- store frames

Beyond these capabilities, you may want your parts to have additional capabilities, such as drawing themselves asynchronously, providing data-transfer capability, supporting scripting, or others. You can add those capabilities by overriding other methods of `ODPart`.

Overriding the Methods of ODPart

Your fundamental programming task in creating an OpenDoc part editor is to subclass the class `ODPart` and override its methods. The following list summarizes the OpenDoc protocols that your part editor can use and lists the sections in this book that describe each protocol more fully. To create and edit full-featured container parts, your editor must support all of these protocols.

The methods of `ODPart` involved in each protocol are shown in the table that follows this list.

■ **Layout.** The layout and imaging protocols together make up the drawing process. Your part uses the layout protocol for frame manipulation and for facet manipulation.

□ Frame manipulation includes adding and removing display frames, setting frame characteristics and order, opening frames into windows, and performing frame negotiation (modifying embedded-frame shapes on request). Your part interacts with its containing part and with its draft object to modify your display frames.

□ Facet manipulation is the adding, altering, or removing of facets of frames that are modified or scrolled into or out of view. You interact with existing facet objects to add or manipulate embedded facets. OpenDoc uses the facet hierarchy constructed by the layout protocol for passing geometric events like mouse clicks to the appropriate part editor.

All parts that are visible must participate in this protocol. The layout protocol is described, along with the embedding protocol, in the section "Frame and Facet Hierarchies" on page 103.

■ **Imaging.** Your part uses the imaging protocol after the layout protocol, to draw itself appropriately in each of its display frames. Drawing may occur asynchronously, it may occur in response to update events, and it may occur when activation or deactivation affects highlighting. Drawing can be to a video display or to a printer. You interact with frames, facets, canvases, transforms, and shapes during the imaging process.

All parts that are visible must participate in this protocol. The imaging protocol is described in the sections "Canvases" on page 131, "Transforms and Shapes" on page 135, "Drawing" on page 158, and "Printing" on page 180.

■ **Activation.** Through this protocol your part activates and deactivates itself (and its frames and facets). Your part interacts with the arbitrator to change ownership of the selection, menu, and keystroke foci, and to notify the parts and frames involved of the changes.

Your part must participate in this protocol if it ever needs to be active or if it needs any of the other focus types. The activation protocol is described in the section "Focus Transfer" on page 207.

■ **User events.** OpenDoc uses this protocol to distribute events such as keystrokes and mouse clicks to the appropriate part editors. The document shell, the arbitrator, and the dispatcher use focus-ownership information and the facet hierarchy to deliver these events to your part.

Your part must participate in this protocol if it handles events. The user-events protocol is introduced in the section "About Event Handling in OpenDoc" on page 189 and is described in more detail in other parts of Chapter 5.

■ **Storage.** Your part uses the storage protocol to write its content and its state information persistently in its document, and subsequently to retrieve it from the document. You interact with your draft object and your part's storage unit when reading and writing your part, and you may also interact with other drafts and storage units when using the clipboard, drag-and-drop, and linking protocols.

All parts must participate in this protocol. The part-storage protocol is described in the sections "Storage Units, Properties, and Values" on page 270 and "Documents, Drafts, and Parts" on page 284.

■ **Binding.** The OpenDoc document shell controls the runtime binding of your part editor to the parts in a document that it can edit. Your part's methods are not called during binding. The binding protocol is discussed in the section "Binding" on page 474.

■ **Linking.** Your part can use the linking protocol to export updatable data to another part or to incorporate or embed an updatable copy of another part's data into your part. If your part is the source of a link, you interact with a link-source object; if your part is the destination of a link, you interact with a link object.

Your part must participate in this protocol if it supports linking. The linking protocol is described in the section "Linking" on page 372.

■ **Embedding.** Your part uses this protocol to embed other parts within itself and to interact with those parts.

Your part participates in this protocol if it is a container part—that is, if it is capable of embedding parts within itself. The embedding protocol is described in the section "Frame and Facet Hierarchies" on page 103.

- **Clipboard.** The clipboard protocol allows the user to use menu commands to move content elements and embedded parts into or out of your part, from or to a system-maintained buffer. Your part interacts with the clipboard object both when copying to the clipboard and when pasting from it.

  Your part must participate in this protocol if it supports clipboard transfer. The clipboard protocol is described in the section "Clipboard Transfer" on page 355.

- **Drag and drop.** The drag-and-drop protocol allows the use of direct manipulation to move content elements and embedded parts into or out of your part or within your part. Your part interacts with the drag-and-drop object.

  Your part must participate in this protocol if it supports drag and drop. The drag-and-drop protocol is described in the section "Drag and Drop" on page 361.

- **Undo.** Your part uses this protocol to give the user the capability of reversing the effects of recently executed commands. Your part interacts with the undo object to perform the reversals.

  Your part must participate in this protocol if it has an undo capability. The undo protocol is described in the section "Undo" on page 260.

- **Extensions.** The extension protocol is a very general mechanism for extending your part's capabilities; it consists of an interface in the form of a specialized extension object that other part editors can access.

  Your part participates in this protocol if it provides OpenDoc extensions. The extensions protocol is described in the section "The OpenDoc Extension Interface" on page 441.

- **Semantic events.** Your part uses the semantic events protocol to make itself scriptable. It interacts with the semantic interface object when receiving scripting messages (semantic events); it interacts with the message interface object when sending scripting messages.

  Your part must participate in this protocol if it is scriptable. The semantic events protocol is described in the section "Scripting and OpenDoc" on page 403.

■ **Memory management.** OpenDoc manages the memory needed for the document containing your part.

In general, your part editor does not need to be concerned with memory management except to make sure that it deletes or releases objects that it has created or obtained. The memory-management protocol and the use of reference counting are further discussed in the section "Creating and Releasing Objects" on page 463.

Table 2-1 lists the methods of `ODPart` that you must override to have a functioning part editor, as well as those that you can optionally override to participate in specific protocols. Note that some protocols, such as layout, imaging, and activation, are required of all part editors, and you must override some or all of the methods associated with them. Other protocols, such as embedding or undo, are not required, and you need not override any of their methods if your parts do not participate. It is, of course, strongly recommended that your parts participate in all protocols that are appropriate to their content model.

Table 2-1   Required and optional `ODPart` overrides

Protocol	Required overrides	Optional overrides
Layout	AttachSourceFrame ContainingPartPropertiesUpdated DisplayFrameAdded DisplayFrameClosed DisplayFrameConnected DisplayFrameRemoved FacetAdded FacetRemoved FrameShapeChanged GeometryChanged Open SequenceChanged	AcquireContainingPartProperties* RevealFrame*
Imaging	CanvasChanged Draw GetPrintResolution HighlightChanged PresentationChanged ViewTypeChanged	AdjustBorderShape* CanvasUpdated*

continued

Table 2-1 Required and optional `ODPart` overrides (continued)

Protocol	Required overrides	Optional overrides
Activation	AbortRelinquishFocus BeginRelinquishFocus CommitRelinquishFocus FocusAcquired FocusLost	
User events	AdjustMenus HandleEvent	
Storage	CloneInto[†] ClonePartInfo Externalize[†] ExternalizeKinds InitPart InitPartFromStorage ReadPartInfo WritePartInfo	somInit[†] somUninit[†]
Binding	ChangeKind	
Memory Management	ReleaseAll[†]	Acquire[†] Purge[†] Release[†]
Linking	LinkStatusChanged	CreateLink EditInLinkAttempted[*] FulfillPromise[‡] LinkUpdated RevealLink
Embedding		CreateEmbeddedFramesIterator[*] EmbeddedFrameUpdated[*] RemoveEmbeddedFrame[*] RequestEmbeddedFrame[*] RequestFrameShape[*] UsedShapeChanged[*]
Clipboard		FulfillPromise[‡]

continued

Table 2-1   Required and optional `ODPart` overrides (continued)

Protocol	Required overrides	Optional overrides
Drag and drop		`DragEnter`
		`DragLeave`
		`DragWithin`
		`Drop`
		`DropCompleted`
		`FulfillPromise`[‡]
Undo		`DisposeActionState`
		`ReadActionState`[‡]
		`RedoAction`
		`UndoAction`
		`WriteActionState`[‡]
Extensions		`AcquireExtension`[†]
		`HasExtension`[†]
		`ReleaseExtension`[†]
Semantic events		`EmbeddedFrameSpec`[*]

[*] Required of all parts that support embedding
[†] Defined in a superclass of `ODPart`
[‡] Optional even if you implement this protocol

Generally, you must override all of the optional methods listed for a given protocol (other than those marked with [‡] in Table 2-1) if you are to participate in that protocol. For example, to participate in the extensions protocol, you must override all three methods `AcquireExtension`, `HasExtension`, and `ReleaseExtension`. The embedding protocol has even further requirements; to support embedding, you must not only override all the optional methods listed for that protocol, but you must override several methods associated with other protocols (marked with [*] in Table 2-1).

Development Scenarios

This section contains a high-level discussion of several possible OpenDoc development scenarios. Reading the scenarios may help you to decide what kinds of OpenDoc component software you are most interested in developing. Specifically, it discusses

- creating a part editor for noncontainer parts

- creating a part editor for container parts

- converting a conventional application into a part editor

- converting a conventional application into a container application

- developing OpenDoc components that are not part editors

Writing an Editor for Noncontainer Parts

Writing a part editor that does not support embedding is somewhat simpler than writing an editor that does. Furthermore, if you are starting from scratch (not modifying an existing application), you are free to consider all aspects of the design of your part editor before you implement anything.

1. **Content model.** Create a content model that defines the functioning of your part editor and the OpenDoc protocols that it participates in. If your parts are to be scriptable (see step 6), your part's content objects and operations must reflect that content model.

2. **Core engine.** Design and implement your core data engine, the set of data structures and behaviors that manifest the basic purpose of your editor.

3. **Storage.** Implement persistent storage in these situations:

   - Use the OpenDoc storage system to store your part editor's data. Your part editor must implement code to initialize a part and to write it back to storage.

   - Implement clipboard and drag-and-drop capabilities to transfer information between parts, using the same OpenDoc storage concepts for data transfer as for persistent storage.

   - Implement linking support, using a combination of event-handling code and storage code (similar to support for document storage, clipboard, and drag and drop).

4. **Drawing.** Give your part the capability of drawing its content, properly transformed and clipped, in whatever combination of facets and frames the content appears, onscreen or offscreen, and for screen display or for printing.

5. **Event handling.** Give your part editor the capability of responding to user events such as mouse clicks and keystrokes. It must also respond properly to activation and deactivation events, and use the OpenDoc menu bar object to manipulate the contents of the menu bar.

6. **Scripting.** To support scripting, you must first define the content model of your parts, as noted earlier (step 1). Then you must implement accessor functions to resolve object specifiers (external references to a part's content objects) as well as semantic-event handlers to perform your part's content operations.

7. **Extensions.** If you plan to extend the capabilities of your parts to communicate with other parts or process information fast, create and attach an extension interface to your part editor. To obtain existing public extension interface designs or to propose a new public interface, contact CI Labs.

8. **Packaging and shipping.** Once your part editor is complete, package one or more stationery documents with your part editor, as templates of your part kind. Provide information (in the form of name-mapping resources on the Mac OS) for the OpenDoc binding process to use, indicating what part kinds are handled, what semantic events are handled, and what extension interfaces are provided.

Once your part editor is complete, you typically create one or more stationery documents, which are empty versions or other kinds of templates for creating parts with your part kind. Stationery documents are commonly blank, but they may have any content you wish, including other embedded parts.

You ship your product as one or more part editors, plus one or more stationery documents, plus accompanying documentation. Users install your part editor into their systems and then, using the stationery, create new documents of your part kind or insert new parts with your part kind into their documents. Rules and conventions for installing part editors and storing documents vary among platforms. For Mac OS platform rules, see Appendix C, "Installing OpenDoc Software and Parts."

Users themselves can create additional, custom stationery documents. Users should be able to exchange documents, including stationery, freely.

Writing an Editor for Container Parts

If your part editor is to support embedding—that is, if its parts are to be container parts—you need to include the following additional steps:

9. **Embedding.** You need to add embedding support to your content model and to storage.

   ☐ Your content model needs to include a type of content element that represents an embedded part. If your part editor supports semantic events, embedded parts must be content objects to which you can pass events.

   ☐ Make sure your parts can store embedded parts, both in their documents and during data transfer. This capability is relatively simple to implement; OpenDoc takes care of most of it.

10. **Layout management.** You need to add support for layout management during event handling and during frame negotiation.

   ☐ Your part editor must be able to maintain updated information on embedded frames and facets, and notify embedded parts of such changes. It must add facets when embedded frames become visible. It must modify or delete facets when embedded frames move or become no longer visible.

   ☐ Your part editor must include support for layout negotiation, including updating the shapes and transforms associated with each visible embedded frame and facet.

For a summary of the issues to consider in creating a part editor for container parts, see Appendix A, "Embedding Checklist."

Converting a Conventional Application to a Part Editor

Creating a part editor from an existing conventional application involves maintaining its core features but repackaging them for the OpenDoc environment.

1. **Content model and core data engine.** You should have your content model and core data engine already in place. You may need to separate your core data engine from other facilities, such as user interface and storage, if it is not already sufficiently separated.

2. **Storage.** You must refit all file I/O and clipboard data transfers into OpenDoc terms, as described for part editors in step 3 on page 93.

Development Overview

3. **Event handling.** Because your part editor will receive its event information from the document shell, you need to remove your event loop and event-handling code.

4. **Scripting.** You can add scripting support, as described for part editors in step 6 on page 94.

5. **Extensions.** You can extend the capabilities of your parts, as described for part editors in step 7 on page 94.

6. **Packaging and shipping.** Package and ship your part editor, as described for part editors in step 8 on page 94.

If your converted application is to be a container part, you need to follow these additional steps:

7. **Embedding.** Add embedding support, as described for part editors in step 9 on page 95.

8. **Layout management.** Add layout-management code, as described for part editors in step 10 on page 95.

Converting a Conventional Application to a Container Application

If you have an existing application, the simplest way to give it some OpenDoc capabilities may be to convert it into an embedding application (also called a **container application**), so that it can embed parts. A container application's documents still belong to it but may also contain embedded frames and data from embedded parts.

A container application performs some tasks of a container part, although it never has to act as an embedded part. It also handles some tasks normally performed by the OpenDoc document shell; the document shell is not executing when a container application's document opens. The container application initializes the session object at startup and disposes of it at shutdown. The container application accepts platform-specific user events, converts them to OpenDoc user events, passes them to the dispatcher, and takes care of events that the dispatcher does not handle.

Here are some general considerations to keep in mind if you develop a container application:

1. **Initialization.** Because the document shell is not available, your container application needs code to initialize the OpenDoc class library.

2. **Storage.** Because all OpenDoc parts in a given document share persistent storage, you must refit all file I/O and clipboard data transfers into

96   Writing OpenDoc Software

OpenDoc terms, as described for part editors in step 3 on page 93. You can use OpenDoc calls to store and retrieve your application's intrinsic data without changing the data format, as long as it is stream-oriented. (The OpenDoc container-application library contains code that helps with reads and writes.) Embedded parts can then also use the regular OpenDoc calls for reading and writing their own data.

Your container application cannot support OpenDoc drafts of its documents (if it uses the container-application library).

3. **Data transfer.** Your container application need do nothing to support clipboard transfer, drag and drop, or linking of content to or from embedded parts. However, for transfers that involve your application's intrinsic content mixed with embedded parts, your application will need to translate between the platform-specific facilities and OpenDoc facilities.

4. **Drawing.** Your basic drawing routines need little modification, except that you need to set up your drawing so that it is properly transformed and clipped in your embedded parts' facets and frames. When your container application receives an update event for synchronous drawing, it draws its own content and then passes the event to the OpenDoc dispatcher so that embedded parts can also redraw.

5. **Event handling.** Because your application takes the place of the document shell, it needs to pass all user events to the OpenDoc dispatcher first—and handle them only if OpenDoc does not.

To make this work, you can have a proxy root part, with a frame and facet that correspond to your document window. Events not handled by actual embedded parts are then passed to the proxy part and therefore back to your application for handling. Other parts of OpenDoc can also communicate with those proxies in a normal fashion, and your application can convert those communications into actions that make sense for your application.

Although OpenDoc supports multiple levels of undo, only one undoable action is preserved when the user switches from an embedded part to your native content. Your container application needs to manage the Undo and Redo menu items itself.

6. **Embedding.** You need to add embedding support, as described for part editors in step 9 on page 95.

7. **Layout management.** You need to add layout-management code, as described for part editors in step 10 on page 95. Your container application does not necessarily have to support frame negotiation.

8. **Scripting.** You can add scripting support, as described for part editors in step 6 on page 94.

To make development of a container application even easier, OpenDoc is distributed with a container-application library (CALib) that contains helpful code. CALib includes support for proxy objects and has other useful features.

Writing Other Types of Component Software

This book primarily describes how to create a part editor. However, you are not limited to that alone. Development of container applications is discussed briefly in the previous section. Using the OpenDoc class libraries, you can also create other kinds of OpenDoc component software:

- **Part viewers** are simply part editors with their editing and saving capabilities removed or disabled. A part viewer should be able to read, display, and print its parts.

  Development issues for part viewers are a subset of those for fully functional part editors. A part viewer can be much smaller than its corresponding editor, and it can be developed from the same code base.

  To encourage data interchange, you should always create a part viewer for every part editor you develop, and you should distribute the viewer widely and without cost or obligation to the user.

- Part **extensions** are objects with which you can extend the programming interface of your part editor. Extensions work in conjunction with part editors, allowing their parts to communicate with and directly manipulate other parts. Extensions are described in Chapter 10, "Extending OpenDoc."

- Document-shell **plug-ins** are extensions to the capabilities of the OpenDoc shell. They are shared libraries that you can write and install. Shell plug-ins are described in the section "Shell Plug-Ins" on page 449.

- Part or document **services** are OpenDoc components that, instead of editing and saving parts in a document, provide specialized services to those parts and documents. Spelling checkers, database-retrieval engines, and network connection services are all examples.

  You develop an OpenDoc service much as you develop a part editor. Like part editors, services are subclasses of `ODPart`. However, services commonly use less of the embedding, layout, and imaging protocols of OpenDoc, and they usually communicate with the parts they serve through an extension interface (a subclass of `ODExtension`). The extension interface is described in Chapter 10, "Extending OpenDoc."

Programming

CHAPTER 3

Frames and Facets

Contents

This is the first of eight chapters that discuss the OpenDoc programming interface in detail. This chapter focuses on the key concepts of how parts use frames and facets to accomplish embedding and to communicate with each other during layout and display.

Before reading this chapter, you should be familiar with the concepts presented in Chapter 1, "Introduction to OpenDoc," and Chapter 2, "Development Overview." For additional concepts related to your part editor's runtime environment, see Chapter 11, "OpenDoc Runtime Features."

This chapter starts with a general discussion of frames and facets, and then describes

- how your part uses its display frames and facets to function as an embedded part in an OpenDoc document

- how your part can negotiate with its containing part for modifications to its display frames

If your part is a noncontainer part, these are the only parts of this chapter you need to read. If, however, you are developing a container part, you also need to read the remainder of this chapter. It describes

- how to negotiate with your embedded parts for modifications to their display frames

- how to otherwise manipulate the frames and facets of your embedded parts

For a general summary of the embedding process, see "Adding an Embedded Part" on page 305. For a summary of embedding capabilities that must be implemented by container parts, see also Appendix A, "Embedding Checklist."

Frame and Facet Hierarchies

The object hierarchy of embedding controls how information is passed among the parts that make up a compound document. Parts and embedded frames make up one hierarchy; facets make up a separate but essentially parallel hierarchy.

Frames and Facets

Figure 3-1 shows a simple example of these hierarchies. The document illustrated in the figure consists of a graphics root part ("draw part"), in which are embedded a clock ("clock part") and a text-processing part ('text part"). The text part has a movie-viewing part ("movie part") embedded within it.

This figure uses the same conventions as the more detailed runtime diagrams presented in the section "Runtime Object Relationships" on page 487. Individual OpenDoc objects are represented by labeled boxes, with the references (pointers in C++) between them drawn as arrows. (Different arrows have different appearances in Figure 3-1 for clarity only; all represent the same kinds of object references.)The embedding structure extends downward, with more deeply embedded objects shown lower in the diagram.

Figure 3-1   Simplified frame and facet hierarchies in a document

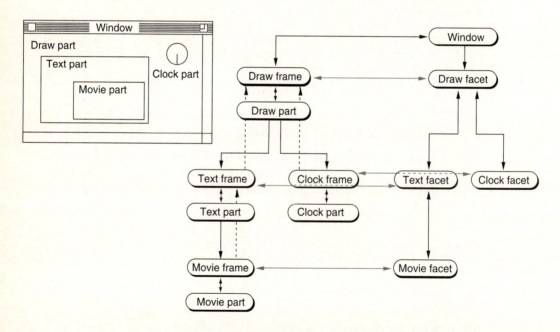

The window object is at the top of Figure 3-1, uniting the two object hierarchies. The window object itself is referenced by the window state object, as shown in Figure 11-5 on page 492.

Frames and Parts

The fundamental structure of embedding in the compound document is represented by the hierarchy on the left in Figure 3-1. The draw part is the root part of the document; it directly references its two embedded frames. Those frames in turn reference their parts, the text part and the clock part. The text part references its one embedded frame, which in turn references its part, the movie part. Each part thus references its own embedded parts only indirectly. (In this case, there is one display frame per part, but there could be more than one.)

Note that each part also has a reference back up the hierarchy to its display frame, and each frame has a direct upward reference up to its containing frame. See Figure 11-6 on page 493 for a more general picture of the object structure of embedding.

The embedding relationship of parts and frames does not have to be the strict hierarchy shown in Figure 3-1. For example, a single part can have frames embedded at different levels, as in Figure 4-18 on page 177.

Parts and frames are stored together in their document. When the document is closed, the states of all the parts and frames are saved. When the document is reopened, all the parts and frames are restored by reading in the saved data.

Facets

The hierarchy on the right in Figure 3-1 is analogous to the one on the left, but it is simpler and more direct. The facet hierarchy is designed for fast drawing and event dispatching. Each facet corresponds to its equivalent frame, but it directly references its embedded facets. (In this case, there is one facet per visible frame, but there could be more than one.)

Whereas frames must exist (at least in storage, if not always in memory) for all embedded parts in a document, facets are needed for only those frames that are visible at any one moment. Because the facet hierarchy is for drawing and event dispatching, there is no need to have facets that can't be drawn and can't accept events.

Facets are ephemeral; they are not stored when a document is saved. Facets are created and deleted by their frames' containing parts, as the facets' frames become visible or invisible because of scrolling, resizing of frames or windows, or opening and closing of windows.

As Figure 3-1 shows, each frame has a direct reference to (and from) its equivalent facet. That frame-to-facet reference is the connection between the two hierarchies. Each part object therefore references its own facets only indirectly, through its display frames. (Your part can, of course, keep its own private list of its facets.)

Working With Your Display Frames and Facets

Your part's **display frames** are the frames in which you draw your part's contents. This section discusses how to request or respond to changes and additions to those frames.

You do not directly create your own part's display frames; your part's containing part does that. When your part is first created or first read into memory from storage, the containing part of your part will in most cases have already provided at least one frame for your part to display itself in. However, it is possible that your part can be instantiated without already having a display frame (see "Adding an Embedded Part" on page 305). Your part should allow for that possibility.

Your part should also allow for the possibility of multiple display frames. Your part must keep a list of its display frames, with enough information so that your part knows how to display itself in each and synchronize their displays when necessary. OpenDoc does not specify the format of that list. It is your responsibility to keep the list and to update each display frame that has been affected by any change to your part.

Responding to Reconnected and Closed Display Frames

When the document containing your part opens and your previously stored display frames are read in and instantiated, OpenDoc calls your part's `DisplayFrameConnected` method. Here is its interface (note that this and all other method prototypes in this book are written in IDL):

```
void DisplayFrameConnected(in ODFrame frame);
```

Your `DisplayFrameConnected` method should update your part's internal list of display frames and other related structures to reflect the addition of the frame. It should assign the frame's used shape, if different from the frame shape itself. The method should also check the frame's *content extent* and update it if necessary, as described in "Content Extent" on page 143. The method should also call the frame's `SetDroppable` method if you wish the frame to be able to accept drops.

Unlike `DisplayFrameAdded` (see page 111), your `DisplayFrameConnected` method does not normally have to create new part info data or a new set of embedded frames for the display frame, because they will have been created earlier.

When your part's document is closed, OpenDoc calls your part's `DisplayFrameClosed` method when it closes your display frame.

```
void DisplayFrameClosed(in ODFrame frame);
```

Your `DisplayFrameClosed` method should

1. update your part's internal list of display frames and other related structures to reflect the closing of the frame

2. relinquish any foci owned by the frame (see "Relinquishing Foci" on page 210)

3. unregister the frame, if your part has registered it for idle time (see "Null Events" on page 196)

4. call the `Close` method of all your embedded frames

If this frame is the root frame of your window and you have previously instructed OpenDoc not to dispose of the platform-specific window structure (see "Allocating Window Memory Efficiently" on page 227), you must dispose of the platform window yourself at this time.

Closing and reconnecting can happen at other times as well:

■ When a part's editor is changed at runtime, OpenDoc calls the `DisplayFrameClosed` method of the editor losing the part and the `DisplayFrameConnected` method of the editor receiving the part.

■ For efficient memory use, a containing part may not always keep frame objects in memory for all of its embedded frames. Instead, as described in the section "Reconnecting and Releasing Embedded Frames" on page 123, it might release frames as they become invisible through scrolling, and recreate them as they become visible. Released frames can then be closed by OpenDoc.

Do not update your persistently stored display frames when your
`DisplayFrameConnected` or `DisplayFrameClosed` methods is called; these
methods should have no effect on stored data. In general, you should write
your part content and frames to storage only when your `Externalize` or
`ExternalizeKinds` methods is called.

Responding to Added or Removed Facets

When your part's containing part has added a facet to one of your part's
display frames, the display frame notifies your part of the addition by calling
your part's `FacetAdded` method. Here is its interface:

```
void FacetAdded(in ODFacet facet);
```

Your `FacetAdded` method must perform certain actions to handle the addition
of the new facet to one of your frames. Some actions depend on the nature and
implementation of your part itself, but others are standard.

1. The `FacetAdded` method should examine the facet's canvas to make sure
    your part editor understands how to draw on that canvas; it should return
    an error if it does not understand.

2. The method should store any private information that it needs as part info
    data in the facet that is being added. Although a facet's part info is not
    persistent, it can hold information (such as a view port reference, for
    example) that the facet needs for display.

3. The method should assign an active shape to the facet, if needed. If you do
    not explicitly assign an active shape, OpenDoc uses the frame shape of the
    facet's associated frame as the active shape.

4. The method should create facets for all embedded frames that are visible
    within the area of the added facet. See "Adding a Facet" on page 124.

When a containing part removes a facet from one of your part's display frames,
the frame notifies your part by calling your part's `FacetRemoved` method, which
has the following interface:

```
void FacetRemoved(in ODFacet facet);
```

Your `FacetRemoved` method must perform certain actions to handle the removal of the facet. In general, this method reverses the actions performed by `FacetAdded`. Typically, the method should at least

1. remove the facets for all embedded frames that were visible in the area of the removed facet

2. delete any part info data that was referenced in the facet

Facets are intended to be ephemeral objects; don't retain references to them when they are no longer needed. Your `FacetRemoved` method should delete all references to the facets that it removes.

Note
If your part is visible in a window, it receives a `FacetAdded` call from its display frame when the window opens, and a `FacetRemoved` call when the window closes. ◆

Resizing a Display Frame

Because of editing operations in your part, or because of an undesirable frame size imposed by your part's containing part, you may wish to change the size or shape of your display frame. You must negotiate this change with the containing part. (For an example of frame negotiation, showing the points of view of both the containing part and the embedded part, see the section "Frame Negotiation" on page 116.)

You start by requesting a new frame size from your part's containing part. Depending on its current contents and other constraints such as gridding, the containing part may grant the requested size, return a different size, or in essence refuse the request by returning a size identical to your current frame size.

To request a new frame size, take these steps:

1. Call the `RequestFrameShape` method of your display frame. The frame in turn calls the containing part's `RequestFrameShape` method to forward the request.

2. The containing part may honor the request, or it may decide on a different (usually smaller) shape. It returns the shape it will let your display frame have. The frame stores it as its frame shape and returns it to you.

3. Use the returned frame shape to update the used shape for that frame. At this time, you can also update the active shape of your frame's facet.

4. If your part does not wish to accept the new shape, it can call the frame's `RequestFrameShape` method again, but with a different shape to avoid endless repetition of these steps. Alternatively, it can request an additional frame, as described in the section "Requesting an Additional Display Frame" (next).

Requesting an Additional Display Frame

Your part may need a display frame in addition to the frame or frames already created by your part's containing part. For example, you may need to flow content into another frame (as when you add another column or page of text), or you may need another frame to display your part with a new presentation.

To request another frame, you can call the `RequestEmbeddedFrame` method of the containing part. You must specify one of your current display frames as the **base frame,** the frame that defines certain characteristics of the new frame.

- The new frame is a **sibling** of the base frame; that is, it is embedded at the same level as the base frame.

- The new frame is in the same frame group as the base frame.

- The new frame has a sequence number within the base frame's frame group, assigned by the containing part. (By convention, the containing part adds the new frame to the end of the sequence in that group.)

You also pass additional information, such as the new frame's view type, presentation, and overlay status (that is, whether it should **overlay,** or float over, the content of the containing part).

The shape you request for the new frame is understood to be expressed in the frame coordinates of the base frame (see "Frame Coordinate Space" on page 136). Thus you can request a position for the new frame that is relative to the base frame (such as above, below, to the side, or overlapping) by specifying an origin that is offset from the base frame's origin. The containing part has ultimate control over frame positioning, however, and is not required to size or place the new frame exactly as you request. Furthermore, the frame shape returned by the containing part is by convention **normalized;** that is, the relative-positioning information has been stripped from it and its origin is at (0, 0).

The containing part responds to this call as described in "Adding an Embedded Frame on Request" on page 120. Your part then responds as described in "Responding to an Added Display Frame" (next).

Responding to an Added Display Frame

When an additional display frame is created, OpenDoc automatically connects it to the part it displays. This automatic connection ensures that frames are always valid and usable; the object that creates the new frame need do nothing beyond creating the frame itself.

To achieve that automatic connection, the part displayed in the frame must respond to this method call, which informs the part that it has a new frame:

```
void DisplayFrameAdded(in ODFrame frame);
```

Your part receives this call when it is first created and has no previously stored display frame, and also when additional display frames are created for it. In response to this call, your part's DisplayFrameAdded method performs the appropriate tasks. Most of them depend on the nature and implementation of your part itself; however, here are some general actions it should take:

1. The method should add the new display frame to your part's list of display frames. This list, like other internal structures, is completely hidden from OpenDoc. You can represent the list any way you choose.

2. The method should validate the view type and presentation of the new frame. Your part should accept any view types that are in the required set of view types, plus any other view types or presentations that you support. The DisplayFrameAdded method should correct these values if necessary, as described in the section "Defining General Display Characteristics" on page 158.

3. The method should assign your part's current *content extent* to the frame, using the frame's ChangeContentExtent method; see "Content Extent" on page 143 for an explanation.

4. The method should assign a used shape for the frame. If you do not specifically assign a used shape, the frame shape is used; a containing part that calls the frame's AcquireUsedShape method receives the frame shape in that case.

5. The method should add any needed part info to the frame, by calling the frame's `SetPartInfo` method. See the section "Part Info" on page 160 for more information.

6. If the frame being added is the root frame of its window, your part may want to activate itself. Part activation is described in the section "How Part Activation Happens" on page 198. (This situation can occur only when your part is first opened into a window, such as a part window; it cannot happen when an additional display frame for the current window is created.)

7. If the frame being added can accept dropped data, the method should call the frame's `SetDroppable` method, passing it a value of `kODTrue`. (Frames, by default, are not droppable.) Otherwise, the frame will not be able to receive data through drag and drop. See "Drag and Drop" on page 361 for more information.

Your part should not perform any layout or imaging tasks as a result of a display frame being added; specifically, it should not at this point negotiate with its containing part for a different frame shape. It should wait until its `FacetAdded` method is called, by which time the containing part has stored the frame shape and the frame has become visible.

Note
OpenDoc calls `DisplayFrameAdded` only when a frame is newly created. When your part opens and its stored display frame is recreated, OpenDoc calls your part's `DisplayFrameConnected` method; see "Responding to Reconnected and Closed Display Frames" on page 106. ◆

Removing a Display Frame

To remove a frame in which your part is displayed, you call the `RemoveEmbeddedFrame` method of your part's containing part (see "Removing an Embedded Frame" on page 122). You can remove only those frames that you have previously requested through calls to your containing part's `RequestEmbeddedFrame` method. Your other display frames can be removed only by your containing part.

When the containing part receives the `RemoveEmbeddedFrame` call, it permanently severs all connection between your part and the frame (and the draft object may delete the frame from storage if its reference count becomes 0). Just before deleting the frame, OpenDoc calls your part's `DisplayFrameRemoved` method (next).

Responding to a Removed Display Frame

Your part's containing part can also initiate removal of one of your display frames, as described in "Removing an Embedded Frame" on page 122. The removal may occur, for example, if your frame is part of a selection that is cut or deleted.

Regardless of whether your part or the containing part initiates the removal, OpenDoc calls your part's `DisplayFrameRemoved` method. This is its interface:

```
void DisplayFrameRemoved(in ODFrame frame);
```

In your `DisplayFrameRemoved` method, take steps such as these:

1. Relinquish any foci owned by the frame (see "Relinquishing Foci" on page 210).

2. Delete any part info that your part had associated with the frame. Set the frame's part info data to null by calling the frame's `SetPartInfo` method.

3. Unregister the frame, if your part had registered it for idle time (see "Null Events" on page 196).

4. Update your part's internal list of display frames and other related structures to reflect the removal of the frame.

5. Remove in turn any embedded frames that your part had been displaying in the removed frame. Check the identity of the embedded frame's containing frame to determine which call to make:

   ▫ If your (removed) display frame is designated as the embedded frame's containing frame, the display frame has not been moved from your part to another object. In this case, call the embedded frame's `Remove` method.

   ▫ If your (removed) display frame is *not* designated as the embedded frame's containing frame, the display frame has been moved from your part to another object. In this case, call the embedded frame's `Release` method.

If this frame is the root frame of your window and you have previously instructed OpenDoc not to dispose of the platform-specific window structure (see "Allocating Window Memory Efficiently" on page 227), you must dispose of the platform window yourself at this time.

Note
OpenDoc calls `DisplayFrameRemoved` only when a frame is permanently removed from your part. When your part closes and OpenDoc stores its display frame, OpenDoc calls your part's `DisplayFrameClosed` method; see "Responding to Reconnected and Closed Display Frames" on page 106. ◆

Grouping Display Frames

As an embedded part, your part does not directly control the frames in which it is displayed. However, you may need to flow text or other content in order through a sequence of separate display frames of your part (as for page-layout purposes). If so, you can request that the containing part create and assign you the needed frames as a sequence in a single frame group. See "Creating Frame Groups" on page 126 and "Displaying Continuous Content in Sequenced Frames" on page 584.

If your part's containing part adds a new frame to your display frame's group or reorders the sequence of one of your display frames within its group (by calling the frame's `ChangeSequenceNumber` method), OpenDoc calls your part's `SequenceChanged` method. This is its interface:

```
void SequenceChanged(in ODFrame frame);
```

Your part can then retrieve the new sequence number of the frame by calling its `GetSequenceNumber` method.

Synchronizing Display Frames

Sometimes, views of your part in two or more separate frames must be **synchronized,** meaning that any editing or other changes to the contents of one (the **source frame**) must force updating of the other. In some cases, such as when you open one of your display frames into a window, you can determine these dependencies internally. In other cases, you cannot. For example, if your

part is an embedded part and your containing part creates multiple views of
your part, your containing part asks you to synchronize those views by calling
your part's `AttachSourceFrame` method. This is its interface:

```
void AttachSourceFrame(in ODFrame frame,
                       in ODFrame sourceFrame);
```

Your `AttachSourceFrame` method should take whatever action is necessary to
synchronize the frames; make sure that the result of any editing in one frame
appears in the other. At a minimum, if the two frames have the same
presentation, the method should duplicate all the embedded frames of one
frame into the other (and attach them to their source frames as well).

It is the containing frame that determines when embedded frames must be
synchronized. See "Synchronizing Embedded Frames" on page 126.

Adopting Container Properties

As described in the section "Transmitting Your Container Properties to
Embedded Parts" on page 127, a containing part can notify its embedded parts
of the *container properties,* the characteristics of its content that it expects the
embedded parts to adopt. For example, if your part is a text part and the user
embeds it in another text part, the containing part may expect your part to
adopt the general text appearance (font, size, stylistic variation, and so on) of
the containing part.

Your part can, of course, adopt only those container properties whose format
and meaning it understands. You obtain the set of container properties
that your containing part makes available for adoption by calling the
`AcquireContainingPartProperties` method of your containing part.

A containing part calls your part's `ContainingPartPropertiesUpdated` method
when it changes any of the container properties available for your part to
adopt. This is its interface:

```
void ContainingPartPropertiesUpdated
                    (in ODFrame frame,
                     in ODStorageUnit propertyUnit);
```

Your `ContainingPartPropertiesUpdated` method should read and adopt any container properties that it understands from the provided storage unit. Then, it should in turn call the `ContainingPartPropertiesUpdated` method of any of your part's own embedded frames (other than bundled frames) that are displayed within the frame passed to `ContainingPartPropertiesUpdated`.

Frame Negotiation

Each part in an OpenDoc document controls the positions, sizes, and shapes of its embedded frames. At the same time, embedded parts may need to change the sizes, shapes, or numbers of the frames in which they are displayed. Read this section if your part expects to negotiate its display frame sizes with its containing part, or if it is a container part and expects to negotiate the sizes of its embedded frames with their parts.

Either party can initiate the negotiation, although the containing part has unilateral control over the outcome. Figure 3-2 shows an example of frame negotiation. In this example, an embedded part with a single display frame requests a larger frame size from its containing part, which has two display frames.

Figure 3-2   An example of frame negotiation with multiple frames

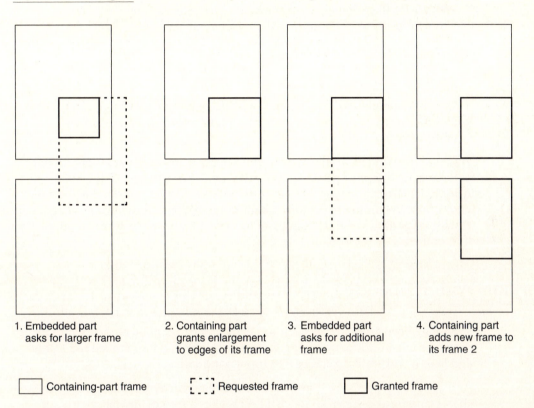

1. Embedded part
   asks for larger frame

2. Containing part
   grants enlargement
   to edges of its frame

3. Embedded part
   asks for additional
   frame

4. Containing part
   adds new frame to
   its frame 2

☐ Containing-part frame   ⌐ ¬ Requested frame   ☐ Granted frame

In this case, the embedded part initiates the frame negotiation. Its frame is wholly contained within frame 1 (the upper frame) of the containing part.

1. The embedded part asks the containing part for a significantly larger frame, perhaps to fit material pasted in from the clipboard. The embedded frame is not concerned with, and does not even know, where or how the larger frame will fit into the containing part's content.

2. The containing part decides, on the basis of its own content model, that the requested frame is too large to fit within frame 1. The containing part instead increases the size of the embedded frame as much as it can, assigns it a place in its content area, and returns the resulting frame to the embedded part.

3. The embedded part accepts the frame given to it. If it were to repeat step 1 and ask for the original larger frame again, the containing part would simply repeat step 2 and return the same frame.

   But the embedded part still wants more area for its display, so it tries a different tack; it requests another display frame, this time to be embedded in frame 2 (the lower frame) of the embedded part.

4. The containing part decides that the requested frame will fit in frame 2. It assigns the frame a place within frame 2 and returns the frame to the embedded part.

Frame negotiation from the point of view of the embedded part is discussed in the sections "Resizing a Display Frame" on page 109 and "Requesting an Additional Display Frame" on page 110. Frame negotiation from the point of view of the containing part is discussed in the sections "Resizing an Embedded Frame" on page 121 and "Adding an Embedded Frame on Request" on page 120.

Working With Embedded Frames and Facets

Read the information in this section if your part can contain embedded parts. It discusses what information your part needs to maintain for embedded frames, and how it creates those embedded frames and facets.

As a containing part, your part needs to maintain current information on the shapes and transforms of all its visible embedded frames and facets. If your part makes changes to them, it should not only update its own information but in some cases also notify the embedded parts of the changes so that they can update their own information. Your part should also support frame negotiation (see "Frame Negotiation" on page 116), to permit embedded parts to request additional frames or changes to the sizes of their existing frames.

If your part is a container part, the user can embed other parts into your part in several ways. Examples include pasting from the clipboard, using drag and drop, choosing the Insert command from the Document menu, or even selecting a tool from a palette.

The overall process of embedding a part is summarized in the section "Adding an Embedded Part" on page 305. The overall process of removing a part is summarized in the section "Removing an Embedded Part" on page 307. Both processes make use of the specific tasks described in this section.

Providing an Embedded-Frames Iterator

Your part must keep a list of all its embedded frames. OpenDoc does not specify the format of this list. However, your part must implement an iterator class (a subclass of `ODEmbeddedFramesIterator`) that gives a caller access to each of the frames in your list of embedded frames. The caller creates an iterator to access your embedded frames by calling your part's `CreateEmbeddedFramesIterator` method, which has this interface:

```
ODEmbeddedFramesIterator CreateEmbeddedFramesIterator(in ODFrame frame);
```

Your implementation of `CreateEmbeddedFramesIterator` must provide `First`, `Next`, and `IsNotComplete` methods, as do other OpenDoc iterators. See "Accessing Objects Through Iterators" on page 471 for additional discussion.

Creating a New Embedded Frame

If your part embeds a part that does not already have its own display frame, you need to create a new embedded frame that will be the embedded part's display frame. Also, if you create an additional view of an existing embedded part (see, for example, "Multiple Views of a Part" on page 577), you need to create and embed a frame to hold the new view.

In these situations, your part—the containing part—initiates the embedded-frame creation. Your method to create an embedded frame calls the `CreateFrame` method of your draft, which returns an initialized frame that has already been assigned to the embedded part. (`CreateFrame` calls the `DisplayFrameAdded` method of the embedded part for this purpose.) This calling sequence ensures that you can use the new frame as soon as the draft returns it.

When you call `CreateFrame`, you specify several features of the new frame, including the following:

- containing frame: the frame (your display frame) that is to contain the embedded frame.

- frame shape: the shape of the frame to be created. Your part can use a default shape, or it can use information supplied with the data you are embedding. See "Frame Shape or Frame Annotation" on page 318 for more information.

- part: the part (your part) in which the frame is to be embedded.

- view type and presentation: the initial view type and presentation the part displayed in the embedded frame is to have.

- subframe: whether or not the embedded frame is to be a subframe of its containing frame (your display frame). See "Using Subframes to Suppress the Active Frame Border" on page 157 and "Using Multiple Facets" on page 174 for examples.

- overlay status: whether or not the frame should overlay, or float over, the containing frame.

Once the reference to the new frame is returned, take these steps:

1. Store it somewhere in your content and add it to your part's list of embedded frames. It's up to you to decide how your part internally stores its content, including its embedded frames.

2. Set the embedded frame's link status appropriately. See "Frame Link Status" on page 377 for more information. If your part does not support linking, you must nevertheless set the new frames' link status (to `kODNotInLink`).

3. If the embedded frame is visible within the containing frame, you must create a facet for it. See "Adding a Facet" on page 124.

Creating an frame should be an undoable action. See "Undo and Embedded Frames" on page 265 for information on how to set a frame's in-limbo flag when you undo or redo its creation.

For more information on the `DisplayFrameAdded` method, see "Responding to an Added Display Frame" on page 111.

Adding an Embedded Frame on Request

As a container part, your part may also need to support creation of an embedded frame when requested to do so by another part. As described in the section "Requesting an Additional Display Frame" on page 110, an embedded part can call your part's `RequestEmbeddedFrame` method to get an additional frame for its content. The embedded part passes the necessary information about the requested frame, as shown in this interface:

```
ODFrame RequestEmbeddedFrame(in ODFrame containingFrame,
                             in ODFrame baseFrame,
                             in ODShape frameShape,
                             in ODPart embedPart,
                             in ODTypeToken viewType,
                             in ODTypeToken presentation,
                             in ODBoolean isOverlaid);
```

Your `RequestEmbeddedFrame` method passes most of this information along to your draft's `CreateFrame` method. The `baseFrame` parameter specifies which of the embedded part's existing display frames is to be the base frame for the new frame; the newly created frame will be a sibling of the base frame and will be in the same frame group as the base frame.

The `frameShape` parameter passed to this method expresses the requested frame shape in the coordinate system of the base frame. By this method, the embedded part can request, by specifying the origin of the frame shape, a relative location for the new frame compared to its base frame. Your `RequestEmbeddedFrame` method should take this information into account when granting the frame shape and assigning an external transform to its facet. Specifically, you should incorporate the positioning information into the external transform (if appropriate, given the nature and state of your intrinsic content), and then return a frame shape that has been normalized—that is, one in which the origin of the frame shape is (0, 0).

Based on information in the existing frame, your `RequestEmbeddedFrame` method should also assign the new frame's group ID and sequence number, by calling its `SetFrameGroup` and `ChangeSequenceNumber` methods. Your part can assign the new frame any sequence number in the frame group, although by convention you should add the new frame to the end of the current sequence. Then the `RequestEmbeddedFrame` method should add the new frame to your part's list of embedded frames. The method should also create a facet for the new frame if it is visible.

Other tasks you perform are the same as when you initiate the creation of the frame (see the previous section, "Creating a New Embedded Frame"). You might implement your `RequestEmbeddedFrame` method in such a way that it calls a private method to actually create the frame. You could then use that same private method in both situations.

Resizing an Embedded Frame

To change a frame's size, the user typically selects the frame and manipulates the resize handles of the frame border. The containing part is responsible for drawing the selected frame border, determining what resize handles are appropriate, and interpreting drag actions on them.

You need to notify an embedded part that its frame has changed in these situations

■ if your part is the containing part of a frame that is resized by the user

- if your part has other reasons to change the size of an embedded frame (for example, to enforce gridding or in response to editing of your own intrinsic content surrounding the frame)

- if the embedded part's display frame has called your `RequestFrameShape` method for frame negotiation

This is the interface to `RequestFrameShape`:

```
ODShape RequestFrameShape(in ODFrame embeddedFrame,
                          in ODShape frameShape);
```

Return the changed shape (the same shape reference passed to you) in the method result. After you change the embedded frame's shape, call the frame's `ChangeFrameShape` method and pass it the new shape. (For efficiency, you can first acquire the embedded frame's existing frame shape, then resize it, then call `ChangeFrameShape`, and finally release your reference to the frame.) The frame in turn notifies its part by calling its `FrameShapeChanged` method. In response, the embedded part may request a different frame size, as discussed in the section "Resizing a Display Frame" on page 109.

Note that resizing may result in your part having to adjust the layout of its own intrinsic content, such as wrapped text.

Removing an Embedded Frame

You may need to remove an embedded frame from your part, either as a direct result of user editing (such as cutting or clearing a selection) or upon request of the part displayed in that frame.

An embedded part requests that you remove one of its display frames by calling your part's `RemoveEmbeddedFrame` method. This is its interface:

```
void RemoveEmbeddedFrame(in ODFrame embeddedFrame);
```

Whether because of editing or by request to `RemoveEmbeddedFrame`, the basic procedure for removing an embedded frame is to remove all its facets, delete it from your private content structures, and call its `Remove` or `Release` method. OpenDoc then notifies the embedded part of the removal by calling its `DisplayFrameRemoved` method, as described in the section "Responding to a Removed Display Frame" on page 113.

Removing an embedded frame should be an undoable action. Therefore, you should add a few steps to the procedure to retain enough information to reconstruct the frame (and all its embedded frames) if the user chooses to undo the deletion. You can follow steps such as these:

1. Remove all of the embedded facets from the frame; see "Removing a Facet" on page 125.

2. Set the frame's containing frame to `KODNULL`, to indicate that the frame is no longer embedded in any part.

3. Place a reference to the frame in an undo action that you add to the undo history, as described in "Adding an Action to the Undo Action History" on page 262. Set the removed frame's in-limbo flag to true, as shown in Table 6-4 on page 266.

4. Remove the frame from your embedded-frames list (with which you allow callers to iterate through your embedded frames; see "Providing an Embedded-Frames Iterator" on page 119).

5. Remove the frame from your other private content structures (except for your undo structures).

If the user subsequently chooses to undo the action that led to the removal of the frame, you can then

1. retrieve the reference to the frame from the undo action, and set its in-limbo flag to false, as shown in Table 6-4 on page 266

2. reestablish your display frame as the frame's containing frame

3. recreate any needed facets for the frame

If the undo action history is cleared, your part's `DisposeActionState` method is called and at that point you can remove the frame object referenced in your undo action. You call the frame's `Remove` method if its in-limbo flag is true; you call the frame's `Release` method if its in-limbo flag is false.

Reconnecting and Releasing Embedded Frames

Your part connects and closes its embedded frames when the document containing your part opens and closes. On opening, when your part calls the draft's `AcquireFrame` method for each embedded frame that you want to display, the frame in turn calls the `DisplayFrameConnected` method of its part. After your part and its embedded frames have been saved, and before the document closes, you call the `Close` method of each of your embedded frames; the frames in turn call the `DisplayFrameClosed` methods of their parts.

The `DisplayFrameClosed` and `DisplayFrameConnected` methods are described in the section "Responding to Reconnected and Closed Display Frames" on page 106.

For efficient memory usage, your part can retrieve and connect only the embedded frames that are visible when its document opens. It can also release and reconnect embedded frames during execution, as the frames become invisible or visible through scrolling or removal of obscuring content. This process is described in the section "Lazy Internalization" on page 471.

Adding a Facet

OpenDoc needs to know what parts are visible in a window and where they are, so that it can dispatch events to them properly and make sure they display themselves. But OpenDoc does not need to know the embedding structure of a document; that is, OpenDoc is not directly concerned with where embedded frames are located and what their sizes and shapes are. Because embedded frames are considered to be content elements of their containing part, each containing part maintains, in its own internal data structures, embedded-frame positions, sizes, and shapes. Therefore, containing parts need to give OpenDoc information about embedded frames only when the frames are visible. Containing parts do this is by creating a facet for each location where one of their embedded frames is visible.

An embedded frame in your part may become visible immediately after it is created, or when your part has scrolled or moved it into view, or when an obscuring piece of content has been removed. No matter how the frame becomes visible, your part must ensure that there is a facet to display the frame's contents. Follow these general steps:

1. If your own display frame has multiple facets, create an embedded facet for each of the facets in which the newly visible embedded frame appears. To do that, iterate through all the facets of your display frame, creating embedded facets where needed.

2. For each needed facet, if it does not already exist, make one by asking the containing facet (your display frame's facet) to create one. Call the containing facet's `CreateEmbeddedFacet` method.

   ☐ In your call to `CreateEmbeddedFacet`, assign the embedded facet a clip shape equal to the embedded frame's frame shape, if the new facet is to be positioned in front of all sibling facets and other content in your part. Otherwise, adjust the clip shape as described in the section "Managing Facet Clip Shapes" on page 151.

   ☐ Assign the embedded facet an external transform, based on your part's internal data on the location of the embedded frame.

   ☐ If you will draw offscreen through this facet, assign the facet a canvas. See "Canvases" on page 131 for an explanation.

3. If you want to receive events sent to but not handled by the part displayed in this facet, set the event-propagating flag of the facet's frame. See "Propagating Events" on page 197 for an explanation.

After you create the facet, OpenDoc calls the embedded part's `FacetAdded` method to notify it that it has a new facet.

Removing a Facet

An embedded frame may become invisible when the containing part has deleted it, scrolled or moved it out of view, or placed an obscuring piece of content over it. In any of these instances, the containing part can then delete the facet because it is no longer needed.

Your part deletes the facet of an embedded frame by calling the containing facet's `RemoveFacet` method. (If the frame that is no longer visible has more than one facet, you need to iterate through all facets, removing each one that is not visible.) OpenDoc in turn calls the embedded part's `FacetRemoved` method to notify it that one of its facets has been removed.

You do not have to delete the facet from memory the moment it is no longer needed; you can instead mark it privately as unused and wait for a call to your `Purge` method before you actually remove it.

Creating Frame Groups

A **frame group** is a set of display frames used in sequence. For example, a page-layout part uses a frame group to display text that flows from one frame to another. Each frame in the frame group has a sequence number; the sequence numbers establish the order of content flow from one frame into the next.

Sequence information is important for a frame group because the embedded part needs to know the order in which to fill the frames. Also your part (the containing part) needs to provide sequence information to the user, and it probably also needs to allow the user to set up or modify the sequence.

Your part creates and maintains the frame groups used by all its embedded parts. To create a frame group, you call the `SetFrameGroup` method of each frame that is to be in the group, passing it a **group ID** that is meaningful to you. You also assign each frame a unique **sequence number** within its group, by calling its `ChangeSequenceNumber` method. You should assign sequence numbers that increase uniformly from 1, so that the embedded part can recognize the position of each frame in the group. You can, of course, add and remove frames from the group, and alter their sequence, with additional calls to `SetFrameGroup` and `ChangeSequenceNumber`. The embedded part displayed in the frame group can find out the group ID or sequence number of any of its frames by calling the frame's `GetFrameGroup` and `GetSequenceNumber` methods.

For further discussion and examples of the user interface to provide for frames in a frame group, see the section "Displaying Continuous Content in Sequenced Frames" on page 584.

Synchronizing Embedded Frames

If your part wants to create multiple similar views of an embedded part, you must ask the embedded part to synchronize those views. Then, if the content of one of the frames is edited, the embedded part will know to invalidate and redraw the equivalent areas in the other frames.

Frame synchronization is necessary because each display frame of a containing part represents a separate display hierarchy. For invalidating and redrawing, OpenDoc itself maintains no direct connection between embedded frames in those separate hierarchies, even if they are exact duplicates that show the same embedded-part content.

Figure 3-3 shows an example. Part A (in frame view type) is opened into a part window. Embedded frame B2, as displayed in the part window, is a duplicate of embedded frame B1 in the original frame. However, unless you synchronize the frames, Part B will not know to update the display of B1 if the user edits the content of B2.

Figure 3-3   Synchronizing frames through `AttachSourceFrame`

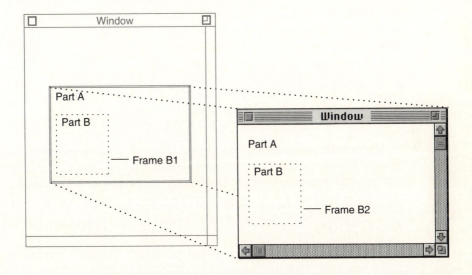

Your part (the containing part) makes the request to synchronize frames by calling the embedded part's `AttachSourceFrame` method. You should call `AttachSourceFrame` as soon as you create the frame that needs to be synchronized with the source frame—that is, before you add any facets to the frame. See the section "Synchronizing Display Frames" on page 114 for a description of how an embedded part responds to `AttachSourceFrame`.

Transmitting Your Container Properties to Embedded Parts

When one part is embedded in another part of the same or a similar part category, the user may prefer that, by default, they share certain visual or behavioral characteristics. For example, if the user embeds a text part into another text part, it might be more convenient for the embedded part to adopt the text appearance (font, size, stylistic variation) of the containing part.

OpenDoc supports the communication necessary for this process by defining the concept of **container properties.** The containing part defines whatever characteristics it wishes to transmit to its embedded parts; embedded parts that understand those container properties can choose to adopt them. Container properties are passed from the containing part to its embedded part in a storage unit; the embedded part reads whatever container properties it understands from the storage unit and adopts them for its own display if appropriate.

Note
Container properties are defined exclusively by individual parts and may apply to only a portion of a part's content. They are therefore generally unrelated to the *properties* of the part's storage unit, as described in the section "Storage-Unit Organization" on page 270. ◆

As the containing part, your part can define whatever container properties it wishes to provide for adoption by embedded parts. Only parts that understand the formats of your container properties, of course, can adopt them.

An embedded part learns what container properties it might adopt from your part by calling your part's `AcquireContainingPartProperties` method. This is its interface:

```
ODStorageUnit AcquireContainingPartProperties(in ODFrame frame);
```

You should return your container properties to the caller in a storage unit.

Whenever your part changes any of the container properties that it expects embedded parts to adopt, it should notify each embedded part (other than bundled parts) of the change by calling the embedded part's `ContainingPartPropertiesUpdated` method.

CHAPTER 4

Drawing

Contents

This is the second of eight chapters that discuss the OpenDoc programming interface in detail. This chapter describes how your part draws itself.

Before reading this chapter, you should be familiar with the concepts presented in Chapter 1, "Introduction to OpenDoc," and Chapter 2, "Development Overview." You should also be familiar with the discussion of frames and facets presented in Chapter 3. For additional concepts related to your part editor's runtime environment, see Chapter 11, "OpenDoc Runtime Features." The discussion in this chapter also assumes that your are familiar with the platform-specific graphics system and drawing commands you need to draw your parts' content. For the Mac OS, this means QuickDraw or QuickDraw GX.

This chapter shows how your part

- uses canvases as drawing destinations

- uses transforms and shapes to lay out its contents

- draws itself to the screen

- prints itself

For a discussion of windows, the display structures within which all your drawing typically takes place, see Chapter 6, "Windows and Menus."

Canvases

Canvases are inherently platform specific. OpenDoc canvas objects are basically wrappers for structures that differ across platforms. This section discusses how to use canvas objects regardless of the platform for which you are developing, with some information specific to the Mac OS platform provided where appropriate.

Using Canvases

The class `ODCanvas` is OpenDoc's wrapper for a platform-specific (or graphics-system-specific) structure that represents a drawing environment. A drawing canvas can refer to anything from a bitmap or a structured display list to a stream of PostScript™ code. It represents the destination for drawing commands, the environment for constructing a rendered image. A canvas has a coordinate system and may retain state information (for example, pen color) that influences how the system interprets drawing commands.

On the Mac OS platform, for example, a canvas could represent an onscreen or offscreen graphics port under the QuickDraw graphics system or a view port under the QuickDraw GX graphics system. A canvas object holds a reference to its graphics port or other system-specific structure, and that structure is *not* deleted when the canvas is released. If you create a canvas, you must create the underlying structure separately, and you are responsible for deleting that structure when the canvas is deleted.

Canvas Features

Canvases are either dynamic or static—that is, they are used either for video display or for printing display, respectively. Your part editor can determine whether it is drawing to a static or dynamic canvas and adjust its procedures accordingly.

Canvases can be onscreen or offscreen. Your part editor can create special effects or improve performance by a drawing a complex image to an offscreen cache and then quickly transferring the completed image to the screen. For added convenience, offscreen canvases maintain clipping and updating information that mirrors their onscreen equivalents.

Canvases are attached to individual facets. See, for example, Figure 4-1, which shows the same document with the same facet hierarchy as in Figure 3-1 on page 104. The document in the figure has two attached canvases:

■ An offscreen canvas is attached to the movie part's facet.

■ An onscreen canvas is attached to the root part's facet. (A canvas attached to the root facet of a window is also called a **window canvas;** every window has a window canvas, assigned to its root facet by OpenDoc when you first register the window.)

Figure 4-1   Facets and canvases

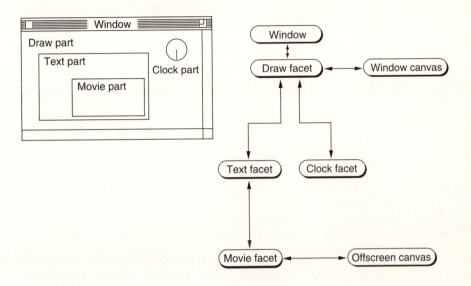

If a particular facet in a window's facet hierarchy has an attached canvas, all of its embedded facets (and their embedded facets, and so on) draw to that canvas. Thus, for most drawing, only a window's root facet needs a canvas. In Figure 4-1, for example, any drawing done to the text facet, draw facet, or clock facet is rendered on the window canvas.

However, if a particular part needs an offscreen canvas, for itself or for an embedded part, it can attach a canvas to a facet anywhere within the hierarchy. Any drawing done to the movie facet in Figure 4-1, for example, is rendered on the offscreen canvas.

The onscreen canvas in Figure 4-1 is the **parent canvas** of the offscreen canvas; that is, it is the canvas immediately above the offscreen canvas in the facet hierarchy. Every canvas has an **owner,** a part that is responsible for transferring images drawn on its canvas to the parent of that canvas. In Figure 4-1, for example, the movie images drawn to the offscreen canvas must be transferred to the window canvas in order to be viewed onscreen. The owner decides when and how to transfer images from a canvas to its parent. The owner of the offscreen canvas in Figure 4-1 might be the movie part or the text part that contains the movie part.

Adding and Removing Canvases

This section describes how to create and delete canvases for your parts. For specific information on using canvases for offscreen drawing, see "Offscreen Drawing" on page 172.

If you want to create a canvas and attach it to a facet, take these steps:

1. Create and initialize the platform-specific drawing structure that underlies the canvas.

2. Create a canvas object, using the `CreateCanvas` method of `ODFacet` or `ODWindowState`. In calling the method you assign the platform-specific drawing structure to the new canvas, and you also define the canvas as static or dynamic, and onscreen or offscreen. (These values cannot change for the lifetime of the canvas.)

3. Designate your part as owner of the canvas by calling the `SetOwner` method of the canvas.

4. Assign the canvas to a facet. Because only the owner of a canvas can remove it from a facet, the timing of assigning the canvas is important:

   □ If your part is a containing part assigning an offscreen canvas to one of its embedded parts, you should assign the canvas when you first create the embedded facet—that is, when you first call the `CreateEmbeddedFacet` method of the embedded part's containing facet. Otherwise, the embedded part may assign a canvas to the facet, precluding you from doing so.

   □ If your part is a containing part and one of its embedded parts has an existing facet with no assigned canvas, you can add one by calling the `ChangeCanvas` method of the embedded facet. When you do so, OpenDoc communicates the change to all embedded parts that use that facet, by calling their `CanvasChanged` methods.

   □ Your part can add a canvas to any of its own display frames' facets at any time, as long as the facet does not already have an assigned canvas. It is probably best to attach the canvas as soon as the facet is created, by calling `ChangeCanvas` from within your part's `FacetAdded` method. If the containing part of your part has already attached a canvas to your new facet, you cannot assign a different canvas to it.

   □ If your part absolutely needs to attach its own canvas to a facet that already has an assigned canvas, you can get around this restriction by creating a subframe of the facet's frame, creating a facet for that frame, and assigning the canvas to that facet.

To remove a canvas from a facet, take these steps:

1. Call the facet's `ChangeCanvas` method, passing it a null value for the canvas reference.

2. Delete the graphics-system-specific structures that the canvas had referenced.

3. Delete the canvas object, by calling `delete` (in C++).

Transforms and Shapes

Unlike windows and canvases, transforms and shapes are not platform specific. The OpenDoc objects that represent them may encapsulate platform-specific structures, but they also give added capabilities. This section discusses how you use transforms and shapes to position and clip embedded parts for drawing.

Transforms and Coordinate Spaces

Both frames and facets employ transforms. It is useful to discuss them in terms of the coordinate spaces they define.

In OpenDoc, an object of the class `ODTransform` is a 3×3 matrix that is used to modify the locations of points in a systematic manner. OpenDoc transforms support the full range of two-dimensional transformations shown in Figure 4-2.

Figure 4-2   What a transform does

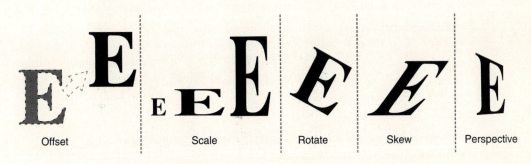

Offset   Scale   Rotate   Skew   Perspective

Drawing

Not all graphics systems support all the features of OpenDoc transforms. Some graphics systems support only offset, or translation, of points; others support offset plus scaling; still others support all transformations. Depending on the graphics system your part editor uses, it may have to do extra work on its own to support features such as scaling or rotation. In such a case, you can create a subclass of `ODTransform`, if desired, that adds those features or even other, more sophisticated transformational capabilities. See "Custom Transform Objects" on page 448 for more information.

A transform can be thought of as defining a coordinate space for the items that it is applied to. OpenDoc uses transforms to convert among two kinds of coordinate space: frame coordinate space and content coordinate space.

Frame Coordinate Space

The **frame coordinate space** is the coordinate system defined by the specification of the frame shape. The frame shape is the basis for the layout and drawing of embedded parts. Suppose, for example, that a frame shape is defined as a rectangle with coordinates of (0, 0) and (100, 100). In a coordinate system with the origin at the upper left—such as that used by QuickDraw and QuickDraw GX—the shape would appear as shown in Figure 4-3.

Figure 4-3   Frame shape (in its own frame coordinates)

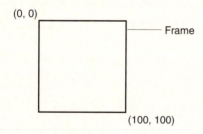

All shapes and geometric information passed back and forth between embedded parts and their containing parts are expressed in terms of the frame coordinate space.

The shapes describing the facet associated with a frame are described in the same coordinate space as the frame; that is, they are in frame coordinates. Thus, in this example, if the clip shape of the facet corresponded exactly to the frame shape, it would have identical coordinates: (0, 0) and (100, 100).

Content Coordinate Space

The **content coordinate space** of a part is the coordinate system that defines locations in the part's content area. It is the local coordinate space of the part itself, and—again, assuming the coordinate systems used by QuickDraw and QuickDraw GX—typically has its origin in the upper-left corner of the part's content.

The **internal transform** of a part's display frame defines the scrolled position (as well as the scaling, rotational, and skew properties) of the part's content within the frame. Applying the display frame's internal transform to a point in content coordinate space converts it to frame coordinate space. Conversely, applying the inverse of the internal transform to a point in frame coordinate space converts it to content coordinate space.

For example, suppose that Figure 4-4 shows the entire contents of a part, and that a portion of it is to be displayed in a frame. If the part's display frame has the dimensions shown previously (in Figure 4-3), and if the frame's internal transform specifies an offset value of (–50, –50), the frame will appear in relation to its part's content as shown in Figure 4-4. Only the portion of the part within the area of frame shape will be displayed when the part is drawn.

Figure 4-4   Frame shape (in content coordinates of its part)

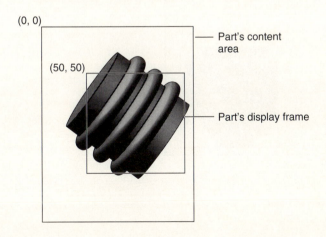

Application of the internal transform in this case means that a point at (50, 50) in content coordinates—the upper-left corner of the display frame—is at (0, 0) in frame coordinates. Conversely, a point at (–50, –50) in frame coordinates is at (0, 0) in content coordinates.

Transformations other than offsets are applied in the same manner; you can scale, rotate, or otherwise transform the contents of the part within its frame by applying the frame's internal transform.

Converting to the Coordinates of a Containing Part

Just as the internal transform of a frame defines the scrolled position of the content it displays, the **external transform** of that frame's facet defines the position of the frame within its containing part.

Applying the external transform of a frame's facet to a point in frame coordinate space converts it to the content coordinate space of the containing part. For example, suppose that the facet and frame of the embedded part in Figure 4-4 have the same shape, and suppose further that the facet's external transform specifies an offset of (150, 75). In relation to the containing part's content area, the embedded part will appear as shown in Figure 4-5.

Figure 4-5   Frame shape (in content coordinates of its containing part)

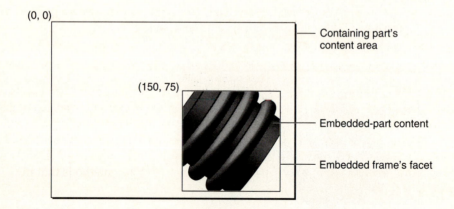

138   Transforms and Shapes

In this case, applying the external transform causes a point at (0, 0) in embedded-frame coordinates—the upper-left corner of the embedded part's frame—to be at (150, 75) in containing-part content coordinates.

(Conversely, applying the inverse of the embedded facet's external transform to a point in content coordinate space converts it to the embedded frame's coordinate space. Thus, in Figure 4-5, a point at (–150, –75) in embedded-frame coordinates is at (0, 0) in the content coordinates of the containing part.)

Transformations other than offsets are applied in the same manner; you can scale, rotate, or otherwise transform the embedded part and its frame within the containing part by applying the facet's external transform.

To convert from the content coordinates of an embedded part to the content coordinates of its containing part, therefore, you need to apply two transforms: the internal transform of the embedded part's display frame, followed by the external transform of that frame's facet. For the example shown in this section, you can see by inspection that the point (50, 50) in the content coordinates of the embedded part (the origin of its display frame) becomes the point (150, 75) in the content coordinates of the containing part. You could also calculate that the point (0, 0) in the content of the embedded part (its upper-left corner) becomes, by application of both transforms, the point (100, 25) in the content of the containing part (outside of the embedded frame and therefore not drawn).

You are not usually concerned with your embedded part's location within the content area of its containing part. You are, however, always interested in your content's location—and your frame's location—on the canvas or in the window in which your part is drawn, as described next.

Canvas Coordinates and Window Coordinates

When your part draws its contents, or when it draws adornments to its frame such as scroll bars, your part is responsible for properly positioning what it draws on its canvas. In setting up the canvas's platform-specific drawing structure, you need to provide information that tells the canvas where, in terms of its own coordinate space, your drawing will take place. OpenDoc doesn't do that for you automatically. It does, however, provide methods that make it fairly simple.

If you were to start from your part's content coordinate space and traverse the embedding hierarchy upward, applying in turn your part's internal transform and external transform, and then applying each internal transform and external transform of each containing frame and facet, up to a facet with an attached canvas, you would arrive at the **canvas coordinate space** or the **window coordinate space** in which your part is drawn.

- If there are no offscreen canvases in the facet hierarchy, the canvas coordinate space is exactly the same as the window coordinate space; to calculate it, OpenDoc applies all transforms up through the internal transform of the root frame. This coordinate space corresponds to the device coordinates of the window canvas. In QuickDraw, for example, it corresponds to the local coordinates of the port in which you are drawing.

- If one or more offscreen canvases are in the facet hierarchy, the canvas coordinate space corresponds to the frame coordinates of the first part above yours in the hierarchy whose facet has an attached canvas. To calculate it, OpenDoc applies all transforms up through the internal transform of the frame whose facet has the canvas. The window coordinate space in this case is unaffected by the presence of an offscreen canvas; it is still defined by the device coordinates of the window canvas.

Figure 4-6 shows a simple example of converting to canvas coordinates and window coordinates. The containing part and the embedded part are the same ones as shown in Figure 4-5 on page 138, and the containing part is in this case the root part of the window. The internal transform of the root frame (the containing part's display frame) specifies an offset of (–50, –50), and the external transform of the root facet is identity.

Figure 4-6   Frame shape (in canvas coordinates and window coordinates)

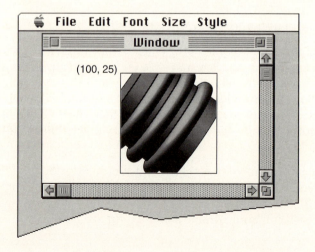

Converting content coordinates to window coordinates means concatenating all the transforms up through the root facet's external transform. Assuming there is no offscreen canvas in Figure 4-6, the point (50, 50) in content coordinates (the origin of the embedded part's frame, as shown in Figure 4-4 on page 137) becomes the point (100, 25) in window or canvas coordinates. If there were an offscreen canvas attached to the embedded facet in Figure 4-6, the canvas coordinates for the origin of the embedded part's frame would be (0, 0).

Normally, you do all your drawing in canvas coordinate space. That way, whether or not you are drawing to an offscreen canvas (which you might not control or even be aware of), your positioning will be correct. However, when you need to draw directly to the window to provide specific user feedback (as described in the section "Drawing Directly to the Window" on page 170) you need to work in window coordinates.

By concatenating the appropriate internal and external transforms, OpenDoc calculates four different composite transforms that you can use for positioning before drawing:

- The composite transform from your content coordinates to canvas coordinates is called your **content transform,** and you apply it when drawing your part's contents on any canvas. You obtain it by calling your facet's `AcquireContentTransform` method.

- The composite transform from your frame coordinates to canvas coordinates is called your **frame transform,** and you apply it when drawing any frame adornment on the canvas. You obtain it by calling your facet's `AcquireFrameTransform` method.

- The composite transform from your content coordinates to window coordinates is called your **window-content transform,** and you apply it when drawing your part's contents directly to the window. You obtain it by calling your facet's `AcquireWindowContentTransform` method.

- The composite transform from your frame coordinates to window coordinates is called your **window-frame transform,** and you apply it when drawing any frame adornment directly to the window. You obtain it by calling your facet's `AcquireWindowFrameTransform` method.

For a description of how to use these transforms when setting up for drawing, see "The Draw Method of Your Part Editor" on page 162.

Transforms and hit-testing

Hit-testing is in a sense the inverse of drawing; it involves a conversion from window coordinates to your part's content coordinates. In most circumstances OpenDoc takes care of this for you. See "Hit-Testing" on page 215 for more information. ◆

Coordinate Bias and Platform-Normal Coordinates

On each platform, OpenDoc uses the platform's native coordinate system, called **platform-normal coordinates,** for stored information and for internal calculations. For example, on Mac OS and Windows platforms, coordinates are measured with the origin at the upper left (of the screen, of a shape, or of a page, for example), with increasing values to the right and downward. Some other platforms use coordinates with an origin at the lower left, with values increasing to the right and upward. Figure 4-7 shows how these two coordinate systems would apply to measurements on a text part's page.

Figure 4-7   Two coordinate systems for measuring position in a part's content

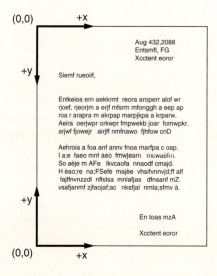

OpenDoc functions consistently on any platform, regardless of the platform's coordinate system, without need for coordinate conversion. However, some platforms allow for simultaneous existence of different coordinate systems. In such a case, a part editor that assumes a particular coordinate system will not function correctly with OpenDoc if the platform-normal coordinate system is different, unless it first accounts for the **coordinate bias,** or difference between its coordinate system and platform-normal coordinates. Likewise, document interchange between platforms using different coordinate systems requires accounting for coordinate bias.

Bias Transforms

Coordinate bias usually takes the form of an offset in the origin, a change in the polarity of one or more axes, and possibly a change in scale. A transformation matrix, called a **bias transform,** is applied to measurements in a part's coordinate system to change them into platform-normal values.

You do not have to calculate bias transforms yourself. When you create a canvas and define its graphics system, OpenDoc uses that information to calculate a bias transform if it is required. In constructing the bias transform, OpenDoc also needs to know your part's content extent (described next).

Content Extent

To convert locations in your part's content between coordinate systems whose origins are offset, the vertical extent of your content (in essence, the height of your part's page) represents the offset between the two coordinate origins. See Figure 4-7 for an example. This **content extent** is the offset needed in the bias transform that performs the conversion.

Because your part may be drawn at any time on a canvas that has a bias transform attached, you should always make the value of your content extent available. When a frame is added to your part, and whenever the content extent of your part changes (such as when you add a new page), you should call your display frame's `ChangeContentExtent` method so that the frame always stores the proper value. (Content extent is stored persistently when a frame is stored.)

A caller constructing a bias transform can obtain the current content extent of your part by calling the `GetContentExtent` method of your part's frame.

The biasCanvas Parameter

The classes `ODFrame` and `ODFacet` include several methods, such as `ChangeInternalTransform` and `ContainsPoint`, that specify shapes or calculate positions on a canvas. Because these calculations necessarily assume a coordinate system, the methods include a parameter, `biasCanvas`, that allows you to specify a canvas whose attached bias transform is to be used to convert between your part editor's coordinates and platform-normal coordinates. Thus, once you set up your offscreen canvas for drawing in your own coordinate system, you can also use it to make sure that all point, frame, and facet geometry is properly converted for you.

In the overwhelming majority of cases, the bias to apply when calling methods of the layout protocol is the bias of your own facet's canvas. In such cases, you pass your own canvas for the `biasCanvas` parameter. (You can pass a null value if you know for certain that the canvas on which your facet draws uses platform-normal coordinates.) Only in special cases do you have to pass the canvas of your containing part, your embedded part, or the root part.

Using Transforms

This section demonstrates some of the basic ways you can use transforms to position and modify the content of your part and embedded parts.

Scrolling Your Part in a Frame

If your part's content area is greater than its frame area, only a portion of the content can be displayed in the frame. The user needs to be able to choose which portion of a part shows through its frame by moving the part's contents—as a unit—in relation to the frame position.

The standard OpenDoc method for supporting this ability involves the Show Frame Outline menu command, which you should place in the Edit menu when the user opens your part's frame into its own part window. In this mode, the user can drag an outline of the frame, positioning it as desired in your part's content area. Another standard method involves a mode in which the user employs a hand-shaped cursor to drag the part within its frame. It is also possible to use page-up and page-down keys or other keyboard input to cause scrolling. For interface guidelines for positioning a part in a frame, see the section "Repositioning Content in a Frame" on page 575.

Providing scroll bars is another way to support scrolling. If your part is the root part of a document window or part window, scroll bars are the standard method. If your part is an embedded part displayed in a frame, scroll bars may or may not be appropriate, depending on the size of your frame and the nature of its contents.

Programmatically, changing the portion of a part displayed in a frame involves modifying the offset (translational setting) of the internal transform of the part's frame and then redrawing. If you don't draw scroll bars within your frame, these are the basic steps:

1. Obtain a reference to your frame's internal transform by calling the frame's `AcquireInternalTransform` method.

2. Call the `MoveBy` method of the transform, passing it the negative of the amount by which you want the frame to scroll.

3. Reassign the changed transform to your frame by calling your frame's `ChangeInternalTransform` method.

4. Release your reference to the transform.

5. Redraw the scrolled frame, as shown in Figure 4-8 and discussed in the section "Drawing When a Part Is Scrolled" on page 165.

Figure 4-8   Scrolling a part by modifying the frame's internal transform

1. Portion of a part in a frame.

2. User specifies a rightward scroll. Move visible portions to the right.

3. Set internal transform, invalidate undrawn portion of facet.

4. Invalidated portion of facet redraws at next update.

For more information on redrawing frames that include scroll bars or other adornments, see the section "Drawing With Scroll Bars" on page 168. For more information on handling scroll bars and interpreting events in them, see the section "Scrolling" on page 216.

Transforming the Image of Your Part

If the graphics system used by your part editor supports all transformations, you can simply modify the internal transform of your display frame to achieve the kinds of special effects shown in Figure 4-2 on page 135. By modifying the internal transform appropriately, you not only can position your part's content in its display frames but you can also scale, rotate, skew, and apply perspective to it.

For example, you could change the scale of your part's content—to support either higher precision in positioning or larger total content area than would otherwise be possible—by including a scale factor in your display frames' internal transforms. Then, to leave embedded parts' displays unaffected by the scaling, you could apply the inverse scaling factor to the external transforms of all embedded facets.

Even if your graphics system does not support features such as rotation or skew, you can still "pre-transform" your images by first applying the internal transform to all drawing coordinates, before passing them to the drawing commands.

Positioning an Embedded Frame

In general, if your part supports embedding, it can store information on the shapes and positions of embedded frames in any format that is convenient for you. When frames become visible, however, OpenDoc needs that positioning information to dispatch events correctly and to place the drawn images of each embedded part correctly.

Thus, when you create a facet for a visible frame embedded in your part, you assign it (when calling the `CreateEmbeddedFacet` method) an external transform whose offset reflects the position of the embedded frame in the coordinate system of your part content. If you later reposition that frame, you need to modify its facet's external transform, if the frame is visible. You can change a facet's external transform, as well as its clip shape, by calling its `ChangeGeometry` method.

Transforming the Image of an Embedded Part

If your graphics system allows, you can use the external transform of a facet embedded in your part to achieve special display effects, regardless of the display intention of the embedded part. By modifying the external transform appropriately, you not only can position the frame within your part's displayed content but also can scale, rotate, skew, and apply perspective to it.

For example, you could make separate embedded frames appear to be the faces of a cube, giving each the proper skew or perspective necessary to achieve the effect, regardless of what is being drawn in each frame by its own part editor.

Using Drawing-Related Shapes

A shape object is an OpenDoc object that is an instance of the class `ODShape`. It is the specification of a two-dimensional shape in a given coordinate space. Different platforms and different graphics systems define shapes differently. Objects of the class `ODShape` are partly wrappers for system-specific shape structures, but they also have the ability to convert among several common shape structures. Most importantly, OpenDoc shapes provide for a platform-independent, polygonal representation of shape data. You are encouraged to represent shapes as OpenDoc polygons wherever possible.

OpenDoc uses shape objects for clipping purposes in drawing and hit-testing. There are four drawing-related shapes: the frame shape and used shape (attached to the frame object), and the clip shape and active shape (attached to the facet object).

Frame Shape

The frame shape is discussed in many places in this book, including earlier in this chapter, in the section "Frame and Facet Hierarchies" on page 103. The frame shape represents the fundamental contract between the embedded part and the containing part for display space. The other drawing-related shapes are variations on the frame shape, and all are defined in the same coordinate system as the frame shape.

A frame shape is commonly rectangular, as shown in Figure 4-9, but it can have any kind of outline, even irregular. An embedded part can request a nonrectangular frame shape if it has a special need for one; for example, a part that displays a clock face might request a round frame shape. It is the containing part's right to comply with or deny any request for a change in frame shape, and it is also the containing part's responsibility to draw that frame's selected appearance, including resize handles if appropriate.

Figure 4-9   A frame shape

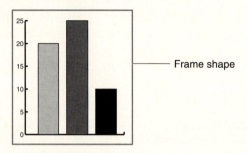

The frame shape is defined by the containing part and is stored in the frame object. Your part (the containing part) can set an embedded frame's frame shape by calling the frame's `ChangeFrameShape` method. Any caller may access the frame shape by calling the frame's `AcquireFrameShape` method.

By convention, your part should use the frame shape when drawing the selected frame border of an embedded part.

Cross-platform representation
The frame shape is stored persistently, and your part may subsequently be displayed under a different graphics system. Therefore, it is important that a frame shape have a platform-neutral (that is, polygonal) representation when it is stored. ◆

Used Shape

An embedded part may need a nonrectangular shape to draw in, may need to change frame shape often, or may want to allow the containing part to draw within portions of its frame. In these cases, the embedded part need not negotiate for an unusual frame shape or continually renegotiate its frame size. Instead, it can define a **used shape** to tell its containing part which portions of its frame shape it is currently using. In Figure 4-10, for example, the embedded part retains a rectangular frame shape but defines a used shape that covers only the content elements it draws. The containing part can then use that information to, perhaps, wrap its content more closely to the used portions of the embedded part. For example, Figure 1-13 on page 57 shows a containing part (a text part) that wraps its text closely to the used shape of an embedded part (a pie-chart part whose frame shape is actually rectangular).

Figure 4-10   A used shape

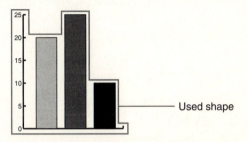

Used shape

The used shape is defined by the embedded part, specified in frame coordinates, and stored in the frame object. Any caller may access the used shape by calling the frame's `AcquireUsedShape` method. If the embedded part has not stored a used shape in its frame, `AcquireUsedShape` returns a copy of the frame shape as a default.

It does not make sense for the used shape to extend beyond the edges of the frame shape, because the clip shape (described on page 151) is based on the frame shape and no drawing occurs outside of the clip shape.

Your part can set its display frame's used shape by calling the frame's `ChangeUsedShape` method. (You can pass a null shape to `ChangeUsedShape` to make your used shape identical to your frame shape. If you do so, be sure to call `ChangeUsedShape` again whenever your frame shape changes.) When you call `ChangeUsedShape`, OpenDoc then calls the `UsedShapeChanged` method of your containing part:

```
void UsedShapeChanged(in ODFrame embeddedFrame);
```

If your part is the containing part in this situation and has wrapped its content to the embedded part's used shape, you can use this method to adjust your content to the new used shape.

Drawing

Active Shape

A facet's **active shape** is the area within a frame in which the embedded part is willing to receive geometry-based (mouse) events. The active shape of a facet is often identical to either the frame shape or the used shape of its frame, as shown in Figure 4-11. The active area of a part is likely to coincide with the area it draws in; events within the frame shape but outside of the used shape are better sent to the containing part, which may have drawn in that area.

Figure 4-11   An active shape

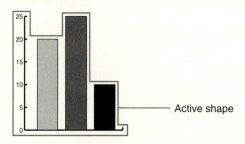

The active shape is defined by the embedded part, specified in frame coordinates, and stored in the facet object. Your part (the embedded part) can set the active shape of its display frame's facet by calling the facet's `ChangeActiveShape` method. Any caller may access the active shape by calling the facet's `AcquireActiveShape` method. If the embedded part has not stored an active shape in its facet, `AcquireActiveShape` returns a copy of the frame's frame shape as a default.

Note that the effective active shape—the active shape as the user perceives it—is the intersection of the active shape and the clip shape (described next). Events within the area of obscuring content or other frames that block the active shape are not passed to the embedded part.

OpenDoc uses the active shape when drawing the active frame border of an embedded part.

Clip Shape

A facet's **clip shape** defines the portion of a frame that is actually to be drawn. The clip shape of a facet is commonly identical to the frame shape of its frame, except that it may be modified to account for obscuring content elements or overlapping frames in the containing part, as shown in Figure 4-12.

Figure 4-12   A clip shape

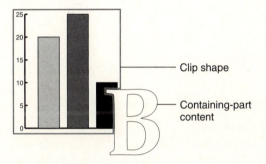

The clip shape is defined by the containing part, specified in frame coordinates, and stored in the facet object. Your part (the containing part) can set the clip shape of an embedded frame's facet by calling the facet's `ChangeGeometry` method. Any caller may access the clip shape by calling the facet's `AcquireClipShape` method.

Managing Facet Clip Shapes

This section describes how your part adjusts the clip shapes of its embedded frames' facets before drawing, to account for overlapping relationships among embedded facets and elements of intrinsic content.

Sibling frames are frames embedded at the same level within a containing frame. They may be frames in a frame group (described in the section "Creating Frame Groups" on page 126), or they may be unrelated frames belonging to different embedded parts. Because sibling frames can overlap each other and can overlap (or be overlapped by) intrinsic content of the containing part, it is the responsibility of the containing part to ensure that clipping occurs properly. Figure 4-13 shows examples of the overlapping relationships that can occur.

Figure 4-13   Overlapping content elements and sibling embedded frames

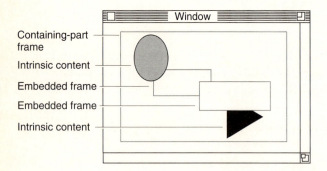

Maintaining a List of Embedded Facets

If your part contains embedded frames, it must maintain a z-ordered (front-to-back) list of the embedded frames and content elements, so that you can reconstruct the overlapping relationships among them. You use that list to update the clip shapes of the facets of your embedded frames.

You control the z-ordering among sibling frames embedded in your part, and you can communicate that information to OpenDoc through the `MoveBehind` and `MoveBefore` methods of the containing facet of the sibling frames' facets. The facet positioning you achieve with `MoveBehind` and `MoveBefore` is reflected in the order in which you or OpenDoc (or any caller) encounters facets when using a facet **iterator** (class `ODFacetIterator`) to access each of the sibling facets in turn (as, for example, when calculating a resulting clip shape).

Calculating the Clip Shapes

If your part contains embedded frames, it performs two related tasks when managing its embedded facets' clip shapes.

■ It must clip all of its embedded facets so that sibling embedded parts don't improperly overwrite each other, the containing part's intrinsic content, or the active frame border. (The section "Adjusting the Active Frame Border" on page 155 describes how to account for the active frame border.)

■ It must clip its own intrinsic content so that it doesn't improperly overwrite embedded parts or the active frame border. This also means taking responsibility for drawing in the area of an embedded frame that is outside the embedded frame's used shape. Because the embedded part does not draw outside of its used shape, it is the containing part's responsibility to do so.

In calculating the clip shapes for your embedded parts' facets, remember these points:

■ A facet's clip shape is affected only by sibling elements, whether they be items of intrinsic content or facets of other embedded frames. Your own display facet's clip shape, and the clip shapes of facets embedded within your embedded parts, have no effect.

■ When one embedded facet obscures another, use the used shape of the obscuring facet's frame to clip the obscured facet.

■ When intrinsic content obscures an embedded facet, make sure to account for all of it—including selection handles, the active frame border, and other adornments.

■ You need to recalculate your embedded parts' clip shapes whenever a content element or an embedded frame is added, deleted, moved, adorned with resize handles, or modified in any way that affects how it is drawn. However, when a given item changes, you need only recalculate the clips of it and the elements *behind* it; the clipping of elements lower in z-order is unaffected.

Your routine to recalculate embedded-facet clip shapes could take steps similar to these:

1. Create a "working clip," a clip shape that at each point in the calculations represents the total unobscured area of your display facet. Start it as a copy of your own display frame's used shape; only content elements within that area need to have their clip shapes recalculated.

2. If the currently active frame is embedded in your part, subtract the active frame border from your working clip. (See "Adjusting the Active Frame Border" on page 155.)

3. Iterate through all your z-ordered content elements, front to back. For each element that is an item of intrinsic content, do this:

☐ Calculate a new clip shape, representing the visible portion of the item, by intersecting the item's shape with the current working clip. Store the new clip shape according to your own content model.

☐ Calculate a mask shape that includes both the (clipped) content item shape and any adornments (such as selection handles) it may have. Modify the working clip by subtracting that mask shape from it, so that elements behind this content item will be obscured.

Likewise, for each element that is an embedded facet, do this:

☐ Get the frame shape for the facet's frame and convert it to your own content coordinates. Intersect it with the current working clip (to account for obscuring content in front), convert it back to embedded-frame coordinates, and assign it as the facet's new clip shape.

☐ Calculate a mask shape by getting the used shape for the facet's frame and converting it to your own content coordinates. Modify the working clip by subtracting that mask shape from it, so that elements behind this embedded frame will be obscured.

Embedded-Part Responsibilities

The containing part is responsible for its embedded facets' clip shapes, but the embedded part has some responsibilities, to ensure that drawing occurs properly:

■ The embedded part must always clip its own drawing operations correctly, using its aggregate clip shape; see "The Draw Method of Your Part Editor" on page 162.

■ The embedded part must never draw outside of its used shape. Only a root part can draw outside of its used shape.

■ When a containing part changes the clip shape of one of its embedded frame's facets, OpenDoc notifies the embedded part of the change by calling the embedded part's `GeometryChanged` method. If the embedded part is drawing asynchronously (see "Asynchronous Drawing" on page 171), its next asynchronous draw must use the new clip shape.

Managing the Active Frame Border

When a part's frame is active, OpenDoc draws the active frame border (shown, for example, in Figure 12-17 on page 525) around the frame. Neither the active part itself nor its containing part needs to draw the border.

However, your active part may need to adjust the clipping of the border shape and also adjust the clipping of its own content to account for the border. Furthermore, your part may need to suppress the drawing of the active border in special instances, such as when creating split-frame views. This section discusses both tasks.

Adjusting the Active Frame Border

The active frame border occupies an area a few pixels wide in the content area of the active part's containing part, and it may overlap or be overlapped by other content elements (embedded frames or intrinsic content) of the containing part (see Figure 4-14). Therefore, it is up to the containing part to make sure that the active frame border is appropriately clipped by elements in front of the active frame, and that elements behind the active frame are appropriately clipped so that they do not draw themselves within the border area.

Figure 4-14   An active frame border that both obscures and is obscured by content

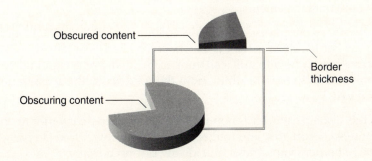

When a new frame acquires the selection focus, or when the active frame changes its frame shape, OpenDoc calculates a new active border shape. It then

Drawing

passes that shape to the active part's containing part by calling the containing part's `AdjustBorderShape` method:

```
ODShape AdjustBorderShape(in ODFacet embeddedFacet,
                          in ODShape shape);
```

Your `AdjustBorderShape` method has two tasks: clip the active border shape to account for obscuring content, and clip any of your own content that is obscured by the border.

When the active frame embedded in your part becomes inactive and thus no longer has the active border around it, OpenDoc notifies your part of the change by calling your part's `AdjustBorderShape` method once more, this time passing a null value for the `shape` parameter. You can then remove the clipping you had previously applied to your obscured content.

Note
If your part receives several consecutive calls to its `AdjustBorderShape` method, your embedded (active) frame has several facets. Consider the active border shape to be the union of all the provided shapes. ◆

In your `AdjustBorderShape` method, you can take steps such as the following. These steps assume that you maintain a field in your part that is a copy of the clipped active frame border, and that your embedded-frame clipping method (see "Managing Facet Clip Shapes" on page 151) uses that active-border field to clip your content elements.

1. If the `shape` parameter is null, you no longer need to maintain an active frame border. Release the border shape you had maintained, set your active-border field to null, call your embedded-frame clipping method to remove the clipping resulting from the presence of the active frame border, and exit.

2. If the `shape` parameter is non-null, copy the shape, convert it to your own content coordinates, and intersect it with your own used shape, so that the active border is not drawn outside of your used shape.

3. To calculate the resultant clipped border shape, iterate through all your z-ordered content elements, starting from the facet of the active frame and working toward the front. (Only items in front of the facet can clip it.)

   □ For each element that is an item of intrinsic content, calculate a mask shape that includes both the item's shape and any adornments (such as selection handles) it may have. Subtract that mask shape from your active-border shape.

□ For each element that is an embedded facet, calculate a mask shape by getting the used shape for the facet's frame, converting it to your own content coordinates, and subtracting it from your active-border shape.

4. If your active-border field is currently null, place a copy of the resulting active-border shape in it. If it is currently non-null, you are calculating a composite border shape from several facets of the active frame; in that case, replace the shape already in the field with the union of itself and the resulting active-border shape.

5. Call your embedded-frame clipping method (see "Managing Facet Clip Shapes" on page 151), so that it recalculates the clip shapes of all items behind the active frame, making sure that they don't overwrite it.

If your `AdjustBorderShape` method does nothing and simply passes back the shape it receives, it must increment the shape's reference count before returning it.

Using Subframes to Suppress the Active Frame Border

OpenDoc draws the active frame border (see, for example, Figure 1-11 on page 55) around a frame of the currently active part. (It actually follows the active shape of the frame's facet, as described in the section "Active Shape" on page 150.) When your part is the active part, OpenDoc automatically draws the active frame border around your part's display frame (the frame that has the selection focus).

Situations may occur in which you do not want the active frame border around your part's display frame, even when it is active. For example, your part's frame may represent a single pane in a split window (see "Using Multiple Facets" on page 174). In this case the entire window should be considered active, not just a single pane.

In such a case you can force OpenDoc to draw the active frame border around your display frame's containing frame instead of your display frame itself. You can call your display frame's `SetSubframe` method to assign it as a subframe of its containing frame. (A frame and a subframe must display the same part.)

You can test whether a frame is a subframe of its containing frame by calling its `IsSubframe` method.

Drawing

Fundamental to OpenDoc is the responsibility of each part in a compound document to draw itself, within the limits of the frame provided by its containing part. Drawing typically occurs when your part editor is asked to draw a particular facet of a particular frame in which its part is displayed. Your part editor is responsible for examining that facet and frame and displaying the correct data, with the appropriate representation, properly transformed and clipped.

Before drawing, your part editor should, if necessary, update the used shapes of its frames and the active shapes of its facets, so that the containing part can lay itself out correctly and so that only the proper events are dispatched to your part by the document shell.

This section begins by discussing how your part defines the general characteristics of its display and outlining several aspects of the basic drawing process. The section then discusses

- drawing with scroll bars

- drawing directly to the window

- drawing asynchronously

- drawing offscreen

- using multiple frames and facets

Defining General Display Characteristics

OpenDoc parts can display themselves in different ways in different frames, or in different ways in the same frame at different times. The part is in control of its display within the borders of its frames, but there are conventions for other parts to request that the part display itself in a particular way.

There are two kinds of display categories. The **view type** of a frame indicates whether the part within it is shown as one of several kinds of icons (standard icon, small icon, or thumbnail view type) or whether the part content itself is drawn within a frame (frame view type). View types are standard values, defined by OpenDoc; any part should be able to draw itself in any of the standard view types.

The **presentation** of a frame describes, for parts in frame view type, how the content is to be represented within the frame. Presentations are defined by parts. You define what types of presentations your part supports, and you assign their values. Examples of presentations are top view, side view, wireframe, full rendering, table, bar chart, pie chart, and tool palette.

View type and presentation are represented as tokenized ISO strings of type `ODTypeToken`. If you create a presentation type, you define it first as an ISO string and then use the session object's `Tokenize` method to convert it to a token.

View Type

You can get and set the view type of your display frames by calling the frame's `GetViewType` and `SetViewType` methods, respectively.

In general, a part is expected to adopt the view type specified by its containing part, according to the guidelines noted in the section "Preferred View Type for Embedded Parts" on page 513. However, another part (such as your part's containing part) can change your frame's view type at any time, and you can change the view type of a frame of another part (such as one of your part's embedded parts) at any time, by calling the frame's `ChangeViewType` method. In response, `ChangeViewType` sets the view type and then notifies the owning part by calling the part's `ViewTypeChanged` method. This is its interface:

```
void ViewTypeChanged(in ODFrame frame);
```

If your part receives this call, it should display itself in the specified frame according to the indicated view type. Parts must support all standard view types. If for some reason your part receives a request for a view type that it does not support, call your display frame's `SetViewType` method to change it back to a view type that you do support. (Calling `SetViewType` does not result in a call to your `ViewTypeChanged` method.)

Note that a change in view type can mean a change in the optimum size for your display frame; see Figure 13-12 on page 573 for an example. Your `ViewTypeChanged` method might therefore call your display frame's `RequestFrameShape` method at this point to initiate frame negotiation.

Presentation

You can get and set the presentation of your own frames by calling the frame's GetPresentation and SetPresentation methods, respectively.

Note that another part (such as your part's containing part) can change your frame's presentation, and you can change the presentation of a frame of another part (such as one of your part's embedded parts), by calling the frame's ChangePresentation method. In response, ChangePresentation sets the presentation and then notifies the owning part, by calling the part's PresentationChanged method. This is its interface:

```
void PresentationChanged(in ODFrame frame);
```

If your part receives this call, and if it supports the indicated presentation, it should display itself in the specified frame accordingly. If it recognizes the indicated presentation but does not support it, or if it does not recognize it, your part should instead pick a close match or a standard default. It should then call the frame's SetPresentation method to give it an appropriate value. (Calling SetPresentation does not result in a call to your PresentationChanged method.)

Part Info

The part info data of a frame is a convenient place for your part to store information about that particular view of itself. The information can be anything from a simple ID to a pointer to a complicated structure or a reference to a helper object. A frame's part info is stored with the frame, not the part. Thus, if the part has many frames and if only a few have been read into memory, only the part info of those frames will take up space in memory.

To assign information to a frame's part info field, use its SetPartInfo method; to retrieve its part info, use its GetPartInfo method. Writing a frame's part info to its storage unit and reading it back in are described in the section "Reading and Writing Part Info" on page 303.

The facet object also contains a part info field, which can hold any kind of display-related information that you wish, such as transforms, color information, pen characteristics, or any other imaging-related data.

To assign information to a facet's part info field, use its SetPartInfo method; to retrieve its part info, use its GetPartInfo method. (A facet's part info is not persistently stored, so there are no methods for reading and writing it.)

Basic Drawing

This section discusses how your part editor performs its drawing tasks in typical situations.

Setting Up

To set itself up properly for display, your part should have previously examined the following information in the given facet and its frame.

- The view type of the frame tells your part whether it should display itself as an icon or whether it should show its contents. Your part should be ready to display itself in the specified frame according to the frame's view type.

- The presentation of the frame tells your part what kind of presentation (as defined by your own part) its content is to have, if it has frame view type. If your part does not support the frame's presentation, substitute a default presentation and call the frame's `SetPresentation` method to give it the correct value.

- Your part may be within a selection in its containing part. If so, it may need to be highlighted appropriately for the selection model of the containing part; see the section "Drawing Selections" on page 166 for more information. You can call the `GetHighlight` method of your facet at any time to see whether you should draw your content with full highlighting, dim (background) highlighting, or no highlighting.

  Alternatively, when your part's `HighlightChanged` method is called, it can record the style of highlighting it has been assigned. It can then in turn call the `ChangeHighlight` method of all facets embedded in the facet whose highlighting has changed, to make sure that they reflect the same highlighting style.

- Check whether you need to draw borders around any link sources and destinations in your part's content, as described in the section "Link Borders" on page 380.

- Both the frame and the facet may have information in their part info fields, placed there by the part itself, that can provide additional display-related information or objects. Use the `GetPartInfo` method to obtain it.

■ Your part should also be aware of the kind of canvas on which it is being drawn. You can call the `GetCanvas` method of the facet to get a reference to the drawing canvas.

If the canvas is dynamic (that is, if the result of calling the canvas's `IsDynamic` method is `kODTrue`), the part is being drawn to an interactive device like a video display. Otherwise, it is being drawn to a static device like a printer (or perhaps a print-preview image onscreen). Your part may display its content differently in each case; for instance, it might display scroll bars only on dynamic canvases, and it might engage in frame negotiation if it is being drawn on a static canvas. For considerations applying to static canvases, see the section "Printing" on page 180.

Your part can make these adjustments from within its `FacetAdded` and `CanvasChanged` methods. When a facet is added, the static/dynamic nature of its canvas is fixed and cannot be changed unless the canvas itself is changed.

The Draw Method of Your Part Editor

Your part must be able to display its content in response to a call to its `Draw` method. This is the method's interface:

```
void Draw(in ODFacet facet, in ODShape invalidShape);
```

When it receives this call, your part editor draws the part content in the given facet. Only the portion within the update shape (defined by the `invalidShape` parameter) needs to be drawn. The update shape is based on previous `Invalidate` calls that were made involving this facet or containing facets, or on updating needed because of part activation or window activation. The shape is expressed in the coordinate system of the facet's frame.

Your part should take steps such as these to draw itself:

1. Your part must make sure that any required platform-specific graphics structures are prepared for drawing and that the drawing context for the facet is set correctly. On the Mac OS using QuickDraw, for example, you must at least do the following:

   ☐ Set the current graphics port. Obtain the graphics-port pointer from the canvas by calling a method such as `GetPlatformCanvas` or `GetQDPort`; pass the returned pointer to the QuickDraw `SetPort` routine.

□ Set the origin of the graphics port to reflect your part's position on the canvas and the scrolled position of your content. Call your facet's `AcquireContentTransform` method to get the proper conversion from your part's content coordinates to canvas coordinates, convert the transform to a QuickDraw offset, and pass that offset to the QuickDraw `SetOrigin` call.

□ Set the clip for drawing your part. Call your facet's `AcquireAggregateClipShape` method to transform and intersect your facet's clip shape with all enclosing clip shapes, resulting in a composite clip shape in frame coordinates. Then convert the aggregate clip shape to a QuickDraw region, and pass that region to the QuickDraw `SetClip` call.

OpenDoc provides a utility library (FocusLib) that facilitates this step for QuickDraw drawing on the Mac OS platform.

2. If your part has placed embedded parts on an offscreen canvas, have the embedded parts draw themselves first; see "Updating an Offscreen Canvas" on page 173.

3. Your part can then draw its contents, using platform-specific drawing commands.

   Your part can alter the normal order of drawing, perhaps to combine overlapping embedded parts and content elements to achieve a sophisticated visual effect.

   □ You can force the drawing of a given embedded part at any point by calling the embedded facet's `Draw` method.

   □ Calling the embedded facet's `DrawChildren` method in addition forces the embedded part's own embedded parts to draw all invalidated portions of themselves immediately.

   □ Calling the embedded facet's `DrawChildrenAlways` method forces the embedded part's embedded parts to draw all of their content immediately, whether or not the content has been invalidated.

IMPORTANT

Unless you are the root part drawing in the root frame, never draw outside of the used shape of your display frame. Your part's containing part may be wrapping its content to the edges of your used shape. ▲

Invalidating and Validating Your Content

To mark areas of your part's content that need redrawing, you modify the update shape of the canvas on which your part is imaged. To do so, you call the `Invalidate` method of your display frames or their facets, passing a shape (`invalidShape`), expressed in your own frame coordinates, that represents the area that needs to be redrawn. OpenDoc adds that shape to the canvas's update shape, and when redrawing occurs once again, that area is included in the `invalidShape` passed to your `Draw` method.

Likewise, to remove previously invalid areas from the update shape of the canvas, you call the `Validate` method of your frame or facet, passing a shape (`validShape`) that represents the area that no longer needs to be redrawn. Validating is not a common task for a part editor to perform. OpenDoc automatically validates all areas that you draw into with your `Draw` method. Also, when you draw asynchronously, you automatically validate the areas that you have redrawn when you call the `DrawnIn` method of the facet.

Drawing on Opening a Window

When a window opens, the facets for all the visible parts of the document are created when the window's `Open` method is called. The root part's `FacetAdded` method is called; it builds facets for its embedded frames and invalidates them. OpenDoc in turn calls the embedded parts' `FacetAdded` methods, so that they can build facets for their own embedded parts, and so on.

Each part editor whose frame is visible in the window (that is, whose frame has an associated facet) thus receives a call to its `Draw` method. The method draws the contents of its frame into the facet, either by using privately cached presentations or by making standard drawing calls, taking into account the frame's and facet's aggregate transforms and clip shapes.

Drawing When a Window Is Scrolled

When the entire contents of a window are scrolled, the scrolled position of the contents is determined by the value of the internal transform of the root part's frame. If any of its embedded frames are made newly visible or newly invisible by scrolling, the root part should create or delete their facets by calling the root facet's `CreateEmbeddedFacet` or `RemoveFacet` method, as described in the sections "Adding a Facet" on page 124 and "Removing a Facet" on page 125.

To force redrawing of those parts of the window that need to be redrawn after scrolling, the root part marks the area that needs to be redrawn as invalid by calling the root facet's `Invalidate` method. That area is then redrawn when an update event occurs.

Redrawing a Frame When It Changes

If your part changes an embedded frame's shape, the embedded part and your part may both need to redraw portions of their content. Take these steps:

1. Change the frame's shape as appropriate, by calling `ChangeFrameShape`. OpenDoc then calls the embedded part's `FrameShapeChanged` method, passing it the new frame shape.

   (Your part may receive a call to its `UsedShapeChanged` method as a result of changing the embedded frame's shape.)

2. Change the clip shape—and external transform, if necessary—of the frame's facet to correspond to the new frame shape and, possibly, new used shape.

3. If there is an undrawn area outside of the new facet shape, invalidate the portions of your own intrinsic content that correspond to the difference between the old and new frame shapes.

When the next update event is generated, the `Draw` methods of the embedded part and your part, as appropriate, are called to draw the invalidated areas.

Drawing When a Part Is Scrolled

When a user scrolls the contents of an embedded part, the containing part takes no role in the repositioning or redrawing. The embedded part sets its frame's internal transform to the appropriate value, as discussed in the section "Scrolling Your Part in a Frame" on page 144, and calls the facet's `Invalidate` method to force the redraw.

If it is your part whose contents are to be scrolled, take these steps:

1. Call your frame's `SetInternalTransform` method, to set the transform's offset values appropriately. How you obtain the offset values you pass to `SetInternalTransform` depends on what kinds of events you interpret as scrolling commands and how you handle them. For example, handling events in scroll bars within your display frames is discussed in the section "Scrolling" on page 216.

4

Drawing

2. If any embedded frames become visible or invisible as a result of the scrolling, create or delete facets for them as described in the sections "Adding a Facet" on page 124 and "Removing a Facet" on page 125.

   You can simply mark unneeded facets as purgeable at this time, actually deleting them only if OpenDoc calls your part's `Purge` method. That way, you can simply reuse any undeleted facets if their frames become visible again.

3. Call your facet's `Invalidate` method to force a redraw at the next update event. You should be able to shift the bits of your frame's image by the scrolled amount and invalidate only the portion of your facet that represents part content scrolled *into* view. On the Mac OS platform, the QuickDraw function `ScrollRect` provides this capability.

Drawing the contents of frames that include scroll bars is more complicated, for two reasons. First, the content must be clipped so that it won't draw over the scroll bars. Second, although the content can be scrolled, the scroll bars themselves should not move. See "Drawing With Scroll Bars" on page 168 for more information.

Drawing Selections

You determine how selecting works and how selections are drawn inside your parts. However, if your part editor supports embedding of other parts, you should support the selection behavior and appearance guidelines described in the section "Selection" on page 562.

When a part embedded within your part is selected, the appearance you give it should be appropriate for your own selection model, but it should also reflect whether the part is selected by itself or is part of a larger selection that includes your own part's intrinsic content.

■ To select an embedded part alone when it is viewed in a frame, the user can perform several actions, such as activating the part and then clicking on its frame border, or using a lasso tool or other selection method supported by the containing part. (Your part should support all selection methods that are appropriate for your content model. Note that when a frame is selected, its part is not active; the menus displayed are those of the containing part.)

   If the part alone is selected, your part (the containing part) should draw the frame border with a standard appearance—typically a gray line, corresponding to the frame shape, with resize handles (usually eight of them) if you permit the user to resize the frame. If you allow nonrectangular frames, such as irregular polygons or circles, you are responsible for putting an appropriate number of resize handles on the frame border.

■ To select an embedded part alone when it is viewed as an icon, the user places the mouse pointer over the part's icon (that is, anywhere within the active shape of the facet displaying the icon) and clicks the mouse button. Because the view type of the facet specifies an icon rather than frame display, OpenDoc sends the mouse-up event to your part (as an event type of `kODEvtMouseUpEmbedded`).

You should, in this case, not draw the frame border of the embedded part at all. Instead, you should notify the part that it is highlighted by calling the `ChangeHighlight` method of the embedded part's facet, specifying a highlighting value of `kODFullHighlight`. It is then up to the embedded part to draw its highlighted appearance, either by using a highlighting color or displaying the selected version of its icon.

■ When an embedded part is enclosed within a range of your selected intrinsic content, its appearance should be analogous to that of the intrinsic content itself. You should draw the frame border with a selected appearance, if appropriate, and you should call the `ChangeHighlight` method of the embedded part's facet, so that the part will know how it should highlight itself.

  □ If your part highlights selections with a highlighting color or inverse video (as text processors typically do), you should not draw frame borders around embedded parts within your selection, and you should set their facets' highlighting value to `kODFullHighlight`.

  □ If your part highlights selections by drawing frame borders around individual objects (as object-based drawing programs typically do), you should draw frame borders with a selected appearance around any embedded parts, and you should set their facets' highlighting value to `kODNoHighlight`.

  □ If your part highlights selections by drawing a dynamic marquee or lasso border around the exact area of the selection (as bitmap-based drawing programs typically do), you should not draw frame borders around embedded parts, and you should set their facets' highlighting value to `kODNoHighlight`.

For definitions and examples of these kinds of highlighting and frame-border appearance, see "Making a Range Selection" on page 564.

Your part should support multiple selection, allowing the user to select more than one frame at a time. Your part should also support Select All on its own contents. Furthermore, it should allow for selection of **hot parts**—parts (such as controls) that normally perform an action (such as running a script) in response to a single click—without executing the action. See "Making Multiple Selections" on page 565 and "Selecting Hot Parts" on page 571 for more specific guidelines.

Drawing With Scroll Bars

This section discusses two methods for providing scroll bars for your parts. These approaches work not only for scroll bars but also for any nonscrolling adornments associated with a frame.

Placing Scroll Bars Within Your Frame

If you create scroll bars for your content inside the margins of your frame, remember that your frame shape includes the areas of the scroll bars. To draw properly, you need to account for the fact that, although your content can scroll, the scroll bars themselves should remain stationary.

The method discussed in this section applies equally well to a root part that needs to put scroll bars in its window.

Clipping and Scrolling Your Content

One approach is to create an extra, private "content shape," as shown in Figure 4-15. The content shape is the same as the frame shape, except that it does not include the areas of the scroll bars.

Figure 4-15   Using a "content shape" within a frame shape for drawing

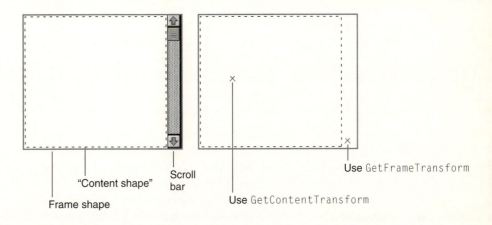

You can define the content shape in terms of frame coordinates, and you can store it anywhere, although placing it in your frame's part info data is reasonable.

When drawing your part's contents—the portion within the area of the content shape—you take the current scrolled position of your content into account. You include the frame's internal transform by using the transform returned by your facet's `AcquireContentTransform` method to set the origin, and you intersect the content shape with the facet's clip shape when drawing. When drawing the scroll bars, however, you ignore the current scrolled position of your content. You use the transform returned by your facet's `AcquireFrameTransform` method to set the origin, and you intersect the frame shape with the facet's clip shape.

Clipping Embedded Frames

One complication of this method is that OpenDoc knows nothing of your content shape and therefore cannot clip the facets of embedded frames accordingly. OpenDoc clips all embedded facets to the area of your frame's facet, but that area includes the scroll bars as well. Thus, embedded parts can draw over the area of your scroll bars.

To avoid this problem, you must set each embedded facet's clip shape to be the intersection of its otherwise-expected clip shape with your content shape.

Placing Scroll Bars in a Separate Frame

To avoid having to define a separate, private "content shape," you can place scroll bars or adornments in completely separate frames from your content. This method, however, requires the overhead of defining more objects, uses more memory, and may possibly affect performance negatively.

You can request one display frame for your part that encloses both the scroll bars and the content. This frame has an internal transform of identity: it does not scroll. You draw the scroll bars directly in this frame.

You then request a second display frame for your part, a frame that can scroll and in which you draw your content. Make the second frame a subframe of the first; that is, make the nonscrolling frame the containing frame of the scrolling frame. Because both frames are display frames of the same part (yours), you must set the `isSubframe` parameter to true when you first create the new frame. This setting notifies OpenDoc that the frame is a subframe so that OpenDoc can draw the active frame border in the correct location—around the facet of the parent frame.

Your part's containing part must, as usual, make separate facets for both frames. Then, when a mouse event occurs in the nonscrolling frame, your part can interpret it and set the internal transform of the scrolling frame accordingly.

With this method, you do not need to take any special care to manage clip shapes of any embedded facets.

A more common use of subframes may be in creating scrollable split windows. See "Drawing With Multiple Frames or Facets" on page 173.

Drawing Directly to the Window

In some circumstances, you may want your part editor to draw interactively, providing feedback for user actions. For example, you may support rubber-banding or sweeping out a selection while the mouse button is held down. If so, your part can draw directly on the root facet's canvas (the window canvas). The window canvas is equivalent to the Window Manager port in QuickDraw terms.

OpenDoc provides several `ODFacet` methods, analogous to those used for drawing to your own canvas, that you can use to draw directly to the window:

■ The `AcquireWindowContentTransform` method, analogous to `AcquireContentTransform`, converts from your part's content coordinate space to window-canvas coordinate space.

■ The `AcquireWindowFrameTransform` method, analogous to `AcquireFrameTransform`, converts from your part's frame coordinate space to window-canvas coordinate space.

■ The `AcquireWindowAggregateClipShape` method, analogous to `AcquireAggregateClipShape`, transforms and intersects your part's facet clip shape with all enclosing clip shapes, resulting in a composite clip shape in window-canvas coordinate space.

Use the values returned by these methods to set up your drawing structure when you must draw directly to the window canvas. When there is no canvas in the facet hierarchy other than the window canvas, the results returned by each of these pairs of methods are the same.

Asynchronous Drawing

Your part editor may need to display its part asynchronously, rather than in response to a call to your `Draw` method. For example, a part that displays a clock may need to redraw the clock face exactly once every second, regardless of whether or not an update event has resulted in a call to redraw. Asynchronous drawing is very similar to synchronous drawing, except that you should make these minor modifications:

1. Determine which of your part's frames should be drawn. Your part can have multiple display frames, and more than one may need updating. Because your part stores its display frames privately, only you can determine which frames need to be drawn in.

2. For each frame being displayed, you must draw all facets. The frame's `CreateFacetIterator` method returns an iterator with which you can access all the facets of the frame. (Alternatively, you can keep your own list of facets.) Draw the part's contents in each of these facets, using the steps listed for synchronous (regular) drawing.

3. After drawing in a facet, call its `DrawnIn` method to tell it that you've drawn in it asynchronously. If the facet is on an offscreen canvas, calling `DrawnIn` allows the drawing to be copied into the window, because the owning part's `CanvasUpdated` method is called.

Offscreen Drawing

There are several situations in which you may want your part to create an offscreen canvas. For example, you may want to increase performance with double-buffering, drawing complex images offscreen before transferring them rapidly to the screen. Alternatively, you may want to perform sophisticated image manipulation, such as drawing with transparency, tinting, or using complex transfer modes.

Parts are likely to create offscreen canvases for their own facets for double-buffering, in order to draw with more efficiency and quality. Parts are likely to create offscreen canvases for their embedded parts' facets for graphic manipulation, in order to modify the imaging output of the embedded part and perhaps combine it with their own output.

Canvases are described in general in the section "Using Canvases" on page 131; this section discusses how to use them for offscreen drawing.

Drawing to an Offscreen Canvas

Drawing on an offscreen canvas is essentially the same as drawing on an onscreen canvas.

- You set up the environment as usual: you obtain the canvas and its pointer to the system-specific drawing structure as usual, and you use your facet's transform and clip information as usual.

- If you draw asynchronously on your facet's offscreen canvas, you must, as for any asynchronous drawing, call the facet's `DrawnIn` method to ensure proper updating of the offscreen canvas to the window canvas. If your part's facet is moved to an offscreen canvas while it is running, OpenDoc calls your part's `CanvasChanged` method, so that your part will know to call `DrawnIn` if it is drawing asynchronously.

- You perform invalidation as usual: you call the `Invalidate` or `Validate` method of your display frames and their facets, to accumulate the invalid area in the update shape of the offscreen canvas.

If you want to bypass the offscreen canvas and draw directly on the window canvas, make sure you obtain the window canvas when setting up the environment. Then use the appropriate facet calls (such as `AcquireWindowContentTransform` instead of `AcquireContentTransform`) when setting the origin and clip.

Updating an Offscreen Canvas

The part that owns an offscreen canvas is responsible for transferring its contents to the parent canvas. Only the part that created the canvas can be assumed to know how and when to transfer its contents. The canvas may have a different format from its parent (one may be a bitmap and the other a display list, for example); the owner may want to transform the contents of the canvas (such as by rotation or tinting) as it transfers; or the owner may want to accumulate multiple drawing actions before transferring.

When a containing part has placed one of its embedded part's facets on an offscreen canvas, it should force the embedded part to draw before the containing part itself draws any of its own contents. This step ensures that the contents of the offscreen canvas are up to date and can be combined safely with the containing part's contents when drawn to the onscreen canvas. You can force your embedded part to draw itself by calling the embedded facet's `Draw` method; you can force your embedded part's own embedded parts to draw themselves by also calling your embedded facet's `DrawChildren` method.

If an embedded part displays asynchronously and uses `Invalidate` or `Validate` calls to modify the update shape of its offscreen canvas, the offscreen canvas calls its owning part's `CanvasUpdated` method to notify it of the change. The owning part can then transfer the updated content immediately to the parent canvas, or it can defer the transfer until a later time, for efficiency or for other reasons.

Drawing With Multiple Frames or Facets

OpenDoc has built-in support for multiple display frames for every part, and multiple facets for every frame. This arrangement gives you great flexibility in designing the presentation of your part and of parts embedded in it. This section summarizes a few common reasons for implementing multiple frames or multiple facets.

Using Multiple Frames

Several uses for multiple frames have already been noted in this book, most of which involve the need for simultaneous display of different aspects or portions of a part's content.

■ A part whose frame is opened into a part window requires a second frame as the root frame of that part window.

- A part that flows text from one frame to another naturally needs more than one frame.

- Parts that allow for multiple different presentations of their content are likely to display each kind of presentation (top view versus side view, wireframe versus rendered, and so on) in a separate frame.

- Parts that display scroll bars, adornments, or palettes in addition to their own content might use separate frames for such items.

In general, the part that is displayed in a set of frames initiates the use of multiple frames. The containing part does, however, have ultimate control over the number and sizes of frames for its embedded parts.

Using Multiple Facets

The use of multiple facets allows a containing part to duplicate, distort, and reposition the content displayed in its embedded frames. Normally, even with multiple facets, all of the facets of a frame display their content within the area of the frame shape, because the frame represents the basic space agreement between the embedded part and the containing part. However, the containing part always controls the facets to be applied to its embedded frames, and so the containing part can display the facets in any locations it wishes.

Drawing an Embedded Frame Across Two Display Pages

Perhaps the most common reason to use multiple facets for a frame is to show an embedded frame spanning a visual boundary between separate drawing areas in a containing frame.

In Figure 4-16, for example, a word-processing part uses a single display frame and facet for a pair of its pages but displays the pages with a visual gap between them. An embedded part's display frame spans the boundary between page 1 and page 2. The word-processing part then defines two facets for its embedded frame: one facet in the display for page 1, and the other in the display for page 2.

Drawing

Figure 4-16   Using two facets to draw a frame that spans a page break

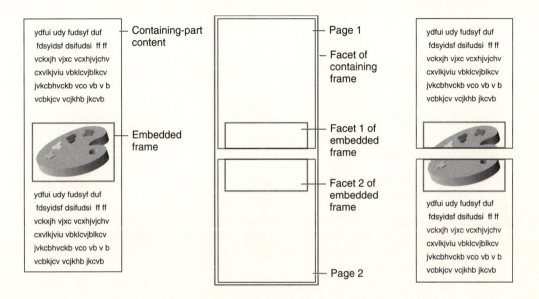

Multiple Views of an Embedded Frame

One simple use of multiple facets is for a containing part to provide a modified view (such as a magnification) in addition to the standard view of an embedded frame. You can also use multiple facets to tile the area of an embedded frame with multiple miniature images of the frame's contents.

A similar but more complex example is shown in Figure 4-17. In this case, multiple facets are used to break up the image in an embedded frame, to allow the tiled parts to be moved, as in a sliding puzzle.

Figure 4-17   Using multiple facets to rearrange portions of an embedded image

Facets are sized and offset to fill
frame shape

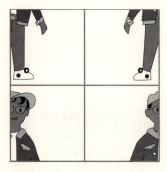

Facet shapes unchanged;
external transforms modified

The clip shapes for the facets in Figure 4-17 are smaller than the frame shape and have offset origins so that they cover different portions of the image in the frame. Initially, as shown on the left, their external transforms have offsets that reflect the offsets in the shape origins, and the facets just fill the area of the frame. Subsequently, as shown on the right, the containing part can cause any pair of facets to change places in the frame simply by swapping their external transforms.

Providing Split-Frame Views

One of the most useful implementations of multiple facets may be for the construction of **split-frame views,** in which the user can independently view and scroll two or more portions of a single document. This use of multiple facets is somewhat more complex than the others presented here, because it also involves use of **subframes,** embedded frames that display the same part as their containing frame. Figure 4-18 shows one example of how to use two subframes to implement a split-frame view.

Figure 4-18   Using subframes to implement a split-frame view

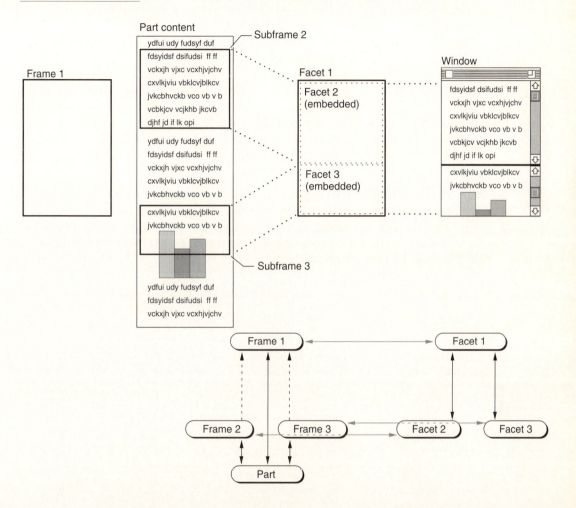

In Figure 4-18, the part to be displayed has one frame (frame 1) and facet (facet 1) that represent its current overall frame size and display. The part creates frames 2 and 3 as embedded frames, specifying that the containing frame for both is frame 1, and also specifying that they are to be subframes of their containing frame. The diagram in the lower right of Figure 4-18 shows the object relationships involved, using the object-diagram conventions described in "Runtime Object Relationships" on page 487.

The part now needs to negotiate for frames 2 and 3 only with itself. It creates facets for them, embedded within facet 1. The part can now position the contents of frame 2 and frame 3 independently, by changing their internal transforms. It uses the external transforms to place facets 2 and 3 within facet 1 as shown. The two facets together fill the area of frame 1 and show different parts of the document.

Note

It is possible to achieve the same effect with only a single subframe. The facet of the parent frame can display one portion of the split view and the facet of the subframe can display the other. ◆

You can also achieve a split-frame view with a somewhat simpler method that does not require the use of subframes. In this case, your part must perform extra work to split its content display. The method relies on multiple facets only for duplicate display of embedded parts. As Figure 4-19 shows, your part has only a single display frame and facet.

Figure 4-19   Implementing a split-frame view using a single display frame

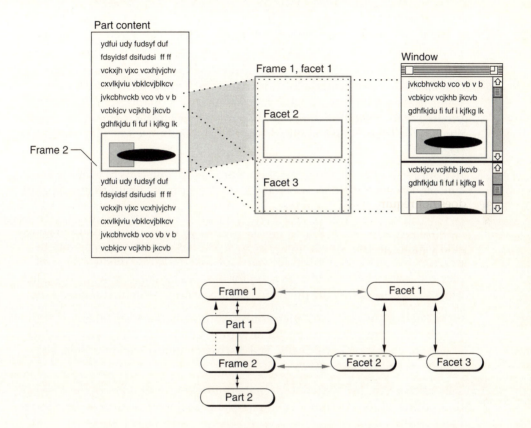

You create two facets (subfacets of your display frame's facet) for each
embedded part that is visible in both halves of the split view. By your own
means, you separate the display of your part's intrinsic content, and at the
same time you apply the appropriate external transforms to each embedded
facet so that embedded parts appear in their proper locations in each portion
of your split view. (The diagram in the lower right of Figure 4-19 shows the
object relationships.)

Printing

To print a document, the user selects Print from the Document menu, and the root part displays a print dialog box (see "Print" on page 251). If the user confirms the print command, the root part then sets up the environment for printing and prints the document. (When your part is the root part, it also handles the Page Setup command, as described in the section "Page Setup" on page 250.)

In printing, part editors in general use normal drawing calls to print their content, although the printer is represented by a canvas object that is separate from the screen display's canvas.

Because any part can be the root part of a document, all parts should in general support the printing commands. The root part has greater responsibility in printing, but all visible embedded parts are asked to draw themselves, and they can adjust their drawing process for the presence of a static canvas. They can also directly access the platform-specific printing structure, if necessary.

OpenDoc does not replace a platform's printing interface; OpenDoc objects provide access to platform-specific structures and provide a context in which you make platform-specific calls. The discussion in this section is therefore largely specific to the Mac OS.

This section first discusses the specific printing responsibilities of the root part, then addresses those of embedded parts, and finally notes aspects of printing that apply to all parts.

Root-Part Responsibilities

If your part is the root part, it defines the basic printing behavior of its document. It sets things up, it allows for any frame negotiation that is to occur, and it makes the platform-specific printing calls. It also controls whether or not embedded parts that use a different imaging or printing system can be printed.

Supporting QuickDraw GX Printing

If QuickDraw GX is installed, you must use it for printing, regardless of whether your own part uses QuickDraw GX for imaging. OpenDoc itself uses QuickDraw GX for imaging if QuickDraw GX is installed, which causes the operating system to assume that all portions of the process (the document) are QuickDraw GX-aware.

Therefore, if QuickDraw GX is installed on the user's system, handle printing in this way:

- When responding to the Page Setup and Print menu commands, display QuickDraw GX dialog boxes instead of the Printing Manager dialog boxes.

- Create a QuickDraw GX job object instead of a Printing Manager print job.

- Install the QuickDraw-to-QuickDraw GX translator, to ensure that parts that do not use QuickDraw GX for imaging (which might include your own part) can still print themselves.

For information on creating a QuickDraw GX job object and displaying QuickDraw GX printing dialog boxes, see the chapter "Core Printing Features" of *Inside Macintosh: QuickDraw GX Printing*. For instructions on installing the QuickDraw-to-QuickDraw GX translator, see the chapter "QuickDraw GX and the Macintosh Environment" of *Inside Macintosh: QuickDraw GX Environment and Utilities*.

Choosing a Frame for Printing

If your part's document uses the same page layout for printing as for screen display, printing is simpler. You use your part's existing display frame (the window's root frame) as the frame for printing. That way, you need not create any new frames, including embedded frames. Using your existing display frame makes most sense in situations where you do not engage in frame negotiation, because you can reuse the same layout after printing.

For greater flexibility, however, you may want to allow the printed version of your document to have a somewhat different layout from the onscreen version. For example, you may want to give embedded parts a chance to remove scroll bars and resize their frames or otherwise lay themselves out differently. To do that, and to retain your original layout for post-printing display, you can create a separate display frame for printing, as described next.

Printing the Document

After you have followed the steps listed in "Page Setup" on page 250 and "Print" on page 251, and once the user has confirmed the print dialog box, your part is ready to print its document. It is assumed that you have created a platform-specific printing structure, such as a print job (if using the Mac OS Printing Manager) or job object (if QuickDraw GX is installed).

You should then take these general steps:

1. If you want to set the resolution for printing, first determine the minimum resolution needed for the portion of the document being printed. Call the GetPrintResolution method of any of your embedded parts that will be printed, and use the highest of the returned values and your own minimum to determine what value to pass to the appropriate function (such as PrGeneral) for setting printer resolution.

2. If you do not change layout or support frame negotiation for printing, skip this step and use your current display frame as the printing frame. Otherwise, create a separate printing frame, like this:

   ☐ Call your draft's CreateFrame method to create a new, nonpersistent frame as a display frame for your part, to be used as the printing frame.

   ☐ Also create new frames for each of your part's visible embedded parts, with the printing frame as their containing frame.

3. Create an external transform and clip shape for your printing facet. Make the clip shape equal to your page size.

4. Create a new facet for the printing frame, using the window state object's CreateFacet method. Assign the transform and clip to the printing facet.

5. Create a static canvas with the printing facet's CreateCanvas method. Use the SetPlatformCanvas method to assign the drawing structure (graphics port if Printing Manager, view port if QuickDraw GX) associated with the printing structure to the canvas. Use the SetPlatformPrintJob method to assign the printing structure itself to the canvas.

6. Assign the canvas to the printing facet by calling the facet's ChangeCanvas method. Notify the printing frame of the presence of the printing facet by calling its FacetAdded method.

   (If you have not created a separate printing frame, each of your embedded parts with a facet is at this point notified of the presence of a static canvas and may attempt frame negotiation. As root part, your part may permit or deny the requests.)

7. Loop through all pages in your part's content area (or the page range specified in the job dialog box) and print each one. For each page, do the following:

   ☐ Reset your printing facet's clip shape and/or transform so that it covers this page.

   ☐ Create facets for your newly visible embedded frames, and release facets for frames no longer in view. At this point, allow frame negotiation with your part's embedded parts if you support negotiation.

   ☐ Invalidate the printing facet's area and force a redrawing, by calling the facet's `Update` method.

8. When finished printing, clean up. Remove the printing facet from the printing frame and release it. Delete the platform-specific structures (such as the print job) that you have created. If you have created a printing frame, remove it by calling its `Remove` method.

Embedded-Part Responsibilities

Embedded parts have these few specific responsibilities in printing.

Engaging in Frame Negotiation

Your part must handle printing properly when it is an embedded part and is assigned a new display frame or facet. It should examine the facet's associated canvas to determine whether it is dynamic or static, and perform frame negotiation if appropriate. On a static canvas, you might engage in a frame negotiation to make all of your part's content visible, or you might need to resize your frame to account for elimination of scroll bars or other items that are appropriate for screen display only.

The best point at which to test for the presence of a static canvas is when your facet is added or when its canvas changes, not when your `Draw` method is called. At drawing time it is too late, for example, to engage in frame negotiation.

Drawing

Responding to GetPrintResolution

Your part may receive a call to its `GetPrintResolution` method as a printing job is being set up. This is its interface:

```
ODULong GetPrintResolution( in ODFrame frame );
```

Your `GetPrintResolution` method should first call the `GetPrintResolution` method of any of its own embedded parts that are visible within the specified frame. It should then return the highest of all returned values and your own part's minimum printing resolution (in dots per inch) as the method result.

Issues for All Parts

Your part draws to the printer canvas just as it draws to its window canvas. Your `Draw` method is called when the facet that displays your part is being imaged. You set up the environment for drawing as usual; you obtain the platform-specific drawing structure from the facet's canvas (using its `GetPlatformCanvas` method), you cast it to the appropriate type (such as `GrafPtr`), and you set its fields properly (with platform-specific calls such as `SetOrigin`).

When your part draws to a static canvas (use the `IsDynamic` method of the canvas to find out), you may not want to draw adornments and interactive features such as scroll bars that are appropriate for screen display only.

On a static canvas you may also want to perform color matching to take into account the characteristics of the device on which you are drawing. When printing using the Mac OS Printing Manager, you can use the ColorSync Utilities calls; when printing with QuickDraw GX, you simply turn on color matching for the view port you are printing to, and draw as usual.

Although all printing canvases are static, not all static canvases are for printing. The presence of a static canvas does not guarantee that a print job or job object exists. You can call the `HasPlatformPrintJob` method of the canvas to find out if a printing structure exists. If it does, it is available through the `GetPlatformPrintJob` method of the printing canvas. You may want to access the print job or job object directly to determine, for example, whether you are printing on a PostScript printer (see the following note).

Clipping on PostScript printers
PostScript printers do not clip correctly to QuickDraw
regions that are not rectangular. If your facet's clip shape
specifies a nonrectangular shape, you must use PostScript
calls to create a polygon to clip to when printing.
Alternatively, you can use the OpenDoc utility library
FocusLib, which creates the polygon for you. ◆

User Events

Contents

This is the third of eight chapters that discuss the OpenDoc programming interface in detail. This chapter describes the OpenDoc event-handling mechanism and discusses how your part editor handles user events to activate itself and to manipulate its user interface.

It is by handling user events that your part editor interacts with the user and cooperates with the user in constructing the compound documents that contain your parts.

OpenDoc distinguishes user events from *semantic events*, the messages related to the OpenDoc scripting extension, although user events can be converted into semantic events. Semantic events are discussed in Chapter 9, "Semantic Events and Scripting."

Before reading this chapter, you should be familiar with the concepts presented in Chapter 1, "Introduction to OpenDoc," and Chapter 2, "Development Overview." For additional concepts related to your part editor's runtime environment, see Chapter 11, "OpenDoc Runtime Features." For detailed design recommendations for your parts' user interface, see Part 3 of this book and also *Macintosh Human Interface Guidelines*.

This chapter starts with a general discussion of user events, and then shows how your part can

- handle mouse events to activate itself

- transfer various types of focus to and from itself

- handle display-related events, for purposes such as hit-testing and scrolling

About Event Handling in OpenDoc

Your OpenDoc part editor is required to respond to a specific set of actions or messages from OpenDoc that, although generated and passed in different ways on different platforms, constitute the majority of user interactions with your parts. In OpenDoc, these messages are called **user events.**

User events in OpenDoc include mouse clicks and keystrokes, menu commands, activation and deactivation of windows, and other events available only on some platforms. This section defines the different types of events and discusses how your part editor's `HandleEvent` method handles them.

How User Events Are Handled

The document shell receives platform-specific events through whatever event-delivery mechanism the underlying platform provides. The shell converts them into the form of OpenDoc user events and passes them to the dispatcher by calling its `Dispatch` method. The dispatcher handles the events it recognizes, using a dispatch module to pass events to individual parts. The `Dispatch` method returns all other events, as well as events passed to parts but not handled by them, to the document shell to handle.

When the OpenDoc dispatcher receives an event intended for your part, it locates a dispatch module for the event. The dispatch module in turn calls your part's `HandleEvent` method. (Your part's `Draw` method can be called indirectly because of an event, through the `Update` method of a window or facet.)

Your part becomes the target for a specific type of user event (other than geometry-based events) by obtaining the *focus* for that event. The OpenDoc arbitrator keeps track of which part owns which foci by consulting a focus module, which tracks, for example, which part is currently active and therefore should receive keystroke events. Foci and focus modules are described further in the section "Focus Types" on page 207.

Geometry-based events, such as mouse clicks, are generally dispatched to the parts within whose frames they occur, regardless of which part currently has the selection focus—that is, regardless of which part is currently active. This permits inside-out activation to occur.

Your part receives some of the information about its events in a platform-specific **event structure.** On the Mac OS platform, the event structure is equivalent to an event record. This is its definition:

```
struct ODEventData {
    short    what;
    long     message;
    long     when;
    Point    where;
    short    modifiers;
};
```

Other information about the event is passed to your part (on the Mac OS platform) in an OpenDoc-defined **event-info structure:**

```
struct ODEventInfo
{
    ODFrame embeddedFrame;
    ODFacet embeddedFacet;
    ODPoint where;
    ODBoolean propagated;
};
```

For any geometry-based event (mouse event) that is passed to your part, the coordinates of the event are passed in the `where` field of the structure. For events in embedded frames that are passed to your part, the frame and facet within which the event occurred are passed in the `embeddedFrame` and `embeddedFacet` fields.

Types of User Events

On the Mac OS platform, your parts must in general handle the types of user events listed in Table 5-1. Not all of these events exist on all other platforms.

Table 5-1   OpenDoc user events (Mac OS platform)

Standard Mac OS events	OpenDoc-defined events
kODEvtNull	kODEvtMenu
kODEvtMouseDown	kODEvtWindow
kODEvtMouseUp	kODEvtMouseEnter
kODEvtKeyDown	kODEvtMouseWithin
kODEvtKeyUp	kODEvtMouseLeave
kODEvtAutoKey	kODEvtBGMouseDown
kODEvtUpdate	kODEvtMouseDownBorder[*]
kODEvtActivate	kODEvtMouseDownEmbedded[*]
kODEvtOS	kODEvtMouseUpEmbedded[*]
	kODEvtBGMouseDownEmbedded[*]

[*] Container parts (parts that can embed other parts) must handle these events.

The following sections describe how you handle each of these kinds of events.

Mouse Events

When the user presses or releases the mouse button while the mouse pointer is in the content area of an OpenDoc window, the dispatcher finds the correct part to handle the mouse event by traversing the hierarchy of facets in the window.

The dispatcher searches depth-first (trying the most deeply embedded facets first) and front-to-back (trying the frontmost of sibling facets first). The dispatcher sends the event to the editor of the first—that is, most deeply embedded and frontmost—frame it finds whose active shape contains the pointer position. In this way the smallest enclosing frame surrounding the pointer location receives the mouse event, preserving the OpenDoc inside-out activation model. None of the part editors of any containing parts in that frame's embedding hierarchy are involved in handling the event.

When the user presses a mouse button while the pointer is within a facet of your part, the dispatcher calls your part's `HandleEvent` method, passing it an event type of `kODEvtMouseDown`. (If your part is in a document in a background process on the Mac OS, the dispatcher passes your `HandleEvent` method an event type of `kODEvtBGMouseDown`.)

When the user releases the mouse button while the pointer is within your facet, the dispatcher again calls your part's `HandleEvent` method, this time passing it an event type of `kODEvtMouseUp`.

The event-dispatching code does not itself activate and deactivate the relevant parts; it is up to the editor of the part receiving the mouse event to decide whether to activate itself or not. See the section "Mouse Events, Activation, and Dragging" on page 198 for information on how your part should handle mouse-down and mouse-up events within its facets for the purposes of part activation, window activation, and drag and drop.

The dispatcher also tracks pointer position at all times when the mouse button is not pressed.

- When the pointer enters a facet of your part, the dispatcher calls your part's `HandleEvent` method, passing it an event type of `kODEvtMouseEnter`.

- Whenever the pointer moves within your facet, the dispatcher calls your part's `HandleEvent` method, passing it an event type of `kODEvtMouseWithin`.

■ When the pointer leaves your facet, the dispatcher calls your part's `HandleEvent` method, passing it an event type of `kODEvtMouseLeave`.

You can use these events to, for example, change the cursor appearance. See "Mouse-Up Tracking" on page 219.

In some situations in the Mac OS platform, OpenDoc redirects or changes mouse events:

■ If the user holds down the Shift key or Command key while pressing or releasing the mouse button, the dispatcher instead sends the event to the frame with the selection focus. This allows users to extend selections by Shift-clicking or Command-clicking.

■ If the mouse event is in the title bar or resize box of a window, the dispatcher converts it to a window event.

■ If the mouse event is in the menu bar, the dispatcher converts it to a menu event.

■ If a frame has the modal focus (see "Acquiring and Relinquishing the Modal Focus" on page 234), mouse events that occur outside of its border are sent to it. However, mouse events that occur within frames embedded within the frame with the modal focus are sent to the embedded frames, as expected.

■ If a frame has the mouse focus (see "Mouse-Up Feedback While Drawing" on page 220), it receives all mouse-within events that occur, regardless of their location.

Mouse clicks within controls associated with your part can be handled in a number of ways, as discussed in the section "Controls" on page 238.

Mouse Events in Embedded Frames

If your part contains embedded frames, the dispatcher can also send you special mouse events that occur within and on the borders of the embedded frames' facets.

The following events occur when your part's frame is the active frame and the embedded frame is selected or bundled or in icon view type, or if the user Shift-clicks or Command-clicks in the embedded frame to extend a selection:

■ When the user presses a mouse button while the pointer is within a facet of the embedded frame, the dispatcher calls your part's `HandleEvent` method, passing it an event type of `kODEvtMouseDownEmbedded`. (If your part is in a document in a background process on the Mac OS, the dispatcher passes your `HandleEvent` method an event type of `kODEvtBGMouseDownEmbedded`.)

■ When the user releases a mouse button while the pointer is within the embedded facet, the dispatcher again calls your part's `HandleEvent` method, this time passing it an event type of `kODEvtMouseUpEmbedded`.

There is one exception to this. If the embedded frame is selected (rather than bundled or in icon view type), and if the mouse-up is *not* part of a Shift-click or Command-click, your part does *not* receive the mouse-up event. In such a case, if the user initiates a drag the mouse-up event is converted to a drop; if the user does not initiate a drag, the mouse-up event is sent to the embedded frame so that it can activate itself. See "Mouse Events, Activation, and Dragging" on page 198 for more information, including how to handle events in a background process.

The following event occurs when the frame embedded within your part is the active frame:

■ When the user presses the mouse button while the pointer is within the active border of a facet of the embedded frame, the dispatcher calls your part's `HandleEvent` method, passing it an event type of `kODEvtMouseDownBorder`.

These events allow your part to activate itself and select or drag the embedded part.

Keystroke Events

When the user presses a key on the keyboard and your part has the keystroke focus, the dispatcher calls your part's `HandleEvent` method, passing it an event type of `kODEvtKeyDown`. When the user releases the key, the dispatcher again calls your part's `HandleEvent` method, this time passing it an event type of `kODEvtKeyUp`.

Exceptions to this convention include keystroke events that are keyboard equivalents to menu commands, which go to your part as menu events, and keystroke events involving the Page Up, Page Down, Home, and End keys, which go to the frame—if any—that has the scrolling focus.

Menu Events

If the user presses the mouse button when the pointer is within the menu bar, or if the user enters a keyboard equivalent to that action, OpenDoc converts the mouse-down or keystroke event into a menu event of type `kODEvtMenu` and calls the `HandleEvent` method of the part with the menu focus.

On the Mac OS platform, the `message` field of the event structure passed to `HandleEvent` specifies the menu and item selected, equivalent to the results of calling the `MenuSelect` or `MenuKey` function of the Menu Manager. In addition, the `HandleEvent` method can obtain a command ID for the menu event by calling the `GetCommand` method of the menu bar object.

Handling individual menu commands is discussed in the section "Menus" on page 242.

Window Events

If the user presses the mouse button while the pointer is within a noncontent portion of the window (such as the close box in the title bar of a Mac OS window), or if the user enters a keyboard equivalent to that action, OpenDoc converts the mouse-down or keystroke event into an event of type `kODEvtWindow` and calls the `HandleEvent` method of the window's root part.

If the root part does not handle the event, the dispatcher returns it to the document shell, which performs the intended action (such as closing the window). However, if your part is the root part it can handle the event if it wishes. For example, it might hide the window rather than closing it.

For window events, the `message` field of the event structure contains the part code—equivalent to the results of the Mac OS `FindWindow` function—describing the part of the window, such as the close box, in which the event occurred.

How to handle window events when your part is the root part is described in the section "Handling Window Events" on page 232.

Activate Events

On platforms such as Mac OS that support activation and deactivation of windows, OpenDoc sends activate events and deactivate events, of type `kODEvtActivate`, to each facet in the window when the window changes state.

If the user clicks in the title bar of an inactive Mac OS window, OpenDoc activates the window and brings it to the front. If the user clicks in the content area of an inactive window, the part at the click location brings the window to the front. Either way, when an active Mac OS window becomes inactive because another Mac OS window has become active, each facet of each part displayed in the window being deactivated receives a deactivate event, and each facet of each part displayed in the window being activated receives an activate event.

User Events

Your part's `HandleEvent` method can use these events to store and retrieve information that allows your part to decide whether or not to activate itself when its window becomes active. See "Handling Activate Events" on page 206 for an explanation.

Update Events

To support redrawing of previously invalidated areas of a window, frame, or facet, OpenDoc handles update events and calls the `Draw` methods of the appropriate parts.

Update events are themselves triggered by the existence of invalid areas, created through changes to the content of parts, the activation of windows, or the removal of obscuring objects such as floating windows.

OpenDoc does not pass update events to your `HandleEvent` method. When an update event occurs that involves a facet of your part, the dispatcher calls the `Update` method of the window, which results in a call to your `Draw` method. For more information, see the section "Invalidating and Updating" on page 216.

Null Events

On platforms such as the Mac OS that support the concept of idle time, OpenDoc permits your part to receive idle-time events, also called null events (type `kODEvtNull`). To receive null events, your part must first call the `RegisterIdle` method of the dispatcher to register each frame that is to receive null events. When you call `RegisterIdle`, you specify an idle frequency. OpenDoc uses the idle frequency to compute the sleep time it passes to `WaitNextEvent`.

Your call to the `RegisterIdle` method might occur in your part's `DisplayFrameAdded`, `DisplayFrameConnected`, or `FacetAdded` methods. You should unregister any idle frames (using the dispatcher's `UnregisterIdle` method) before the frames are deleted. You might make the call in your part's `DisplayFrameClosed` and `DisplayFrameRemoved` methods.

Other Events

Other Mac OS–specific events are handled in these ways:

- The suspend and resume operating-system events (type `kODEvtOS`) are passed to your part editor's `HandleEvent` method. Your part should not normally relinquish the selection focus or other foci upon receiving a suspend event.

- Disk-inserted events (kODEvtDisk) are not distributed to parts.

- Mouse-moved events are converted to the OpenDoc user event types kODEvtMouseEnter, kODEvtMouseWithin, and kODEvtMouseLeave, as described under "Mouse Events" on page 192.

Propagating Events

A containing part can set a flag in an embedded frame that allows the containing part to receive events not handled by the embedded frame. If your part contains embedded frames with that flag set, your HandleEvent method receives the events originally sent to them. OpenDoc sets the propagated field in the eventInfo structure (see page 191) to true when passing a propagated event to your part.

Whenever you add a facet to a frame, you can check the state of the flag by calling the frame's DoesPropagateEvents method. You can then set or clear the flag by calling the frame's SetPropagateEvents method.

This is a specialized feature of OpenDoc, not likely to be used by most part editors. You might use it to manipulate embedded selections; for example, you could use tab-key events to allow the user to tab between embedded parts that do not themselves support tabbing or otherwise handle tab-key events.

If you do not set the event-propagating flag for any of your embedded frames, your HandleEvent method receives only those embedded-frame events described under "Mouse Events in Embedded Frames" on page 193.

The HandleEvent Method of Your Part Editor

The dispatcher calls your part's HandleEvent method to pass it a user event meant for your part. This is the method's interface:

```
ODBoolean HandleEvent(inout ODEventData event,
                      in ODFrame frame,
                      in ODFacet facet),
                      inout ODEventInfo eventInfo);
```

Your implementation of `HandleEvent` might be similar to this:

1. Set the result flag to `kODFalse`.

2. Obtain the part info data from the frame or facet to which the event was directed, if you have stored relevant information there.

3. Execute a `switch` statement with one case for each event type. Pass execution to the appropriate handler for each event type. Set the result flag to `kODTrue` if an individual handler handles the event.

4. Return the result flag as the method result.

Your individual event handlers should function as described in other sections of this chapter. Each should return `kODTrue` to `HandleEvent` if it handles an event, and `kODFalse` if it does not.

Mouse Events, Activation, and Dragging

This section discusses how your part should respond to mouse-down, mouse-up, and activate events in order to activate your part or your window, initiate a dragging operation, or create a selection. Your `HandleEvent` method (see the previous section, "The HandleEvent Method of Your Part Editor") should dispatch events to routines that perform the actions described here.

Follow these procedures to ensure that your parts behave in accordance with the user-interface guidelines given in the sections "Activation" on page 559 and "Using Drag and Drop" on page 598. Some of these instructions are specific to the Mac OS; on platforms without activation events and the concept of active windows, the procedures to follow may be somewhat different.

For other information about creating and modifying selections, see "Mouse-Down Tracking and Selection" on page 218.

How Part Activation Happens

A part's frame activates itself in these situations:

■ when it receives a mouse event within its content area

■ when its window first opens and the part has stored information specifying that the frame should be active on opening

■ when its window becomes active and the part has stored information specifying that the frame should be active upon window activation

■ when data is dropped on the part as a result of a drag-and-drop operation

■ when it has another reason for becoming active (such as the need to display a selection, such as a link source, to the user)

The part activates itself by acquiring the selection focus (see "Focus Types" on page 207) for one of its display frames. The part is then responsible for displaying its contents appropriately (for example, by restoring the highlighting of a selection) and for providing any menus, controls, palettes, floating windows, or other auxiliary items that are part of its active state. The part must also obtain ownership of any other foci that it needs. OpenDoc draws the active frame border around the frame with the selection focus.

Typically, one part is deactivated when another is activated. A part is expected to deactivate itself when it receives a request to relinquish the selection focus, plus possibly other foci. The deactivating part is responsible for clearing its selections—an inactive part in the active window should not maintain a background selection—and for removing any menus and other items that were part of its active state. OpenDoc removes the active frame border from around the (now inactive) part and draws it around the part that currently has the selection focus.

Mouse events that cause part activation can also cause window activation and can lead to dragging of part content. Figure 5-1 illustrates some of the elements you must consider in handling mouse-down events for these purposes. As the following sections explain, your part should handle mouse events according to whether your part is active or inactive, whether it is in an active or inactive window, and whether the event location corresponds to one of the elements— such as the active frame border or an embedded part's icon—that are shown in Figure 5-1.

Figure 5-1   Elements related to mouse events in active and inactive windows

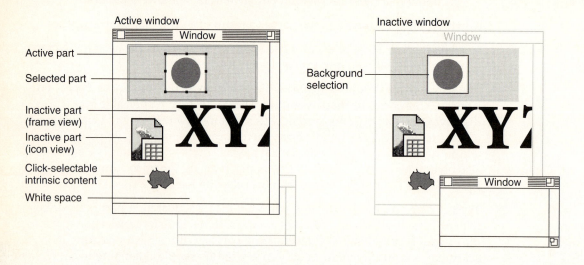

Note these points from Figure 5-1:

- Embedded parts can be represented by either frames or icons. Frames can be active or inactive, and inactive frames can be either selected or unselected. (Figure 5-1 does not show that inactive frames can also be bundled.)

- There can be only one active frame in the active window, and no active frame in an inactive window (except that a dialog box can appear in front of a window that contains the active part).

- All selected items must be within the active frame.

- A selection in the active window becomes a background selection if the window becomes inactive.

- A selection (either foreground or background) can consist of either intrinsic content or an embedded frame or icon, or a combination of both.

- "Click-selectable intrinsic content" in Figure 5-1 means any item of intrinsic content that can be selected by a single mouse click, such as a graphics object in a draw part.

- "White space" in Figure 5-1 means any location in the content area of a part that is neither click-selectable intrinsic content nor an embedded part frame or icon. It includes empty space, but also includes content (such as text or painting) that requires a sweeping gesture, rather than a single click, for selection.

- An inactive window may be in the current process (if, for example, it is a part window of the active document) or in a background process (if, for example, it is a window of another document).

The event-handling guidelines given here are designed to provide the user with maximum consistency and flexibility when activating parts and when dragging selections. These guidelines are summarized more briefly in the sections "Activating Parts" on page 559 and "Activating Windows" on page 561.

Handling Mouse-Down Events

Table 5-2 describes how your part editor's `HandleEvent` method should respond to each of the mouse-down events sent to it by OpenDoc. Mouse-up event handling is described in the section "Handling Mouse-Up Events" on page 205.

The information in Table 5-2 is grouped first by event type. The situations under which your part receives each type of event are listed in the sections "Mouse Events" on page 192 and "Mouse Events in Embedded Frames" on page 193, and can also be inferred from the descriptions in Table 5-2.

Several situations described in Table 5-2 require your part to initiate a drag operation. See the section "Initiating a Drag" on page 364 for instructions.

Table 5-2   Handling mouse-down events

Frame and window state	Event location: Action to take
Event type = `kODEvtMouseDown`	
Active part, active window	*In white space:* Remove any existing selection, and—if consistent with your part's content model—place an insertion point at the mouse location. Treat any mouse movement before the mouse-up as a sweeping selection gesture. *In selection or selectable item of intrinsic content:* Maintain the existing selection around the mouse location, or select the item at the mouse location. If the user moves the mouse pointer before releasing the button, initiate a drag operation on the selection. *If Shift key or Command key is down:* Extend (or retract) any preexisting selection appropriately.
Inactive part, active window	*In white space:* Activate your part; obtain at least the selection focus, but do not yet display palettes or menus. Treat mouse movement before the mouse-up as a sweeping selection gesture. *In selectable item of intrinsic content:* Activate your part; obtain the selection focus and any other foci you need, but do not yet display your palettes. Highlight the item at the mouse location. If the user moves the mouse pointer before releasing the button, initiate a drag operation on the selected item. *If Shift key or Command key is down:* (You do not receive this event. OpenDoc does not permit the user to Shift-click or Command-click outside of the active frame.)
Inactive part, inactive window (curr. process)	*In white space or selectable item of intrinsic content:* Do nothing. (Wait for mouse-up before activating.) Return true from `HandleEvent`. *In background-selected intrinsic content:* If the user moves the mouse pointer before releasing the button, initiate a drag operation on the background selection.

continued

Table 5-2   Handling mouse-down events (continued)

Frame and window state	*Event location:* **Action to take**

Event type = `kODEvtMouseDownEmbedded`

Active part, active window	*In selected frame, bundled frame, or frame with icon view type embedded in your part:* Select—or maintain as selected—the embedded frame or icon. If the user moves the mouse pointer before releasing the button, initiate a drag operation on the selection. (Your part receives the mouse-down event for any location in a bundled or selected embedded frame, even if that location corresponds to a more deeply embedded frame.)
	In unselected, unbundled frame embedded in your part: (You do not receive this event; OpenDoc sends it to the embedded part at the mouse location.)
	If Shift key or Command key is down: Extend (or retract) any preexisting selection to include (or exclude, if previously selected) the frame or icon enclosing the mouse location.
Inactive part, active window	*In bundled frame or frame with icon view type embedded in your part:* Activate your part; obtain the selection focus and any other foci you need, but do not yet display your palettes or menus. Highlight the embedded frame or icon at the mouse location. If the user moves the mouse pointer before releasing the button, initiate a drag operation on the selected frame or icon.
	In unbundled frame embedded in your part: (You do not receive this event; OpenDoc sends it to the embedded part at the mouse location.)
	If Shift key or Command key is down: (You do not receive this event. OpenDoc does not permit the user to Shift-click or Command-click outside of the active frame.)
Inactive part, inactive window (curr. process)	*In background-selected frame, bundled frame, or frame with icon view type embedded in your part:* Do nothing on mouse-down, unless the user moves the pointer before releasing the button. If so, initiate a drag operation on the frame or icon.
	In unselected, unbundled frame embedded in your part: (You do not receive this event; OpenDoc sends it to the embedded part at the mouse location.)

continued

Table 5-2   Handling mouse-down events (continued)

Frame and window state	Event location: Action to take
Event type = `kODEvtMouseDownBorder`	
Inactive part, active window	*On active frame border embedded in your part:* Activate your part; obtain the selection focus and any other foci you need, but do not yet display your palettes or menus. Highlight the (previously active, now selected) frame at the mouse location. If the user moves the mouse pointer before releasing the button, initiate a drag operation on the frame.
Event type = `kODEvtBGMouseDown`	
Inactive part, inactive window (bkgd. process)	*In white space or intrinsic content:* Do nothing, and return `kODFalse` from `HandleEvent`. The Mac OS Process Manager activates the window's process.
	In background-selected intrinsic content: If the user moves the mouse pointer before releasing the button, initiate a drag operation on the background selection. Otherwise, return false from `HandleEvent`.
	Do not perform any task other than initiating a drag in this situation; attempting to switch process or interact with the user can cause a crash.
Event type = `kODEvtBGMouseDownEmbedded`	
Inactive part, inactive window (bkgd. process)	*In background-selected frame, bundled frame, or frame with icon view type embedded in your part:* Do nothing on mouse-down, unless the user moves the pointer before releasing the button; if so, initiate a drag operation on the frame or icon.
	Do not perform any task other than initiating a drag in this situation; attempting to switch process or interact with the user can cause a crash.
	In unselected, unbundled frame embedded in your part: (You do not receive this event; OpenDoc sends it to the embedded part at the mouse location.)

Handling Mouse-Up Events

Table 5-3 describes how your part editor's `HandleEvent` method should respond to each of the mouse-up events sent to it by OpenDoc. Mouse-down event handling is described in the section "Handling Mouse-Down Events" on page 201.

The information in Table 5-3 is grouped by event type; the situations under which your part receives these types of event are listed in the sections "Mouse Events" on page 192 and "Mouse Events in Embedded Frames" on page 193, and can also be inferred from the descriptions in Table 5-3.

Table 5-3   Handling mouse-up events

Frame and window state	Event location: Action to take
Event type = `kODEvtMouseUp`	
Active part, active window	*In white space or intrinsic content:* If necessary, complete any activation you may have started on receiving a prior mouse-down event: obtain any needed foci that you do not already have; display your palettes and menus if they are not already displayed. Prepare for editing at the insertion point or selection.
Inactive part, active window	*At any location:* Activate your part; obtain the selection focus and any other foci you need, and display your palettes and menus. Prepare for editing at the insertion point or selection. (This event is not sent to you if it occurs within a nonbundled embedded frame.)
Inactive part, inactive window (curr. process)	*In white space or intrinsic content:* Activate your part's window by calling the `Select` method of the window. Do not activate your part yet; see "Handling Activate Events" on page 206 for an explanation.
Inactive part, inactive window (bkgd. process)	(OpenDoc does not send this event to windows in background processes.)

continued

Table 5-3   Handling mouse-up events (continued)

Frame and window state	Event location: Action to take

Event type = kODEvtMouseUpEmbedded

Active part, active window	*In bundled frame or frame with icon view type embedded in your part:* If necessary, complete any activation you may have started on receiving a prior mouse-down event: obtain any needed foci that you do not already have; display your palettes and menus if they are not already displayed. Prepare for editing at the insertion point or selection.
	In selected frame embedded in your part: (You do not receive this event. If a drag occurs after mouse-down, OpenDoc absorbs the subsequent mouse-up. If no drag occurs, OpenDoc sends the mouse-up to the embedded selected frame so that it can activate itself.)
Inactive part, active window	*In bundled frame or frame with icon view type embedded in your part:* Activate your part or complete any activation you may have started on receiving a prior mouse-down event: obtain any needed foci that you do not already have; display your palettes and menus if they are not already displayed. Prepare for editing at the insertion point or selection.
Inactive part, inactive window (curr. process)	*In bundled frame, background-selected frame, or frame with icon view type embedded in your part:* Activate your part's window by calling the Select method of the window. Do not activate your part yet; see "Handling Activate Events" (next section) for an explanation.
Inactive part, inactive window (bkgd process)	(OpenDoc does not send this event to windows in background processes. If the prior mouse-down event has caused a process switch, this mouse-up event is then sent to the current process, as it should be. If a drag has occurred, this mouse-up event does not happen.)

Handling Activate Events

As noted in the section "Activate Events" on page 195, your part receives an activate event for each of its facets when your window becomes active, and a deactivate event when your window becomes inactive.

When a window becomes inactive, the part that holds the selection focus is likely to relinquish that focus (on request by another part) but can still maintain, as a background selection, any selection it had been displaying. Conversely, when a window becomes active, the part that had held the selection focus when the window became inactive normally regains the selection focus. That part may or may not be the part that actually activated the window.

This part-activation convention requires that your part respond to activate and deactivate events by recording or retrieving stored information on its focus transfers; see the section "On Window Activation" on page 214 for more information.

Activate events in a window go first to the most deeply embedded facets and last to the root facet. This dispatch order gives the root part the opportunity to obtain the selection focus if no embedded part has done so. It also allows the root part to override any activation actions taken by embedded parts.

Focus Transfer

Part activation is the process of making a part and frame ready for editing. As noted previously, activation typically occurs when the user clicks the mouse button when the pointer is within a frame that is not currently active, but it also happens when a window opens, when a window is activated, and as a result of drag-and-drop operations.

In the OpenDoc model of part activation, part editors use the concept of *focus* to activate and deactivate themselves (rather than being activated and deactivated by OpenDoc) and to arbitrate the transfer of several types of shared resources among themselves.

Focus Types

A part makes itself the recipient of a certain type of user event or other action by obtaining the focus for it. A **focus** is a designation of ownership of a given shared resource, feature, or event type; for example, the frame that owns the keystroke focus receives all keystroke events until it passes ownership of the keystroke focus to another frame.

Focus types are defined as ISO strings. Table 5-4 lists the standard set defined by OpenDoc.

Table 5-4   Focus types

Constant	ISO string	Description
kODKeyFocus	"Key"	Keystroke events are sent to the frame with this focus.
kODMenuFocus	"Menu"	Menu events are sent first to the frame with this focus.
kODSelectionFocus	"Selection"	Shift-click and Command-click mouse events are sent to the frame with this focus. OpenDoc draws the active frame border around all facets of this frame.
kODModalFocus	"Modal"	The frame that owns this focus is notifying other frames that it is the only current modal frame.
kODScrollingFocus	"Scrolling"	Scrolling-specific keystroke events (such as Page Up and Page Down) are sent to the frame with this focus.
kODClipboardFocus	"Clipboard"	The frame that owns this focus has access to the clipboard.
kODMouseFocus	"Mouse"	The frame that owns this focus receives all mouse-within events whenever the pointer moves, and all mouse-down and mouse-up events, regardless of which facet the pointer is within.

To obtain event foci, part editors request them by name from the arbitrator. (You obtain access to the arbitrator by calling the GetArbitrator method of the session object.)

You need to convert focus names into tokens before using them in any method calls. You call the Tokenize method of the session object to convert ISO strings to tokens.

Foci may be manipulated singly or in groups called focus sets. A **focus set** is an OpenDoc object (of class `ODFocusSet`) listing a group of foci that a part editor wants to obtain or release as a group.

Foci are owned by frames. In general, mouse events anywhere within the content area of an OpenDoc window always go to the most deeply embedded frame that encloses the click point. However, Shift-click and Command-click events, regardless of their location, are sent to the frame with the selection focus to allow for extending selections.

OpenDoc does not require that the same frame own the selection focus, keystroke focus, and menu focus, although this is most often the case. Also, OpenDoc does not require that the selection focus be in an active window, although this is usually the case, at least on the Mac OS platform.

In most cases, when a frame is activated the part editor for that frame requests the selection focus, keystroke focus, and menu focus. A frame with scroll bars might also request the scrolling focus. Your part editor might create a focus set ahead of time, perhaps during part initialization, that includes the tokenized names of the foci that your part expects to request when it becomes active. You use the arbitrator's `CreateFocusSet` method to create the focus set.

A simple part, such as a small text-entry field in a dialog box, might request only the selection focus and keystroke focus on receiving a mouse-up event within its frame area. An even simpler part, such as a button, might not even request the selection focus. It might simply track the mouse until the button is released, and then run a script, never having changed the menu bar, put up palettes or rulers, or become active.

Your part editor can define additional focus types as needed. You can define other kinds of focus, perhaps to handle other kinds of user events (such as input from new kinds of devices). To create a new kind of focus, you need to create a new kind of **focus module,** the OpenDoc object that the arbitrator uses to determine focus ownership. Chapter 10, "Extending OpenDoc," describes how to use focus modules to extend OpenDoc's focus management.

Foci may be exclusive or nonexclusive. All of the standard foci defined by OpenDoc are **exclusive,** meaning that only one frame at a time can own a focus. But if you create a new kind of focus, you can make it **nonexclusive,** meaning that several frames could share ownership of it.

Arbitrating Focus Transfers

This section discusses how to request or relinquish foci to activate or deactivate your frames.

Requesting Foci

A part can request, for one of its frames, ownership of a single focus or a set of foci. You request a focus by calling the arbitrator's `RequestFocus` method; you request a focus set by calling the arbitrator's `RequestFocusSet` method. If the request succeeds, your part's frame obtains the focus or focus set.

The arbitrator's `RequestFocus` and `RequestFocusSet` methods perform a two-stage transaction in transferring a focus or focus set:

1. The arbitrator first asks the current owning frame of each focus if it is willing to relinquish the focus, by calling the `BeginRelinquishFocus` method of the frame's part.

2. If any owner of the focus is unwilling to relinquish it, the arbitrator cancels the request by calling each part's `AbortRelinquishFocus` method. In this case, `RequestFocus` or `RequestFocusSet` returns false.

3. If all focus owners are willing to relinquish, the arbitrator calls each part's `CommitRelinquishFocus` method. In this case, `RequestFocus` or `RequestFocusSet` returns true.

Relinquishing Foci

A part can relinquish foci either on request or when a change to its state (such as the closure of its frame or a completion of a method) warrants it. An active part might unilaterally relinquish certain foci (such as the clipboard focus) as soon as it is finished handling an event, but it might not relinquish other foci (such as the selection focus) until another part asks for them. Nevertheless, most parts willingly relinquish the common foci when asked.

Relinquishing foci on request is a two-step process, because multiple foci requested as a focus set must all be provided to the requestor simultaneously; if one is not available, none need be relinquished. Your part editor participates in the process through calls to its `BeginRelinquishFocus`, `CommitRelinquishFocus`, and `AbortRelinquishFocus` methods.

1. In your `BeginRelinquishFocus` method, you need do nothing other than return `kODTrue` or `kODFalse`, basing your decision on the type of focus and

the identities of the frames (current and proposed focus owners) passed to you. In most cases you can simply return `kODTrue`, unless your part is displaying a dialog box and another part is requesting the modal focus. In that case, because you do not want to yield the modal focus until your dialog box window closes, you return `kODFalse`. See "Acquiring and Relinquishing the Modal Focus" on page 234 for more information.

2. Your part's `CommitRelinquishFocus` method verifies that you have actually relinquished the focus type you responded to in `BeginRelinquishFocus`. The method should take appropriate action, such as removing menus or palettes, disabling menu items, removing highlighting, and performing whatever other tasks are part of losing that type of focus. Remember that the focus may possibly be moving from one frame to another of your part, so the exact actions can vary.

3. If, after your part responds with `kODTrue` to `BeginRelinquishFocus`, the focus is actually not transferred from your frame, OpenDoc calls your part's `AbortRelinquishFocus` method. If your part has done anything more than return the Boolean result in `BeginRelinquishFocus`, it can undo those effects in the `AbortRelinquishFocus` method.

4. If your part is one of several focus owners called to relinquish the foci of a focus set, and if you return `kODFalse` to `BeginRelinquishFocus`, your `CommitRelinquishFocus` method is not called (because you chose not to give up the focus). However, your `AbortRelinquishFocus` method is still called (because all owners of a focus set are notified if any one refuses to relinquish the focus).

Your part does not relinquish its focus on request only. For example, in your part's `DisplayFrameClosed` and `DisplayFrameRemoved` methods, you should include a call to the arbitrator's `RelinquishFocus` or `RelinquishFocusSet` method to unilaterally relinquish any foci owned by the frame that you are closing. When your part closes, its `ReleaseAll` method should likewise relinquish all of its foci. When your part finishes displaying a modal dialog box, it should relinquish or transfer the modal focus; when your part finishes accessing the clipboard, it should relinquish the clipboard focus.

Transferring Focus Without Negotiation

There are some situations in which the normal process of requesting and relinquishing foci is not used. Another piece of software interrupts your part's execution, and your part loses a focus without being given a chance to relinquish it, or gains focus without having asked for it. To handle those situations, your part editor must implement versions of the methods `FocusAcquired` and `FocusLost`. The arbitrator calls these methods when your part has just acquired, or just lost, a specified focus without having negotiated the transaction.

For example, a containing part, to support keyboard navigation, might call `FocusAcquired` in turn on each of its embedded parts as the user makes successive keystrokes. Or, if a custom input device with its own focus type were in use and then became detached, the part using the device might receive a call to its `FocusLost` method.

These are the interfaces to `FocusAcquired` and `FocusLost`:

```
void FocusAcquired(in ODTypeToken focus,
                   in ODFrame ownerFrame);

void FocusLost(in ODTypeToken focus,
               in ODFrame ownerFrame);
```

Your `FocusAcquired` and `FocusLost` methods should perform any actions that your part editor deems appropriate in response to having just acquired or lost a focus.

The arbitrator's methods `TransferFocus` and `TransferFocusSet` allow you to initiate a transfer of focus ownership without negotiation. A part can use these calls to transfer focus among parts and frames that it controls directly. For example, in a modal dialog box consisting of several parts, these methods can be used to transfer a focus from the outer part (the dialog box) directly to an inner part (such as a text field) and back.

When focus is transferred with `TransferFocus` or `TransferFocusSet`, the arbitrator generally calls the `FocusAcquired` method of the new frame's part and the `FocusLost` method of the previous frame's part. However, when the frame performing the transfer (the frame representing the part that calls `TransferFocus`) is the frame receiving or losing the focus, its `FocusAcquired` or `FocusLost` method is not called.

Calling your own `FocusAcquired` **and** `FocusLost`
It might seem natural to call your own `FocusAcquired`
method when your request for foci succeeds, or to
call your own `FocusLost` method from your own
`CommitRelinquishFocus` method. A better practice,
however, is to have related methods call a shared
private method, so that you maintain a clear separation
between public and private interfaces. ◆

Recording Focus Transfers

Different frames may need different sets of foci when activated. Selection focus, keystroke focus, and menu focus are commonly needed together. However, a frame with scroll bars might also need the scrolling focus, and a frame for a modeless dialog box might not want the selection focus.

OpenDoc does not save or restore focus assignments. Therefore, during deactivation of windows and frames, and during closing of windows, you can record the state of focus ownership so that you can restore it at a later activation or reopening. Your display frame's part info is an appropriate place to keep that information. Your part's initialization method might create a focus set with those foci, to use whenever your display frames become active.

On Frame Activation

When a previously inactive frame in a window becomes active, the part editors involved should—besides negotiating the focus transfer—record the gain or loss of selection focus for the respective frames. If you maintain that information, your activation and deactivation routines can check the state and exit quickly if no change in the active state is needed.

- If you are activating your part's frame, you might record, in a Boolean flag with a name such as `fHasRequiredFoci` in the frame's part info data, the fact that the frame has the selection focus. You can perform this action in your `FocusAcquired` method, after its call to the arbitrator's `RequestFocusSet` method succeeds.

- If you are deactivating your part's frame, you might set the `fHasRequiredFoci` flag in the frame's part info data to false. You can perform this action in your `FocusLost` method and/or your `CommitRelinquishFocus` method.

On Window Activation

As mentioned in "Activate Events" on page 195, all parts displayed in a window receive an activate event when the window becomes active, and a deactivate event when the window becomes inactive.

When an active facet of a frame of your part becomes inactive through window deactivation, your part's `HandleEvent` method can—upon receiving the deactivate event—store a flag in the facet's part info field to note that the facet was active before window deactivation. Your part then can also maintain, as a background selection, any selection it had been displaying.

Conversely, when a facet of a frame of your part receives an activate event because of window activation, your part's `HandleEvent` method can examine the state of the flag in the part info field to determine whether it was the active part when the window became inactive. If so, it should request the selection focus, reset the flag, and convert any background selection it may have maintained into a foreground selection.

On Closing and Reopening Documents

Normally, the root part of a newly opened window should activate itself as a matter of course. However, if an embedded part had the selection focus when the window closed, the root part can—if it chooses to—allow the embedded part to recapture that focus when the window reopens.

When the state of a window is saved in a document and the document is subsequently reopened, the root part recreates the window. If you want to restore the selection-focus state of your part (plus perhaps the selection itself), you can save the selection and the state of the selection-focus flag in your frame's part info data when the window is closed, and restore them when the window is opened (when your part's `DisplayFrameConnected` method is called).

If your part is the root part in this situation, you can either grant the embedded part's request for the selection focus at this time, or you can acquire the selection focus yourself, when your own `DisplayFrameConnected` method is called. (The root part is called last.)

Display-Related Events

Your part editor needs to respond to events that select or change the position or visibility of your intrinsic content, by highlighting or preparing to move or redraw the content. This section discusses general event-handling issues related to drawing and highlighting. Display concepts are described more completely in Chapter 4, "Drawing."

Just as with intrinsic content, your part editor is responsible for knowing what embedded frames look like and when they become visible or invisible. When update events or events related to scrolling or editing cause an embedded frame to become visible, your part is responsible for creating facets for those frames. If events cause an embedded facet to move, your part must modify the facet's external transform to reflect the move. If the embedded facet moves so as to become no longer visible, your part is responsible for deleting the embedded facet from its containing facet (or marking it as purgeable).

Hit-Testing

Hit-testing is the interpretation of mouse events in terms of content elements within a frame. For example, when the user clicks somewhere within your part's content area to select an item or to set an insertion point, you must use the click location to decide which item has been selected or which characters correspond to the insertion point. You can then highlight the proper item or draw the text caret at the proper location.

Coordinate conversion is necessary to assign content locations to hit-testing events, and in that sense hit-testing is the inverse of drawing. Coordinate conversion and the application of transforms during drawing are discussed in the section "Transforms and Coordinate Spaces" on page 135.

If the user clicks in a facet of your part's frame, OpenDoc applies the inverse of all external transforms from the root facet to your facet, passing you the mouse event in your part's frame coordinates. It is then your responsibility to apply the inverse of your own internal transform to the event location, to convert it to the content coordinates of your part.

If the entire content of your part's frame is scrolled, the application of your frame's internal transform yields the correct location for everything within the frame. If, however, your part has drawn scroll bars or other nonscrolling items within the frame, it is important not to apply the internal transform to events over those items. See "Scrolling" on page 216 for more information.

Invalidating and Updating

On the Mac OS platform, when keystroke or mouse events involved with editing have changed the visible content of your part, you should invalidate the affected areas (by calling your frame's `Invalidate` method), so that an update event will be generated to force a redraw. If the same presentation of your part is displayed in more than one frame (see "Synchronizing Display Frames" on page 114), you are responsible for invalidating those frames as well, if necessary.

Sometimes a portion of a window needs to be redrawn because it has been invalidated by actions taken by the documents' parts or by the system (as when a window is uncovered). In this case, the document shell receives notification of that fact and passes an update event to the dispatcher, which calls the `Update` method of the window. The window in turn calls the `Update` method of its root facet.

The root facet's `Update` method examines all of the root facet's embedded facets (and their embedded facets, and so on) and marks each one that intersects the area that must be updated. Then, each facet that needs to be redrawn calls the `Draw` method of its frame's part, passing it the appropriate shape that represents its portion of the area to be updated.

Your part can, if desired, modify the order in which embedded parts draw their content, by making explicit calls to the `Draw`, `DrawChildren`, and `DrawChildrenAlways` methods of an embedded facet. See "The Draw Method of Your Part Editor" on page 162 for more information.

Scrolling

The scrolled position of a part's contents within a frame is controlled by the frame's internal transform. (The transform object can also support scaling, translation, rotation, and perspective transformations of a frame's contents. See, for example, Figure 4-2 on page 135.)

In general, the user specifies the amount of scrolling to apply to a frame. The part editor then modifies the offset specified in the frame's internal transform. (Depending on the new scrolled position of the part's contents, the part editor may also have to add or remove facets for embedded frames that have become visible or obscured by the scrolling.)

There are a number of ways for your part editor to support scrolling:

- It can create scroll bars for its content, placing them at the margins of its display frames.

- It can create scroll bars, sliders, or other kinds of controls and place them outside of its frame, as separate frames, or as elements in a floating window.

- It can support autoscrolling, by tracking the mouse pointer when the user moves it beyond your part's frame while holding down the mouse button.

- It can support the standard user-interface method for positioning a part in a frame, using the Show Frame Outline command and Reposition Content in Window command. Both commands are described in the section "Repositioning Content in a Frame" on page 575.

Each of these methods requires different event handling by your part to achieve the same result: a modified internal transform for the frame. Your part then draws the scrolled display as described in the section "Scrolling Your Part in a Frame" on page 144.

Event Handling in Scroll Bars Within Your Frame

You can create scroll bars for your content inside the margins of your frame. One approach to handling events in those scroll bars is to create an extra, private "content shape" within your frame, as described for drawing in the section "Placing Scroll Bars Within Your Frame" on page 168. The content shape is the same as the frame shape, except that it does not include the areas of the scroll bars.

When interpreting mouse events in your frame, you must take the current scrolled position of your content into account for content editing, but not for scroll-bar manipulation. Thus, for points within your content shape you apply the inverse of the frame's internal transform to mouse events, whereas outside the content shape (in the scroll bar area) you do not. See Figure 5-2.

Figure 5-2   Using a "content shape" within a frame shape to handle events

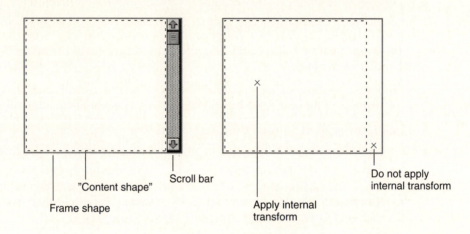

Mouse events within the scroll bar area specify how to set the frame's internal transform; based on the transform's new value, you then redraw your part's content (and the scroll bar slider). Mouse events within the area of the content shape specify how to select or edit the appropriately scrolled content.

Event Handling in Scroll Bars in Separate Frames

If you place scroll bars or adornments in frames that are separate from your display frame (see "Placing Scroll Bars in a Separate Frame" on page 170), you avoid having to define a separate content shape. Your part has one display frame that encloses both the scroll bars and the content; you draw the scroll bars directly in this frame, and you draw the content in a subframe. Only the subframe's internal transform changes.

When a mouse event occurs in the nonscrolling frame, your part interprets it and sets the internal transform of the scrolling subframe accordingly.

Mouse-Down Tracking and Selection

A selection exists only in the context of a particular part. The boundary of a selection cannot span part boundaries; all of its margins must be in the same part. However, a selection can include any number of embedded frames (which themselves can include any number of more deeply embedded frames).

Selections are typically created through mouse events, or keyboard-modified mouse events, within an already active frame or a frame that has been made potentially active by an initial mouse-down event within its area. When a mouse-down event occurs, OpenDoc passes the pointer location, in the frame coordinates of the most deeply embedded frame enclosing the event location, to the part displayed in that frame. If a drag-selection occurs (that is, if a drag-and-drop operation does not occur), the subsequent mouse-up event location is passed in the same coordinates to the same part. Thus, the active frame is not changed simply because the cursor passes across a frame boundary while the user is making a selection.

The selection actions your part takes during mouse-down tracking depend on your content model. Specific user-interface conventions for providing selection facilities and highlighting selections are discussed in the section "Selection" on page 562 of this book and in *Macintosh Human Interface Guidelines*. You should provide feedback to the user while the dragging is in progress.

Your part editor should support extending selections through Shift-clicking and Command-clicking, following the guidelines described in the sections "Extending a Selection" on page 567 and "Making a Discontiguous Selection" on page 567. Because selection is possible only within one part at a time, a part editor can extend a selection outside of its display frame boundary only to items within another of its own display frames.

If your part is a containing part and allows the user to drag selected content, including embedded frames, dragging may lead to frame negotiation. If an embedded frame is clipped by the edge of a page, for example, you may need to change its size.

Selected frames should be highlighted appropriately, as described in the section "Drawing Selections" on page 166.

Mouse-Up Tracking

OpenDoc calls your part's `HandleEvent` method whenever the mouse pointer enters, moves within, or leaves a facet of a display frame of your part and the mouse button is up (not pressed). Your part can use this method call to display a custom cursor while the pointer is within your part's frames.

Your `HandleEvent` method is passed an event of type `kODEvtMouseEnter` when the pointer enters your part's facet, allowing you to swap the pointer for a cursor specific to your application, if desired. When it receives a `kODEvtMouseLeave` event, however, your `HandleEvent` method can perform whatever actions it deems appropriate, but it need not restore the cursor to the appearance it had before the kODEvtMouseEnter event occurred. OpenDoc will restore the default cursor.

Your HandleEvent method is passed an event of type kODEvtMouseWithin only when the cursor changes position within your facet. More specifically, on the Mac OS platform the method is called only when the cursor moves out of the current **mouse region,** an area (by default a size of 1 pixel square) that you can set by calling the dispatcher's SetMouseRegion method. If, for example, you need a special cursor for a facet but do not need the cursor to change shape anywhere within the facet, you can make the mouse region equal to the intersection of the facet's active shape and clip shape. In this case, you receive the kODEvtMouseEnter and kODEvtMouseLeave events when the cursor moves into and out of that facet, but not the kODEvtMouseWithin event when the cursor moves within the facet.

If you do set the mouse region, the first kODEvtMouseEnter, kODEvtMouseLeave, or kODEvtMouseWithin event that you receive resets the mouse region to its default size. You need to recalculate this region and call SetMouseRegion again if you still need a nondefault mouse region. (You can invalidate the current mouse region and cause it to revert to the default at any time by calling the dispatcher's InvalidateFacetUnderMouse method.)

Your part is responsible for providing the appropriate cursor appearances as defined by OpenDoc. Table 12-1 on page 536 shows the standard cursors and describes the situations in which they should be employed. For example, if your part is the containing part of the currently active part, your handler for kODEvtMouseWithin events should change the cursor to a hand when it is over the active border.

Mouse-Up Feedback While Drawing

In certain modal situations, such as when drawing polygons or connected line segments, the user typically draws by clicking the mouse button once for each successive vertex or joint. (The user might complete the polygon and exit the mode by double-clicking or by clicking in the menu bar or another window.) During the drawing operation, while the mouse button is up, the part editor must provide feedback to the user, showing a potential line segment extending from the last vertex to the current mouse position.

Your part can support this kind of drawing feedback by requesting the mouse focus (kODMouseFocus) when the user clicks to make the first vertex after selecting the appropriate drawing mode (perhaps from a tool palette that you maintain). Your part then receives kODEvtMouseWithin events when the mouse moves, regardless of which facet the cursor travels over. The facet passed to your HandleEvent method is the one in which the initial mouse-down event occurred. Receiving these events allows you to provide visual feedback regardless of where the user moves the mouse pointer.

Your part also receives all mouse-down and mouse-up events until it relinquishes the focus. In addition, as long as your part holds the mouse focus, OpenDoc sends no kODEvtMouseEnter and kODEvtMouseLeave events to any facet.

When the user completes the drawing operation, relinquish the mouse focus.

If the user clicks on the desktop or on another document's window, your part receives a suspend event and should exit the mode (relinquish the mouse focus). Also, if the user clicks in the menu bar, you must relinquish the mouse focus and redispatch the event if you want the menu to appear.

International Text Handling

For text input using Roman and other 1-byte script systems, the normal event-handling mechanism of OpenDoc is sufficient; your part receives keystroke events, converts them to characters in memory, and draws them as text glyphs on the screen.

To support text input in 2-byte script systems such as Chinese, Japanese, and Korean, OpenDoc on the Mac OS platform uses the Script Manager, Text Services Manager, and Dictionary Manager. Your parts can use these system software facilities to offer the user both bottomline input and the extra convenience of inline input.

The Script Manager, the Text Services Manager, and the Dictionary Manager are all described in detail in *Inside Macintosh: Text*. This section summarizes only how your part must use the Text Services Manager differently than a conventional application does.

Because it shares application responsibilities with the document shell and other parts of OpenDoc, your part does both less and more than a conventional application when it uses the Mac OS Text Services Manager.

■ OpenDoc itself takes care of basic initialization and event handling. It calls the `InitTSMAwareApplication`, `CloseTSMAwareApplication`, `TSMEvent`, and `SetTSMCursor` functions.

■ OpenDoc does not provide support for any other international text-handling facilities, such as the TSMTE extension. To use such an extension, your part is responsible for checking for its existence and accessing it.

■ To support inline input, your part needs to provide the required Apple event handlers through a semantic interface extension, as described in Chapter 9, "Semantic Events and Scripting." Because it is a part, it cannot directly install Apple event handlers in the same manner as a conventional application.

■ Whenever a part loses the keystroke focus, OpenDoc calls the Text Services Manager function `UseInputWindow` to reestablish the default convention of bottomline input (that is, input using an input window). Therefore, if your part wants to use inline input, it must itself call `UseInputWindow` every time it receives the keystroke focus, to override that default and specify inline input.

■ Like a conventional application, your part makes normal text-processing calls to the Text Service Manager, such as `ActivateTSMDocument`, `FixTSMDocument`, and `DeactivateTSMDocument`.

CHAPTER 6

Windows and Menus

Contents

This is the fourth of eight chapters that discuss the OpenDoc programming interface in detail. This chapter describes how your part editor can present and manipulate some of the major elements of its user interface.

This chapter is a continuation of the previous chapter: it discusses programming issues involved with your part's user interface. Detailed design guidelines and recommendations for how your user interface should look and act are presented in Part 3 of this book and also in *Macintosh Human Interface Guidelines*.

Before reading this chapter, you should be familiar with the concepts presented in Chapter 1, "Introduction to OpenDoc," and Chapter 2, "Development Overview." For additional concepts related to your part editor's runtime environment, see Chapter 11, "OpenDoc Runtime Features."

This chapter discusses the following topics:

■ windows

■ dialog boxes

■ controls

■ menus

■ undo

Windows

Windows are platform-specific data structures through which documents display themselves. This section discusses how to use OpenDoc window objects (which are basically wrappers for those structures) regardless of which platform you are developing for. Some information specific to the Mac OS is also provided where appropriate. For more detailed Mac OS programming information on windows, see *Inside Macintosh: Macintosh Toolbox Essentials*.

Creating and Using Windows

The OpenDoc class `ODWindow` is a wrapper for a pointer to a platform-specific window structure. For some operations, your part editor must retrieve the window pointer from the `ODWindow` object and use the platform's facilities. In most cases, however, the interface to `ODWindow` provides the capability you need for interacting with your windows.

The Window State Object

There is a single instantiated window state object (class ODWindowState) for each OpenDoc session. The window state consists of a list of the currently existing window objects. You can access all open windows in a session through the window state.

The document shell and dispatcher use the window state to pass events to parts so that they can activate themselves, handle user input, and adjust their menus as necessary. A part may be displayed in any number of frames, in any window of a document. The dispatcher uses the window state to make sure that it passes events to the correct part, no matter what window encloses the active frame and how many other frames the part has.

Normally, your part editor calls the window state only when it creates new windows, when it needs access to a particular window, and when it needs access to the base menu bar object.

If for some reason your part needs access to all windows, you can create an ODWindowIterator object, which gives you access to all windows referenced by the window state.

Creating and Registering a Window

To receive events in a window, you generally must create an OpenDoc window object for it. (You may not be able to create an OpenDoc window for a Mac OS modal dialog box, but you can pass an event filter routine to it and therefore receive Mac OS events.) Windows in OpenDoc are created and maintained through the window-state object, which you access through the session object.

You first create a window with platform-specific calls; you then call the window state object to create an OpenDoc window object describing the platform-specific window. You call either of two methods:

- You call the RegisterWindow method of ODWindowState when you create a window that is not a root window or that has not yet been written to storage.

- You call the call the RegisterWindowForFrame method of ODWindowState when you create a root window from a previously stored root frame. (RegisterWindowForFrame takes fewer parameters than RegisterWindow because the frame passed in with the method already contains some of the needed information.)

A window has an *is-root* property. If the property is true, the window is a **root window,** which is the same as a **document window.** The root part of a root window is the root part of its document, and the document cannot close as long as the root window is open. If a window's is-root property is false, the window may be either a **part window** that has been opened from a **source frame** within a root window, or it may be a dialog box, palette, or other utility window. OpenDoc permits multiple document windows for a single document, as long as the root part provides a user interface to support this feature. The document shell closes a document when the document's last document window (root window) is closed.

Windows also have a *should-save* property that, if true, specifies that the state of the window is saved persistently after the window closes. Usually, only document windows should be marked as should-save.

The creator of a window can specify the view type and presentation of the **root frame,** the frame that displays the root part. The view type specifies whether the root part should draw itself as an icon, and the presentation specifies what kind of appearance the part content should have if not drawn as an icon. View type and presentation are suggestions to the part editor that draws within that frame. View type and presentation are described in more detail in the section "Defining General Display Characteristics" on page 158.

OpenDoc assumes that each window has a single canvas, which is attached to the window's **root facet,** the facet created for the root frame. On the Mac OS platform, the root frame in the window has the same shape as the window's content region: it includes window scroll bars but excludes the window's resize box, if present.

Your part should create windows as invisible and then make them visible as described in "Opening a Window" on page 228.

Allocating Window Memory Efficiently

On the Mac OS platform, you can save on the total amount of memory required for your part's document by allocating your windows in system memory rather than in the application heap. If you do so, however, you are responsible for disposing of the platform-specific window structure yourself. Follow these steps:

1. Allocate the platform-specific window in temporary memory, by using calls such as this:

```
WindowPtr myWindow = GetNewCWindow(kWINDID,

 (Ptr)ODNewPtr(sizeof(WindowRecord)),
                                   (WindowPtr)-1L);
```

(`ODNewPtr` is a function of the ODMemory utility library, supplied with OpenDoc; when called in this manner it allocates the pointer in temporary memory.)

2. When registering the window and retrieving the OpenDoc window object, pass a value of `kODFalse` for the `shouldDispose` parameter of `RegisterWindow` or `RegisterWindowForFrame`. This value tells OpenDoc not to dispose of the underlying platform-specific window.

3. Add code to your `DisplayFrameClosed` and `DisplayFrameRemoved` methods to dispose of the platform-specific window if the frame being removed or closed is a root frame.

Opening a Window

After creating a window, your part editor typically makes calls to these three methods, in this order:

1. the window's `Open` method, which creates the root facet

2. the window's `Show` method, which makes the window visible

3. the window's `Select` method, which brings the window to the front

Window IDs

Your part editor should not maintain references to `ODWindow` objects for accessing OpenDoc windows, because the document shell or the window state object can close a window and invalidate the reference. Instead, the window state assigns window IDs that are valid for the length of a session. Use the window's `GetID` method to get the ID of a window when you create it, and then pass that ID to the window state's `AcquireWindow` method for subsequent access to the window.

Closing a Window

If your part editor needs to close a window programmatically, it calls the
window's `CloseAndRemove` method. That method closes the window, releases
the window object and disposes of the platform-specific window structure,
deletes the root facet and canvas, and removes the root frame from the
document. It also makes any necessary platform-specific calls to dispose of the
window itself.

Storing and Retrieving Window Characteristics

Whenever a document is saved, OpenDoc writes certain information into a
storage unit referenced from the storage unit of the window's root frame. The
window's bounding rectangle, title, and other characteristics are saved in a
property of type `kODPropWindowProperties` in that storage unit.

When you create a root window, you retrieve that information from the stored
frame and use it to specify the platform-specific window's characteristics. You
can use functions of the WinUtils utility library (provided with OpenDoc) to
extract that information, or you can access the frame's storage unit directly. The
`kODPropWindowProperties` property contains a persistent reference to another
storage unit, which (for Mac OS windows) contains the properties listed in
Table 6-1.

Table 6-1   Window characteristics stored in a root frame

kODPropWindowRect	kODPropWindowIsResizable
kODPropWindowTitle	kODPropWindowIsFloating
kODPropWindowProcID	kODPropWindowIsRootWindow
kODPropWindowHasCloseBox	kODPropShouldShowlinks
kODPropWindowRefCon	kODPropSourceFrame
kODPropWindowIsVisible	

6

Windows and Menus

Making sure a window is onscreen

If your part is a root part that recreates a previously stored document window, you must make sure that the window is visible onscreen. Your document may have been moved from one system to another with a different monitor configuration or size. You may need to move or resize the window to fit its new environment. ◆

The Open Method of Your Part Editor

Opening your part means creating a window for it and displaying it in the window. You have to open a window only if your part is to be the root part of that window.

Your part itself initiates the opening of a window when the user selects the View in Window command from the Edit menu (see "View in Window" on page 259), and when it creates its own dialog boxes. Otherwise, your part opens a window only when your part's `Open` method is called. This is the interface to the `Open` method:

```
ODID Open(in ODFrame frame);
```

The `Open` method is called in these circumstances.

- When your part is initially created—when it has no previously stored frame or window information—OpenDoc calls your part's `Open` method and passes a null value of `kODNULL` for the `frame` parameter.

- When your part is an embedded part whose frame is selected, and the user chooses the Open Selection command from the Document menu, your part's containing part calls your part's `Open` method and passes a reference to the selected frame in the `frame` parameter.

- When your part is the root part of a document being opened, OpenDoc calls your part's `Open` method and passes a reference to the root frame in the `frame` parameter.

In your implementation of `Open`, you can take steps similar to the following, depending on the circumstances under which it was called.

1. *If you are creating an initial window* (`frame` = null), skip this step and go to step 2.

   ☐ *If you are opening a frame into a part window* (`frame` = an embedded frame), check whether the window already exists. If you have created the part window previously and saved its window ID, pass that ID to the `AcquireWindow` method of the window state object. If the method returns a valid window, bring the window to the front and exit. If the window does not yet exist, go to step 2.

   ☐ *If you are opening a stored document into a window* (`frame` = a root frame), read in the saved window data from the storage unit of the frame passed to the method (see "Storing and Retrieving Window Characteristics" on page 229).

2. Create a platform-specific window and register it with the window state object, as described in the section "Creating and Registering a Window" on page 226.

   ☐ *If you are opening a stored document into a window*, apply the stored characteristics to the platform-specific window. Call the window state object's `RegisterWindowForFrame` method.

   ☐ *If you are opening a frame into a window or creating an initial window*, apply your default characteristics to the platform-specific window. Call the window state object's `RegisterWindow` method.

3. Get the window's window ID and save it for future reference.

4. Open and bring the window to the front, as described in "Opening a Window" on page 228. *If you are opening a stored document into a window*, skip this step because there may be more than one window to open and OpenDoc determines which window is to be frontmost.

Note
You are not absolutely required to open a window when your `Open` method is called. Your part does whatever is appropriate, given its nature and the conditions under which the method is called. For example, if your part is a very simple sound player, it might simply play its sound and never create a window. ◆

Handling Window Events

To receive events in the windows that it creates, your part must create an `ODWindow` object for each platform-specific window it uses, including dialog boxes (except for modal dialog boxes; see "Modal Dialog Boxes" on page 234).

The document shell handles most Mac OS window events outside of the content region—for example, events in the title bar or resize box. Nevertheless, the OpenDoc dispatcher first sends a `kODEvtWindow` event to the root part. If the part editor of the root part wishes to override the action that the document shell would otherwise take, the root part can intercept and act on the event. In situations such as zooming, in which the window content might affect the action to be taken, the root part should intercept and handle the event.

Table 6-2 lists the window events that a root part can intercept and handle. These event types are passed in the `message` field of the event structure.

Table 6-2   Window event types

Constant	Event location for Mac OS window
kODMDInDrag	In the drag region (title bar)
kODMDInGrow	In the resize box (lower-right corner of window)
kODMDInGoAway	In the close box (left edge of title bar)
kODMDInZoomIn	In the zoom box (right edge of title bar)
kODMDInZoomOut	In the zoom box (right edge of title bar)

If your part handles a window event, its `HandleEvent` method must return true. If it does not handle an event, its `HandleEvent` method must return false so that the document shell can handle the event.

Zooming

On platforms that support window zooming, the root part should handle the events `kODMDInZoomIn` and `kODMDInZoomOut` and define the appropriate window size. The document shell cannot know the appropriate window-size limits for zooming in or out. Your part can handle the zoom-in and zoom-out events by using platform-specific functions to adjust the window shape appropriately, and then calling the `AdjustWindowShape` method of the window. (Your part will subsequently receive calls to its `FrameShapeChanged` and `GeometryChanged` methods, notifying it that its frame and facet shapes have been changed accordingly.)

Note that the new window size might trigger a frame negotiation, and it may also require the root part to create or delete facets.

Resizing

The document shell usually resizes windows, although the root part can intercept and handle the event (`kODMDInGrow`). The document shell relies on default size limits for windows, so if your part allows—for example— very small window sizes, it may have to intercept this event and handle the resizing itself.

When a window is resized, the active part does not change, but the part editor for the root frame is informed of the resizing through calls by OpenDoc to its s `FrameShapeChanged` and `GeometryChanged` methods. The root part can then do any necessary invalidation and subsequent redrawing, including creation of new facets if embedded parts have become visible because of the resizing.

Closing

The document shell handles a mouse click in the close box of a window or user selection of the Close menu item (or its keyboard equivalent). The document shell closes the window, after which the window cannot be reopened. However, if the part editor of the root part wishes merely to hide its window rather than close it (for example, if it is a palette), the part editor can intercept this event (`kODMDInGoAway`) and call the `Hide` method of the window.

If the window is a document window and is the only one open for that document, the document shell closes the document.

If your part editor needs to close a window programmatically, it can call the window's `CloseAndRemove` method. The window is closed and the window object is released.

Dragging

The document shell handles some platform-specific window-moving actions, such as dragging of a window by its title bar. No event handling is required of the window's root part, although the root part can intercept and handle this event (kODMDInDrag) if it needs to constrain the movement of the window for some reason.

Parts in other windows may need to be updated because of the window's move; they receive update events as appropriate.

Modal Dialog Boxes

When your part editor displays a Mac OS modal dialog box or alert box, it does not need to create an ODWindow object, as with a regular window. However, it should still request the modal focus (using its own display frame as the modal-focus owner), and it can still receive Mac OS events by providing an event filter.

In addition, your part must ensure that Mac OS floating windows are properly deactivated. To do so, your part must deactivate the front window before displaying a modal dialog box and it must reactivate the front window after dismissing it.

Your part can, as an alternative to handling a dialog box through the Mac OS ModalDialog or Alert function, create and register its own dialog window, request the modal focus for the window's root frame, and handle the dialog box without using either of those Dialog Manager routines.

Acquiring and Relinquishing the Modal Focus

A frame displaying a modal dialog box should own the **modal focus,** a focus type that exists to constrain certain events.

For example, a mouse click outside the frame that has the modal focus still goes to that frame. If your part's frame has the modal focus and the user clicks outside the frame, your part's HandleEvent method is called and passed a facet of kODNULL. The method should check for a null facet in this situation and either alert the user with a beep or dismiss the dialog box, as appropriate.

A click in a frame embedded within the frame that has the modal focus goes to the embedded frame. This behavior may facilitate the construction of dialog boxes and other controls from multiple parts.

Your part obtains and relinquishes the modal focus as it does other foci; see "Requesting Foci" on page 210 and "Relinquishing Foci" on page 210.

In general, your part should not be willing to relinquish the modal focus on request. If your part is displaying a modal dialog box, you probably do not want any other modal dialog box to be displayed at the same time. To make sure that your part retains the modal focus, your part editor's `BeginRelinquishFocus` method should return `kODFalse` if the requested focus is `kODModalFocus` and the proposed new owner of the focus is not one of your own display frames.

When you have finished displaying a modal dialog box, you can directly transfer it to its previous owner by calling the arbitrator's `TransferFocus` method, as noted in "Handling a Simple Modal Dialog Box" on page 235.

Event Filters

With Mac OS modal dialog boxes, your part editor's dialog-box event filter controls which events you receive while a dialog box or alert box is displayed. To pass received null events, update events, and activate events on to OpenDoc or other windows for handling, your event filter can send them to the OpenDoc dispatcher by calling its `Dispatch` method.

Your event filter should not pass other events, such as mouse events, to the dispatcher.

Handling a Simple Modal Dialog Box

To display a simple Mac OS modal dialog box or alert box, you can take these steps:

1. Get a reference to the frame that currently owns the modal focus by calling the arbitrator's `GetFocusOwner` method. Request the modal focus from the arbitrator, using its `RequestFocus` method. If you obtain the focus, proceed.

2. Install your dialog event filter function.

3. Create the dialog box, using a Dialog Manager function such as `GetNewDialog` or a utility function such as `ODGetNewDialog` (from the DlogUtil utility library provided with OpenDoc). One advantage of using `ODGetNewDialog` is that it positions the dialog box in relation to your part's document window, rather than to any part windows that may be open.

4. To handle Mac OS floating windows properly, deactivate the currently active window and any associated floating windows by calling the `DeactivateFrontWindows` method of the window state object.

5. Handle the dialog box with a Dialog Manager call such as `ModalDialog`. Act on the results and, when you finish, dispose of the dialog box with a Dialog Manager call such as `DisposeDialog`.

6. Reactivate the previously active window (to restore floating windows) by calling the window state's `ActivateFrontWindows` method.

7. Remove your dialog event filter function.

8. Restore the modal focus to its previous owner by calling the arbitrator's `TransferFocus` method.

By always saving and restoring the owner of the modal focus, your part can use this approach for nested modal dialog boxes, such as a dialog box that is built from several embedded parts.

Handling a Movable Modal Dialog Box

In OpenDoc, to implement a full-featured Mac OS movable modal dialog box—that is, one that allows process switching—you must create a window object (`ODWindow`) to contain it. To display the dialog box, you can take these steps:

1. Use platform-specific methods to create the structures for the dialog box.

2. Create a window object, using the window state's `RegisterWindow` method. Give it properties appropriate for your modal dialog box, such as nonpersistent and floating.

3. Request the modal focus for the root frame of the dialog window.

4. Adjust menus as necessary for the presence of the dialog box.

5. Call the `Open`, `Show`, and `Select` methods of the modal dialog window.

6. Handle events in the dialog box through your normal event-handling mechanism.

To make sure you dismiss the movable modal dialog box at the right time, you can take actions such as these when you receive a mouse-down event in the dialog box:

1. Determine whether the event applies to your dialog box and, if so, what item the user selected.

2. If the user has chosen to close the dialog box, relinquish the modal focus and call the window's `CloseAndRemove` method to delete the window and its root frame.

3. Re-enable any menus or menu items that you disabled for display of the dialog box.

Note
It is also possible to create a modal dialog box that is
movable but does not support process switching. To do so,
use a filter function and other functions in the utility
library DlogUtil provided with OpenDoc. ◆

Modeless Dialog Boxes

Modeless dialog boxes are more like regular windows than modal dialog boxes
are. They can be activated and deactivated, and they need not be dismissed for
your part to become active and editable.

Showing the Dialog Box

To display a modeless dialog box in OpenDoc, you must create a window
object (`ODWindow`) to contain it. To display the dialog box, you can take steps
such as these:

1. In case the dialog window already exists, try to get a reference to it by
   passing its ID (previously stored in your part) to the window state's
   `AcquireWindow` method. If it does not yet exist, create the platform-specific
   structures for the dialog box and create a window object with the window
   state's `RegisterWindow` method. Call the window's `Open` method.

2. Call the window's `Show` and `Select` methods to make it visible and active.

3. If you do not already have the window ID of the dialog window, get it by
   calling the window's `GetID` method. Save it for use in step 1 the next time
   the user chooses the action that brings up the modeless dialog box.

Closing the Dialog Box

When the user clicks the close box of a modeless dialog box, you may hide the
dialog window rather than close it, so that it is not destroyed. This is an
optimization that allows you to quickly redisplay the dialog box.

In your part's `HandleEvent` method, you can respond in this general way to a
mouse click in a window's close box:

1. From the frame or facet passed to `HandleEvent`, obtain information that can
   identify the window. For example, get a reference to the window object in
   which the event occurred (by calling the facet's `GetWindow` method), or

examine the frame's presentation or part info data for identifying characteristics.

2. Compare that information to stored information that defines your modeless dialog box. For example, get a reference to your modeless dialog's window object (by passing its ID to the window state's `AcquireWindow` method), or check a stored value that defines your modeless dialog's presentation.

3. If the two are the same, hide the window instead of closing it.

Hiding a Dialog Box When Deactivating a Frame

When your part is deactivated, it should hide any of its modeless dialog boxes.

When your part relinquishes the selection focus, it can get a reference to the dialog window (by passing its ID to the window state's `AcquireWindow` method), call the window's `IsShown` method to see if it is currently being shown, and then save that shown state and hide the window.

When your part reacquires the selection focus, it can retrieve a reference to the dialog window by passing its ID to the window state's `AcquireWindow` method. Then, if the dialog window had been visible at deactivation, your part can once again show it.

Controls

This section discusses what kinds of controls you can use, how you can construct them, and how to handle events within controls. It also discusses two specific issues for palettes: how to share them among instances of your part, and how to use them to embed parts within your part.

Design Issues for Controls

Controls in OpenDoc have the same function as in conventional applications: they are graphical objects that allow the user to interact with and manipulate documents in a variety of ways. However, there are some differences:

■ In a conventional application, controls typically apply to the entire document. They are always present unless dismissed explicitly. In an OpenDoc document, however, each part may have its own set of controls, and thus controls can appear and disappear rapidly as the user edits. This rapid change can be irritating if it is not carefully managed.

■ In a conventional application, finding the space in which to display a control may be less of a consideration than in OpenDoc. It may be a challenge for small embedded parts to find sufficient space to display rulers, scroll bars, and palettes.

■ In OpenDoc, you can construct controls as independent parts, assemblages of parts, different frames of a single part, or content elements of a part. You thus have more flexibility in constructing user-interface elements than is possible with conventional applications.

■ OpenDoc controls can have attached scripts or can communicate with each other, or with other parts, using the OpenDoc extension mechanism. Thus, your OpenDoc controls can be far more integrated and context-sensitive than standard controls.

Standard types of controls you might wish to include with your parts include

■ buttons, radio buttons, and checkboxes

■ scroll bars, sliders, or other gauges

■ pop-up menus

■ rulers

■ tool bars

■ status bars

■ palettes

Rulers usually reflect some settings of the current selection context and contain controls that allow the user to change these settings. Tool bars are like rulers, but they often trigger actions instead of changing settings. Status bars display the progress of some long-running operation or suggest actions to users.

In conventional applications, rulers, tool bars, and status bars commonly occupy the margins of the window. In an OpenDoc document, controls can appear within the frame they apply to, or in separate frames outside the frame they apply to.

A ruler for a text part, for example, can be an additional frame associated with the part. Events in the ruler are handled by the part's editor. Alternatively, the ruler may be its own part with its own editor. In this case, the text part editor must maintain a reference to the ruler part and be able to communicate with it through semantic events or some other extension mechanism.

A ruler that is a separate part can have its own embedded parts, such as buttons. The ruler part must then be able to communicate with its embedded controls as well as with the part that it services.

Palettes often contain editing tools but can also contain choices for object attributes such as color or line width. Palettes commonly float freely beside or over the document, although they can also be fixed at the window margins. Palettes might also be pop-up, pull-down, or tear-off menus.

If all parts in a document can communicate with each other, they can coordinate the drawing and hiding of palettes or other controls, to avoid irritating the user. For example, all parts in a document can share a single palette. The various parts negotiate for space within the palette, and they draw or erase only those tools that change as the active part changes.

Handling Events in Controls

How you handle events in a control depends on how you design the control.

- If a control like a ruler is within the active frame, it might not have its own frame, and the active part editor handles any events in the ruler.

- If a control has its own frame, it might be another display frame of the active part. In this case also, the active part editor handles the event in the control.

- If a control is a separate part, its own part editor handles the event and updates the state of the part. Updates might trigger scripts or calls to the extension interfaces of other parts. Likewise, the part itself can receive queries from other part editors, in the form of semantic events or calls to its extension interface.

Sharing Palettes and Utility Windows

The user-interface guidelines presented in the section "Palettes and Toolbars" on page 531 state that you should hide any visible palettes, modeless dialog boxes, or other utility windows when your part becomes inactive or its document closes, and restore them—in the same positions—when the part becomes active once again or the document reopens. In addition, if your part editor maintains multiple parts in a document and the active state switches from one to another of them, any visible utility windows that apply to both parts should remain steadily visible, without any flicker caused by hiding and immediate restoring.

One way to implement this behavior for a utility window is to follow, in general, steps such as these:

■ Make the window globally accessible to your parts by keeping its reference and its state in an object that each of your parts acquires on initialization and releases on closing.

■ Have the global object create the window in a normal manner the first time it is to be displayed. When the user closes the window, the global object can simply hide it by calling its `Hide` method. If the user subsequently needs to redisplay the window, the global object can reshow it by calling its `Show` method.

■ When your part relinquishes the selection focus, its `CommitRelinquishFocus` method can check whether the part that is receiving the focus also belongs to your part editor and has a presentation that uses the same utility window. There are a number of ways to check this, such as by examining the presentation, part info, or even the part kind associated with the newly active frame.

■ When your part acquires the selection focus, it notifies the global object of that fact. The global object in turn calls the `ChangePart` and `SetSourceFrame` methods of the utility window's frame to assign the new part and frame to the utility window. The new part can then adjust the content of the utility window if needed, and also show or hide other palettes or dialog boxes.

Using a Tool Palette to Embed Parts

An example of an OpenDoc-specific use of controls is to allow the user to embed parts by selecting items from a palette. Using a palette in this way, your part can create embedded parts from scratch rather than by reading in existing part data.

Your part can provide a palette, menu, or dialog box from which the user selects an item that specifies a part kind. As in many conventional applications, your palette could display a set of tools to the user—drawing tools, painting tools, text tools, and so on. In this case, however, selecting an item from the palette actually means that a new part of that kind is to be embedded in your part. The section "Creating Parts From Tool Palettes" on page 556 describes interface guidelines for presenting such a palette to the user.

The items could represent existing stationery documents in the user's system, or they could simply represent individual part kinds for which editors exist. If you are creating parts from scratch, follow steps such as these once the user has made a selection from your palette:

1. Create the new part by calling your draft's `CreatePart` method, passing it the part kind that the user selected.

2. Call the new part's `Externalize` method (see "The Externalize Method" on page 298) so that the part can create and write initial data to the properties in its storage unit.

3. Create a new embedded frame for the part, as described in "Creating a New Embedded Frame" on page 119.

4. Give the new frame the proper link status, as described in "Frame Link Status" on page 377.

5. If the new frame is visible, assign facets to it, as described in the section "Adding a Facet" on page 124.

6. Notify your containing part and your draft that there has been a change to your part's content; see "Making Content Changes Known" on page 307.

Menus

While an OpenDoc document is open, three entities share responsibility for the menu bar at any given moment. The operating system provides any system-wide menus, the OpenDoc document shell creates the Document menu and the Edit menu, and individual part editors can create other menus as needed. (Part editors can also, with restrictions, add appropriate items to the Document and Edit menus.)

Different platforms have different conventions for enabling and disabling menus and menu items. In an OpenDoc document, the document shell, the root part, and the part with the menu focus together control which menu commands are available to the user. As each part becomes active, the OpenDoc document shell and the root part update their own menu items, and the active part editor takes care of the rest.

Basic event handling for menu events is described in the section "Menu Events" on page 194. When the user chooses a menu item, the document shell either handles the command itself or dispatches a menu event to the active part; the part receives the event as a call to its `HandleEvent` method.

This section discusses general issues of setting up and working with menus and then describes how to handle individual menu events for the standard OpenDoc menus (the Document menu and the Edit menu).

Setting Up Menus

This section describes how your part editor can set up and use menus and menu items.

The Base Menu Bar

When it first opens a document, the document shell creates a menu bar object (type `ODMenuBar`) and installs it as the **base menu bar,** containing the default set of menus shared by all parts in the document. The document shell installs the base menu bar by calling the window state's `SetBaseMenuBar` method. The base menu bar contains different menus and items on different platforms, but on the Mac OS the Apple menu, the Document menu, and the Edit menu are always installed.

Adding Part Menus to the Base Menu Bar

When your part initializes itself, or when it first obtains the menu focus, it should create its own menu bar object, as follows:

1. It should copy the base menu bar using the window state's `CopyBaseMenuBar` method.

2. It should add its own menu structures, by using menu bar methods such as `AddMenuBefore` and `AddMenuLast`.

If necessary, your part editor can add items to the end of the Document and Edit menus, but you should avoid altering the existing items. See the section "Document Menu" on page 539 and "Edit Menu" on page 543 for more specific guidelines.

Sharing a menu bar among your parts

You can share a single menu bar object among several
instances of your part, using the Mac OS Code Fragment
Manager's per-context globals. You might define a
reference-counted C++ object that can hold the data, as
described for palettes in the section "Sharing Palettes and
Utility Windows" on page 240. ◆

Registering and Retrieving Command IDs

OpenDoc specifies menu items with position-independent command IDs so
that a part can dispatch to a menu item's command handler without reference
to the item's position in its menu. On the Mac OS platform, parts should
register a command ID for each menu and item, using the menu bar object's
`RegisterCommand` method. For better localizability, your part editor should save
the mapping from menu items to command IDs and store it in a resource.

The OpenDoc document shell registers command IDs for all items in the
standard menus, including the Document and Edit menus. Constants for all the
standard menu command IDs are listed in the *OpenDoc Class Reference for the
Mac OS*. If you define your own menu commands, use only ID numbers above
20000, as noted in "Mac OS Menu IDs" (next).

On the Mac OS platform, the menu event dispatched to a part contains a
menu-number/item-number pair that together determine which command the
user chose. To convert that information to a command ID before dispatching it
to your individual menu-item handlers, call the `GetCommand` method of the
menu bar object.

If you pass `GetCommand` a menu-number/item-number pair that you have not
yet registered, the method returns a **synthetic command ID,** an ID that it
manufactures. Your code can test the returned command ID (by calling the
menu bar's `IsCommandSynthetic` method) and, if it is synthetic, dispatch by
menu-number/item-number pair rather than by command ID. (If the user
chooses a disabled item or a menu item separator, the `GetCommand` method
returns `kODNoCommand`.)

Reorganizing the Document and Edit menus on a platform without position-
independent menu-item IDs is not recommended. If your part editor does
reorganize them, however, you need to re-register the command numbers so
that the document shell can still handle menu items correctly.

Mac OS Menu IDs

On the Mac OS platform, you must identify each menu with a menu ID. A menu ID is a positive short value; negative values are reserved by the operating system. Hierarchical menus must have IDs of 255 or less.

All menus in the menu bar must have unique menu IDs. Therefore the document shell, the active part, and any shell plug-ins or services that also have menus must cooperate to ensure that there are no conflicts. Please follow the conventions shown in Table 6-3 to ensure that your menu IDs do not conflict with those of others.

Table 6-3   Mac OS Menu ID ranges

Type of software	Menu ID range	
Container applications or document shell	*Flat menus:*	255–16383
	Hierarchical menus:	0–127
Services or shell plug-ins	*Flat menus:*	16384–20000[*]
	Hierarchical menus:	128–193[*]
Part editors	*Flat menus:*	20001–32767
	Hierarchical menus:	194–255

[*] Dynamically assigned

A shell plug-in or service may have to adjust its menu ID dynamically at runtime, because another service or plug-in with that menu ID may already be installed. The plug-in should choose an ID, look for an installed menu with that ID, and—if it is found—add 1 to the ID and try again.

Obtaining the Menu Focus

When your part activates itself, it should request the menu focus (along with other foci) if it wants to use menus. See "Requesting Foci" on page 210 for more information.

Once your part has the menu focus, it should first call the menu bar's `IsValid` method to check whether the base menu bar that it has copied is still valid (unchanged). If it is not, your part should recopy it and add any part-specific menus to it. Then, your part should call the menu bar's `Display` method to make the menu visible and active.

Enabling and Disabling Menus and Commands

When the user clicks in the menu bar, the OpenDoc dispatcher determines which part has the menu focus and calls that part's `AdjustMenus` method. It also calls the root part's `AdjustMenus` method, if the root part does not have the menu focus.

Your part's `AdjustMenus` method can use methods of the menu bar object such as `EnableCommand` or `EnableAndCheckCommand` to change the appearance of your menu items, or it can make platform-specific calls to directly enable, disable, mark, or change the text of its menu items. For convenience, you can also use the menu bar object's `EnableAll` and `DisableAll` methods to enable or disable all menus at once. In addition, you can enable or disable an entire individual menu by calling the `EnableCommand` method and passing it a special command ID such as `kODCommandAppleMenu`, `kODCommandDocumentMenu`, or `kODCommandEditMenu`.

Your `AdjustMenus` method typically acquires the clipboard focus and enables the Cut, Copy, Paste, and Paste As items in the Edit menu. It also assigns the proper menu string to the *Selection* Info menu item (see page 254) and the *Editor* Preferences menu item (see page 259) in the Edit menu. On the Mac OS platform, it also places and enables its About *Editor* command in the Apple menu.

Menus and Movable Modal Dialog Boxes

When you display a movable modal dialog box, you should disable all menus except for the (Mac OS) Apple menu and Application menu. If the dialog box contains an editable text field, however, you may leave the Cut, Copy, and Paste commands from the Edit menu enabled. You can accomplish this conveniently by first calling the `DisableAll` method of the menu bar, followed by individual `EnableCommand` calls to reenable the individual commands you need.

When you dismiss the movable modal dialog box, you must of course reenable the disabled menus.

Menus and Read-Only Documents

When your draft permissions (see "Drafts" on page 285) specify that your document is read-only, your part editor needs to disable these menu commands:

■ Cut, Paste, Paste As, and Clear in the Edit menu

■ Insert in the Document menu

■ any part-specific content-editing commands

This situation can occur when the user views an early draft of a document, or when a document is stored on read-only media.

Part viewers should disable these commands at all times.

Menus and the Root Part

In all OpenDoc documents, the root part is responsible for printing. The root part therefore should handle the Page Setup and Print items from the Document menu, even if an embedded part has the menu focus.

To allow the root part access to these menu events, the dispatcher passes menu events to the root part if they are not handled by the part with the menu focus. Also, OpenDoc calls the root part's `AdjustMenus` method before it calls the `AdjustMenus` method of the part with the menu focus, so that the root part can adjust the state of those menu items.

When your part's `AdjustMenus` method is called, it should check whether your part is the root part and whether it has the menu focus. If it is the root part but does not have the menu focus, it should adjust only the Page Setup and Print items. If it is an embedded part with the menu focus, it should not adjust those items.

Likewise, when your part's `HandleEvent` method is called, it should first check whether your part is the root part. If it is the root part, `HandleEvent` should return false if it is passed any menu events but Page Setup and Print. If it is an embedded part, `HandleEvent` should return false if it is passed Page Setup or Print.

The Document Menu

This section describes how your part editor should interact with the Document menu. The OpenDoc document shell handles most Document menu commands, as described in "The Document Shell and the Document Menu" on page 503. Individual part editors must respond only to the commands Open Selection, Insert, Page Setup, and Print. The Document menu is illustrated in Figure 12-27 on page 540.

If your part editor wishes to add items to or otherwise modify the Document menu when your part is active, please note the restrictions listed in the section "Document Menu" on page 539 of Chapter 13, "Guidelines for Part Display." That section also gives guidelines on the appearance of the Document menu (including keyboard equivalents) and shows the dialog boxes presented to the user as a result of executing Document menu commands.

Open Selection

The user chooses the Open Selection command to open the user's selection (in an open OpenDoc document) into its own window.

The active part handles this command. If the selection consists of an embedded part's frame or icon, Open Selection is equivalent to the View in Window command in the Edit menu (see "View in Window" on page 259), except that it applies to a selected part within the active frame, rather than to the active frame itself.

Your part need not support this command for intrinsic content; if it does, it can open a second window to display the selected intrinsic content.

If the selection is one or more embedded parts, you should open each one into a part window. Your routine that handles the Open Selection command should take these steps for each selected frame:

1. From your private data structures, determine which of your embedded frames is the selected one. (Each embedded part, even if displayed in an icon view type, has a frame.)

2. Call the `AcquirePart` method of the selected frame, followed by the `Open` method of the part returned by the `AcquirePart` method. The `Open` method is described in the section "The Open Method of Your Part Editor" on page 230.

Insert

The user chooses the Insert command from the Document menu to select a document and embed it as a part within your part. When the user chooses the command, OpenDoc passes the menu event to your part's `HandleEvent` method.

In your routine to handle the Insert command, you should follow these steps:

1. Display a file-access dialog box and let the user select the document to insert. From the returned information, use your own procedures (or functions of the PlatformFile utility library supplied with OpenDoc) to obtain a file specification. Then call the storage system's `AcquireContainer` method to obtain the OpenDoc container object for the specified file.

2. If the file represents an OpenDoc document, `AcquireContainer` returns a non-null value. In that case, you can call the `GetDocument` method of the container and iterate through the drafts of the document (using its `AcquireBaseDraft` and `AcquireDraft` methods) to get a reference to the document's latest draft.

3. Use that draft's `AcquireDraftProperties` method to get a storage unit containing the draft's properties. From that storage unit, get a persistent reference to the root part's storage unit. Convert that persistent reference into the storage-unit ID of the root part itself (using the draft's `GetIDFromStorageUnitRef` method).

4. Once you have the root part's storage unit ID, you can either embed the root part or incorporate it as intrinsic content. The procedure is essentially identical to pasting from the clipboard or other data-transfer object:

   □ If you are incorporating, follow the steps described in "Incorporating Intrinsic Content" on page 344.

   □ If you are embedding, follow the steps described in "Embedding a Single Part" on page 347.

5. After you have inserted the document, release the objects you have created (root-part storage unit, draft, document, container) in the opposite order from which you created them.

6. Notify OpenDoc and your containing part that there has been a change to your part's content; see "Making Content Changes Known" on page 307.

Your part should disable the Insert item when its draft permissions are read-only; see "Menus and Read-Only Documents" on page 247.

Page Setup

The root part of the window handles the Page Setup command. Root parts are responsible for overall document features such as page size and characteristics. When the user chooses this command and your part is the root part of the active window, OpenDoc passes the command information to your part's `HandleEvent` method.

Your routine to handle the Page Setup command should follow the normal procedure for displaying and storing page-setup information. If you use the Mac OS Printing Manager, for example, you take these steps:

1. Call the `PrOpen` function to open the current printer driver.

2. If you previously stored the print settings for this document, retrieve them from your part's storage unit; otherwise, create a new print record.

3. Call the `PrStlDialog` function to display the current printer's style dialog box (Figure 6-1), passing it a handle to the print record.

4. If `PrStlDialog` returns `true`, save the modified print record in your part's storage unit, in a property named `kODPropPageSetup`.

5. Call `PrClose` to close the current printer driver.

Figure 6-1   Page Setup dialog box

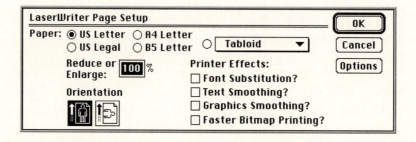

IMPORTANT

If QuickDraw GX is installed, you must display the QuickDraw GX Page Setup dialog box instead of the Mac OS Printing Manager dialog box, even if your own part does not use QuickDraw GX for imaging. ▲

For more information on page setup using the Mac OS Printing Manager, see the chapter "Printing Manager" in *Inside Macintosh: Imaging With QuickDraw*. For information on page setup using QuickDraw GX, see the chapter "Core Printing Features" in *Inside Macintosh: QuickDraw GX Printing*.

Print

The root part of the window handles the Print command. Root parts are responsible for defining the printing behavior of their documents. When the user chooses this command and your part is the root part of the active window, OpenDoc passes the command information to your part's `HandleEvent` method.

Your routine to handle the Print command should set up for printing. If you use the Mac OS Printing Manager, for example, you take these steps:

1. Retrieve any previously stored print settings (such as page-setup information) as a print record from a property named `kODPropPageSetup` in your part's storage unit.

2. Call the `PrJobDialog` function to display the job dialog box (Figure 6-2) for the current printer, to allow the user to set the page range and change any of the current settings.

3. If the `PrJobDialog` function returns `true` (if the user does not cancel printing), your part editor should follow the procedure for printing a document described in the section "Printing" on page 180.

Figure 6-2   Job dialog box

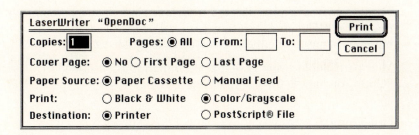

IMPORTANT

If QuickDraw GX is installed, you must display the QuickDraw GX Print dialog box instead of the Mac OS Printing Manager job dialog box, even if your own part does not use QuickDraw GX for imaging. ▲

For more information on job dialog boxes using the Mac OS Printing Manager, see the chapter "Printing Manager" in *Inside Macintosh: Imaging With QuickDraw*. For information on print dialog boxes using QuickDraw GX, see the chapter "Core Printing Features" in *Inside Macintosh: QuickDraw GX Printing*.

The Edit Menu

Most items in the Edit menu are handled by individual part editors. Most apply to the current selection in the currently active part. The Edit menu is illustrated in Figure 12-28 on page 543 and Figure 12-30 on page 549.

If your part editor wishes to add items to or otherwise modify the Edit menu when your part is active, please note the restrictions listed in the section "Edit Menu" on page 543. That section also gives guidelines on the appearance of the Edit menu (including keyboard equivalents).

Undo, Redo

The user chooses the Undo or Redo command from the Edit menu to reverse the actions of recently executed commands, including previous Undo or Redo commands.

The document shell handles the Undo and Redo items, passing control to the undo object. The undo object, in turn, calls the `UndoAction` or `RedoAction` methods of any part editors involved in the undo or redo.

Your part should respond to these commands as described in the section "Undo" on page 260.

Cut, Copy, Paste

The user chooses the Cut, Copy, or Paste command from the Edit menu to place data on the clipboard or to retrieve data from the clipboard.

Your part should handle the Cut and Copy commands as described in the section "Copying or Cutting to the Clipboard" on page 359. Your part should handle the Paste command as described in the sections "Handling Pasted or Dropped Data" on page 336 and "Pasting From the Clipboard" on page 360.

Your part should disable the Cut and Paste items when its draft permissions are read-only; see "Menus and Read-Only Documents" on page 247.

Paste As

The user chooses the Paste As command from the Edit menu to specify how clipboard data is to be pasted into the active part. When the user selects the command, OpenDoc passes the command information to your part's `HandleEvent` method.

Your routine to handle the Paste As command should prepare to read from the clipboard, like this:

1. Acquire the clipboard focus and gain access to its content storage unit, following the initial steps described in "Pasting From the Clipboard" on page 360.

2. Display the Paste As dialog box (see Figure 8-3 on page 337) by calling the `ShowPasteAsDialog` method of the clipboard object. Pass the function the active frame into which the paste is to occur.

3. If the method returns a result of true, the user has pressed the OK button; use the results of the interaction (passed back to you as a structure of type `ODPasteAsResult`) to determine which kind of pasting action to take. The section "Handling the Paste As Dialog Box" on page 337 lists the kinds of pasting that the user can specify. Then read the appropriate kind of data from the clipboard, continuing with the procedures shown in the section "Pasting From the Clipboard" on page 360.

Drag and drop
Your part editor's `Drop` method can also display the Paste As dialog box. See "Dropping" on page 368 for more information. ◆

Your part should disable the Paste As item when its draft permissions are read-only; see "Menus and Read-Only Documents" on page 247.

Clear

The user chooses the Clear command from the Edit menu to delete the selected content from the active part.

Your routine to handle the Clear command should remove the items that make up the selection from your part content. That may involve deleting embedded parts as well as intrinsic content. See, for example, "Removing an Embedded Part" on page 307.

Your part should disable the Clear item when its draft permissions are read-only; see "Menus and Read-Only Documents" on page 247.

Select All

The user chooses the Select All command from the Edit menu to make the current selection encompass all of the content of the active part.

Your routine to handle the Select All command must include all of your part's content in the selection structure that you maintain, and it must highlight the visible parts of it appropriately.

Selection Info

The user chooses the *Selection* Info command from the Edit menu to display a dialog box containing standard information about the current selection, whether it is an embedded part, a link source, a link destination, or intrinsic content. When the user chooses the command, OpenDoc passes the command information to your active part's `HandleEvent` method. Your routine to handle the *Selection* Info command should display a dialog box that describes the characteristics of the current selection.

Even before the user chooses this command, your part needs to make sure that the menu item contains the correct text. Whenever your part is made active, and whenever the selection changes, your `AdjustMenus` method should update the name of this menu item as follows:

- If the current selection consists of an embedded frame, set the name of the menu item to "Part Info…".

- If the current selection consists of a link border (either source or destination), set the name of the menu item to "Link Info…".

■ If the current selection contains intrinsic content of your part, and if you support an Info dialog box of your own, set the name of the menu item to "*myContent* Info...", where *myContent* is a brief, meaningful word or phrase describing the selection content.

■ If there is no selection or insertion point, set the name of the menu item to "Part Info..." and disable the menu item.

Noncontainer, nonlinking parts

If your part supports neither embedding nor linking and does not provide a dialog box to give information on selected intrinsic content, it should at all times set the name of the menu item to "Part Info..." and disable it. ◆

In your routine to handle the *Selection* Info command, you can take the following steps, depending on which of the above four selection states prevails. In general, you determine what the current selection is and act accordingly.

■ If the current selection is an embedded frame border, display the Part Info dialog box for the part in that frame, using the `ShowPartFrameInfo` method of the Info object (class `ODInfo`). You obtain a reference to the Info object by calling the session object's `GetInfo` method. Figure 6-3 shows an example of the dialog box. OpenDoc handles all changes made by the user and updates the information in the storage units for the embedded part and frame, including performing any requested translation.

OpenDoc determines the information it displays in the Part Info dialog box by reading the part's **Info properties,** the set of properties—separate from the part's contents—that can be displayed to, and in some cases changed by, the user. All stored parts include them. If your part creates an extension to the Part info dialog box (see "The Settings Extension" on page 444), it can define and display additional Info properties.

Figure 6-3   The Part Info dialog box

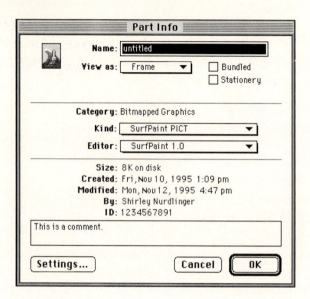

■ If your part supports linking and the current selection is the border of a link source, obtain from your own data structures a reference to the appropriate link-source object and then display the Link Source Info dialog box, using the ShowLinkSourceInfo method of the link-source object. Figure 6-4 shows an example of the dialog box.

Figure 6-4   The Link Source Info dialog box

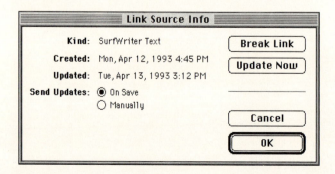

You can either permit or prohibit changes to the displayed information; if your draft is read-only, OpenDoc automatically prohibits any changes. If you allow changes and the method returns true, handle the results like this:

☐ If the user has decided to break the link, release the link source as described in the section "Breaking and Cutting Links" on page 397.

☐ If the user has decided to update the link immediately, update the link source from your part's content. See "Updating a Link at the Source" on page 389 for procedures to follow. (This option is available only if the auto-update setting is Manually, and if the update ID you passed to `ShowLinkSourceInfo` does not match the update ID in the link-source object.)

☐ The default auto-update setting for a link source is On Save. If the user has decided to change the auto-update setting from On Save to Manually, change the auto-update status of the link source accordingly.

☐ If the user has changed the auto-update setting from Manually to On Save (but has not explicitly decided to update immediately), change the auto-update status of the link source accordingly. Then obtain the update ID from the link source (by calling its `GetUpdateID` method) and, if it is different from your currently stored update ID for the source content, store the new ID and update the link source.

■ If your part supports linking and the current selection is the border of a link destination, obtain from your own data structures a reference to the destination's link object and a pointer to the link info structure associated with it. (See "Link Info" on page 380.) Then display the Link Destination Info dialog box, using the `ShowLinkDestinationInfo` method of the link object. Figure 6-5 shows an example of the dialog box.

Figure 6-5   The Link Destination Info dialog box

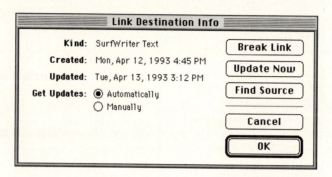

You can either permit or prohibit changes to the displayed information; if your draft is read-only, OpenDoc automatically prohibits any changes. If you allow changes and the method returns true, handle the results like this:

☐ If the user has decided to break the link, release the link as described in the section "Breaking and Cutting Links" on page 397.

☐ If the user has decided to update the link immediately, update your part's content from the link data. See "Updating a Link at the Destination" on page 387 for procedures to follow. (This option is available only if the auto-update setting is Manually, and if the update ID in your link info structure does not match the update ID in the link object.)

☐ If the user has decided to view the source of the link, call the link object's `ShowSourceContent` method.

☐ If the user has changed the auto-update setting of the link, update your link info structure accordingly. If the change is to specify automatic updating, and if your part is not already registered for updates to other destinations of the same link, call the link object's `RegisterDependent` method so that your part will be notified when updates occur.

■ If the current selection is a portion of your part's intrinsic content and your part supports one or more Info dialog boxes of your own, you can display the appropriate dialog box and handle user selections yourself.

■ If there is no current selection, or if the selection is intrinsic content and your part does not support its own Info dialog box, no selection information is available. You should have disabled the menu item as described at the beginning of this section, in which case your method to handle the *Selection Info* command is not called.

Editor Preferences

The user chooses the *Editor* Preferences command from the Edit menu to bring up the **Preferences** dialog box in which the user can view and change preferences for the part editor of the active part.

Even before the user chooses this command, your part needs to make sure that the menu item contains the correct text. Whenever your part is made active, your `AdjustMenus` method should update the name of this menu item to *"myEditor* Preferences", where *myEditor* is the name of your part editor.

Your routine to handle the *Editor* Preferences command should display a dialog box whose contents show the user-controllable global settings that affect all of your part editor's parts. Figure 12-29 on page 547 shows an example of a Preferences dialog box.

View in Window

The user chooses the View in Window command from the Edit menu to open the active part in its own part window. When the user chooses the command, OpenDoc passes the command information to your part's `HandleEvent` method.

Your routine to handle the View in Window menu command should take steps like these:

1. Check whether the window already exists. If you have created the part window previously and saved its window ID, pass that ID to the `AcquireWindow` method of the window state object. If the method returns a valid window, bring it to the front.

2. If the window does not currently exist, create a platform-specific window and register it with the window state object, as described in the section "Creating and Registering a Window" on page 226. Get its window ID and save it for future reference.

3. Open and bring the window to the front, as described in "Opening a Window" on page 228.

Do not call your part's own `Open` method in this situation.

When you create the part window, size and position it as recommended in the section "Viewing Embedded Parts in Part Windows" on page 573. You can also add an item to the Edit menu to display a movable outline of your part's frame in the window, as described in the section "Show Frame Outline" (next).

Show Frame Outline

Your part should add the Show Frame Outline command to the Edit menu when your part's content area is greater than the area of its display frame, the frame is opened into a part window, and the part window is active.

The user chooses this command to reposition your part's content—that is, to change the portion of it displayed in the frame in the document window. In the part window, display a 1-pixel-wide black-and-white border around the content currently visible in the display frame in the document window, and allow the user to drag the frame outline. See the section "Repositioning Content in a Frame" on page 575 for more information and illustrations.

Undo

The Undo command (and its reverse, Redo) is a common feature on many software platforms. It is designed to allow users to recover from errors that they recognize soon after making them. OpenDoc offers a flexible and powerful undo capability.

Multilevel, Cross-Document Capability

Most systems support only a single-level Undo command; that is, only the most recently executed command can be reversed. Therefore, in most platforms undo is restricted to a single domain. A complex operation that involves transferring data from one document to another, for example, cannot be completely undone.

OpenDoc, by contrast, supports multiple levels of undo and redo; there is no limit, other than memory constraints on the user's system, to the number of times in succession that a user can invoke the Undo command. OpenDoc also allows for interdocument undo and redo. Together, these enhancements give users greater flexibility in recovering from errors than is possible with simpler undo capabilities.

The OpenDoc undo feature does not offer infinite recoverability. Some user actions clear the undo **action history,** the cumulative set of reversible actions available at any one time, resetting it to empty. A typical example is saving a document; the user cannot "unsave" the document by choosing Undo, and no actions executed prior to its saving can be undone. As a part developer, you can decide which of your own actions are undoable, which ones are ignorable for undo purposes, and which ones reset the action history. In general, actions that do not change the content of a part (such as scrolling, making selections, and opening and closing windows) are ignorable and do not need to be undoable. Non-undoable actions that require clearing the action history are few; closing your part (see "Closing Your Part" on page 308) is one of them.

Choosing Redo reverses the effects of the previous Undo command. Redo is available only if the user has previously chosen Undo, and if nothing but ignorable actions have occurred since the user last chose Undo or Redo. Like Undo, Redo can be chosen several times in succession, limited only by the number of times Undo has been chosen in succession. As soon as the user performs an undoable action (such as an edit), OpenDoc clears the redo action history and the Redo command is no longer available until the user chooses Undo once again.

To implement this multilevel undo capability that spans different parts and different documents, OpenDoc maintains a centralized repository of undoable actions, stored by individual part editors as they perform such actions. Undo history is stored in the undo object, an instantiation of the class `ODUndo`, created by OpenDoc and accessed through the session object's `GetUndo` method. Your part editor needs access to the undo object to store undoable actions in it or retrieve them from it.

The importance of multilevel undo

Your part must support multiple levels of undo. If your part supports only a single-level Undo command, other parts that support multilevel undo will lose their undo history when they interact with your part. You should support multiple levels of undo if you support the Undo command at all. ◆

Implementing Undo

To implement support for undo in your part editor, you need to save information to the undo object that allows you to recover previous states of your part. Also, your part editor needs to implement the following methods:

- `UndoAction`
- `RedoAction`
- `ReadActionState`

■ WriteActionState

■ DisposeActionState

The undo object calls your part's UndoAction and RedoAction methods when the user chooses, respectively, the Undo and Redo items from the Edit menu.

The undo object calls your part's DisposeActionState method when an undo action of yours is removed from the undo action history. At that point, you can dispose of any storage needed to perform the specified undo action.

WriteActionState and ReadActionState

The WriteActionState and ReadActionState methods of ODPart exist to support a future cross-session undo capability. OpenDoc can call these methods when it needs you to store persistently or to retrieve your undo-related information. Version 1.0 of OpenDoc does not support cross-session undo, however, so you need not override these methods. ◆

Adding an Action to the Undo Action History

If your part performs an undoable action, it should call the undo object's AddActionToHistory method. Your part passes an item of **action data** to the method; the action data contains enough information to allow your part to revert to its state just prior to the undoable action. The action data can be in any format; OpenDoc adds it to the action history in the undo object and passes it back to your part if the user asks your part to undo a command.

The item of data that you pass to AddActionToHistory must be of type ODActionData, which is a byte array. When you create the item, you can either copy the data itself into the byte array or you can copy a pointer to the data into the byte array; either way, you then pass the byte array to AddActionToHistory.

You also pass two user-visible strings to the AddActionToHistory method. The strings consists of the text that you want to appear on the Edit menu, such as "Undo Cut" and "Redo Cut". You must also specify the data's action type, described under "Creating an Action Subhistory" on page 264.

In general, you add most editing actions to the action history unless their data is so large that you cannot practically recover the pre-action state. Actions such as opening or closing a document, or ignorable actions such as scrolling or selecting, should not be added the action history.

You decide what constitutes a single action. Entering an individual text character is not usually considered an action, although deleting or replacing a selection usually is. The sum of actions performed between repositionings of the insertion point is usually considered a single undoable action.

Adding Multistage Actions

Some transactions, such as drag and drop, have at least two stages—a beginning and an end. To add such a transaction to the undo history, your part must define which stage you are adding, by using the **action types** kODBeginAction and kODEndAction. (For undoable actions that do not have separate stages, you specify an action type of kODSingleAction when calling AddActionToHistory.)

In the case of drag and drop, the sequence is like this:

- The source part calls AddActionToHistory at the beginning of a drag, specifying an action type of kODBeginAction to add a **beginning action.**

- The destination part calls AddActionToHistory when the drop occurs, adding a single-stage action to the undo history by specifying kODSingleAction.

- The source part once again calls AddActionToHistory after the completion of the drop (when the drag-and-drop object's StartDrag method returns), specifying an action type of kODEndAction to add an **ending action.**

Similarly, if the user selects the Paste With Link checkbox in the Paste As dialog box (see Figure 8-3 on page 337), the part receiving the paste and creating the link destination adds the beginning action and ending action, whereas the source part adds a single action when it creates the link source.

As the case of drag and drop demonstrates, parts can add single-stage actions to the undo history during the time that a multistage undoable action is in progress—that is, between the times AddActionToHistory is called with kODBeginAction and with kODEndAction, respectively. These actions become part of the overall undoable action.

Menu strings and multistage actions
The strings you can provide when calling AddActionToHistory are ignored if the action type is kODBeginAction. Furthermore, any strings you provide for subsequent single actions are ignored. Once you have created a beginning action, only the strings passed for the action type kODEndAction appear in the menu. ◆

You can remove an incomplete two-stage action from the undo action history—without having to clear the entire history—by using the `AbortCurrentTransaction` method. See "Clearing the Action History" on page 265.

Creating an Action Subhistory

In general, the undoable actions a user performs while a modal dialog box is displayed—as long as the actions do not clear the undo action history of your document—should not affect the action history previous to that modal state. After dismissing the dialog box, the user should be able to undo actions performed before the modal dialog box was displayed—even though at this point the user could not undo actions taken while the modal dialog box was open.

To implement this behavior, you can put a mark into the action history that signifies the beginning of a new **action subhistory.** To do so, call the `MarkActionHistory` method of the undo object. To clear the actions within a subhistory, specify `kODRespectMarks` when you call the `ClearActionHistory` method. To clear the whole action history, specify `kODDontRespectMarks` instead.

For every mark you put into the action history, you must put an equivalent call to `ClearActionHistory` to clear that subhistory.

Undoing an Action

When the user chooses to undo an action added to the action history by your part, OpenDoc calls your part's `UndoAction` method, passing it the action data you passed in earlier. Your part should perform any reverse editing necessary to restore itself to the pre-action state. (When a two-stage transaction involving your part is undone, OpenDoc calls both your part and the other part or parts involved, so that the entire compound action—including any single-stage actions that occurred between the beginning and ending actions—is reversed.)

Redoing an Action

When the user chooses to redo an action of your part, OpenDoc calls your part's `RedoAction` method, passing it the same action data that you had passed in earlier, when the original action was performed. In this case, your task is to reachieve the state represented by the action data, not reverse it. (When a two-stage transaction involving your part is redone, OpenDoc calls both your part and the other part or parts involved, so that the entire compound action—including any single-stage actions that were undone between the beginning and ending actions—is restored.)

Clearing the Action History

As soon as your part performs an action that you decide cannot be undone, it must clear the action history by calling the undo object's `ClearActionHistory` method. Actions that cannot be undone, and for which the action history should be cleared, include saving a changed document and performing an editing operation that is too large to be practically saved. Ignorable actions, such as scrolling or selecting, should not affect the action history.

If your part initiates a two-stage action and, because of an error, must terminate it before adding the second stage to the action history, it can remove the incomplete undo action by calling the undo object's `AbortCurrentTransaction` method. `AbortCurrentTransaction` clears the beginning action and any subsequent single actions form the undo stack without clearing the entire action history.

OpenDoc itself clears the action history when it closes a document.

Undo and Embedded Frames

Every frame has a flag, the **in-limbo flag,** that determines whether the frame (and any of its embedded frames) is actually part of the content of its draft, or whether it is currently "in limbo" (referenced only in undo action data). When a frame is initially created, whether through `CreateFrame` or by cloning, its in-limbo flag is cleared (`kODFalse`).

Whenever your part cuts, pastes, or drag-moves an embedded frame, you must keep a reference to that frame in an undo action. When you first perform the data transfer involving the frame, and when you perform subsequent actions with the frame (including undo and redo), you must set the frame's in-limbo flag accordingly. OpenDoc requires the correct flag settings to properly handle moved and deleted objects.

Table 6-4 shows how to set the flag properly for each situation and how to dispose of the frame referenced in your undo action when your part's `DisposeActionState` method is called.

Table 6-4   Setting a frame's in-limbo flag

Action	Set flag to...	If undone, set flag to...	If redone, set flag to...	When `DisposeActionState` is called
Creating a frame	(leave as is)	kODTrue	kODFalse	If kODTrue, call Remove If kODFalse, call Release
Deleting, cutting, or starting a drag-move*	kODTrue	kODFalse	kODTrue	If kODTrue, call Remove If kODFalse, call Release
Copying a frame	(leave as is)	(Do not create an undo action for this situation)		
Pasting or dropping a moved (not copied) frame	kODFalse (but save prior value)	(restore prior value)	kODFalse (but save prior value)	If kODFalse, call Release If prior value = kODTrue, call Release Otherwise, call Remove
When `StartDrag` returns	kODFalse (if drag was a copy or if drop failed; else leave as is)	(leave as is)	kODFalse (if drag was a copy or if drop failed; else leave as is)	(nothing)

* "Starting a drag-move" in this case means starting a drag in any situation in which a move is a possible outcome.

You set the value of a frame's in-limbo flag by calling its `SetInLimbo` method and passing either kODTrue or kODFalse. You can determine the value of a frame's in-limbo flag by calling its `IsInLimbo` method.

When you re-embed a frame in performing an undo or redo action, you must also reset its link status appropriately. See "Frame Link Status" on page 377 for more information.

CHAPTER 7

Storage

7

Contents

This is the fifth of eight chapters that discuss the OpenDoc programming interface in detail. This chapter describes the external storage facilities OpenDoc uses and provides. OpenDoc relies on a system of persistent storage that is built upon the native file-storage facilities of each of the individual OpenDoc platforms. The same fundamental storage concepts and structures are used consistently for document storage and for data transfer (clipboard transfer, drag and drop, and linking, described in the next chapter).

Before reading this chapter, you should be familiar with the concepts presented in Chapter 1, "Introduction to OpenDoc," and Chapter 2, "Development Overview." For additional concepts related to your part editor's runtime environment, see Chapter 11, "OpenDoc Runtime Features."

This chapter introduces the general architecture of the OpenDoc storage system, including how parts are stored, and then describes how your OpenDoc part editor can use that architecture to store and retrieve its own content.

The OpenDoc Storage System

The OpenDoc storage system is a high-level mechanism for persistent or ephemeral storage that allows multiple part editors to share a single document effectively. The storage system is implemented on top of the native storage facilities of each platform that supports OpenDoc.

The OpenDoc storage system effectively gives each part its own data stream for storage and supports reliable references from one stream to another. The system includes a robust annotation mechanism that allows many pieces of code to access information about a given part without disturbing its format.

The identity of a part is consistent within a session; it is unique within its draft and testable for equality with other part identities. Parts can persistently reference other objects in the same draft, including other parts, thus allowing runtime object structures to be saved and reconstructed in a future session.

Parts have more than just their content to store persistently. *Properties* are used to store both the content of the part and supplemental information. OpenDoc defines a standard set of properties for all parts, and you can assign additional properties to a given part. The name of the preferred part editor is one example of a standard property that can be stored with a part.

The storage system allows OpenDoc to swap parts out to external storage if memory is required for other parts. When a part is first needed, its part editor reads it from external storage into memory. When it is no longer needed, the draft can delete it. If the part is needed again at a later time, the storage system can either return the in-memory part to the part editor or—if the part has been deleted because of low memory—bring the part once again into memory from storage. When it reads or writes its parts, your part editor may not know whether the data is currently being transferred to or from memory, or to or from external physical storage.

Storage Units, Properties, and Values

The OpenDoc storage system is not an object-oriented database. It is a system of structured storage, in which each unit of storage can contain many streams. This design eases the transition for developers working with existing code bases, which generally assume stream-based I/O.

The controlling storage object is the **storage system** object, which instantiates and maintains a list of containers. The containers are objects in the **container suite,** a platform-specific storage implementation. (On the Mac OS platform, version 1.0 of OpenDoc is released with the **Bento container suite,** a container suite that is based on **Bento,** a storage technology can be used with or independently of OpenDoc.)

Each **container** object in a container suite can hold one or more **document** objects, each of which in turn contains one or more **draft** objects. Each draft contains a number of **storage unit** objects, each of which is much like a directory structure in a typical file system (although multiple storage units might be physically stored in a single file, or perhaps not stored in files at all). Storage units hold the streams of stored data.

The runtime relationships among these storage objects are diagramed in Figure 11-9 on page 497.

Storage-Unit Organization

You can visualize a storage unit as a set of **properties,** or categorized groups of data streams. A property is identified by its **property name,** an ISO string. Each property consists of a number of streams called **values,** each of which stores a different representation of the same data, in a format identified by a named type (a **value type,** also an ISO string). Thus, there can be several properties (named categories) in a single storage unit, and several values (typed streams) in a single property.

Figure 7-1 shows these relationships through a simplified diagram of the organization of a storage unit.

Figure 7-1   The organization of a storage unit

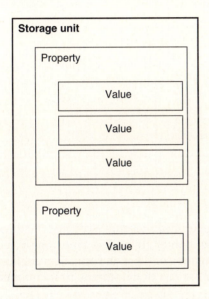

Figure 7-2 is a simplified diagram of a specific storage unit in use. The storage unit contains a figure caption. The part that owns this storage unit has created a contents property, which contains the primary data of this storage unit, as well as a name property, which names the item stored in this storage unit. This particular storage unit has three representations of the contents property (the text of the caption) as three different types of values: it own custom styled text, plain text in a standard (international) text format, and a bitmap. The storage unit has only one representation of the name property.

Figure 7-2   An example of a storage unit with several properties and values

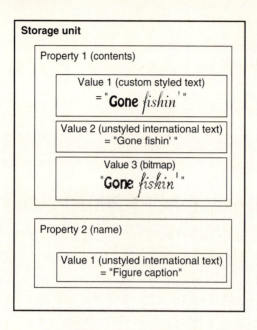

A caller that accesses this storage unit can read or write just the data of immediate interest. In the storage unit of Figure 7-2, for example, a caller could access only the value representing one of the data formats in the contents property without having to read the rest of the storage unit into memory.

A caller can learn the part kinds of the data stored in the storage unit without having to read any of the contents into memory, even if the part editor that stored the data is not present.

Fundamental to the OpenDoc storage system is the concept that all values within a property are analogous, or equivalent, representations of the same data. Every value in the contents property in Figure 7-2, for example, is a complete representation of the item's contents (the caption text), expressed in the type of data that the value holds.

Values in a storage unit can include references to other storage units, as described in the section "Persistent References" on page 279. Thus, storage units can be arranged in ordered structures such as hierarchies; OpenDoc stores the embedding structure of a document in this way.

Standard Properties

A basic feature of the OpenDoc storage system is that storage units are inspectable—that is, one can extract the data (values) of the various properties of a storage unit without first having to read the entire file or document that the storage unit is part of, and without having to understand the internal format of the data in any of the values. For example, if the storage unit for an embedded part includes a property that holds the part's name, you can extract that name without having to read all the data of the part, even if you do not understand how to read or display the part's contents.

To make the inspectability of storage useful across parts, documents, and platforms, OpenDoc publicly specifies certain standard properties, with constant definitions such as kODPropContents and kODPropName, that all part editors can recognize. Documents, windows, frames, and parts all have basic structures, defined by properties, that are accessible from both the stored and in-memory states. This accessibility allows OpenDoc and part editors to read only the information that is needed in a given situation and thus increase performance. Table 7-2 on page 288 and Table 7-3 on page 291 list many of the common standard properties that might be found in storage units.

Using storage-unit methods, you can access the values of any known property of any storage unit.

OpenDoc ISO string prefix
All public ISO string constants defined by OpenDoc include a prefix that identifies them as OpenDoc ISO strings. This is the prefix:

```
+//ISO 9070/ANSI::113722::US::CI LABS::
```

Following the prefix is a designation that represents either OpenDoc as a whole, a specific platform, or a specific developer (company name). Therefore, the full ISO string definition for the property kODPropContents, for example, is

```
+//ISO 9070/ANSI::113722::US::CI LABS::OpenDoc:Property:Contents
```

All defined property names and data types should include the OpenDoc ISO string prefix. Value types in a storage unit (such as part kinds) should not. ◆

Creating Properties and Values

If you have a reference to a storage unit, you can add a property to it and then add several values to that property. For the example illustrated in Figure 7-2 on page 272, for example, you might use statements such as these (in which the storage unit reference is su):

```
su->AddProperty(ev, kODPropContents);
su->AddValue(ev, kCustomTextKind);
su->AddValue(ev, kODIntlText);
su->AddValue(ev, kMyBitmapKind);
```

These statements add the property kODPropContents to the storage unit and give it one standard (kODIntlText) and two custom (kCustomTextKind and kMyBitmapKind) value types. The kODPropContents property is a standard property name; you can add your own custom property and value types to a storage unit, using statements such as this:

```
su->AddProperty(ev, kPropMyAnnotations);
su->AddValue(ev, kMyAnnotationsType);
```

These statements only set up the storage unit to receive data of a particular type; you then need to store the data explicitly in the values. To do so, you must first focus the storage unit, setting it up so that the data you write is placed in the desired value of the desired property.

Focusing a Storage Unit

Because any storage unit can contain a number of properties, and any property a number of values, finding the exact piece of data in an OpenDoc document can be more complex than finding it in a conventional document. OpenDoc allows you to **focus** a storage unit, that is, access the desired data stream (defined by property name and value type) within it before reading or writing.

You focus on a particular stream by calling the storage unit's Focus method and providing some combination of the following three types of specification:

- name: property name or value type

- index: the position of the property in the storage unit or the value in the property

- **position code:** a code that allows you to specify, for example, the next or previous sibling (a sibling is another value in the same property, or another property in the same storage unit)

If you are not focusing by relative position, you specify a position code of kODPosUndefined when you call the Focus method. For example, all of the following calls focus on the first value of the contents property of the storage unit shown in Figure 7-2:

- the names of the property and value

```
su->Focus(ev,
        kODPropContents,          // property name
        kODPosUndefined,
        kCustomTextKind,          // value type
        0,
        kODPosUndefined);
```

- the name of the property and the indexed position (1-based), within its property, of the value

```
su->Focus(ev,
        kODPropContents,          // property name
        kODPosUndefined,
        kODNULL,
        1,                        // value index
        kODPosUndefined);
```

- the relative positions, compared to the current focus, of the property and value

```
su->Focus(ev,
        kODPropContents           // property name
        kODPosUndefined,
        kODNULL,
        0,
        kODPosFirstSib);          // position code
```

- the storage-unit cursor that specifies the property/value pair you want

```
su->FocusWithCursor(ev, cursor);   // storage-unit cursor
```

A **storage-unit cursor** is an OpenDoc object that may be convenient if you frequently switch back and forth among specific property-and-value combinations. You can create a number of objects of class ODStorageUnitCursor, initialize them with the storage-unit foci you need, and pass a storage-unit cursor to the `Focus` method each time you wish to switch focus.

You can set up a storage-unit cursor either by explicitly specifying the property and value of its focus, or by having it adopt the current focus of an existing storage unit.

Once you have focused the storage unit, you can read and write its data, as described next.

Manipulating the Data in a Value

To read or write the data of a value, remove data from a value, or insert data into a value, you first focus the storage unit on that particular value.

- To write data at a particular position in a value, call the `SetOffset` method to set the position of the insertion point in the value's stream, followed by the `SetValue` method to write the data.

  The `SetValue` method takes a buffer parameter of type of type `ODByteArray`; see "Handling Byte Arrays and Other Parameters" on page 469 for more information on byte arrays. For example, to write information from the buffer pointed to by `dataPtr` into the value at the position `desiredPosition`, you could set up the byte array `myData` as shown and then call two methods:

  ```
  ODByteArray MyData;

  myData._length = dataSize;
  myData._maximum = dataSize;
  myData._buffer = dataPtr;

  su->SetOffset(ev, desiredPosition);
  su->SetValue(ev, &myData);
  ```

- To read the data at a particular position in a value, call the `SetOffset` method, followed by the `GetValue` method to read the data. To read information from the position `desiredPosition` in the value into a buffer specified by the byte array `myData`, you could make these calls:

  ```
  su->SetOffset(ev, desiredPosition);
  su->GetValue(ev, &myData);
  ```

  You could then extract the data from the buffer pointed to by `myData._buffer`.

- To read or write data at the current offset in a value, simply call `GetValue` or `SetValue` without first calling `SetOffset`.

■ The SetValue method overwrites any data at and beyond the offset specified. To *insert* data at a particular offset, without overwriting any data already in the value, call the InsertValue method (after having called SetOffset, if necessary).

■ To append data at the end of a value, call GetSize to get the size of the value, then call SetOffset to set the mark to the end of the stream, and finally call SetValue to write the data into the stream.

■ To remove data of a particular size from a particular position in a value, call SetOffset to set the mark to the desired point in the stream, and then call DeleteValue to delete data of a specified length (in bytes) from the stream.

IMPORTANT

If you change the data in one value of a property, remember that you must make appropriate changes to all other values of that property. All values must be complete and equivalent representations—each according to its own format—of the information the property represents. ▲

Iterating Through a Storage Unit

To examine each of the properties of a storage unit in turn, access them in this way:

1. Call the Focus method of the storage unit, passing null values for property name and value type, and kODPosAll for position code. The null values plus kODPosAll "unfocus" the storage unit (that is, focus it on all properties).

2. Get the number of properties in the (unfocused) storage unit by calling its CountProperties method.

3. Focus on each property in turn by iterating through them using a relative-position method of focusing.

```
su->Focus(ev,
        kODNULL,
        kODPosNextSib,        // position code
        kODNULL,
        0,
        kODPosUndefined);
```

To examine in turn each of the values in a property of a storage unit, you access them in a similar way:

1. Focus the storage unit on the desired property by calling its `Focus` method and passing the desired property name and `kODPosAll` for relative position of value. Using `kODPosAll` focuses the storage unit on all values of that property.

2. Get the number of values in the property by calling the `CountValues` method of the focused storage unit.

3. Focus on each value in turn by iterating through them using a relative-position method of focusing for the values while maintaining the same property position.

```
su->Focus(ev,
         kODNULL,
         kODPosSame,              // position code
         kODNULL,
         0,
         kODPosNextSib);          // position code
```

Removing Properties and Values

You can remove a property from a storage unit by

1. Focusing on the property to be removed: call the `Focus` method and pass it a specific property name and a value position of `kODPosAll`

2. Removing the property: call the `Remove` method of the focused storage unit

You can remove a value from a property in a storage unit by

1. Focusing on the value to be removed: call the `Focus` method and pass it a specific property name and a specific value type

2. Removing the value: call the `Remove` method of the focused storage unit

Storage-Unit IDs

At runtime, the draft object assigns an identifier to each of its storage units. A **storage-unit ID** is a nonpersistent designation for a storage unit that is unique within its draft (storage-unit IDs are not unique across drafts and do not persist across sessions). You can use the ID to identify storage units, to compare two storage units for equality at runtime, and to recreate persistent objects from their storage units.

Whereas object references can be used only with instantiated OpenDoc objects, storage-unit IDs are more general—they can refer to either the runtime object or its persistently stored equivalent (its storage unit).

For purposes in which the object or its storage unit as a whole is passed or copied, an ID is better than a runtime object reference. For example, storage-unit IDs are used when cloning persistent objects (see "Persistent References and Cloning" on page 282). Using a storage-unit ID ensures that the copying occurs even if the storage unit's object is not in memory at the time. However, OpenDoc first looks for the object in memory; if it is there, OpenDoc uses it rather than its storage unit.

You generally create a persistent object from storage by passing a storage-unit ID to the object's factory method (such as `ODDraft::AcquireFrame` and `ODDraft::AcquirePart`). You can also conveniently retrieve persistent objects that may or may not have been purged (such as frames scrolled out of and then back into view) by retaining the storage-unit ID for the object when you release it, and then supplying that ID when you need it again. Note also that, in discussions that refer to *part ID* or *object ID* for any persistent object, the ID being referred to is the same as a storage-unit ID.

Storage-unit IDs are not persistent. Therefore, to get the correct storage-unit ID when creating a stored persistent object, a caller must have access to another, more permanent means of identifying a storage unit. For that purpose, OpenDoc uses *persistent references* (described next). OpenDoc provides methods (such as `ODDraft::GetIDFromStorageUnitRef`) for obtaining a storage-unit ID from a persistent reference, and vice versa (such as `ODStorageUnit::GetStrongStorageUnitRef`).

Persistent References

A **persistent reference** is a number, stored within a given storage unit, that refers to another storage unit in the same document (see Figure 7-3). The reference is preserved across sessions; if a document is closed and then reopened at another time or even on another machine, the reference is still valid.

Figure 7-3   Persistent references in a storage unit

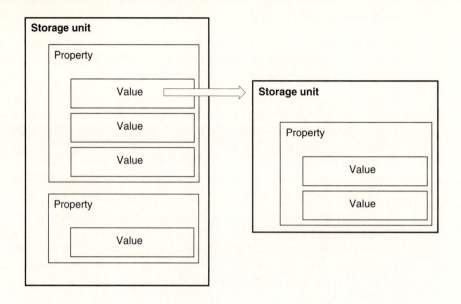

Persistent references allow data to be placed in multiple storage units. The storage units reflect the runtime objects whose data they store; the persistent references permit the reconstruction of the runtime relationships among those objects in subsequent sessions.

Persistent References in OpenDoc

OpenDoc uses persistent references in several situations, including these:

- The stored data in a draft includes a list of persistent references to the root frames of all windows. When a document is opened, the root frames can then be found and their windows reconstructed.

- A stored frame has a persistent reference to its part. When a frame is read into memory, it can then find the part it displays.

- A stored part has persistent references to all of its embedded frames. When a part is read into memory, it can then find all of the embedded frames that it contains. Persistent references to embedded frames are essential to embedding; parts have no access to their embedded parts except through embedded frames.

- A stored part also may have persistent references to all of its display frames. When a part is read into memory, it can then find all of the frames that display it.

- Parts can also use persistent references for hierarchical storage of their own content data.

Figure 7-4 is a simplified diagram showing the persistent references among stored objects in an OpenDoc document. (The difference between the strong and weak persistent references referred to in the figure is explained in the section "Persistent References and Cloning" on page 282.)

Figure 7-4   Persistent references in a document

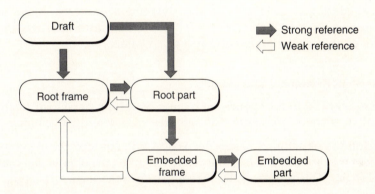

Creating Persistent References

To create a persistent reference, you first focus the storage unit on the value whose data stream is to hold the reference and then call the storage unit's `GetStrongStorageUnitRef` or `GetWeakStorageUnitRef` method, passing it the storage-unit ID of the storage unit that is to be referred to. You then store the returned reference in the focused value, in a format consistent with the type of the value. Such a reference is then said to be *from* the value *to* the referenced storage unit.

A persistent reference is a 32-bit value of type `ODStorageUnitRef`. You can create and store a virtually unlimited number of persistent references in a storage-unit value; each persistent reference that you create from a particular value is guaranteed to be unique. Do not try to inspect or interpret a persistent reference; the classes `ODStorageUnit` and `ODStorageUnitView` provide methods for manipulating them.

IMPORTANT

The scope of a persistent reference is limited to the value in which it was originally created and stored. Do not store it in a different value; it will almost certainly no longer refer to the correct storage unit. ▲

Once a persistent reference is no longer needed, you should remove it from the value in which it was written. Extra persistent references threaten the robustness and efficiency of execution.

A storage unit is aware of all persistent references that it holds, even those that a part editor may have stored within its contents property. OpenDoc provides an iterator class, `ODStorageUnitRefIterator`, through which a caller can retrieve all persistent references in a given value.

Persistent References and Cloning

There are two kinds of persistent references, **strong persistent references** and **weak persistent references.** They are treated differently in cloning.

To **clone** an object is to make a deep copy of it: not only the object itself is copied but also all objects that it references (plus the objects that they reference, and so on). This process is described further in the section "Cloning" on page 321.

In a clone operation, copies are made of all storage units referenced with a strong persistent reference in the object being cloned. Storage units referenced with a weak persistent reference are not copied. The use of weak persistent references allows you to clone only portions of a document or other structure of referenced storage units. Figure 7-5, which shows the persistent references among a stored frame and part plus their embedded frame and part, illustrates how cloning gives different results, depending on which objects you clone and which references are strong and which are weak.

Figure 7-5   Cloning objects with strong and weak persistent references

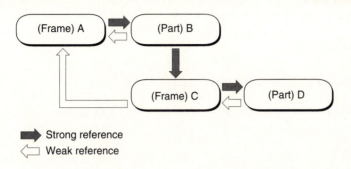

For example, if you were to clone the containing frame (A) in Figure 7-5, all four objects in the figure would be cloned, representing the containing frame and part plus its embedded frame and part. If, however, you were to clone the containing part (B), only the part plus its embedded frame and part (C and D) would be cloned, even though the containing part includes a persistent reference back to its display frame (A). Likewise, if you were to clone the embedded frame (C), only that frame and its part (D) would be cloned.

You define a persistent reference as weak or strong by calling either the `GetStrongStorageUnitRef` or the `GetWeakStorageUnitRef` method of the storage unit that is to hold the reference.

Stored display frames
It is recommended, although not necessary, that you store your part's display frames persistently. If you do store display frames, however, make sure that your part's persistent references to them are weak references. ◆

Main and Auxiliary Storage Units

Every part (or other persistent object) has a single **main storage unit,** whose `kODPropContents` property stores the content of that object. In most cases, you can simply write all of your part's data as a stream into that one storage unit. It is possible, however, to create **auxiliary storage units** that hold additional data related to the data in a main storage unit.

The procedure involves creating a strong persistent reference to the auxiliary storage unit and storing it in your main storage unit. You can subsequently retrieve the reference and convert it into an object reference to the auxiliary storage unit. See the section "Creating Additional Storage Units" on page 301 for more information.

Prefocused Access With Storage-Unit Views

A storage-unit view is an OpenDoc object that represents a prefocused access to a storage unit. The class `ODStorageUnitView` has most of the functionality of the class `ODStorageUnit`, except that it has no methods for accessing different properties and values. A storage-unit view does not in itself store data; each storage-unit view is associated with a specific storage unit that actually does the storing. Calls to access the storage unit view are passed to its associated storage unit.

Several methods of several OpenDoc classes take a storage-unit view as a parameter. The `ODPart` methods `FulfillPromise`, `ReadPartInfo`, `WritePartInfo`, `ReadActionState`, and `WriteActionState`, for example, all make use of storage-unit views. When one of your methods receives a storage-unit view as a parameter, the method can read from the storage-unit view or write to it without first focusing on any property or value, or locking the storage unit.

You can, if you wish, create storage-unit views to pass prefocused storage units among your software components or to any OpenDoc objects whose methods take storage-unit views.

Documents, Drafts, and Parts

Compound documents are fundamental to OpenDoc, and each compound document is represented by a document object. As noted previously, documents are composed of one or more drafts. This section discusses the relationship of documents to drafts and to parts, describes how part data is stored, and discusses the objects that a document contains.

The document object is responsible for creating and deleting drafts, for storing the identity of the current draft, and for collapsing multiple drafts into one. Your part editor rarely interacts directly with its document object. However, see "Creating a New Document" on page 292 for information on creating a document object.

Drafts

A **draft** is a specific version of an OpenDoc document. Multiple drafts can be maintained within a single document. There is always at least one draft, the **base draft,** within a document. An individual draft can be extracted from a document and placed in a new document for editing.

Drafts are created by users with the help of the document shell, and maintained by the container suite. Figure 1-16 on page 62 shows an example of the Drafts dialog box, with which the user views and manipulates the drafts of a document. A user can save the current state of the document as a new draft at any time. In general, your part editor can ignore the existence of separate drafts in a document. The data you read or write is always associated with the currently open draft.

Methods of `ODDocument` allow access to drafts by draft ID or by object reference and relative position in the document. Drafts have a specific set of properties, including creation date, modification date, and user name. Each draft object privately maintains whatever information it needs to distinguish itself from its predecessor draft.

The draft object is responsible for creating and tracking frame objects, part objects, link-related objects, and storage units. It also manages the cloning process and flags changes to the content of any of its parts. Typically, it is to perform these tasks—and not to manipulate a draft as a version of a document—that your part editor interacts with its draft object.

Only one user can edit a draft at a time, and only the most recent draft of a given document can be edited. (Drafts cannot be changed if other drafts are based on them.) To enforce this limitation, each open draft has an associated set of **draft permissions**. They specify the class of read/write access that your part editor has to the draft. Table 7-1 lists the draft permissions recognized by OpenDoc.

Table 7-1   Draft permissions

Constant	Explanation
kODDPExclusiveWrite	Read access and exclusive-write access
kODDPReadOnly	Read-only access
kODDPSharedWrite	Read access and shared-write access
kODDPTransient	Navigation-only access (no read or write access)
kODDPNone	No access

Note

The Bento container suite supports only the kODDPReadOnly and kODDPExclusiveWrite draft permissions. ◆

When your part initializes itself, or at least before attempting to modify any of its data, it should get the permissions of its draft (by calling the draft's GetPermissions method) and behave accordingly. For example, your part editor should not attempt to make changes to a part when its draft has been opened as read-only. Also, certain menu items should be disabled when the user views a read-only draft; see "The Document Menu" on page 248 and "The Edit Menu" on page 252 for descriptions.

Storage Model for Parts

Parts, like other persistent objects, have a storage unit in which they can write their state persistently. At the same time, parts are directly involved in many other OpenDoc actions (such as binding, data translation, and data transfer) and thus must satisfy additional storage requirements to ensure that they can share their data with other objects as needed. Here are some of the requirements your parts must meet:

■ Your part must be able to store multiple representations of its content. Each must be a full representation of the content; it cannot contain just that data that differs from the data in another representation.

■ A caller must be able to extract a single, full representation from your part's storage unit without having to understand the format of any of the representations.

- A caller must be able to remove all but one representation from your part's storage unit, without having to understand the format of any of the representations.

- You must store your part's representations in order of **fidelity,** the faithfulness of the representation to that of your part editor's native format. Store them in descending order, with your part editor's highest-fidelity format first.

- It must be possible to distinguish the fundamental content of your part from any annotations to it or information about it. OpenDoc—or any caller with access to your storage unit—can delete these annotations and items of information from memory at any time, without writing them to storage, and therefore you *cannot* use them to store actual content. You can, however, use them to store noncritical optimizations such as caches.

- Because property names are ISO strings, only simple property-naming conventions, such as prefixes to establish ownership, are possible. For example, "SurfWriter Corporation" might use the prefix "Surf:" to identify all the ISO strings whose format and meaning it controls. OpenDoc-defined strings have the OpenDoc ISO string prefix; see the note "OpenDoc ISO string prefix" on page 273.

To meet these requirements, your part must create a contents property, defined by the property name `kODPropContents`, in your storage unit. In that property, you need to create—for every representation you wish to store—a value whose type is the part kind of the representation. (Part kind is described in the section "Part Kinds Stored in a Part" on page 475.) Into each of these values, you must write one and only one representation of your part's contents, using the data format appropriate to that part kind. Order the values by fidelity.

Do not store any part content outside of the contents property. Make sure that all other properties in your part's storage unit are for annotations or extra information rather than for content. Your part's contents property can, however, include persistent references to other storage units that contain additional content data.

To help you decide which data you should store as content and which you should not, consider that content includes any data that the user should be able to save as well as any data that should persist across different part editors, different machines, and different platforms.

This storage model offers greater flexibility than is available for application storage in the file systems of many platforms. If your applications use only a single stream to store all of their contents, your equivalent part can simply store everything in a single value in the contents property of its storage unit. If your applications use resources, multifork files, or some other form of structured storage, your equivalent part can use multiple storage units referenced from a value in the contents property of your part's main storage unit.

Because you can add more storage units at any time and save references to them in any value, you can construct an arbitrarily complex structure for your stored data. Each additional storage unit can have multiple properties, and each property can have multiple values. (Remember that different values within the same property should be used only for different representations of the same data.)

What a Draft Contains

Table 7-2 shows some of the kinds of information that can be stored persistently as properties of the various objects that make up the storage units in a draft of an OpenDoc document. Note that some of the storage units shown in Table 7-2 reflect the objects and persistent references shown in Figure 7-4 on page 281, as well as the runtime object references shown in the section "Runtime Object Relationships" on page 487. This list is not complete, nor are all properties shown here required to be present. Furthermore, some properties should not be accessed by part editors. For more information on these and other standard properties, see "Types and Constants" in the *OpenDoc Class Reference for the Mac OS*.

Table 7-2   Data stored in a draft

Property	Description
Any Storage Unit	
kODPropObjectType	Type of object stored in this storage unit (draft, frame, part, and so on)
Draft Storage Unit	
kODPropRootPartSU	Strong persistent reference to the root part of this draft

continued

Table 7-2   Data stored in a draft (continued)

Property	Description
Frame Storage Unit	
`kODPropPart`	Strong persistent reference to the part displayed in this frame
`kODPropContainingFrame`	Weak persistent reference to the containing frame of this frame
`kODPropFrameShape`	Frame shape of this frame
`kODPropPartInfo`	Part info (part-specific data) associated with this frame
`kODPropPresentation`	Presentation of the part displayed in this frame
`kODPropInternalTransform`	Internal transform of this frame
`kODPropFrameGroup`	Group ID of the frame group this frame belongs to
`kODPropSequenceNumber`	Sequence number of this frame in its frame group
`kODPropLinkStatus`	The link status (in-source, in-destination, or not in link) of this frame
`kODPropIsRoot`	True if this frame is root frame in window
`kODPropIsSubframe`	True if this frame is a subframe
`kODPropIsOverlaid`	True if this frame is overlaid
`kODPropDoesPropagateEvents`	True if this frame's part propagates events

(Other standard frame properties are listed in Table 7-3 on page 291.)

Part Storage Unit

Property	Description
`kODPropContents`	Part content (the actual stored data of this part)
`kODPropDisplayFrames`	Weak persistent references to the display frames of this part

(Other standard part properties are listed in Table 7-3 on page 291.)

continued

Table 7-2   Data stored in a draft (continued)

Property	Description
Clipboard or Drag-and-Drop Storage Unit	
kODPropContents	The contents of the clipboard (or drag-and-drop object)
kODPropSuggestedFrameShape	Suggested shape for frame, if contents are embedded at destination
kODPropLinkSpec	A link specification
kODPropContentFrame	(Exists if data is a single embedded frame)
kODPropProxyContents	Suggested adornments to apply to frame (if data is a single embedded frame)
Link Storage Unit	
kODPropLinkSource	Weak persistent reference to the link-source object associated with this link object
Link-Source Storage Unit	
kODPropLink	Weak persistent reference to a link object associated with this link-source object
kODPropSourcePart	Weak persistent reference to the part that contains (or last contained) the source data for this link
kODPropLinkContentSU	Strong persistent reference to the contents storage unit for the linked data
kODPropChangeTime	The date and time of this link's last update
kODPropUpdateID	The update ID for this link's last update
kODPropAutoUpdate	True if link is to be updated automatically

Your part editor is responsible for reading and writing only the data that is stored persistently by your parts; OpenDoc takes care of persistent storage of the other objects listed in Table 7-2. Basically, each of the objects can read and write itself.

Info Properties

Some of the standard properties associated with a part (or, in some cases, its frame) are made visible to the user, either for information purposes only or to allow the user to modify them. This set of properties, called **Info properties,** is displayed in the Part Info dialog box and Document Info dialog box. The last-modified date and time (kODPropModDate) is an example of an Info property that the user cannot change; the name of the part (kODPropName) is an example of an Info property that the user can change. Certain items displayed in the dialog box (such as part category and part size) are not storage-unit properties at all, but are calculated at runtime or obtained from other sources of information.

Table 7-3 lists the standard Info properties defined for version 1.0 of OpenDoc.

Table 7-3   Standard Info properties

Property	Explanation
kODPropName	The user-assigned name of the part
kODPropViewType	The view type of the part in the currently selected frame (a frame property)
kODPropIsFrozen	True if the part is bundled, false if not (a frame property)
kODPropIsStationery	True if the part is stationery, false if not
kODPropIconFamily	The icons that represent this part
kODPropPreferredKind	The user-specified part kind for the data of this part
kODPropPreferredEditor	The user-specified preferred editor for editing this part (the ID of the editor that last wrote this part to persistent storage)
kODPropCreateDate	The date and time at which this part was originally created
kODPropModDate	The date and time at which this part was last modified
kODPropModUser	The name of the user who last modified this part
kODPropComments	Comments entered by the user into this part's Part Info dialog box

Your part editor can define additional Info properties and store them in the part's content or attach them as properties to its parts' storage units. You can then display them to the user in a **Settings dialog box,** accessible from the Part Info dialog box. See "The Settings Extension" on page 444 for more information.

Container Properties

If your part contains embedded parts, you may want the embedded parts to adopt, by default, some of your current display settings or behavior. For example, if your part is a text part, it may be appropriate for other text parts embedded in it to have the same text characteristics (font, size, style, and so on) unless the user overrides them.

You can define such a set of characteristics as properties and attach them to your parts' storage units. These **container properties** then become available to embedded parts for adoption. See "Adopting Container Properties" on page 115 and "Transmitting Your Container Properties to Embedded Parts" on page 127 for more information.

Creating a New Document

Under most circumstances, your part editor never creates a document. Other parts of OpenDoc, such as the document shell, handle document creation when the user chooses a menu command such as New or drags a part to the desktop.

If, however, your part editor provides its own document-creation interface to the user, or if it caches its own data in separate OpenDoc documents, then it must use methods of the container suite to create those documents.

In your document creation method, you can follow steps such as these:

1. Create a file, following whatever platform-specific procedures are required by the file system in use.

2. Create an OpenDoc container, document, and draft for the file. Call the session object's `CreateContainer` method, then the container's `AcquireDocument` method, and then the document's `AcquireBaseDraft` method.

3. Create the root part. Call the base draft's `CreatePart` method, then obtain the root part's storage unit and assign it to the draft. Call the draft's `Externalize` method to save the storage unit.

4. Assign the proper file type to the file. On the Mac OS platform, this involves giving it a file type (an `OSType`) that represents the root part's part kind and assigning the document a creator type (`'odtm'`) that is the signature of the OpenDoc document shell.

5. Release the objects you have created: the root part, the draft, the document, and the container. Finally, delete the platform-specific file object that you created. (This action does not delete the file from persistent storage.)

Reading and Writing Your Part

In OpenDoc, **reading** an object (also called *internalization*) is the process of initializing (or re-initializing) the object by bringing its stored data into memory from persistent storage. Conversely, **writing** (also called *externalization*) is the process of copying an object's essential data to persistent external storage. In general, when a document is opened, its objects are read into memory. As the user edits the document, the objects are modified. When the user saves the document, the modified objects are written back to storage. (As noted earlier, the container suite controls how data is physically stored; reading and writing may not necessarily involve an immediate transfer of data between memory and an external physical storage medium.)

This section discusses how your part reads and writes its own content data, as well as related OpenDoc objects, such as frames, that it uses.

Your part editor must be able to read any parts whose data formats (part kinds) it recognizes. You are not required to read the entire contents of your part into memory at once, and you needn't write it all to storage at once. However, reading must put your part in a state in which it can accept events and handle requests, and writing it must ensure that changes made by the user are not lost.

Your part editor should never change the part kind of any part you handle except as a result of an explicit user request. Any translations required to make a part readable, whether performed by OpenDoc or by your part editor, are first selected by the user. See "Binding" on page 474 and "Translation" on page 333 for more information.

Initializing and Reading a Part From Storage

Any part must be able to read itself (reconstruct itself in memory by reading its stored data). To maximize performance, OpenDoc requires reading and writing only when absolutely necessary. A part is not instantiated and read into memory until its draft's `CreatePart` or `AcquirePart` method has been called—meaning that the part editor is needed for tasks such as drawing, editing, frame negotiation, or script execution. When a part is read in, OpenDoc has already bound it to a part editor according to its part kind (and loaded the part editor if it is not already in memory).

Whenever a document in which your part is visible is opened, or whenever your part is added to a document, your part's data must be read into memory. Note that OpenDoc parts should always be ready to work from an empty storage unit as well. The two fundamental methods that your part must implement for initializing itself are `InitPart` and `InitPartFromStorage`.

The somInit Method

When your part object is first created (or recreated from storage), and before receiving a call to its `InitPart` or `InitPartFromStorage` method, your part receives a call to its System Object Model (SOM) object constructor `somInit`. The `somInit` method is inherited from the `somObject` class of SOM; when you subclass `ODPart`, you must override `somInit`.

Your `somInit` method should initialize (clear) your part object's instance variables. You must not perform any tasks in this method that might fail. You can set pointer variables to null and assign appropriate values to numeric variables. If you have any initialization code that can potentially fail, your part's `InitPart` or `InitPartFromStorage` method must handle it.

The InitPart Method

The `InitPart` method is called only once in your part's lifetime, by your draft's `CreatePart` method, when your part is first created and has no previously stored data to read. (If your part is created from stationery, this method is never called.) This is its interface:

```
void InitPart(in ODStorageUnit storageUnit,
              in ODPart partWrapper);
```

One possible approach to `InitPart` is to take steps such as these:

1. Call your inherited `InitPart` method, which in turn calls its inherited `InitPersistentObject` method to initialize the information your part needs as a persistent object. (Your classes' initialization methods should always call their superclasses' initialization methods.)

2. If your part stores its data in multiple part kinds, add a contents property (type `kODPropContents`) and a value (of your highest-fidelity part kind) to the storage unit passed to you, thus preparing your part for eventual writing of its data. Add values for other part kinds also, if appropriate. Initialize the values if necessary.

3. If your part stores more than one part kind, add a preferred-kind property (type `kODPropPreferredKind`) to the storage unit passed to you. Write into a value of that property an ISO string representing your editor's highest-fidelity part kind. Normally, that part kind should equal the type of the first value in your contents property.

4. Save, in a field (such as `fSelf`) of your part, the contents of the `partWrapper` parameter passed to this method. It represents an object reference through which OpenDoc interacts with your part. See "The Part-Wrapper Object" on page 461 for more information.

5. Initialize any data pointers or size values that your part maintains.

At this point you might mark your part as clean (unchanged). You could use a "dirty flag" for this purpose, which you initialize as cleared, and then set whenever you change your part's content.

Note
Another approach to `InitPart` is to defer all writing (such as that in steps 2 and 3) until your part's `Externalize` method is called. ◆

The InitPartFromStorage Method

The `InitPartFromStorage` method is similar to `InitPart`, except that `InitPartFromStorage` also reads in data. Your draft's `AcquirePart` method calls your `InitPartFromStorage` method and supplies a storage unit from which the part reads itself. Your part retrieves, from the `kODPropContents` property of the storage unit, the value (specified by part kind) that represents the data stream you wish to read. This is the interface to `InitPartFromStorage`:

```
void InitPartFromStorage(in ODStorageUnit storage unit,
                         in ODPart partWrapper);
```

In your `InitPartFromStorage` method, take steps like these:

1. Call your inherited `InitPartFromStorage` method. That method calls its inherited `InitPersistentObject` method, which initializes the persistent-object information previously stored for your part.

2. Determine the appropriate part kind of data to read in.

   ☐ Your editor may be reading in a part that was created or previously edited by a different editor (see "The Binding Process" on page 480). Focus on the `kODPropPreferredKind` of the storage unit passed to you, and retrieve the part's **preferred kind** (the part kind you should read, if possible). This part kind may or may not equal the type of the first value in the part's contents property.

   ☐ If the `kODPropPreferredKind` property does not exist or if you cannot read data of that part kind, find the highest-fidelity (earliest in storage order) part kind that you can read

   (If there is no preferred kind, take the kind that you can read to be the preferred kind. Use that preferred-kind designation later, when you write to storage.)

If the data is non-OpenDoc file data to which your part editor has just been bound because of a drop operation (see "Accepting Non-OpenDoc Data" on page 371), you can take the following steps (on the Mac OS platform). Otherwise, go on to step 3.

   ☐ Find, in the contents property, a value type representing the file type. If the item is a text file, for example, OpenDoc will have provided the value type (OpenDoc ISO prefix followed by) "MacOS:OSType:FileType:TEXT".

   ☐ Assuming your part can read data of that file type, you can then obtain the file's `HFSFlavor` structure (defined by the Mac OS Drag Manager) from a value of type (ISO prefix plus) "MacOS:OSType:ScrapType:hfs ", also provided in the contents property by OpenDoc.

   ☐ Using information in the `HFSFlavor` structure (such as the file specification), you can then make file-system-specific calls to open the file and process its contents into a buffer in memory. If you must store the data immediately and the draft permissions allow you to do so, write the data into an appropriate value or values in your part's contents property. Otherwise, you can wait until your `Externalize` method is called before writing it to your storage unit.

Skip to step 7 (you have already read the data into your part).

3. Focus the storage unit on its contents property and on the value containing the part's preferred kind, if you can read that kind. If you cannot read the preferred kind, focus on the highest-fidelity part kind that you can read. (Even if you do not read in the preferred kind at this stage, do not yet change the value in the `kODPropPreferredKind` property.)

4. Read the data into your part's buffer, using the `GetValue` method.

5. Read in additional objects as needed—that is, as persistent references within your main storage unit's `kODPropContents` property lead you to information stored elsewhere. See, for example, "Creating Additional Storage Units" on page 301, "Storing and Retrieving Embedded Frames" on page 302, and "Reading Linked Content From Storage" on page 392.

6. If your part's display frames have been stored, read them in as discussed in "Storing and Retrieving Display Frames" on page 302.

7. Call your draft's `GetPermissions` method and save the results in a field of your part. Respect the permissions in later attempts to write to the draft. See "Drafts" on page 285 for more information.

8. Save, in a field (such as `fSelf`) of your part, the contents of the `partWrapper` parameter passed to `InitPartFromStorage`. The parameter represents a reference (pointer) through which OpenDoc calls back to your part. See "The Part-Wrapper Object" on page 461 for more information.

9. Initialize any data pointers or size values that your part maintains. At this time you might, if you maintain a dirty flag, mark your part as clean (unchanged).

Writing a Part to Storage

Your part must be able to write itself (write its data to persistent storage, typically external storage such as a disk) when instructed to do so. This instruction may come at any time, not just when the user saves or closes your document. To maximize performance, OpenDoc requires writing only when absolutely necessary.

■ A part is not written to storage until the user performs a save operation on its document, causing the part's `Externalize` method to be called. If the user does not perform a save operation on a document, no changes to any of its parts are permanently recorded.

■ When its document is saved or closed, no writing is required of a part if it has not been altered since it was read into memory.

Your part editor can follow these policies strictly, or it can deviate from them as necessary. For example, you can write out your part at any time, without waiting for the user to save the entire document. Note, however, that no matter how many times your part writes its data to storage, none of those changes will become persistent unless the user performs a save.

This section discusses the `Externalize` and `ExternalizeKinds` methods of your part editor. Another method that involves writing your part data to storage is the `CloneInto` method, described in the section "The CloneInto Method of Your Part Editor" on page 327.

The Externalize Method

A caller instructs your part to write its data to storage by calling your part's override of its inherited `Externalize` method. Your part then writes its data to its storage unit.

As a minimum, your part must write one property: `kODPropContents`. The `kODPropContents` property contains your part's intrinsic data. You can write your part's data in multiple part kinds, representing multiple data formats, in the `kODPropContents` property. Each format is a separate stream, defined as a separate value in the property, and each value must be a complete representation of your part's contents.

You can add other properties and values as annotations to your part's storage unit, and you can access them for your own purposes. However, remember that during the binding process, OpenDoc considers only the value types of `kODPropContents` when assigning an editor to a part.

The fundamental method that your part must override for writing its data to storage is the `Externalize` method, inherited from the class `ODPersistentObject`. This is its interface:

```
void Externalize();
```

In a simple `Externalize` method, you might take these basic steps:

1. Call the inherited `Externalize` method, to make sure that the appropriate persistent-object information for your part is written to storage.

2. Examine your part to see whether it is dirty—that is, whether the content has been changed since the last write. If it is clean (unchanged), take no further action.

3. Get a reference to your main storage unit by calling your part's inherited `GetStorageUnit` method.

4. Your editor may be writing a part that was created or previously edited by a different editor (see "The Binding Process" on page 480). If so, you need to prepare the contents property of the part to match the part kinds and fidelity order that your part editor uses. (This step is required only the first time you write a part after your editor has been first bound to it.)

   □ Remove any values in the storage unit that represent kinds that your part editor does not support or does not intend to save.

   □ Add values if necessary, so that values for all part kinds that your part editor intends to include are present. Make sure the values are in fidelity order, and make sure that the preferred part kind, determined when you read the part in, is one of the values that you write.

5. Focus the storage unit on the contents property and on each of the part kinds of the data you are writing in turn. Write your data to the storage unit, using its `SetValue` method. Write one value for each part kind of data you store.

   If your part is a container part, you write persistent references to your embedded frames as part of writing your content. See "Storing and Retrieving Embedded Frames" on page 302.

6. Store references to your display frames, as described in "Storing and Retrieving Display Frames" on page 302.

7. Mark your part as clean (unchanged).

Typically, in writing your content you might write out just two values: one in the preferred part kind, and another in a standard, widely recognized part kind useful for data interchange. If your part editor supports many kinds, you might allow the user to select a single default kind, to avoid the creation of very large files full of redundant data.

IMPORTANT

Do not change the preferred kind that was specified when you read the part, even if you can easily convert the data to a higher-fidelity part kind. (You can, however, store a higher-fidelity part kind in addition to the preferred kind, if you wish.) Changing the preferred kind is implicit translation, and translation should always be controlled by the user. Maintain the preferred kind until the user instructs you to change it, as in the examples described in "Binding With Translation" on page 484. ▲

Your part can write its contents to its storage unit at any time, not just in response to a call to its `Externalize` method. However, changes to any parts in a document are actually made persistent only when the user performs an explicit save, and thus only when `Externalize` is called. If your part updates its storage unit but the user never saves the document, your changes are lost.

The ExternalizeKinds Method

Your part's `ExternalizeKinds` method can be called whenever your part is expected to save its data with a specific set of formats. For example, OpenDoc calls `ExternalizeKinds` when the user saves a copy of your part's document in multiple formats. A document-interchange utility or service might call the `ExternalizeKinds` method of all parts in a document to create a version of the document in which all data is written in one or more common standard part kinds.

When your part's `ExternalizeKinds` method is called, it is passed a list of part kinds. This is the method's interface:

```
void ExternalizeKinds(in ODTypeList kindSet);
```

The method should write as many of the specified part kinds as it supports, as well as your part's preferred kind. The method should ignore part kinds on the list that it does not support, and it should remove values (other than the preferred kind) from its storage unit that are not on the list. Just like `Externalize`, the `ExternalizeKinds` method should always write the part kinds in proper fidelity order, and it should not change the preferred kind.

Creating Additional Storage Units

Your part can use persistent references to create an auxiliary storage unit for keeping additional data. The auxiliary unit must be referenced from your part's main storage unit, using a strong persistent reference. In brief, you can follow these steps:

1. Call the `CreateStorageUnit` method of your part's draft to create the storage unit to hold the data.

2. Focus your part's main storage unit on the value in your contents property that is to contain the persistent reference. (It is not necessary to create a separate value to hold the reference.)

3. Create the persistent reference by calling the `GetStrongStorageUnitRef` method of your main storage unit.

4. Store the reference anywhere in the value; the only requirement is that you be able to recognize and retrieve the reference later. Write the value to persistent storage by calling the `SetValue` method of your main storage unit.

Your part can later retrieve the auxiliary storage unit from the main storage unit, in this way:

1. Focus the main storage unit on the value that contains the persistent reference.

2. Read the value, using the `GetValue` method of your main storage unit. Retrieve the persistent reference from the value's data.

3. Get the storage-unit ID of your auxiliary storage unit from the persistent reference by calling the `GetIDFromStorageUnitRef` method of your main storage unit.

4. Get the storage unit itself by passing its ID to the `AcquireStorageUnit` method of your draft.

How you store the data in your auxiliary storage unit is completely up to you. You can define your own properties, or you can keep the kinds of properties used in your main storage unit. If you define your own property names, avoid using constants for them that start with `kOD`; only OpenDoc-defined constants should use those characters.

Storing and Retrieving Display Frames

As noted in the section "Working With Your Display Frames and Facets" on page 106, your part should keep a private list of its display frames. It is further recommended that your part persistently store those display frames when it writes itself to storage and retrieve them when it reads itself from storage. Your part may need information on currently nonvisible, uninstantiated display frames so that it can perform frame synchronization (page 114) or frame negotiation (page 116).

If your part object includes a field that is a list of display-frame objects, your `InitPart` method can first create the field, and your `DisplayFrameAdded`, `DisplayFrameRemoved`, `DisplayFrameConnected`, and `DisplayFrameClosed` methods can add or delete elements of the list, as appropriate.

In this list you can keep additional information about the frames, such as what portion of your content (like a page number) each displays. That way, you can create only those frames that you currently need to manipulate, using the techniques described in "Lazy Internalization" on page 471.

You should store your list of frames in an annotation property in your part's storage unit. Your `Externalize` method should create a property with the name `kODPropDisplayFrames` in your storage unit and should write the frame list as weak storage unit references into a value of that property.

When reading your part from storage, your `InitPartFromStorage` method can focus on the `kODPropDisplayFrames` property and value, and read the list of stored display frames back into your display-frame field. (Be sure your `ReleaseAll` method releases any remaining display frames in that field; see "The ReleaseAll Method" on page 308.)

Storing and Retrieving Embedded Frames

Your part does not explicitly store the data of embedded parts; their own part editors take care of that. You do not even explicitly store the frame objects that you use; OpenDoc takes care of that. You do, however, store persistent references to the frames that are embedded in your part.

The process of storing an embedded frame for your part is simple. All you need to do is store a strong persistent reference to the embedded frame object; OpenDoc takes care of storing the frame itself. You follow the same steps that you take when creating and storing a reference to any storage unit (described in "Creating Additional Storage Units" on page 301):

1. Focus your storage unit on your contents property and on the value that is to contain the persistent reference to the embedded frame.

2. Create the persistent reference and place it in your contents data.

3. Write the data back into the value.

When your part is reinstantiated at a later time, your part can then retrieve the frame this way:

1. Focus the storage unit on the value containing the persistent reference.

2. Retrieve the reference.

3. Get the storage-unit ID of the frame.

4. Recreate the frame itself, by calling your draft's `AcquireFrame` method.

5. If you have previously stored information regarding a change to the frame's link status (see "The LinkStatusChanged Method of Your Part Editor" on page 378), set the frame's link status at this time. Link status is described in the section "Frame Link Status" on page 377.

For efficient memory use, you can create only those embedded frames that you currently need to manipulate or display, using the techniques described in "Lazy Internalization" on page 471.

Reading and Writing Part Info

As noted in the section "Part Info" on page 160, you can use the part info data of a frame or facet to store any display-related information you want to associate with that particular frame or facet. Because frames are persistent objects and facets are not, a frame's part info can be stored persistently, whereas a facet's part info cannot.

Just as you store multiple representations of your part's data, you should store multiple representations of your frames' part info, so that other editors can potentially read your part info as well as your part content. In that case, you should give your part info formats names equivalent to the part kinds with which they are associated. For example, if you write part data whose part kind is "SurfCorp:SurfWriter:StyledText", your associated part info data should be written in a value whose type is "SurfCorp:SurfWriter:StyledText:PartInfo".

If you also write your part data in a standard format such as PICT, RTF, or JPEG, you would not write associated part info for those formats, because they have no associated part info format.

As with other changes to the contents of your part's draft, any time you place or modify information in your display frame's part info data, you should follow the procedures listed in "Making Content Changes Known" on page 307. (If your frame is a nonpersistent frame, however, you do not need to make changes to it known.)

Whenever your document is saved, your part's `WritePartInfo` method is called for each of your part's display frames. Here is its interface:

```
void WritePartInfo(in ODPointer partInfo,
                   in ODStorageUnitView storageUnitView);
```

On receiving this call, you could first examine your part's own part-info dirty flag (if you have defined one) to see if this frame's part info has changed since it was read in from storage. If so, focus on as many values in the provided storage unit view as is appropriate and write your current part info into them. (Then clear the dirty flag.)

Conversely, whenever a display frame of your part is read into memory, your part's `ReadPartInfo` method is called. Here is its interface:

```
ODPtr ReadPartInfo(in ODFrame frame,
                   in ODStorageUnitView storageUnitView);
```

On receiving this call, you should allocate a structure to hold the part info, focus on the appropriate value in the provided storage-unit view, and read the data into your part-info structure. (Then initialize your part-info dirty flag to clean.)

Your part also writes part info data when its display frames are cloned; see "The ClonePartInfo Method of Your Part Editor" on page 329 for more information.

Changing Your Part's Content

Users can change the content of your part through a variety of standard editing actions involving keyboard input, menu commands, scripting, and so on. How you can support those tasks on the Mac OS platform is described throughout this book, with additional information in *Inside Macintosh* and other programming texts.

This section summarizes the content-changing tasks of adding and removing embedded parts, and it notes the ways in which you must keep OpenDoc and other parts informed when you make content changes of any kind.

Adding an Embedded Part

Embedding is a process that can combine elements of storage, layout, data transfer, menu handling, and control manipulation. This section summarizes the embedding process; the summary is presented in this chapter because embedding involves such a fundamental change to a part's storage configuration.

In terms of the stored persistent objects involved, embedding breaks down to these basic alternatives:

- Your part embeds either a new or preexisting frame into its content.

- The embedded frame displays the content of either a new or preexisting part.

You create a new frame to embed by calling your draft's `CreateFrame` method; you obtain an existing frame to embed by calling your draft's `AcquireFrame` method. In situations where you must explicitly instantiate the part object to embed, you create a new part by calling your draft's `CreatePart` method, or you obtain an existing part by calling your draft's `AcquirePart` method.

Detailed procedures for embedding a part within your part are described in the sections "Pasting From the Clipboard" on page 360, "Dropping" on page 368, "Insert" on page 249, and "Using a Tool Palette to Embed Parts" on page 241.

See those sections for more information. In summary, however, you perform these tasks when you embed:

1. You decide, based on your own part's content model and on information accompanying the transferred data, what area to give to the embedded part for display.

   ☐ You retrieve or define a frame shape for the embedded frame. (The part to be embedded may or may not arrive with a suggested frame or frame shape.)

   ☐ You decide where to position the embedded frame in your part's content; based on that position, you eventually create an external transform to use for positioning the facets of the embedded frame.

2. For each of your own part's display frames that is to show the embedded part, you create or retrieve a part object (if necessary), and then you create or retrieve a frame object.

   ☐ If the part you are embedding is already attached to a frame, ignore this step. If not, you must manipulate the part itself. Either retrieve the part object (as when embedding pasted content that has no preexisting frame or adding a new frame to an existing embedded part) or create a new part object (as when creating a new part from a palette).

   The embedded part is stored in your part's draft, but not in your part itself.

   ☐ Either retrieve the supplied frame object (as when embedding pasted content that comes with a display frame) or create a new frame object (as when adding a new frame to an existing embedded part or creating a new part from a palette). If you retrieved or created a part the previous step, attach that part to the frame.

   You store a reference to the frame somewhere in your part's content. The frame object itself is stored in your part's draft, but not in your part.

3. If the embedded part's frame is presently visible, you create a new facet (or facets) to display the embedded part.

4. As necessary or appropriate, you perform other tasks related to embedding, such as those described in the section "Working With Embedded Frames and Facets" on page 118. Finally, you notify OpenDoc and your own containing part that you have changed your part's content.

Removing an Embedded Part

To remove an embedded part from your part, you must remove all the facets of the part's display frame (your embedded frame), release or remove the embedded frame, and redisplay your own part's content. Follow the instructions in "Removing an Embedded Frame" on page 122.

This procedure illustrates the fact that your part is not actually concerned with removing embedded parts themselves. Under user instruction or for other reasons, your part may have reason to remove one or more embedded frames; once the last display frame of a given embedded part is removed from your part, that part is no longer embedded in your part.

Making Content Changes Known

Whenever you make any significant change to your part's content, whether it involves adding, deleting, moving, or otherwise modifying your intrinsic content or your embedded frames, you must make those changes known to OpenDoc and to all containing parts of your part.

- Call your draft's `SetChangedFromPrev` method. This call marks the draft as dirty, giving your part the opportunity to write itself to storage when the draft is closed.

- Call the `ContentUpdated` method of each of your part's display frames in which the change occurred, passing it an identifying update ID, obtained in one of three ways:

  □ returned from a call to the session object's `UniqueChangeID` method (if the content change originated in your part's intrinsic content)

  □ propagated from a link destination (see "Link Update ID" on page 374)

  □ propagated from a call to your `EmbeddedFrameUpdated` method (see "The EmbeddedFrameUpdated Method of Your Part Editor" on page 380)

  Calling `ContentUpdated` notifies your containing parts—and their containing parts, and so on—that your content has changed. The notification is necessary to allow all containing parts to update any link sources that they maintain.

You should call these methods as soon as is appropriate after making any content changes. You may not have to make the calls immediately after every minor change; it may be more efficient to wait for a pause in user input, for example, or until the active frame changes.

In addition to sending these notifications, you must of course also update your part's display if appropriate. This updating may involve adding or removing facets, adjusting intrinsic content, and invalidating areas that need to be redrawn.

Closing Your Part

When the user closes the document containing your part, or when your part is deleted from its containing part, OpenDoc calls your part's `ReleaseAll` method, followed by its `somUninit` method. (If, when closing a document, the user specifies that changes be saved, your part's `Externalize` method is called before `ReleaseAll`.)

The ReleaseAll Method

The `ReleaseAll` method is inherited from `ODPersistentObject`. Its purpose is to ensure that all your part's references to other objects and ownership of shared resources are relinquished before your part is itself deleted from memory. As a minimum, your override of the `ReleaseAll` method should

- call the `Release` methods of all reference-counted objects to which your part has references, including iterating through your part's private lists of embedded frames and display frames and releasing each one (at this point, all of them should have been released anyway)

- remove any link specifications your part has written to the clipboard

- fulfill any promises your part has written to the clipboard

- relinquish all foci that your part owns

- clear the undo stack if your part has written any undo actions to it

- call the `BaseRemoved` method of any of your part's extensions

- call the `PartRemoved` method of any embedded-frames iterators your part has created

Your part should not write itself to storage from within its `ReleaseAll` method.

Your part's Release method, inherited from ODRefCntObject, is called under different circumstances from ReleaseAll. For information on implementing a Release method, see the section "Reference-Counted Objects" on page 466.

The somUninit Method

After it completes ReleaseAll, your part receives no subsequent method calls except to its System Object Model (SOM) object destructor somUninit. The somUninit method is inherited from the somObject class of SOM; when you subclass ODPart, you must override somUninit.

Your somUninit method should dispose of any storage created for your part object by the somInit method and any other storage related to additional instance variables of your part initialized during execution. In this method, do not perform any tasks that could fail.

CHAPTER 8

Data Transfer

Contents

8

Data Transfer

This is the sixth of eight chapters that discuss the OpenDoc programming interface in detail. It describes how OpenDoc provides support for data-transfer operations.

Before reading this chapter, you should be familiar with the concepts presented in Chapter 1, "Introduction to OpenDoc," and Chapter 2, "Development Overview." You should also be familiar with OpenDoc storage concepts, as presented in the previous chapter. For additional concepts related to your part editor's runtime environment, see Chapter 11, "OpenDoc Runtime Features."

This chapter describes general issues common to all data-transfer methods and then describes how your part can support

- clipboard data transfer

- drag-and-drop data transfer

- linking

Storage Issues for Data Transfer

This section introduces some of the storage-related concepts used in clipboard transfer, drag and drop, and linking, which are described in the remaining sections of this chapter.

For the purposes of this section, the term *data-transfer object* means any of the following: the clipboard or drag-and-drop object (when reading or writing data), a link-source object (when writing linked data), or a link object (when reading linked data).

Data Configuration

When a part places data on the clipboard or other data-transfer object, it writes a portion or all of its intrinsic content to the data-transfer object, and it also can cause the contents of one or more embedded parts to be written.

Whatever the nature of the data, once it is written to the data-transfer object it can be considered an independent part. It has its own intrinsic content and it may contain embedded parts. In writing or reading the data, your part is directly concerned only with the characteristics (such as part kind) of the intrinsic content that is transferred. Any embedded parts are transferred unchanged—as embedded parts—during the process.

The storage unit that holds the data-transfer object's intrinsic content is called its **content storage unit.** It is equivalent to a part's main storage unit (see "Main and Auxiliary Storage Units" on page 283). Any embedded parts in the transferred data, and any other OpenDoc objects, have their own storage units.

Note
A link object or a link-source object is a persistent object, and as such has its own main storage unit. That storage unit is not the same as its content storage unit. Always access the content of a data-transfer object by calling its `GetContentStorageUnit` method. ◆

More specifically, the data-transfer object's intrinsic content is stored in the contents property (type `kODPropContents`) of the content storage unit. When writing to a data-transfer object, your part can store data in multiple formats in different values of the contents property. As with any part, each value in the contents property must be complete; it must not depend on other properties or other values of the property.

Your part accesses other properties besides the contents property in a data-transfer object. For example, when your part writes data to a data-transfer object, it may also write—into a separate property—a frame object or a frame shape for the destination part to use when constructing a display frame. See "Annotations" (next) for more information.

Objects in memory take precedence over their stored versions in data transfer. If the user cuts or copies a part's frame to the clipboard or other data-transfer object, the moved data represents the current state of the part, including any edits that have not yet been saved to disk.

Annotations

This section discusses the items, in addition to part content, that you can write to or read from the storage unit of a data-transfer object.

Link Specification

When copying content to the clipboard or drag-and-drop object, a part advertises its ability to create a link by writing a **link specification** in addition to content. When you copy data to the clipboard or drag-and-drop object, you should create a link specification—using your draft's `CreateLinkSpec` method—in case the user chooses to link to the data when pasting or dropping it in the destination. The sections "Writing Intrinsic Content" on page 341 and "Writing a Single Embedded Part" on page 342 specify when you should write a link specification.

Write the link specification onto the content storage unit of the clipboard or drag-and-drop object as a property with the name `kODPropLinkSpec`. The data in a link specification is private to the part writing it. The data you place in your link specification is returned to your part if and when your part's `CreateLink` method is called to create the link. All that your part needs from the link specification data is sufficient information to identify the selected content.

Because the link specification is valid only for the duration of the current instantiation of your part, the link specification can contain pointers to information that you maintain.

Link specifications are not necessary in the following situations:

- when you place content on the clipboard as a result of a cut operation. You cannot link data that is no longer in your part. (Because you cannot know at the start whether a drag will be a move or a copy, you should always write a link specification when you write data to the drag-and-drop object.)

- when you write all or a portion of a link destination (or any of your part's content, if your part itself is in a link destination) to the clipboard or drag-and-drop object. Creating a link in that situation could make your link destination the source of another link. That configuration is technically possible but generally bad practice. (See Table 8-4 on page 400 for an explanation.)

- when your draft permissions are read-only (see "Drafts" on page 285). You would not be able to establish links to other parts of the same (read-only) document, and any links to other documents would be broken when your draft closed.

- when you are writing to a link-source object. Link specifications are for the clipboard or drag-and-drop object only. Link specifications are transitory, whereas links are persistent.

When you write a link specification to the clipboard, obtain and save the clipboard update ID (see "Clipboard Update ID" on page 357). You must remove a link specification from the clipboard if your source data changes and the clipboard data therefore no longer reflects it; you need the update ID to test for that situation. See "Removing a Link Specification From the Clipboard" on page 357. (You never need to remove a link specification from the drag-and-drop object, because it is valid only during the course of a single drag operation.)

Note
The kODPropLinkSpec property is not copied when the storage unit containing it is cloned. ◆

Frame Shape or Frame Annotation

When you place intrinsic content (with or without embedded frames) on the clipboard or other data-transfer object, there is no frame associated with that content. You should, nevertheless, write a frame shape to the data-transfer object to accompany the content; the shape is a suggestion to any part that reads the data and must embed it as a separate part. You write the frame shape into a property named kODPropSuggestedFrameShape in the data-transfer object's content storage unit.

Likewise, if your part receives a paste or drop from the data-transfer object and embeds the intrinsic data, your part should examine the kODPropSuggestedFrameShape property to get the source part's suggested frame shape for the data. If the kODPropSuggestedFrameShape property does not exist, use your own part-specific default shape.

If you place one of your embedded parts (in the form of a single embedded frame) on the clipboard or other data-transfer object, you must place the frame object there also. You write the frame into a property with the name kODPropContentFrame in a storage unit of the data-transfer object's draft.

Likewise, if your part receives a paste or drop from the data-transfer object, you can note from the presence of the kODPropContentFrame property that the data represents a single frame that should be embedded (according to the guidelines presented in "Embedding Transferred Data" on page 593), and you can retrieve the frame from the property.

When you transfer a single embedded frame, you can specify the frame location relative to your part's content (that is, the offset specified in the external transform of the frame's facet) by incorporating the offset into the frame shape that you write. Then, the receiving part of the paste or drop can, if appropriate to its content model, use that offset to construct an external transform.

Note

Neither the `kODPropSuggestedFrameShape` nor the `kODPropContentFrame` property is copied when the storage unit containing it is cloned. ◆

Proxy Content

When you write a single embedded frame to a data-transfer object, you can optionally write any intrinsic data that you want to associate with the frame. The intrinsic data might be a drop shadow or other visual adornment for the frame, or it might be information needed to reconstruct the frame as a link source or link destination.

This information is called **proxy content.** To write it, you add a property (of type `kODPropProxyContents`) to the data-transfer object and write your data into it as a value that your part recognizes. If the transferred part is subsequently embedded into a part that also recognizes that value and knows how to interpret it, the added frame characteristics can be duplicated.

Likewise, if your part receives a paste or drop and embeds the single part, you can note from the presence of the `kODPropProxyContents` property that proxy content for that frame exists. If your part understands the format of the proxy content—which you should be able to determine by examining the value types in the property—you can read it and duplicate the frame characteristics.

Note

The `kODPropProxyContents` property is not copied when the storage unit containing it is cloned. ◆

Cloning-Kind Annotation

When a single embedded part is written to a data-transfer object, its containing part writes a property with the name `kODPropCloneKindUsed` to the data-transfer object. The property specifies the kind of cloning transaction used to clone the embedded part. The embedded part, if it writes a promise instead of actual data to the data-transfer object, uses the information in the `kODPropCloneKindUsed` property when it later fulfills the promise.

For more information, see "Writing a Single Embedded Part" on page 342 and "Fulfilling a Promise" on page 331.

Mouse-Down Offset Annotation

If your part initiates a drag operation (see "Initiating a Drag" on page 364), you need to create a property of type `kODPropMouseDownOffset` in the drag-and-drop object's storage unit. Write into that property a value that specifies the location of the mouse-down event that triggered the drag. The value should be of type `ODPoint` and should contain the offset from the origin of the content being dragged. (On the Mac OS, the origin of any shape is its upper-left corner.)

If your part receives a drop, it should likewise check for the presence of the `kODPropMouseDownOffset` property. If the property exists, and if taking it into account is consistent with your part's content model, use it to locate the dropped content in relation to the mouse-up event that marks the drop.

Note
The `kODPropMouseDownOffset` property is not copied when the storage unit containing it is cloned. ◆

Clonable Data Annotation Prefix

In some situations an entity may need to store properties in the storage unit of a part or other object without the knowledge or cooperation of the part itself. For example, a service such as a spelling checker might store a dictionary of exceptions as a property of a part's storage unit. The part is unaware of the existence of that property, but the spelling checker would want the dictionary cloned whenever the part is cloned.

When a storage unit itself is cloned (see "Cloning," next), all its properties are copied, no matter who wrote them into the storage unit. However, the in-memory version of an object is given preference over its storage unit during cloning, because recent, unsaved changes to the object should be included in the cloning operation. Unfortunately, when an in-memory object clones itself, any of its properties that the object itself is unaware of are not cloned, because it does not know to write them into the destination storage unit.

To get around this difficulty, OpenDoc defines the property prefix constant `kODPropPreAnnotation`, whose value is the OpenDoc ISO prefix plus "OpenDoc:Annotation:". When the property prefix constant is part of a property name (such as, for example, the OpenDoc ISO prefix plus "OpenDoc:Annotation:Exceptions") in an object's storage unit, OpenDoc always copies that property when the object is cloned, even if the object being cloned is in memory and regardless of whether the object is aware of the existence of the property.

Therefore, if you store data in another object that the object itself does not use but that you want to be cloned along with the object, make sure you store it in a property whose name starts with the string defined by `kODPropPreAnnotation`.

Cloning

You should always transfer data to and from the clipboard or other data-transfer object in the context of cloning. This section describes how cloning works, what the scope of a cloning operation is, and how to implement your part editor's `CloneInto` method.

To clone an object is to copy the object itself as well as the objects that it references, plus any objects that those objects reference, and so on. Typically, copies are made of all storage units—or their equivalent, instantiated persistent objects—that are referenced with strong persistent references, starting with the object being cloned. Storage units referenced only with weak persistent references are not copied. See the section "Persistent References" on page 279 and Figure 7-5 on page 283 for more information on how strong and weak persistent references affect cloning.

Actually, each object that is cloned during the operation decides—if it is in memory at the time—which of its own storage unit's properties and which of its referenced objects should be included. If the object is not currently instantiated, all of its storage unit's properties and all of its strongly referenced objects are copied.

The Cloning Sequence

All persistent objects have a `CloneInto` method by which they clone themselves, but your part editor should not call the `CloneInto` method of any object directly. Instead, you clone an object by calling the `Clone` (or `WeakClone`) method of its draft object. The `Clone` method in turn calls the `CloneInto` method of the object involved. (Your parts, as persistent objects, must provide a `CloneInto` method. See "The CloneInto Method of Your Part Editor" on page 327 for more information.)

Cloning is a multistep transaction, designed so that it can be terminated cleanly if it fails at any point. You perform a clone by calling the following three methods, in order.

BeginClone

First, call the `BeginClone` method of the draft object of the data to be cloned. If you are transferring data from your part, call your part's draft object; if you are transferring data from a data-transfer object, call that object's draft object. `BeginClone` sets up the cloning transaction.

(If you are cloning because your part is receiving a paste or drop, you must also specify the destination frame, the display frame of your part that is receiving the paste or drop.)

When you call `BeginClone`, you are returned a **draft key,** a number that identifies that specific cloning transaction. You pass that key to the other cloning methods that you call during the transaction. You also specify (in the `kind` parameter to the `BeginClone` method) the kind of transaction to be performed, so that OpenDoc can maintain the proper behavior for linked data being transferred. Table 8-1 lists the kinds of cloning transactions that OpenDoc recognizes. The section "Transfer Rules for Links and Link Sources" on page 398 explains how these different types of transactions result in different behavior for links.

Table 8-1   Kinds of cloning transactions

`kind` **parameter**	**Meaning**
`kODCloneCopy`	Copy object from source to data-transfer object
`kODCloneCut`	Cut object from source to data-transfer object
`kODClonePaste`	Paste object from clipboard to destination
`kODCloneDropCopy`	Copy object to the destination of a drop
`kODCloneDropMove`	Move object to the destination of a drop
`kODCloneToLink`	Copy object from source to update a link source
`kODCloneFromLink`	Copy object from link to update a destination

Even when transferring only intrinsic content (and not actually cloning any objects), you should still bracket your transfer with calls to `BeginClone` and `EndClone`. That way, you notify OpenDoc of the kind of operation (such as cut or copy) that is being performed, and you ensure that the right actions occur at both the source and destination of the transfer.

Clone

For each object that you are cloning, call the draft's `Clone` method. `Clone` allows the draft object to specify and recursively locate all objects to be cloned. It calls the `CloneInto` method of the object to be copied, which results in calls to the `CloneInto` methods of all referenced objects, and so on. For example, when `Clone` calls the `CloneInto` method of a part, the part clones its embedded frames; the embedded frames in turn clone the parts they display, and so on.

(You sometimes call the draft's `WeakClone` method instead of `Clone`, especially when you are cloning within the context of your own `CloneInto` method. See "The CloneInto Method of Your Part Editor" on page 327 for more information.)

Take these steps when calling the `Clone` method:

1. First, obtain an object ID to pass to `Clone`.

   □ If you are cloning from a data-transfer object into your draft, make sure that the object you are cloning is valid. Starting with the persistent reference that specifies the object to be cloned, call the `IsValidStorageUnitRef` method of the storage unit or storage unit view that contains the persistent reference. Never assume that a persistent reference is valid.

   Then, get the object's ID (see "Storage-Unit IDs" on page 278) from the persistent reference by calling the `GetIDFromStorageUnitRef` method of the storage unit.

   □ If you are cloning from your draft into a data-transfer object, your access to the objects to be cloned may be through object references instead of persistent references. In that case, get an object ID by calling the referenced object's `GetID` method.

2. Pass the object ID to the `Clone` method.

3. Save the resulting object ID that `Clone` returns, along with the IDs returned from other calls to `Clone`, until cloning is complete and you have called `EndClone`. (See "EndClone," next.)

   (If you are not actually cloning objects but simply reading or writing intrinsic data, this is the point at which to read or write, instead of calling `Clone`.)

In cloning, the in-memory version of an object takes precedence over its stored version. For this reason, an object does not need to be written to storage prior to being cloned. If the object is in memory, its `CloneInto` method is called to perform the clone; if the object is not in memory, its storage unit performs the clone operation.

This convention also means that, if an object is in memory, properties attached to its storage unit that the object itself does not know about might not be copied, unless they are specially named. See "Clonable Data Annotation Prefix" on page 320 for an explanation.

Null IDs when cloning links

The `Clone` method returns a value of `kODNullID` if the desired object cannot be cloned. For example, `Clone` does not allow you to clone a link object or link-source object into a link, and it returns `kODNullID` if you attempt to do so. In this case, because you cannot clone the object, you should delete any data associated with it that you have written into the data-transfer object. However, in the case of a link or link source, you should still write the content formerly associated with the object, but as unlinked content. ◆

Annotation properties not cloned

When data is cloned from a data-transfer object, most of the annotation properties (such as `kODPropLinkSpec`) that the source part may have added to the content storage unit are not transferred, because they make no sense as properties outside of the data-transfer object. If you clone a storage unit from a data-transfer object and need these properties, you must read them from the data-transfer object's storage unit, not from the cloned storage unit. ◆

EndClone

Finally, call the draft's `EndClone` method. `EndClone` commits to and actually performs the cloning operation. After `EndClone` completes, you can then use or reconnect the cloned objects.

1. Pass each returned object ID that you have saved to your draft's `IsValidID` method to determine if the object was cloned.

2. If `IsValidID` returns true, you can at this point reconstruct either the cloned object in memory or a persistent reference to it:

   ☐ If you are cloning from a data-transfer object into your draft and `IsValidID` returns true, call your draft's `Acquire`*Object* method to read in the object and obtain a reference to it.

   ☐ If you are cloning from your draft into a data-transfer object and if `IsValidID` returns true, call the `GetStrongStorageUnitRef` or `GetWeakStorageUnitRef` method of the cloned storage unit, as appropriate. Store the persistent reference in the appropriate location in the contents property of the cloned storage unit.

3. If `IsValidID` returns false, the object was not cloned and you should exclude it from the data you are reading or writing.

If, at any time after calling `BeginClone`, the operation cannot be completed, you can terminate the transaction by calling the `AbortClone` method instead of `EndClone`.

IMPORTANT

You cannot instantiate and use any cloned object until the entire cloning operation is complete. If you are cloning several parts and link objects, for example, you cannot call `AcquirePart` or `AcquireLink` until you have cloned all of the objects and `EndClone` has successfully returned. ▲

The Scope of a Clone Operation

For cloning, the **scope** defines the set of objects that are to be included in the cloning operation. Scope is expressed in terms of a frame object or its storage unit.

Because a part can have more than one display frame and because each frame can include a separate set of embedded frames and parts, it is important to specify the frame whose enclosed objects are to be cloned. Otherwise, extra embedded parts or other objects not needed by the copy may be included unnecessarily. (You can specify null for the scope of a clone if you want all objects copied, regardless of what display frame they are associated with.)

In the example shown in Figure 8-1, the user has selected some content in the root part that includes display frame 1 of embedded part A. The root part writes its intrinsic content and then clones part A, passing it a scope of frame A1. Any content that belongs only to frame A2 (such as part C) is not included in the clone.

Figure 8-1   Scope in cloning

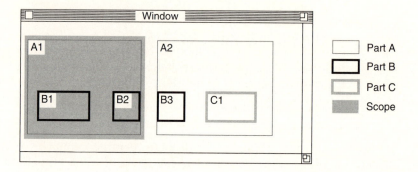

Scope changes during the course of a clone. Continuing the example shown in Figure 8-1, Figure 8-2 demonstrates how part A clones itself in the context of the scope (frame A1) specified by the root part. Part A writes the intrinsic content of its display frame A1 and then clones part B twice, first passing it a scope of frame B1 and then a scope of frame B2. Part B thus gets called to clone itself twice, with different scopes. Any content of B within frames B1 and B2 is included, but any content that belongs only to frame B3 is not.

Figure 8-2   Change in scope as more deeply embedded parts are cloned

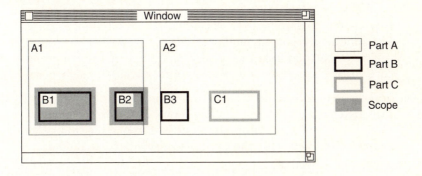

The CloneInto Method of Your Part Editor

If your part is an embedded part that is written to the clipboard (or other data-transfer object), your part's override of its inherited `CloneInto` method is called by your draft's `Clone` method. This is the interface to `CloneInto`:

```
void CloneInto(in ODDraftKey key,
               in ODStorageUnit toSU,
               in ODFrame scope);
```

Your `CloneInto` method is passed a draft key for the clone operation and a frame that defines the scope of the cloning. The method should write your part's intrinsic content to the provided storage unit, and it should clone in turn any objects (such as embedded frames or auxiliary storage units) that it references. It needn't clone any objects or write any data that is outside the scope.

Note
Do not implement your `CloneInto` method by writing your part to storage and then cloning your storage unit. Doing so would levy performance penalties because of the extra time needed to store your data. Also, it could result in the copying of unneeded objects because the scope of the clone would be ignored. ◆

To support efficient data transfer, your part should, if possible, write a promise (see "Promises" on page 330) instead of writing its actual intrinsic data when `CloneInto` is called. It is possible to write a promise only when your part is placed into the data-transfer object as a single, stand-alone frame with no surrounding intrinsic content of its containing part. In any other situation, your `CloneInto` method might have been called to help fulfill a promise, in which case writing a promise would be inappropriate.

You can determine whether you can write a promise by examining the provided storage unit. If it contains a property with the name `kODPropContentFrame`, your part alone is stored in the storage unit's contents property, and you can write a promise instead of actual data.

When you write a promise, be sure to identify (to yourself) the display frame or frames of your part that are within the scope of the clone operation, so that your `FulfillPromise` method can write the proper content when it is called.

Take these general steps in your `CloneInto` method:

1. Check whether your part has already been cloned in this operation. Because an object can be referenced more than once, its `CloneInto` method can be called more than once in a single cloning operation. In general, if a contents property already exists in the storage unit passed in the method, your part has already been cloned and there is no need to repeat the process.

   An exception to this rule occurs when scope is significant. If your part is called to clone itself with different scopes during the same operation (see, for example, Figure 8-2 on page 327), it may have to write additional data each time its `CloneInto` method is called.

2. Call your inherited `CloneInto` method.

3. If it does not already exist, add a property named `kODPropContents` to the provided storage unit.

   (You do not have to call `BeginClone`; that method will already have been called. Also, you do not have to add properties other than the contents property; OpenDoc will add your part's name and any other needed annotations.)

4. Check whether you can write a promise. Look for a property with the name `kODPropContentFrame` in the storage unit. (It is not required that any value yet exist in the property; the caller of your `CloneInto` method may write the value after cloning completes.)

5. Focus on the contents property, and write a value for each part kind you support. Either write a promise or the data of your part itself, using either the storage unit's `SetPromiseValue` or `SetValue` method, respectively.

(For data transfer, it is especially important to write a standard format in addition to your own native part kind, because the ultimate destination of the transferred data is unknown.)

6. Clone all objects that your part references (and that are within the scope of the cloning operation), as follows:

   ☐ For each object to which your part has a strong persistent reference, call your draft's `Clone` method to clone the object, passing the same draft key that was passed to your `CloneInto` method. Pass a new scope, if appropriate; for example, if you are cloning an embedded frame (and thus its part), that frame is the new scope.

   ☐ For each object to which your part has a weak persistent reference, call your draft's `WeakClone` method, passing the appropriate draft key and scope.

   (Calling `WeakClone` does not by itself cause an object to be copied; it only ensures that, if the object ends up being copied because of an existing strong persistent reference to it, your part's weak persistent reference will be maintained across the cloning operation.)

The ClonePartInfo Method of Your Part Editor

Whenever your part's display frame is cloned during data transfer, the frame calls your part's `ClonePartInfo` method.

```
void ClonePartInfo(in ODDraftKey key,
                   in ODInfoType partInfo,
                   in ODStorageUnitView storageUnitView,
                   in ODFrame scope);
```

You should respond to this method call by writing your part info into the provided storage unit view (regardless of the state of your part-info dirty flag) and cloning any objects referenced in your part info data.

Promises

Clipboard transfer, drag and drop, and linking can all make use of promises. A **promise** is a specification of data to be transferred at a future time. If a data transfer involves a very large amount of data, the source part can choose to write a promise instead of actually writing the data to a storage unit. When another part retrieves the data, the source part must then fulfill the promise. The destination part does not know that a promise is being fulfilled; it simply accepts the data as usual.

The format of a promise is completely determined by the source part. The only restriction is that the promise must be able to be written to a storage-unit value.

You are encouraged to write promises in place of actual data in most cases; it minimizes memory requirements and increases performance.

Writing a Promise

Your part can follow these steps to write a promise when it is the source of a data transfer—that is, when it responds to a mouse-down event that initiates a drag, or when it copies data to the clipboard, or when it updates a link source.

1. Gain access to the content storage unit of the data-transfer object. See, for example, the initial steps under "Copying or Cutting to the Clipboard" on page 359, "Initiating a Drag" on page 364, and "Updating a Link at the Source" on page 389. Focus the storage unit on the contents property (kODPropContents).

2. Prepare your promise. It can have any content and format you decide; you must be able to read it later and reconstruct the exact data that is to be transferred.

3. Write the promise into a single value of the storage unit, using the storage unit's SetPromiseValue method. Your promise must include at least this information:

   □ A specification of the actual content that is to be delivered later.

   □ A specification of the display frame (or frames) of your part involved in the data transfer. When you fulfill the promise, you can then supply the proper scope for the cloning operation.

   □ A specification of the proper kind of cloning transaction (such as kODCloneCopy or kODCloneCut) to apply when you fulfill the promise.

4. Write other needed information. You needn't at this stage clone any frames or read any actual content into the data-transfer object. However, you should—as usual—create a link specification, obtain an update ID, write a suggested frame shape, and so on, as described in "Writing Intrinsic Content" on page 341 and "Writing a Single Embedded Part" on page 342.

Each promise you write is for a single part kind. You can write several promises representing data of several kinds, so that the destination part has a better chance of being able to incorporate the data instead of embedding it. (Because promises are private data, the actual content of all of your promises can be the same, regardless of the part kind being promised. When you are called to fulfill the promise, you can inspect the provided storage-unit view object to find out which part kind is needed.)

Because a promise is valid only for the duration of the current instantiation of your part, the promise can contain pointers to information that you maintain.

Getting Data From a Value Containing a Promise

When the `Drop` method of a destination part retrieves the data from a drop, or when a destination part reads data from the clipboard (using the `GetValue` or `GetSize` method of the dragged data's or clipboard's storage unit), the source part is called to fulfill the promise. The destination part does not even know that a promise is being fulfilled; it follows the procedures described in the section "Reading From a Data-Transfer Object" on page 344 and uses the same code whether the value contains a promise or not.

Fulfilling a Promise

OpenDoc calls your source part's `FulfillPromise` method when a promise must be fulfilled, passing it a storage-unit view object that contains the data of the promise. This is its interface:

```
void FulfillPromise(in ODStorageUnitView promiseSUView);
```

In your implementation of the method, take steps similar to these:

1. Examine the private information that you wrote into the promise earlier, to determine what data to write.

2. Look for a property named `kODPropCloneKindUsed` in the storage-unit view passed to you. Your containing part may have placed the property there if your part was being cloned as a single embedded frame when your part

wrote the promise. If the property exists, it contains a value of type
kODCloneKind that specifies the kind of cloning transaction (such as
kODCloneCopy or kODCloneCut) that you must use in fulfilling the promise.

If the property does not exist, use information that you saved when you
wrote the promise to determine the kind of cloning transaction to use.

3. Begin a cloning operation (call to BeginClone).

4. Retrieve the actual data that the promise represents and write it into the
   provided storage-unit view object, following the steps described in "The
   Cloning Sequence" on page 321. You can clone frames and other objects as
   usual at this time.

5. End the cloning operation (call EndClone).

When your FulfillPromise method completes, the destination part receives
the data.

When you fulfill a promise, be sure to supply the source content that was
selected at the time the promise was written, even if that content no longer
exists in your part.

If fulfilling your promise requires cloning, you must specify the scope and the
appropriate kind of cloning transaction. If you have saved that information in
the promise itself, extract it and pass it to your draft's BeginClone and Clone
methods, respectively.

At some times your part may have to fulfill a promise on its own, without its
FulfillPromise method having been called. For example, when your part
closes, your part's ReleaseAll method (see "Closing Your Part" on page 308)
must fulfill all outstanding promises. To fulfill a promise in that manner, your
part must always keep a record of the promises (and their update IDs) that it
has written. Then, in ReleaseAll, it can

- access the clipboard content storage unit and verify the clipboard update ID
  against the part's stored update ID

- access each value that it has written and verify that it is a promise by calling
  the storage unit's IsPromiseValue method

- extract the promise from the value, fulfill it, and write the fulfilled data back
  into the value

You can also force fulfillment of one of your promises by focusing on the
promised value and calling the GetSize method of its storage unit. That causes
your FulFillPromise method to be called immediately.

Translation

The OpenDoc translation object, implemented on each platform as a subclass of `ODTranslation`, is a wrapper for platform-specific translation services. OpenDoc and part editors can use the translation object to convert part data from one format (part kind) to another.

Through the translation object, OpenDoc maintains information on what kinds of translations are available on the user's system. OpenDoc and part editors can then use the translation object to perform any requested translations, rather than directly calling the platform-specific translation service.

Translation should generally occur only with explicit user approval and instruction. OpenDoc initiates translation in the situations described in the section "Binding With Translation" on page 484. Your part editor can initiate translation in these situations:

- When embedding or incorporating parts through clipboard paste or through drag and drop, your part editor performs translation if the user specifies—in the Paste As dialog box—a part kind that requires translation. See the section "Handling the Paste As Dialog Box" on page 337 for more information.

- Your part editor performs translation when updating a link destination for which the user specified translation in the Paste As dialog box when originally creating the link.

The user specifies the specific translation to perform by selecting a new part kind in the kind pop-up menu (see Figure 8-4 on page 338) of the Paste As dialog box.

To set up the information in the pop-up menu, OpenDoc examines each part kind in the part and determines, from the translation object, the new part kinds (supported by available editors) to which the original part kind can be translated. OpenDoc then presents those choices to the user.

Once the user selects a part kind, your part editor calls the translation object to perform the translation. It is possible for the user to request translation to a part kind that your part editor cannot read. In such a case, you perform the translation but embed the data as a part, and another editor (also chosen by the user) is then bound to the data that you have translated.

The translation object allows only one-step translation; conversion can be only from the existing part kind directly to the part kind selected by the user. Note also that translation applies only to the outermost (intrinsic) portion of the data; parts embedded within it are not translated.

For detailed procedures to follow in translating transferred data, see "Translating Before Incorporating or Embedding" on page 351.

Converting between part kinds and Mac OS file types
The translation object provides some services in addition to translation. For example, suppose you have part data expressed as a Mac OS file type and you need to express it as a part kind (ISO string). You can use the `GetISOTypeFromPlatformType` method of the translation object to find out if there is a part kind equivalent to that file type. To convert in the opposite direction, you can use the `GetPlatformTypeFromISOType` method instead. ◆

Handling Cut Data

The user can remove data from your part by selecting the Cut command or by using drag and drop to move (rather than copy) data from your part into another part. In this event, you need to take extra steps to account for the fact that the data is still valid but is no longer in your part, and also to allow the action to be undone. Keep these points in mind:

■ Cutting must be an undoable action. If the data cut from your part includes references to objects such as embedded frames or link objects, you should retain those references in an undo action (see "Adding an Action to the Undo Action History" on page 262). However, your part's content should release its references to the objects. Set the in-limbo flag of each cut embedded frame appropriately (see Table 6-4 on page 266).

Once the objects are no longer needed for undo support, OpenDoc calls your `DisposeActionState` method. You should then either release them entirely or remove them from your draft, depending on whether other valid references to them remain. (Follow the guidelines listed in Table 6-4 on page 266.) See also "Undo for Clipboard" on page 358 and "Undo for Drag and Drop" on page 364 for related information.

■ When you cut an embedded frame to a data-transfer object, call the `SetContainingFrame` method of the cut frame, setting its containing frame to null and severing it from your part's embedding hierarchy.

■ Remove the facets of the cut frame. To access the facets of a frame that the user has drag-moved out of your part, use the embedded-facet iterator of your own display facet. For each facet to be removed, call its containing facet's `RemoveFacet` method and then delete the facet object itself, as described in the section "Removing a Facet" on page 125.

■ If you have more than one frame displaying an embedded part, remember that removing the embedded part from one of your display frames does not automatically remove it from the others. If the removed frame is synchronized with embedded frames in your other display frames, for example, you must remove those embedded frames also.

■ Do not create a link specification for the data you have cut; the data no longer belongs to your part.

■ If the data you cut to the data-transfer object includes a link source, you must call the `SetSourcePart` method of the link source object in your own draft, passing it a null value. That action relinquishes your part's ownership of the link source (except that you retain a reference to it in your undo data). Even if you write a promise instead of actual data, call `SetSourcePart` at this time; don't wait until the promise must be fulfilled.

■ If you write a promise to the clipboard when cutting data from your part, you can later fulfill that promise using either a `kODCloneCut` or `kODCloneCopy` transaction (unless the storage-unit view contains a `kODPropCloneKindUsed` property; see "Fulfilling a Promise" on page 331). You have this flexibility because the same promise may need to be fulfilled during a paste immediately following the cut, or to subsequent pastes that do not follow the cut. Therefore, you must take all cut-specific actions at the time you write the promise (or, if the cut is undone, when you handle the undo action).

■ If you have cut data from your part and cloned it to the clipboard or drag-and-drop object, OpenDoc may use the actual objects that were cut from your draft—not clones of them—when providing the data to be pasted or dropped into a destination. Therefore, it is important to release, rather than delete, objects (embedded frames, links, and so on) that you cut from your part. Likewise, if you paste data into your part and then the user selects Undo, make sure that you release rather than delete the objects that you remove in the course of reversing the paste operation.

Handling Pasted or Dropped Data

When data is pasted or dropped into a part, the part receiving the data can either embed the data as a separate part or incorporate the data as intrinsic content. The part may also in some circumstances translate the data, or it might even refuse to accept the pasted data.

This section discusses how OpenDoc and your part editor make these decisions, both with and without explicit user intervention. It also discusses when your part editor might explicitly translate data.

Default Conventions

In the absence of other instructions, OpenDoc expects your part to follow these specific conventions when pasting data from the clipboard or when accepting dropped data during a drag-and-drop operation. The conventions are explained further in the user-interface guidelines given in the sections "Incorporating Transferred Data" on page 593 and "Embedding Transferred Data" on page 593.

- If the transferred data consists of an arbitrary portion of the source part's intrinsic content—plus possibly one or more embedded parts—the destination part either incorporates or embeds that outer intrinsic content, according to these rules:

    □ If any of the representations of the outer data are of a part kind directly readable by the destination part editor, the editor should incorporate the outer data into the intrinsic content of the destination part and embed any parts that were embedded in the outer data.

    □ If none of the representations of the outer data is readable by the destination part editor, the editor should transfer the data as a single part (plus any embedded parts), and embed the part in a frame in the destination.

- If the transferred data represents a single embedded frame that was cut or copied (or dragged), the destination part editor should embed the data as a separate part into the destination part, regardless of whether its part kind is different from or identical to that of the destination.

The destination part should place clipboard data at the insertion point; it should place dropped data at the point where the user releases the mouse button. Note also that a pasted or dropped part takes on the view type that its containing part prefers it to have; see "Preferred View Type for Embedded Parts" on page 513 for guidelines.

Handling the Paste As Dialog Box

The Paste As dialog box allows the user to override OpenDoc and specify whether transferred data is to be embedded, incorporated, or translated and then embedded or incorporated. It also allows the user to create a link to the source of the transferred data.

When the user chooses the Paste As command in the Edit menu (see "Paste As" on page 253), the active part calls the clipboard's ShowPasteAsDialog method to display the Paste As dialog box, shown in Figure 8-3. A part at the destination of a drop also displays this dialog box if the user holds down the Command key while performing a drop; see "Dropping" on page 368.

Figure 8-3   The Paste As dialog box

The user can select the following options from the dialog box:

■ Paste with Link. The user can request that a link be created between the source and destination data. This option is not available if no link specification accompanies the data to be pasted. Disable this option if your part does not support linking.

■ Get Updates [of a link] Automatically/Manually. If the user creates a link, the user selects one of these options to specify whether updates are to be automatic or manual. See "Automatic and Manual Updating" on page 375 for more information.

■ Merge with Contents. If the user selects this option, the destination part editor is expected to incorporate the data if at all possible, even if doing so requires translation and great loss of information (such as converting text to a bitmap).

When your part editor displays the dialog box, it can check the part kinds available in the data-transfer object and specify whether this option is enabled and whether it is selected by default. Disable this option if your part cannot incorporate the data even after translation.

■ Embed As. If the user selects this option, the source data must be embedded in the destination as a separate part, even if incorporation is possible.

When your part editor displays the dialog box, it can check the part kinds available in the data-transfer object and specify whether this option is enabled and whether it is checked by default. Disable this option if your part does not support embedding.

If the user selects Embed As, the user can also make the following selections:

☐ Kind [of pasted data]. With this option, the user can override OpenDoc's default pasting decision and explicitly specify a destination part kind from a pop-up menu. If translation to other part kinds is possible, the user can select the Translate To command from the Kind pop-up menu shown in Figure 8-4.

Figure 8-4   The Kind pop-up menu in the Paste As dialog box

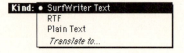

The user can then choose a translated part kind from the Translation for Paste dialog box shown in Figure 8-5.

Figure 8-5   The Translation for Paste dialog box

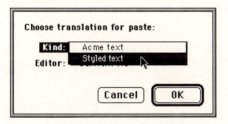

This option (choosing part kind) is not available if the transferred data consists of a single frame that is being moved (not copied) from its original source. The moved frame may not be the only frame displaying its part, and changing its kind would then affect the display in the other parts, which may not be the user's intent.

☐ Editor. From the Editor pop-up menu, the user can specify a new editor for the part. Only part editors that can read the currently selected part kind appear in the menu.

☐ View type. From a pop-up menu, the user can choose the view type the embedded part is to have: frame, large icon, small icon, or thumbnail.

The ShowPasteAsDialog method returns the user's choices to your part in an ODPasteAsResult structure:

```
struct ODPasteAsResult
{
    ODBoolean    pasteLinkSetting;
    ODBoolean    autoUpdateSetting;
    ODBoolean    mergeSetting;
    ODTypeToken selectedView;
    ODType       selectedKind;
    ODType       translateKind;
    ODEditor     editor;
};
```

Depending on the contents of the returned structure, your part either creates a link to its source or does not, either accepts the data as it is or translates it, and either embeds or incorporates the transferred data:

■ If the user has chosen to create a link, respond as described in the section "Creating a Link at the Destination" on page 383. If you create a link, take into account the automatic/manual update setting as well as the other Paste As settings selected by the user.

■ If the user has chosen to translate the data but is not creating a link, respond as described in the section "Translating Before Incorporating or Embedding" on page 351.

■ If the user is not creating a link or translating, read the transferred data in either of two ways:

☐ If your part can directly read any of the part kinds in the data-transfer object's content storage unit, and if the user has not selected Embed As, incorporate the data. Follow the instructions in the section "Incorporating Intrinsic Content" on page 344.

☐ If your part cannot directly read any of the part kinds in the storage unit, or if the user has selected Embed As, follow the instructions in the section "Embedding a Single Part" on page 347.

Writing to a Data-Transfer Object

You write data to a data-transfer object when the user cuts, copies, or drags data from your part or when you create or update the source of a link. This section discusses how to place that data into the data-transfer object.

This section does not discuss how your part handles cutting (or moving) differently from copying. Cutting involves removing data from your part, including possibly one or more frames of embedded parts. Removing an embedded frame is discussed in the section "Removing an Embedded Part" on page 307; other issues related to cutting operations are discussed in the section "Handling Cut Data" on page 334.

Writing Intrinsic Content

Intrinsic content plus possibly one or more embedded parts is the most general configuration of data that you can place into a data-transfer object. If the data to be written consists of a combination of your part's intrinsic content plus embedded parts, you need to write your own intrinsic content, and you need to clone the embedded frames as well. If the data includes link sources or destinations, you need to clone those objects also. These are the basic steps to take, regardless of whether or not your intrinsic content is accompanied by embedded frames and other objects:

1. Gain access to the data-transfer object and prepare to write to it. (See, for example, the initial steps under "Copying or Cutting to the Clipboard" on page 359, "Initiating a Drag" on page 364, and "Updating a Link at the Source" on page 389.)

2. Start the cloning operation, as described under "Cloning" on page 321. Specify the appropriate kind of cloning operation, using one of the constants listed in Table 8-1 on page 322.

3. Write your content to the data-transfer object. For intrinsic content, add a property with the name `kODPropContents` to the data-transfer object's content storage unit. Write your data into that property, in a value specified by the data format (part kind) of your intrinsic content.

   As you encounter persistent references to objects (embedded frames, link-source objects, link objects, auxiliary storage units, and so on), clone the objects to the data-transfer object by calling your draft's `Clone` method. Write persistent references to the newly cloned objects.

   Instead of writing actual data, you should if possible write a promise to the data-transfer object. See the section "Promises" on page 330 for more information.

4. If your editor supports other part kinds, write or promise additional versions of your data as separate values in that same property, so that users can incorporate a version of your content into several different part kinds.

5. End the cloning operation.

6. If possible, add a suggested frame shape for the data (see "Frame Shape or Frame Annotation" on page 318), in case the data is embedded as a separate part in its destination.

7. If appropriate, create a link specification as described in the section "Link Specification" on page 317.

8. Perform any closing tasks specific to the kind of data-transfer object you are writing to. (See, for example, the final steps under "Copying or Cutting to the Clipboard" on page 359, "Initiating a Drag" on page 364, and "Updating a Link at the Source" on page 389.)

In this process, any link sources or link destinations are correctly written to the data-transfer object, subject to the constraints listed in Table 8-3 on page 399. (However, you must also write the necessary accompanying link-related information, as described in the section "Writing Linked Content to Storage" on page 391.)

If this operation is a cut rather than a copy, note the additional considerations listed in the section "Handling Cut Data" on page 334.

Writing a Single Embedded Part

When the data that you place into the data-transfer object consists of a single frame of an embedded part—with no surrounding intrinsic content of the containing part (your part)—you must treat the operation as a special case. The identity of the data as a single, separate part must be preserved.

The content storage unit of the data-transfer object should end up with a duplicate of the embedded part; the nature of your part (the containing part) generally has nothing to do with the operation. However, you can write some data associated with the frame itself, if you wish; see step 4 of the following list.

In summary, you take these steps:

1. Gain access to the content storage unit of the data-transfer object and prepare to write to it. (See, for example, the initial steps under "Copying or Cutting to the Clipboard" on page 359, "Initiating a Drag" on page 364, and "Updating a Link at the Source" on page 389.)

2. Start the cloning operation, as described under "Cloning" on page 321. Specify the appropriate kind of cloning transaction, using one of the constants listed in Table 8-1 on page 322.

   In addition, create a property with the name `kODPropCloneKindUsed`, containing a value of type `kODCloneKind`, in the content storage unit. Write the kind of cloning transaction you are using into that value. (The embedded part, if it writes a promise, will use that value later, when fulfilling the promise.)

3. Clone the embedded part into the data-transfer object by calling your
   draft's `Clone` method. Unlike with writing intrinsic content, you do not
   add a `kODPropContents` property (the embedded part itself does that) or a
   `kODPropSuggestedFrame` property (you instead add a `kODPropContentFrame`
   property).

   Be sure to perform the cloning operation in this order:

   □ Add a property with the name `kODPropContentFrame` to the data-transfer
     object's content storage unit. The presence of this property notifies the
     destination part that the data being transferred is a frame without
     surrounding intrinsic content, and also informs the embedded part (the
     part being cloned) that it can write a promise instead of its actual content.

     (It is important *not* to clone the frame yet. Wait until you've cloned the
     embedded part, or else the part itself will be cloned into the wrong
     storage unit.)

   □ Clone the embedded part into the data-transfer object's content
     storage unit.

   □ Clone the embedded part's frame into the data-transfer object's draft (into
     any storage unit other than the content storage unit). This cloning
     operation must occur *after* the embedded part is cloned.

   □ Add a value of type `kODWeakStorageUnitRef` to the `kODPropContentFrame`
     property of the data-transfer object's content storage unit. Create a weak
     persistent reference from that value to the cloned frame. This reference
     allows a destination part, upon recognizing the `kODPropContentFrame`
     property, to locate the frame for the part in the data-transfer object.

4. Optionally, write any intrinsic data you want associated with the frame
   (such as a drop shadow or other visual adornment) as proxy content. Add
   a property (of type `kODPropProxyContents`) to the data-transfer object, and
   write your data into it as a value that you recognize. If the transferred part
   is subsequently pasted into a part that also recognizes that value and
   knows how to interpret it, those special characteristics of the frame can
   be duplicated.

5. If the embedded part is the entire source or destination of a link, you need to
   write additional proxy content, as described in "Writing Linked Content to
   Storage" on page 391.

6. If appropriate, write a link specification into the data-transfer object, as
   described in the section "Link Specification" on page 317.

7. Perform any closing tasks specific to the kind of data-transfer object you are writing to. (See, for example, the final steps under "Copying or Cutting to the Clipboard" on page 359, "Initiating a Drag" on page 364, and "Updating a Link at the Source" on page 389.)

If this operation is a cut rather than a copy, note the additional considerations listed in the section "Handling Cut Data" on page 334.

Reading From a Data-Transfer Object

You read from a data-transfer object when the user pastes or drops data into your part or when you create or update the destination of a link. This section discusses how to extract that data from the data-transfer object.

When you place transferred data into your part, what you do with the data depends on how the part kinds of the transferred data relate to the part kind of your part (the destination part).

Incorporating Intrinsic Content

As the destination of a data transfer, your part incorporates the intrinsic content of the data-transfer object into your own part's intrinsic content (and embeds whatever embedded parts the transferred content contains) if all of these conditions apply:

- The intrinsic content of the transferred data is stored in at least one part kind that you can incorporate into your part.

- The user has not specified Embed As in the Paste As dialog box.

- The data-transfer object's content storage unit does *not* contain a property named kODPropContentFrame. (If it does, the transferred data consists of a single embedded frame without surrounding intrinsic content, and the data should be embedded; see "Frame Shape or Frame Annotation" on page 318.)

When incorporating transferred data, you should read the highest-fidelity part kind possible—that is, the first value (in storage order) that your part editor understands. If the transferred data includes a kODPropPreferredKind property, however, it takes precedence over fidelity; you should attempt to read it first.

Incorporating involves reading intrinsic content plus possibly cloning embedded frames, links, and other objects. Figure 8-6 summarizes the steps involved.

Figure 8-6   Incorporating the content of a data-transfer object

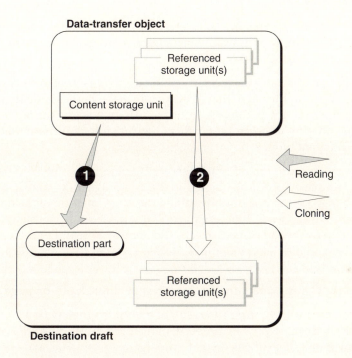

1. Read content into your part
2. Clone referenced storage units into your draft

Here, in more detail, are the basic steps to take when incorporating:

1. Gain access to the data-transfer object and prepare to read from it. (See, for example, the initial steps under "Pasting From the Clipboard" on page 360, "Dropping" on page 368, "Insert" on page 249, and "Updating a Link at the Destination" on page 387.)

If you are incorporating translated data, you already will have cloned the data into a temporary storage unit in your draft, and you already will have translated it. Take these steps:

- ☐ In the `kODPropContents` property of that storage unit, focus on the value that corresponds to the translated part kind. Read the data into your part, following your own content model.

- ☐ Skip to step 5.

2. Start the cloning operation, as described in "BeginClone" on page 322. Specify the appropriate kind of cloning operation, using one of the constants listed in Table 8-1 on page 322.

3. In the `kODPropContents` property of the data-transfer object's content storage unit, focus on the value that corresponds to the highest-fidelity part kind that you can incorporate into your part. (It may not be the highest-fidelity value present in the property.) Read the data into your part, following your own content model.

   As you encounter persistent references to objects—embedded frames, link-source objects, link objects, auxiliary storage units, and so on—clone each object into your draft by calling the `Clone` method of the data-transfer object's draft (see "Clone" on page 323). Adjust your persistent references to point to the newly cloned objects. (Remember to retain the cloned object IDs for instantiation after cloning is complete, rather than reconstructing the objects yet.)

4. End the cloning operation, as described in "EndClone" on page 325.

5. If you are incorporating as a result of a drop, there may be a `kODPropMouseDownOffset` property in the data-transfer object's content storage unit. If so, focus on that property, read its value, and—if appropriate for your content model—use the value to position the incorporated data in relation to the drop location.

   (If you are incorporating translated data, you must read this property from the original data-transfer object, not the cloned storage unit.)

6. If the cloning was successful, instantiate each cloned embedded frame (with your draft's `AcquireFrame` method) and call the frame's `SetContainingFrame` method, to make your part's display frame (the frame that received the data transfer) the containing frame of the new embedded frame.

   Create additional embedded frames as necessary, if your part's content model specifies that the new part is to appear in more than one of your display frames. If you do create new frames, synchronize them with the first (source) frame; see "Synchronizing Display Frames" on page 114 for more information.

7. Change each new frame's link status to reflect its current location. Link status is described in the section "Frame Link Status" on page 377. If your part does not support linking, you must nevertheless change your cloned embedded frames' link status (to `kODNotInLink`).

8. If any of the objects that you have cloned into your part is a link-source object or link object, follow the procedures described in the section "Reading Linked Content From Storage" on page 392 to make sure that the objects are valid.

9. If any newly embedded frame is visible, assign a facet or facets to it, as described in the section "Adding a Facet" on page 124.

10. Perform any closing tasks specific to the kind of data-transfer object you are reading from. (See, for example, the final steps under "Pasting From the Clipboard" on page 360, "Dropping" on page 368, "Insert" on page 249, and "Updating a Link at the Destination" on page 387.)

(If you are incorporating translated data, you can at this time remove the cloned temporary storage unit from your draft.)

Embedding a Single Part

As the destination of a data transfer, your part embeds the entire contents of the data-transfer object as a single part (plus whatever embedded parts it contains) if any of these conditions apply:

■ The intrinsic content is of a part kind that you cannot incorporate.

■ The user has specified Embed As in the Paste As dialog box.

■ The transferred data consists of a single embedded frame without surrounding intrinsic content (regardless of its part kind). In this case the data-transfer object's content storage unit contains a property named `kODPropContentFrame`, which serves as a signal that the data consists of a single frame and should be embedded, even if it is of a part kind that you can incorporate. See "Frame Shape or Frame Annotation" on page 318.

Embedding data from a data-transfer object as a single part involves, basically, cloning the content storage unit into your draft and then providing a frame and facets for the new part. Figure 8-7 summarizes the steps involved.

Figure 8-7　　Embedding the content of a data-transfer object

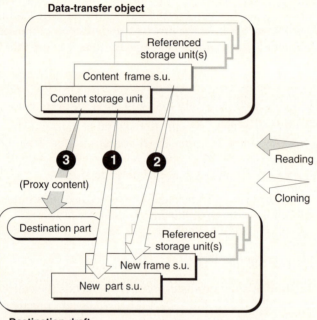

1. Clone content storage unit into a new part in your draft (referenced storage units are cloned also)
2. Clone content frame (if present) into your draft
3. Read proxy content (if present) into your part

Here, in more detail, are the basic steps to take when embedding:

1. Gain access to the data-transfer object and prepare to read from it. (See, for example, the initial steps under "Pasting From the Clipboard" on page 360, "Dropping" on page 368, "Insert" on page 249, and "Updating a Link at the Destination" on page 387.)

If you are embedding translated data, you already will have cloned the data into a new storage unit in your draft, and you already will have translated it. Skip to step 6.

2. Start the cloning operation, as described under "The Cloning Sequence" on page 321. Specify the appropriate kind of cloning operation, using one of the constants listed in Table 8-1 on page 322.

3. Clone the data-transfer object's content storage unit into a new storage unit in your draft, using the Clone method of the data-transfer object's draft.

4. If there is a property named kODPropContentFrame in the original storage unit, read the storage-unit reference it contains and use that reference to clone the new part's frame from the data-transfer object's storage unit into your draft. (Cloning the data-transfer object's content storage unit alone does not copy the frame, because the reference is a weak persistent reference.)

5. End the cloning operation.

6. If any of the following conditions apply, notify the embedded part's future part editor that it should use a specific part kind when reading the part:

   □ if the data has been translated

   □ if this embedding has occurred as a result of a user selection in the Paste As dialog box and the user has chosen a part kind that is not the preferred kind

   □ if a preferred kind property does not exist and the user has chosen a part kind that is not the highest-fidelity (first) value stored in the transferred storage unit's contents property

   In any of these cases, create a property with the name kODPropPreferredKind in the cloned storage unit (if the property does not already exist) and write into it a value that specifies the part kind the editor should use.

7. If this embedding has occurred as a result of a user selection in the Paste As dialog box and the user has chosen a specific part editor to edit the part, add a property with the name kODPropPreferredEditor to the cloned storage unit, and write into it the editor ID (returned in the editor field of the ODPasteAsResult structure) of the preferred editor.

8. If the original storage unit contains a property with the name kODPropProxyContents, that property contains any proxy content that the part's original containing part wanted associated with the frame, such as linking information or a drop shadow or other visual adornment. (This

property is absent if the transferred data includes any intrinsic content in addition to the embedded frame.)

Focus the original storage unit on the kODPropProxyContent property and read in the information from the data-transfer object (not from the cloned storage unit). You must understand the format of the proxy content in order to use it; it is subsumed in your own part's intrinsic content to be associated with the frame. If you don't understand the format, ignore the data.

9. If you are embedding as a result of a drop, there may be a property named kODPropMouseDownOffset in the content storage unit of the data-transfer object (not the cloned storage unit). If so, focus on that property, read its value, and—if appropriate for your content model—use the value to position the embedded data in relation to the drop location.

10. Recreate the new part's frame—if it has been provided in the kODPropContentFrame property—using your draft's AcquireFrame method, and call its SetContainingFrame method to assign your part's display frame (the frame that received the data transfer) as the containing frame.

    If no frame was provided, you need to create one:

    ☐ Obtain the suggested frame shape—if it exists—from the data-transfer object (not from the cloned storage unit). It is in a property named kODPropSuggestedFrameShape. If it is not there, use a default frame shape.

    ☐ Instantiate the new part; pass the cloned storage unit's ID to your draft's AcquirePart method.

    ☐ Create the frame for the part, using your draft's CreateFrame method.

11. Change the link status of the new frame to reflect its current location. If your part does not support linking, you must nevertheless change your new embedded frame's link status (to kODNotInLink).

12. If the newly embedded frame is visible, assign facets to it, as described in the section "Adding a Facet" on page 124.

13. Perform any closing tasks specific to the kind of data-transfer object you are reading from. (See, for example, the final steps under "Pasting From the Clipboard" on page 360, "Dropping" on page 368, "Insert" on page 249, and "Updating a Link at the Destination" on page 387.)

Translating Before Incorporating or Embedding

If you must translate transferred data before incorporating or embedding it in your part, follow the steps listed here before following those in the sections "Incorporating Intrinsic Content" on page 344 and "Embedding a Single Part" on page 347. The OpenDoc translation service is described in general in the section "Translation" on page 333.

Basically, you translate by first cloning the data into a storage unit in your own draft, then modifying it, and then completing the data transfer. When you translate transferred data, always write the translated data into a storage unit in your own draft; do *not* write it back into the original data-transfer object. Subsequent readers of the data cannot tell a translated value from a value written by the data's original part editor.

These are the general steps you might follow:

1. Gain access to the data-transfer object that contains the untranslated data and prepare to read from it. (See, for example, the initial steps under "Pasting From the Clipboard" on page 360, "Dropping" on page 368, "Insert" on page 249, and "Updating a Link at the Destination" on page 387.)

   (If you are creating a link, remember that you read the data from the newly created link object, not the clipboard or drag-and-drop object that contained the link specification.)

2. Start the cloning operation, as described under "Cloning" on page 321. Specify the appropriate kind of cloning transaction, using one of the constants listed in Table 8-1 on page 322.

3. Clone the data-transfer object's content storage unit into a new storage unit in your draft, using the `Clone` method of the data-transfer object's draft.

4. If there is a property named `kODPropContentFrame` in the original storage unit, you should embed the data (unless the user explicitly specified incorporation in the Paste As dialog box). Read the storage-unit reference the property contains and use that reference to clone the new part's frame from the data-transfer object's draft into your draft. (Cloning the data-transfer object's content storage unit alone does not copy the frame, because the reference is a weak persistent reference.)

5. Access the storage unit of the cloned-but-untranslated data, and focus on its contents property. Add a value whose value type is the part kind you are translating to.

6. Create two storage-unit views: one focused on the original untranslated value, and the other focused on the translated value you have just created.

7. Gain access to the translation object (by calling the session object's `GetTranslation` method), and then call the translation object's `TranslateView` method, passing it the two storage-unit views. The translation object performs the translation and writes the new data into the new value.

8. Delete the storage-unit views.

Complete the transfer of the translated data in either of two ways, depending on whether you are incorporating or embedding, and whether you are creating or updating a link.

■ If your part can directly read the part kind of the translated data (and if the user has not selected Embed As from the Paste As dialog box), incorporate it. Follow the steps in the section "Incorporating Intrinsic Content" on page 344.

Figure 8-8 summarizes the steps involved. As the figure shows, you read the content into your part from the cloned temporary storage unit, not the original data-transfer object, and you remove the temporary storage unit from your draft when the transfer is complete.

Figure 8-8   Translating and then incorporating the contents of a data-transfer object

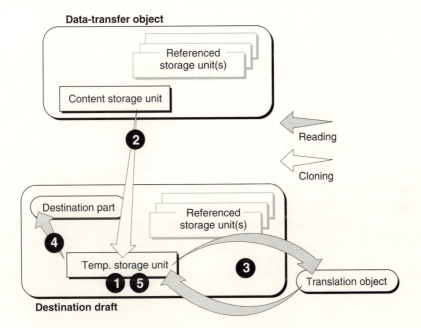

1. Create a temporary storage unit in your draft
2. Clone content storage unit into temporary storage unit
   (referenced storage units are cloned also)
3. Translate content of temporary storage unit
4. Read translated content into your part
5. Remove temporary storage unit from your draft

■ If your part cannot directly read the part kind of the translated data (or if the user has selected Embed As from the Paste As dialog box), follow the instructions in the section "Embedding a Single Part" on page 347.

Reading From a Data-Transfer Object   353

Figure 8-9 summarizes the steps involved in this case. The cloned storage unit is not temporary, but becomes the new embedded part's storage unit. Note also that you must read proxy content from the original data-transfer storage unit, not the cloned one.

Figure 8-9　　Translating and then embedding the contents of a data-transfer object

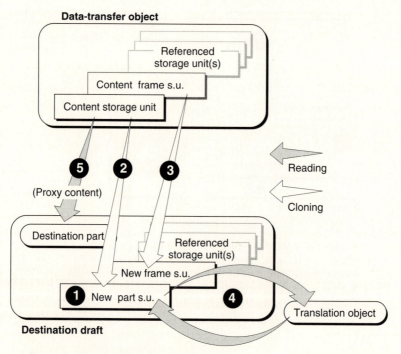

1. Create a storage unit for the new part
2. Clone content storage unit into the new part
   (referenced storage units are cloned also)
3. Translate content of new part
4. Clone content frame storage unit (if present)
5. Read proxy content (if present) from data-transfer object

Clipboard Transfer

The clipboard commands Cut, Copy, and Paste constitute a common mechanism for transferring data within and across conventional documents, even documents of different data formats. For OpenDoc documents, these commands perform the same tasks, but with added capabilities.

- The commands operate on embedded parts as well as intrinsic content. The data copied to or pasted from the clipboard can contain any number of parts, of any part kinds. The parts may be displayed in frames or represented as icons.

- The Paste and Paste As commands can either embed parts or incorporate data as intrinsic content.

- The Paste and Paste As commands can cause a portion of one part's intrinsic content to become, when copied and then pasted into another part, a separate, embedded part on its own.

- The Paste As command can create a persistent link to the source of the data being pasted.

- The Paste As command also allows the user to override decisions on incorporating versus embedding that would normally be made by OpenDoc.

As with data placed in a conventional clipboard, if your part editor stores multiple formats on the clipboard—including standard formats—the user has a greater chance of being able to incorporate (rather than embed) the data into more kinds of parts.

Clipboard Concepts

This section discusses some basic clipboard operations common to both reading and writing, such as acquiring the clipboard focus and using the clipboard update ID. It also presents some special considerations related to updating the clipboard and cutting data from your part.

Enabling the Cut and Paste menu items

OpenDoc does not permit changes to your draft (and therefore your part's content) if the draft permissions are read-only. You should check your draft permissions (see "Drafts" on page 285) before enabling the Cut, Paste, or Paste As items in the Edit menu or before allowing the user to perform a cut or paste operation using keyboard equivalents. ◆

Acquiring and Relinquishing the Clipboard Focus

Your part can access the clipboard only when your part is in the foreground process; access from a background process is meaningless. Furthermore, to be thread-safe, you must always acquire the clipboard focus before writing or reading clipboard data. As long as you hold the clipboard focus, no other part should access or modify the data.

Typically, your part needs to inspect the contents of the clipboard before deciding whether to enable Edit menu items, so your `AdjustMenus` method can include a call to the arbitrator's `RequestFocus` method to acquire the clipboard focus.

After acquiring the clipboard focus, you can access the clipboard when responding to a menu command (or its keyboard equivalent) with your `HandleEvent` method by calling the session object's `GetClipboard` method. You should then unilaterally relinquish the clipboard focus in your `HandleEvent` method, after having handled the clipboard command. (Your `HandleEvent` method is always called after `AdjustMenus` is called, even if the user does not choose a menu command.)

These are the steps you take to acquire the clipboard focus and prepare to write to the clipboard or read from it:

1. Acquire the clipboard focus, using the Arbitrator's `RequestFocus` method (as described in "Requesting Foci" on page 210).

2. Gain access to the clipboard object, using the session object's `GetClipboard` method.

3. If you are writing to the clipboard, remove any existing data on the clipboard with the clipboard's `Clear` method. (Do not take this step if you are reading from the clipboard.)

4. Gain access to the clipboard's content storage unit, using the clipboard's
   `GetContentStorageUnit` method.

You relinquish the clipboard focus unilaterally by calling the arbitrator's
`RelinquishFocus` method.

Clipboard Update ID

Whenever you copy data to the clipboard, you should get and save the
clipboard's current **update ID,** a number used to identify this particular
instance of clipboard contents. You typically obtain the update ID in this
situation by calling the clipboard's `ActionDone` method. In other situations, you
may need to inspect the clipboard's current update ID; you can do so by calling
the clipboard's `GetUpdateID` method.

If a link specification that you have written to the clipboard becomes invalid
because of changes to your content that was copied to the clipboard, you
must remove the link specification from the clipboard, as described under
"Removing a Link Specification From the Clipboard" (next). You can examine
the clipboard's current update ID at any time and compare it with your saved
update ID; if they are identical, the clipboard has not changed.

Removing a Link Specification From the Clipboard

If your part copies some of its content to the clipboard and the user then
modifies the equivalent content in your part (without copying anything else to
the clipboard), the clipboard data no longer matches the source data in your
part. The potential link represented by the link specification you wrote in the
clipboard therefore no longer reflects the content at the source of the link. If
your source content has changed to the extent that creating a link is no longer
feasible, your part must remove the link specification.

By saving the update ID of the clipboard whenever you copy data to it, you can
check that ID against the current update ID of the clipboard whenever your
source data changes to the extent that creating a link to the previous data is
impossible. If the IDs match, the clipboard still contains the data that you
placed in it, and you should remove the link specification.

You can follow these steps to remove a link specification:

1. Acquire the clipboard focus as described in the section "Acquiring and Relinquishing the Clipboard Focus" on page 356.

2. Get the clipboard's update ID and compare it to your stored update ID. If they don't match, skip to step 5.

3. Access the clipboard's content storage unit. (Unlike when writing to the clipboard, do not clear the clipboard data.)

4. Focus the storage unit on the link-specification property (type `kODLinkSpec`) and remove that property, using the storage unit's `Remove` method. Be sure to focus on the entire property (by specifying a null value type), so that you remove the entire property and not just one value.

5. Relinquish the clipboard focus.

Undo for Clipboard

If your part supports cutting or pasting, it must also support undoing those operations. (Note that data transfer between parts is undoable only if both parts involved have undo support.) Undo support in general is described in the section "Undo" on page 260.

Whenever your part performs a cut, copy, or paste operation, it must call the clipboard's `ActionDone` method to notify the clipboard of the kind of cloning transaction that took place. `ActionDone` returns a clipboard ID that identifies the current clipboard contents. Save that update ID.

When your part cuts an object to the clipboard, it should remove the object from its content data structures. However, your part should not release the object, but instead save a reference to the object in an undo action. (For a cut embedded frame, you also set its in-limbo flag to true, as shown in Table 6-4 on page 266.) Then, if the user chooses the Undo command and your part's `UndoAction` method is called, your part should

■ reinstate the object in your part's content structures (and setting its in-limbo flag to false)

■ notify the clipboard that the cut was undone, by calling the clipboard's `ActionUndone` method, passing it the update ID returned to you when you called `ActionDone` after cutting the data to the clipboard

If the user subsequently chooses the Redo command and your part's
`RedoAction` method is called, your part should

- once again remove the object from its content data structures (and reset its in-limbo flag to true)
- notify the clipboard that the cut was redone, by calling the clipboard's `ActionRedone` method, passing it the same update ID

Calling `ActionDone`, `ActionUndone`, and `ActionRedone` notifies the clipboard
whether it is involved in a cut, a copy, or the restoration of a cut or a copy; the
clipboard's internal handling of its objects differs in each case.

If and when your part's `DisposeActionState` method is called, you can at that
point release (not remove from your draft) the object referenced in your undo
action. (For an embedded frame, you either release or remove it, as shown in
Table 6-4 on page 266.)

To undo a cut, copy, or paste operation requires the restoration of the previous
state of the document involved, but it does not require the restoration of the
previous state of the clipboard. Therefore, if you redo a paste operation that has
been undone, you cannot assume that the clipboard once again contains the
original data that had been pasted. You must implement the redo from
your own data. For this reason, you should retain a copy of pasted data in a
private cache.

Copying or Cutting to the Clipboard

You write data to the clipboard as a result of the user selecting the Cut
command or the Copy command from the Edit menu (or their keyboard
equivalents). These are the basic steps to take:

1. Acquire the clipboard focus and access the clipboard's content storage unit, as described in the section "Acquiring and Relinquishing the Clipboard Focus" on page 356.

2. Write the data to the clipboard.

    □ If the selection consists of a combination of your part's intrinsic content plus zero or more embedded parts, you need to write your own intrinsic content to the clipboard, and you need to clone the embedded frames and parts as well (or you can write a promise). Follow the steps listed in the section "Writing Intrinsic Content" on page 341.

    □ If the selection consists of a single frame of an embedded part with no surrounding intrinsic content, you need to clone the part and provide a frame for it. Follow the steps listed in the section "Writing a Single Embedded Part" on page 342.

In either case, when you call the `BeginClone` method, specify either `kODCloneCopy` or `kODCloneCut`, depending on whether you are copying or cutting the data to the clipboard.

3. When you have finished, call the clipboard's `ActionDone` method, specifying either `kODCloneCopy` or `kODCloneCut`. Save the clipboard's current update ID (see "Clipboard Update ID" on page 357), which is returned from `ActionDone`, in case you later have to undo the cut or copy, remove a link specification, or fulfill a promise you wrote.

4. If this operation was a cut rather than a copy, it must be undoable. Add a single action to the action history, as described in "Adding an Action to the Undo Action History" on page 262. Be sure to follow the special instructions in the section "Handling Cut Data" on page 334, including setting the in-limbo flag of any cut frame to true.

5. Delete the cut selection from your part's content.

6. Relinquish the clipboard focus (see "Acquiring and Relinquishing the Clipboard Focus" on page 356).

Pasting From the Clipboard

You read data from the clipboard as a result of the user selecting the Paste command or the Paste As command from the Edit menu. These are the basic steps to take:

1. Acquire the clipboard focus and access the clipboard's content storage unit, as described in the section "Acquiring and Relinquishing the Clipboard Focus" on page 356. (Do not clear the clipboard data, of course.)

2. Read the data from the clipboard.

   □ If the data consists of intrinsic content plus zero or more embedded frames, and if the intrinsic content is of a part kind that you can incorporate into your part, you need to read the intrinsic content and possibly clone embedded parts, links, or other objects. Follow the steps listed in the section "Incorporating Intrinsic Content" on page 344.

   □ If you need to embed the data as a single part with no surrounding intrinsic content, you need to clone the part and either extract its frame or create a frame for it. Follow the steps listed in the section "Embedding a Single Part" on page 347. That section lists the conditions under which you must embed rather than incorporate clipboard data.

In either case, when you call the `BeginClone` method, specify `kODClonePaste`.

3. Pasting must be an undoable operation. Call the clipboard's `ActionDone` method, specifying `kODClonePaste`. Save the current clipboard update ID, returned by `ActionDone`, in a single undo action (see "Adding an Action to the Undo Action History" on page 262), so that you can undo the paste operation if necessary. If you are pasting an embedded frame, follow the instructions listed in Table 6-4 on page 266: save the current value of the frame's in-limbo flag and then set the flag to false.

4. Notify OpenDoc and your containing part that there has been a change to your part's content; see "Making Content Changes Known" on page 307.

5. Relinquish the clipboard focus (see "Acquiring and Relinquishing the Clipboard Focus" on page 356).

Drag and Drop

The OpenDoc drag-and-drop facility allows users to move or copy data through direct manipulation. Users can drag items from one location in a part or document (or the desktop) to another location in the same or a different part or document (or to the desktop).

Drag-and-Drop Concepts

Drag and drop provides a direct-manipulation alternative to the clipboard. The fundamental user-level operations—copying and moving—are similar in drag and drop and in clipboard transfer, and they are similar across all platforms.

User Interaction

The user typically initiates a drag by positioning the mouse pointer over some selected (or single-click-selectable) content, pressing and holding down the mouse button, and then moving the pointer. The user can hold down a modifier key while pressing the mouse button or while releasing the mouse button to force a drag to be a copy (called a **drag-copy**) or a move (called a **drag-move**).

As the user moves the mouse pointer, an outline of the selected item (provided by the source part, drawn by OpenDoc) is dragged to the new location. When the user releases the mouse button, the item is placed (dropped) at the pointer location. The part beneath the pointer is notified that something has been dropped on it. At this point, the destination part behaves essentially as it does when pasting from the clipboard; it makes the same decisions regarding embedding versus incorporating data and handling links. The source part may have to delete the items if the operation was a move, or do nothing if it was a copy.

Parts can restrict the dropped content they will accept to specific part kinds. To indicate that it can accept a drop, a part provides appropriate feedback to the user once the pointer enters its facet.

For frames and icons that are being dragged, OpenDoc provides specific behavior and appearance for the item being dragged. For intrinsic content that is being dragged, your part editor is responsible for defining behavior and providing user feedback. You should follow the guidelines given in the section "Using Drag and Drop" on page 598.

The user can move an active frame by dragging its border. By moving the mouse pointer to the active frame border and pressing the mouse button, the user selects the frame and can start dragging immediately.

The user can move a selected frame by moving the pointer anywhere within it and pressing the button to start a drag. Also, if a frame is bundled, the user can drag it by pressing the mouse button while the pointer is anywhere in the interior of the frame, whether or not the frame is already active or selected.

When the user releases the mouse button, the frame and its part are dropped at the new location. After a frame is dropped, it becomes selected. The destination may adjust the drop location of a frame to reflect constraints such as gridding (in a graphics part) or text position (in a text part).

Move Versus Copy

OpenDoc follows these conventions for drag and drop:

■ When a user drags an item within a document, the item is moved, not copied. Note that a window boundary is not always a document boundary; dragging an item to or from a part window, but still within the same document, results in a move.

- When the user drags an item across a document boundary, the item is copied, not moved.

- When the user employs drag and drop to move a frame, the moved frame displays the original part if the destination is in the same document. However, if the destination is in a different document, the source frame is deleted, and a new part (and new frame displaying the contents) is created at the destination.

OpenDoc supports a mechanism to allow the user to force a copy or move operation by pressing modifier keys. See "Force-Move and Force-Copy" on page 604 for specific guidelines.

Dragging stationery

Stationery parts may be copied exactly like other parts. However, if you drag-move stationery into a part whose preferred view type for embedded parts is frame view, a copy is "torn off" the stationery pad and displayed in a frame. The stationery part remains in its original location, unchanged. ◆

Droppable Frames

Each frame has a `SetDroppable` method, through which the part displayed in the frame controls whether or not the frame can (in general) accept dropped data. When a display frame is added or reconnected to your part, you can call `SetDroppable` and pass either `kODTrue` or `kODFalse` to allow or prohibit dropping. (When initially created, frames are not droppable.) You can call `SetDroppable` again at any time to change the state of the frame.

OpenDoc calls the `IsDroppable` method of the frame before making any of the drag-related method calls `DragEnter`, `DragWithin`, `DragLeave`, and `Drop` to your part. If your display frame is not droppable, your part does not receive any of these calls.

Your part's display frame does not have to be droppable for you to initiate a drag *from* it.

Undo for Drag and Drop

If your part supports dragging and dropping data, it must also support undoing that operation. (Note that data transfer between parts is undoable only if both parts involved support undo.) Undo support in general is described in the section "Undo" on page 260.

For drag and drop, undo involves a multistage action. The part initiating the drag begins the action, the part receiving the drop adds a single action, and the initiating part completes the action when the drop is complete. See the section "Adding Multistage Actions" on page 263 for more information.

If drag and drop involves embedded frames, be sure to set the dragged frames' in-limbo flags appropriately when initiating a drag, when dropping, and when the drag completes. See Table 6-4 on page 266 for details.

Initiating a Drag

In response to a mouse-down event at the appropriate location, the part receiving the mouse event (the source part) has the choice of initiating a drag.

You should follow the procedures listed under "Handling Mouse-Down Events" on page 201 in deciding whether to initiate a drag operation. On the Mac OS platform, you can call the Drag Manager function `WaitMouseMoved`, which returns true if the mouse pointer has moved enough to trigger a drag operation. (`WaitMouseMoved` returns false if a mouse-up occurs without the mouse pointer having moved sufficiently.)

To initiate a drag, your part (the source part) should follow these steps:

1. Call the `GetDragAndDrop` method of the session object to gain access to the `ODDragAndDrop` object. Then call the `Clear` method and the `GetContentStorageUnit` method of the drag-and-drop object to get an empty storage unit into which to copy the dragged data.

   Note that there is no drag-and-drop focus or lock to be acquired. Only one part at a time can initiate and complete a drag. Version 1.0 of OpenDoc on the Mac OS platform does not support asynchronous dragging.

2. Write the dragged data (or write a promise) into the drag-and-drop storage unit:

   ☐ If the data is intrinsic content—with or without one or more embedded parts—follow the procedure outlined in the section "Writing Intrinsic Content" on page 341.

☐ If the data is a single embedded part, follow the procedure outlined in the section "Writing a Single Embedded Part" on page 342.

In either case, when you call the `BeginClone` method, specify `kODCloneCut` even if you are initiating a drag-copy. (The user can override the move-versus-copy conventions when dropping the data.)

3. Create a property with the name `kODPropMouseDownOffset` in the drag-and-drop storage unit. Write into the property a value (of type `kODPoint`) that specifies the offset of the mouse from the origin (upper-left corner on the Mac OS platform) of the selection or item being dragged. This offset allows the destination part to locate the item correctly in relation to the mouse-up event when the item is dropped.

4. If there are frames that should not accept a drop from this drag—such as any frames that are themselves being dragged—call the frames' `SetDragging` method and pass it a value of `kODTrue` to notify OpenDoc that it should not allow them to be drop targets.

5. If the drag involves an embedded frame, follow the instructions listed in Table 6-4 on page 266; set the frame's in-limbo flag to true if a drag-move is possible.

6. Add a beginning action to the undo action history (see "Adding Multistage Actions" on page 263), to allow the user to undo the drag if necessary.

7. Initiate the drag by calling the drag-and-drop object's `StartDrag` method. When you call `StartDrag`, you are responsible for providing OpenDoc an image, such as an outline, for it to display to the user as dragging feedback. (On the Mac OS, you provide a handle to a drag region in global coordinates, as required by the Drag Manager.)

The `StartDrag` method completes when the drop occurs; see "Completion of StartDrag" on page 372.

Operations While a Drag Is in Progress

As long as the mouse button remains pressed, the drag is in progress. Potential destination parts need to perform certain actions during dragging, when the pointer is within their facets.

On Entering a Part's Facet

Any facet that the mouse pointer passes over during a drag represents a potential drop destination, if the facet's frame is droppable. OpenDoc calls a part's DragEnter method when the pointer enters one of its droppable frames' facets during a drag.

```
ODDragResult DragEnter(in ODDragItemIterator dragInfo,
                       in ODFacet facet,
                       in ODPoint where);
```

On receiving a call to its DragEnter method, your part (the potential destination part) should take these steps:

1. Examine the part kinds of the dragged data, using a drag-item iterator (class ODDragItemIterator) passed to your part. Inspect the part kinds in each item's storage unit and determine whether or not you can accept the dragged data. An iterator is necessary in case non-OpenDoc data is being dragged; see "Accepting Non-OpenDoc Data" on page 371.

   If your part cannot accept all the dragged items, you should not accept a drop at all.

2. If your part can accept a drop, provide the appropriate feedback to the user, such as adorning your part's frame border or changing the cursor appearance. See "Destination Feedback (for Drag and Drop)" on page 528 and "Providing Destination Feedback" on page 602 for illustrations and specific recommendations. Otherwise, take no action.

   When the user initiates a drag from within your frame, you should not display destination feedback as long as the mouse pointer has not yet left your frame, although you should provide feedback if the mouse pointer returns to your frame after having left it. To help you know when to display feedback, OpenDoc on the Mac OS platform defines the drag attribute kODDragIsInSourceFrame (see "Drag Attributes and the Drop Method" on page 368), which, if returned, means that the mouse pointer has not yet left the source frame.

   You can draw the drag feedback on your own or with the help of platform-specific services such as the Mac OS Drag Manager's ShowDragHilite function.

3. Examine the current state of the machine, if desired, to obtain any relevant information (such as whether the user has pressed a modifier key since initiating the drag).

If you return kODFalse from this method, OpenDoc assumes you cannot accept a drop and will not subsequently call your DragWithin, DragLeave, or Drop methods as long as the mouse pointer remains in this facet.

While Within a Part's Facet

OpenDoc calls the potential destination part's DragWithin method continuously while the mouse pointer remains inside the facet.

```
ODDragResult DragWithin(in ODDragItemIterator dragInfo,
                        in ODFacet facet,
                        in ODPoint where);
```

In response, the part can do any desired processing inside its display. For example, if a part allows objects to be dropped only in individual hot spots, it may change its feedback based on the pointer location.

Calls to a part's DragWithin method also give the part an additional chance to examine the state of the user's system. For example, the part may want to find out whether the user has pressed a modifier key during the drag operation.

If you return kODFalse from this method, OpenDoc assumes you no longer wish to accept a drop in this facet. It will not make additional calls to your DragWithin method and will not call your DragLeave or Drop method as long as the mouse pointer remains in this facet.

On Leaving a Part's Facet

OpenDoc calls the DragLeave method of a potential destination part when the mouse pointer leaves a droppable facet.

```
void DragLeave(in ODFacet facet,
               in ODPoint where);
```

In response, the part might remove the adornment on its frame or restore the cursor appearance to its original form.

Dropping

If the user releases the mouse button while the pointer is within a facet, OpenDoc calls the `Drop` method of the facet's part. This is its interface:

```
ODDropResult Drop(in ODDragItemIterator dropInfo,
                  in ODFacet facet,
                  in ODPoint where);
```

The potential destination part then decides whether it can receive the dragged object. If it accepts the data, it either incorporates it or embeds it. This section describes how to design your drop method, how to accept a drop of non-OpenDoc data, and what the source part (the part that initiated the drag) should do after the drop occurs.

Drag Attributes and the Drop Method

The OpenDoc human interface guidelines specify when a drop should be considered a move and when it should be considered a copy; see "Dropping" on page 603. The destination part can inspect the OpenDoc drag attributes (by calling the `GetDragAttributes` method of the drag-and-drop object) to determine how to handle the drop. Drag attributes are bit flags, and more than one can be set at a time. Table 8-2 lists the defined OpenDoc drag attributes. The first two apply during the drag operation; the rest apply at the drop.

Table 8-2   Drag attributes

Constant	Description
kODDragIsInSourceFrame	The item being dragged has not yet left the source frame of the drag.
kODDragIsInSourcePart	The item being dragged has not yet left the source part of the drag.
kODDropIsInSourceFrame	The drop is occurring in the source frame of the drag.
kODDropIsInSourcePart	The drop is occurring in the part displayed in the source frame of the drag (though not necessarily in the source frame itself).

continued

Table 8-2   Drag attributes (continued)

Constant	Description
kODDropIsMove	This drag-and-drop operation is a move.
kODDropIsCopy	This drag-and-drop operation is a copy.
kODDropIsPasteAs	The destination part should display the Paste As dialog box (the user has held down the Command key while dropping).

In your `Drop` method, you might follow steps similar to these:

1. Use the `ODDragItemIterator` passed to you to determine whether you can handle the drop, as described in the section "On Entering a Part's Facet" on page 366. (Alternatively, you can set a "can-drop" flag in `DragEnter` or `DragWithin` that you inspect at this point.)

2. Examine the drag attributes to see, for example, whether this is a move or a copy and whether or not to display the Paste As dialog box.

3. If the drag attribute `kODDropIsPasteAs` is set (that is, if the user held down the Command key when the drop occurred), take these steps before reading from the drag-and-drop object:

   □ Call the `ShowPasteAsDialog` method of the drag-and-drop object to display a Paste As dialog box (see Figure 8-3 on page 337).

   □ If the `ShowPasteAsDialog` method returns a result of true, the user has pressed the OK button; use the results of the interaction (passed back as a structure of type `ODPasteAsResult`) to determine what action to take. The section "Handling the Paste As Dialog Box" on page 337 lists the kinds of pasting that the user can specify.

4. Depending on the nature of the data and the user's instructions, you may either incorporate the data or embed it, you may first translate it, and you may create a link to its source.

   □ If you are creating a link, follow the steps in "Creating a Link at the Destination" on page 383. Take into account the automatic/manual update setting, as well as the other Paste As settings chosen by the user.

   □ If you are translating but not creating a link, follow the steps in "Translating Before Incorporating or Embedding" on page 351.

□ If you are simply incorporating the data, follow the steps in "Incorporating Intrinsic Content" on page 344.

□ If you are simply embedding the data, follow the steps in "Embedding a Single Part" on page 347.

In all of these cases, you initially read the data from the drag-and-drop object, and you specify the following kinds of clone transactions:

□ If a move is specified (the drag attribute `kODDropIsMove` is set), use a clone transaction of `kODCloneDropMove`—unless the user has specified that a link be created. Creating a link takes precedence over specifying a drag-move; therefore, use a clone transaction of `kODCloneDropCopy` in this case.

□ If a copy is specified (the drag attribute `kODDropIsCopy` is set), use a clone transaction of `kODCloneDropCopy`

Note
The destination part can override a drag that is a move and force it to be a copy. It cannot, however, override a copy and force it to be a move. ◆

5. Add a single action to the action history (see "Adding an Action to the Undo Action History" on page 262) so that the user can undo the drop. The section "Adding Multistage Actions" on page 263 describes why this action must be a single-stage action.

   If the drop involves an embedded frame, follow the instructions listed in Table 6-4 on page 266: save the current value of the frame's in-limbo flag and then set the flag to false.

6. If it is not already active, activate the frame in which the drop occurred, and select the dropped content.

7. Notify OpenDoc and your containing part that there has been a change to your part's content; see "Making Content Changes Known" on page 307.

When it completes, your `Drop` method should return an appropriate result (of type `ODDropResult`), such as `kODDropCopy`, `kODDropMove`, or `kODDropFail`. OpenDoc in turn passes that information on to the source part; see "Completion of StartDrag" on page 372.

Accepting Non-OpenDoc Data

When your part's `Drop` method is called, it is passed a drag-item iterator so that you can access all drag items in the drag-and-drop object. If OpenDoc data has been dragged, there is only one drag item in the object. If the data comes from outside of OpenDoc (such as from the Mac OS Finder), there may be more than one item. It is the responsibility of the destination part to iterate through all the drag items to find out whether it can accept the drop.

You can examine the contents property of the storage unit of each dragged item to determine the kind of data the property contains. On the Mac OS, for example, if the drag was initiated in the Finder and the dragged item is a file, the contents property of the item's storage unit contains a value whose type is the OpenDoc ISO prefix followed by "MacOS:OSType:FileType:" followed by the Mac OS file-type designation. If the item is a text file, for example, the value type is (ISO prefix plus) "MacOS:OSType:FileType:TEXT". If you can read data of that type, you can incorporate it into your part. Otherwise, you may be able to embed it as a separate part.

- To access a file whose data you intend to incorporate, you can obtain the item's `HFSFlavor` structure (defined by the Mac OS Drag Manager) from a value of type (ISO prefix plus) "MacOS:OSType:ScrapType:hfs " in the contents property of the item's storage unit. You can then use that information to make file-system-specific calls to open the file and process its contents into your part.

- To embed dropped non-OpenDoc data as a part, you treat it just as you would OpenDoc data. You follow the procedures described in the section "Embedding a Single Part" on page 347, specifying a cloning operation of `kODCloneDropCopy` or `kODCloneDropMove` for the content storage unit of the dropped data. OpenDoc locates and binds a part editor to the data. That part editor itself then must obtain the item's `HFSFlavor` structure, access the file, read its data, and incorporate the data into the part's contents.

For more information, see the Mac OS Drag Manager documentation and *Inside Macintosh: Files*.

Completion of StartDrag

If your part is the source part of this drag, your call to the drag-and-drop object's `StartDrag` method completes after the destination's `Drop` method completes. You can now, based on the return value of `StartDrag`, confirm whether the operation was a move or a copy or whether it failed. Take these steps:

1. Whether it was a move or a copy, add an ending action to the undo action history (see "Adding Multistage Actions" on page 263), so that the user can undo the entire transaction, from initiating the drag to dropping the data. If it was a move, note any applicable special considerations given in "Handling Cut Data" on page 334.

   If the completed drag was initiated as a drag-move but ended up being a drag-copy, and if it involved an embedded frame, follow the instructions listed in Table 6-4 on page 266 (reset the frame's in-limbo flag to false).

2. If it was a move, delete the dragged content from your part and notify OpenDoc and your containing part that there has been a change to your content. See "Making Content Changes Known" on page 307.

3. Whether it was a move or a copy, call your source frame's `SetDragging` method once again, this time passing it a value of `kODFalse` to notify OpenDoc that the frame can once more be a drop target.

Asynchronous drag and drop
Version 1.0 of OpenDoc on the Mac OS does not support asynchronous drag and drop. For future compatibility, however, OpenDoc provides the `ODPart` method `DropCompleted`. This method is called to notify the source part of the completion of a drag that it initiated. The method provides the same drop results that `StartDrag` returns for a synchronous drag. ◆

Linking

Linking is a mechanism for placing information into a part and allowing that information to be updated whenever source information in another location changes.

Linking support in OpenDoc is a combination of event-handling code and storage code. It uses the same data-transfer mechanisms as the clipboard and drag and drop, but it also includes a set of notification calls that keep the transferred data synchronized with its source.

Some aspects of linking are closely related to other data-transfer concepts. Link specifications, used in writing data to the clipboard or drag-and-drop object, are described in the section "Link Specification" on page 317. The interactions between cutting and pasting and the preservation of link-related objects are listed in the section "Transfer Rules for Links and Link Sources" on page 398.

Link Concepts

Linking requires the cooperation of one or two parts with several linking-related objects. Figure 8-10 is a schematic illustration of the objects and data involved in linking. The figure shows a link between two separate parts (which can be in the same document or in different documents), although links can also occur within a single part.

Figure 8-10   Objects and data involved in linking

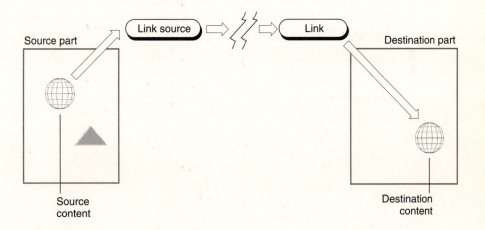

The user creates a link by requesting it during a paste or drop operation. The part that contains the source of the information to be linked is called the **source part.** The content that is to be copied and sent to another part is called the

source content or **source.** The source part creates an object, the **link source,** and places into it a copy of the source data; that copy is stored in the same document as the source part.

The part that is the intended destination of the information to be linked is called the **destination part.** The content that is actually copied into the destination part is called the **destination content** or **destination.** The draft object of the destination part creates an object, the **link,** that is stored in the same document as the destination part. For a link within a single document, the link object and the link-source object share the same copy of the source data. For cross-document links, the two objects use separate storage units that each have a copy of the linked content, although the existence of separate storage units does not affect your part's interactions with either object.

The link-source object contains references to all link objects for which it is the source. (Within a given document, there is only one link object associated with each link source, even if the source is linked to multiple destinations in the document.) The user is free to edit the source of a link; when a change occurs in the source part and the link needs to be updated, the source part copies the source content into the link-source object. The destination part then copies the content from the link object into the destination itself.

OpenDoc links are unidirectional; changes are propagated from the source to the destination only. You should not permit users to edit any link destinations that you maintain; such edits would be overwritten when the link is updated.

Whether it contains the source or the destination of a link, your part is responsible for defining the exact content that constitutes the linked data and for knowing what visual area it covers in your part's display. Linked data, whether source or destination, is part of your own content; you store and manipulate it according to your own content model, and under your own control.

Link Update ID

Each link source and each link destination—that is, every region of content that is the source or destination of a link—must have an associated **update ID.** The source part determines the update ID associated with the link and updates the ID each time the source changes. The destination part stores the update ID of the link that was current at the time the destination was last updated through the link.

Whenever the content in your part changes—for instance, in response to a series of keystroke events—you need to assign a new update ID to all link sources directly affected by that change. Note that all link sources affected by a given change must have the *same* update ID. You obtain a new update ID by calling the session object's `UniqueChangeID` method.

When you update a link source, you can save the update ID in your source content and use it later to determine whether your source content and the content of the link-source object are identical.

A **circular link** or **recursive link** can occur when changes to a link's destination directly or indirectly affect its source. To avoid endless sequences of updates, it is important that your part take these steps:

- Whenever your part updates a link destination that also participates in a link source, it must propagate the update ID passed to it. Your part must update the affected source with the update ID passed to the destination, rather than calling `UniqueChangeID`.

- Whenever a content change to your part results from an update to a link destination, your part must—when it calls its frame's `ContentUpdated` method—propagate the update ID passed to it.

- Whenever your part updates a link source manually (on explicit user instruction), it should not propagate an existing update ID. It should always call `UniqueChangeID` to get a new update ID.

Automatic and Manual Updating

OpenDoc informs destination parts when the sources of their links have been updated. The update notification can be

- **automatic,** which means immediately (if the source is in the same document as the destination) or whenever the user saves the source document (if the source is in a different document)

- **manual,** which means only when instructed to do so by the user

The user selects whether updating is to be automatic or manual, either in the Paste As dialog box when the link is first created, or in the Link Source Info and Link Destination Info dialog boxes after the link exists.The user must select both on-save updating at the source and automatic updating at the destination if automatic updating is to occur.

The user initiates a manual update by pressing the Update Now button in either the Link Source Info or Link Destination Info dialog box. Note, however, that manual updating applies to each half of the link separately:

■ Pressing the Update Now button in the Link Source Info dialog box updates the link source object from the source data, but it does not result in an update notification being sent to the destination part (unless the user has specified automatic updating at the destination).

■ Pressing the Update Now button in the Link Destination Info dialog box updates the link destination from the contents of the link object, but it does not update the link source object from the source data.

For link sources, the link source object retains information about whether updating is to be automatic or manual. For link destinations, it is up to the destination part to save that information (see "Link Info" on page 380), because the same link object can supply several destinations with different settings.

To be notified automatically of changes to the source of a link, your destination part calls the link object's `RegisterDependent` method, supplying it the update ID of the last content it read from the link. Each link object maintains a private registry of dependent parts and calls their `LinkUpdated` methods whenever the link source changes. Your part should respond to this method call by updating its destination content from the link object, as described in "Updating a Link at the Destination" on page 387.

If updating is to be automatic, your part should register for update notification when it first creates the link (passing an update ID of `kODUnknownUpdate`) and whenever your part reads itself from storage (passing the appropriate stored update ID from its link info structure). Be sure you are prepared to receive a notification when you call `RegisterDependent`, because your `LinkUpdated` method may be called before `RegisterDependent` returns. You can unregister and re-register as desired, but be careful not to register more than once at a time with the same link, even if it serves more than one destination in your content.

If your draft permissions (see "Drafts" on page 285) are read-only, you should not register for update notification. Even if you do register, you do not receive notifications.

Updating a manual link without user instruction
If you maintain a link source set for manual updating, the
state of your source content at any given time may be
different from the contents of the link-source object. If
another destination is added to the link, you must update
the link-source object—even though the user has not
explicitly requested the update—so that the new
destination and all existing destinations will show the
same content. ◆

Frame Link Status

All frames have a **link status** that describes the frame's participation in links.
Parts are responsible for setting the link status of all frames that they embed;
the link status indicates whether the frame is in the source of a link, in the
destination of a link, or not involved in any link. Parts can use this information
to decide whether to allow editing of linked data, and whether to allow
creation of a link within an existing link. See Table 8-4 on page 400 for a list of
the possible combinations.

When to Change Link Status

In general, any time that you create a link involving an embedded frame or add
an embedded frame to your part, you should set the frame's link status.

- When your part creates a link source, it should call the `ChangeLinkStatus`
  method of each the embedded frames within the content area of the link
  source, passing it the value `kODInLinkSource`.

- If you add embedded frames to a link source, call `ChangeLinkStatus` for each
  new frame, passing it the value `kODInLinkSource`.

- If pasting and creating a link destination in your part involves adding
  embedded frames at the destination, call `ChangeLinkStatus` for each new
  frame, passing it the value `kODInLinkDestination`. (This situation may arise
  either during a paste-with-link involving embedded frames, or during an
  update of a link destination that includes embedded frames.)

- Any time you embed a frame outside of any link source or destination that
  you maintain, set its status to `kODNotInLink`.

- If you break a link but keep the embedded data at the source or destination,
  set the status of each frame that was formerly linked to `kODNotInLink` (unless
  it is also in a source; see next item).

■ Destinations take precedence over sources. If one of your embedded frames is contained in a link destination that you maintain, and that destination is itself contained in a link source that you maintain, your should set the embedded frame's status to `kODInLinkDestination`. If you later break that link destination (but not its enclosing link source), set the frame's status to `kODInLinkSource` **rather than** `kODNotInLink`.

IMPORTANT

If you do not support linking, you must nevertheless set the link status of your embedded frames (to `kODNotInLink`). ▲

The `ChangeLinkStatus` method changes the value of the frame's link status, if necessary, and calls the `LinkStatusChanged` method of the frame's part, so that the part can change the link status of any of its own embedded frames.

When you set the link status of a frame in any of these situations, you need to take into account only the links that your part maintains; you can ignore your own display frame's link status. OpenDoc automatically adjusts the link status of frames that you embed to account for your display frame's status.

You can examine the link status of a frame by calling its `GetLinkStatus` method.

The LinkStatusChanged Method of Your Part Editor

Your own part's `LinkStatusChanged` method is called by the `ChangeLinkStatus` method of any of your display frames, whenever the display frame's link status is changed. This is its interface:

```
void LinkStatusChanged(in ODFrame frame);
```

Your implementation of `LinkStatusChanged` should iterate through all of your part's embedded frames, calling each one's `ChangeLinkStatus` method.

■ The link status of embedded frames already in links that you maintain cannot change; sources will remain sources, and destinations will remain destinations. Therefore, you do not need to call `ChangeLinkStatus` for them.

■ You can set the link status of embedded frames not involved in links that you maintain to be equal to your display frame's link status. However, you can also just set their link status to `kODNotInLink`, letting OpenDoc adjust their link status if necessary.

It is important to make this call to all of your embedded frames, so that they can in turn to call their parts' `LinkStatusChanged` method to change the link status of more deeply embedded frames, and so on.

You needn't call the `ChangeLinkStatus` method of all of your embedded frames immediately upon receiving a call to `ChangeLinkStatus`. If you instantiate frame objects only when needed for display (see "Lazy Internalization" on page 471), you can internally record which frames are affected, and then set their link status when you bring them into memory.

Note
If the user attempts to edit the content of any of your display frames whose link status is `kODInLinkDestination`, you should disallow the attempt. See "Editing a Link Destination" on page 395 for details. ◆

Content Changes in Embedded Frames

Because linked content can contain embedded frames, there must be a way for an embedded part to inform its containing part that its content has changed, so that the link can be updated.

The ContentUpdated Method

Any time a content change occurs in one of your part's display frames, you should follow the procedures described in the section "Making Content Changes Known" on page 307. Part of the procedure is to call the frame's `ContentUpdated` method. The `ContentUpdated` method then calls the `EmbeddedFrameUpdated` method of your part's containing part, informing it that the content of one of its embedded frames has changed. If your display frame is involved in a link source maintained by your part's containing part, the containing part can then choose to update the link-source object with the new data.

(This `ContentUpdated` method is unrelated to the `ContentUpdated` method of `ODLinkSource`, discussed in the section "Updating a Link at the Source" on page 389. However, you pass the same update ID to both `ContentUpdated` methods when a content change to your part is entirely due to a content change to its link source.)

The EmbeddedFrameUpdated Method of Your Part Editor

Your part's `EmbeddedFrameUpdated` method is called by the `ContentUpdated` method of any of your embedded frames whenever the content of the frame's part has changed. This is its interface:

```
void EmbeddedFrameUpdated(in ODFrame frame,
                          in ODUpdateID change);
```

The method is passed a reference to the embedded frame and an update ID identifying the modification. You should respond by saving the update ID and updating any link-source objects you maintain that involve that frame (and whose updating is automatic). When updating the link source, pass it the update ID you received in the call to this method.

Your `EmbeddedFrameUpdated` method should also call the `ContentUpdated` method of your own display frames that contain the embedded frame. In this way, the change is propagated upward throughout the embedding hierarchy.

Link Borders

If your part contains the source or destination of a link, you are responsible for drawing an appropriate border around the linked content area when requested to do so. Any time that the user selects any content within the link or checks the Show Links setting in your document's Document Info dialog box, you need to show the border of the link source or destination whenever you draw. For recommended appearances for the link border, see the sections "Link Borders" on page 530 and "Showing Link Borders and Selecting Links" on page 611.

Whenever you draw your part's content in a facet, first call the `ShouldShowLinks` method of the facet's window. If `ShouldShowLinks` returns `kODTrue`, draw borders around any link sources and destinations.

Link Info

The link info structure (type `ODLinkInfo`) contains fields that hold information about the nature of a link, such as the part kind of its intrinsic data, its creation date, and its update ID. Your part should allocate and maintain a link info structure for every link destination that it contains.

Here is the structure's definition:

```
struct ODLinkInfo
{
    ODType      kind;
    ODTime      creationTime;
    ODTime      changeTime;
    ODUpdateID  change;
    ODBoolean   autoUpdate;
};
```

You fill in the fields of the link info structure when you first create a link, you store it privately, and you update it as needed.

When you display the Link Destination Info dialog box, you pass a link info structure to the `ShowLinkDestinationInfo` method of the link object that represents your link destination.

If you move or copy a link destination, you transfer the link info along with it so that the new destination can maintain the same characteristics as the original.

For an example of the Link Destination Info dialog box and instructions on how to handle user interaction with it, see the section "Selection Info" on page 254.

Linking and Undo

Just as the basic data-transfer actions (cutting, pasting, and dropping) should be undoable, so should their variations that involve linked data. The user should be able to undo (and redo) any of these actions:

■ pasting or dropping content and creating a link to its source

■ pasting or dropping content that contains existing linked data

■ deleting or cutting content that includes one or more link sources or destinations

■ breaking a link at its source or its destination (through the Link Info dialog boxes)

When a link is created, the part receiving the data and creating the link destination adds a beginning action and ending action to the undo action history (see "Adding Multistage Actions" on page 263), whereas the source part adds a single action to the history when it creates the link source.

Edits to the source content of a link must also—like any edits to the content of your part—be undoable. However, updating a link source object from its source content does not need to be an undoable action.

- If the link source is updated manually, undoing or redoing changes to source content has no effect on the link source object. A manually updated link source always reflects the state of the source content at the last update.

- If the link source is updated automatically, changes to source content accomplished through an undo or redo action should cause you to update the link source as usual. (Be sure to use the update ID associated with the restored or redone content when updating.) Furthermore, automatic updating is not a user action; since it is not performed by user command, it likewise cannot be undone.

Likewise, updating the destination content of a link from its link object does not need to be an undoable action.

- Editing the content at the destination of a link is not generally permitted. Because undoing or redoing an update to a destination would constitute editing the destination, you should never put the update action in the undo or redo stacks.

- You can, however, allow changes to the destination content that can be maintained across a link update, such as a style applied to the entire destination. Such nonediting changes can be undoable or ignorable, depending on your part's content model.

When you delete or cut content that includes a link source or destination, or when you break a link, follow the procedures outlined in the section "Breaking and Cutting Links" on page 397 to make sure that you can undo the actions.

Manipulating Links

This section describes some of the basic procedures you follow in creating links, reading and writing linked data, and updating links.

Related information is described as part of general data-transfer considerations earlier in this chapter. Creating and removing link specifications are described in the sections "Link Specification" on page 317 and "Removing a Link Specification From the Clipboard" on page 357.

Both the source part and destination part of a link, or even separate destination parts of a single source, may attempt to access linked data simultaneously.

Therefore, many methods of the classes `ODLinkSource` and `ODLink` require that you provide a key before accessing the storage unit containing the content of a link. You obtain the key by first calling the `Lock` method of the link-source object or link object involved.

Creating a Link at the Destination

A link is created when the user decides—using the Paste As dialog box—to link rather than statically transfer data while performing a paste. The destination part—the part receiving the paste or drop—retrieves the link specification from the clipboard or drag-and-drop object and calls its draft's `AcquireLink` method. The draft in turn calls the `CreateLink` method of the source part (the part that placed the data in the clipboard or drag-and-drop object).

If your part is the destination part that creates a link to pasted data from the data's source, you can use the following steps. It is assumed that you have previously called the `ShowPasteAsDialog` method of the clipboard or drag-and-drop object (see "Handling the Paste As Dialog Box" on page 337) and are ready to act on the results of the Paste As dialog box. For clipboard transfer, this means that you have already acquired the clipboard focus (see "Acquiring and Relinquishing the Clipboard Focus" on page 356).

1. Focus the clipboard or drag-and-drop storage unit on the link specification it contains. Use your draft's `CreateLinkSpec` method to instantiate the link specification, then call the link specification's `ReadLinkSpec` method to have it read itself from the storage unit.

2. This link-creation procedure should be undoable. If the data transfer for this link is a paste from the clipboard, add a beginning action to start a multistage transaction. That way, if the user decides to reverse the paste, both the paste and this link creation will be undone together. (Do nothing here if this data transfer is a drop.)

3. Pass the link specification to your draft's `AcquireLink` method to construct the link object from the link specification.

4. Create a link-info structure (type `ODLinkInfo`) to associate with the link destination, as described in the section "Link Info" on page 380. Initialize its update ID (to `kODUnknownUpdate`), set its creation time to the current time, set its modification time to the modification time of the link object, and give it a part kind and an auto-update setting that reflect the user's choices in the Paste As dialog box.

5. Add this link object to whatever private list of link destinations you maintain. Store the information you need to associate this link object with its link info structure and with the link-destination content in your part.

   If you have translated the data that now makes up your link destination, you also need to record the part kind that it was translated *from*. You will have to translate the data again for each subsequent update to the link, and you will need to know which part kind in the data to read and translate.

6. If the user has specified auto-updating in the Paste As dialog box, *and* if your part has not already registered with this link object in connection with other link destinations, call the link's `RegisterDependent` method. Otherwise, manually update the link at this time by performing whatever actions your part's `LinkUpdated` method would perform (see "Updating a Link at the Destination" on page 387).

7. To ensure that this link-creation procedure is undoable, take either of these steps:

   □ If the data transfer for this link was a paste from the clipboard, add an ending action to the action history at this time, to complete the two-stage action started in step 2.

   □ If the data transfer for this link is a drop, you only need to add a single action to the undo action history. If the user undoes the drop, this link will be deleted also.

8. Call the `ChangeLinkStatus` method of any of your part's newly embedded frames that are within the linked content area, passing them the value `kODInLinkDestination`.

Never read the link content from the storage unit of the clipboard or drag-and-drop object when creating the link; always read link content from the link object's storage unit.

Every time the link is updated, your part (the destination part) must discard the data in the link destination and read it again from the link object. This process can entail discarding embedded parts and creating them anew from the updated link content. See "Updating a Link at the Destination" on page 387 for details.

Your destination part must be able to draw a border around the link content area when asked to do so, as described in "Link Borders" on page 380. Parts embedded in linked data are not involved in the maintenance of the link; even in the case of a link destination that consists of a single embedded part, you draw the link border around the embedded part's frame.

Note that only the draft should call CreateLink; if your part is a destination part that needs a link to be created, you should call your draft's AcquireLink method.

Creating a Link at the Source

When the user decides to create a link to data that your part placed on the clipboard or drag-and-drop object, the destination part's draft calls the CreateLink method of your part (the source part). The draft passes back the data of the link specification that your part originally wrote when it placed the data on the clipboard or drag-and-drop object. This is the interface to CreateLink:

```
ODLinkSource CreateLink(in ODByteArray data);
```

When your source part's CreateLink method is called, the method should duplicate in a link-source object all of the content that your part originally wrote (or wrote promises for) to the clipboard or drag-and-drop object.

In your source part's CreateLink method, you can follow these general steps:

1. Examine your own structures to see if the link-source object already exists. CreateLink may have been called as a consequence of another destination being added to this link source, as described in "Replacing Link-Source Content in CreateLink" on page 386.

   □ If the link-source object does exist, it may not contain a complete set of promises or data. In that case, you need to write the remaining part kinds to it. You can do so by updating the link source in a particular manner. Skip to step 5.

   (If the link-source object does exist and does contain a complete set of promises or data, you could return the existing link-source object and take no further action. However, it may be simpler just to just rewrite all part kinds than to test to see if you have a complete set.)

   □ If the link-source object does not yet exist, continue with step 2.

2. Create a link source object by calling your draft's CreateLinkSource method.

3. Add this link-source object to whatever private list of link sources you maintain. Store the update ID and any other information you need to associate this link-source object with the link-source content in your part.

Data Transfer

8

4. Call the `ChangeLinkStatus` method of any of your part's embedded frames that are within the linked content area, passing them the value `kODInLinkSource`.

5. Update the link source. Follow the steps listed in "Updating a Link at the Source" on page 389.

6. Creating a link source needs to be undoable. Add a single action to the undo action history so that you can remove the link source if the user decides to undo its creation.

7. Unlock the link-source object.

8. Increment the reference count of the link-source object and return a reference to the link-source object as the method result. (The caller is responsible for releasing the link-source object when it is no longer needed.)

If it intends to create a link, a destination part cannot inspect your link specification to determine the available part kinds of the intrinsic content; instead, it learns what part kinds are available by inspecting the contents property of the clipboard or drag-and-drop storage unit that accompanies the link specification. Your source part should therefore write the same content representations into the link-source content storage unit that it originally wrote into the clipboard or drag-and-drop content storage unit, because the destination part may be expecting any of those part kinds.

Replacing Link-Source Content in CreateLink

If your part's `CreateLink` method is called and the link-specification data provided describes an existing link source that you maintain, your part must ensure that all content kinds that you support are available at the destination. If your part writes promises to the link source, you can ensure that all kinds are promised by replacing the current content in your link-source object. The procedure for replacing is similar to the regular updating procedure, except that you pass an existing update ID to the link-source object's `Clear` method, and you do not call the link-source object's `ContentUpdated` method. See "Updating a Link at the Source" on page 389 for details.

If the link source is set for manual updates, and if your part has written promises to the link-source object, and if the source content has changed since the last update, your part may have to perform an explicit update—without waiting for user instruction—at this time.

Updating a Link at the Destination

When a source part updates its link-source object and calls the object's
`ContentUpdated` method, the link-source object immediately notifies its
associated link objects of the change (except for link objects in other documents,
which do not receive the notification until the source document is saved). The
link destinations receive notification of the change in this manner:

■ If the user has selected automatic updating of a link destination associated
with one of the notified link objects, the link object associated with the
updated source immediately notifies the destination part of the change by
calling its `LinkUpdated` method.

■ If the user has selected manual updating, the destination part is not notified.
In this case, it updates the destination only on user instruction, as described
in "Automatic and Manual Updating" on page 375.

If your part contains the destination of a link and has registered as a dependent
of the link (by calling the link's `RegisterDependent` method), OpenDoc
automatically calls your part's `LinkUpdated` method whenever the link object
receives notification of an update to the source. This is the interface to
`LinkUpdated`:

```
void LinkUpdated(in ODLink updatedLink,
                 in ODUpdateID change);
```

You can perform automatic updates in your part's `LinkUpdated` method, and
manual updates in response to a user command in the Link Destination Info
dialog box (see "Selection Info" on page 254).

It is not always necessary to update immediately, during execution of
`LinkUpdated` or when manually instructed to do so by the user. For example, if
the destination has scrolled offscreen but is still registered as a dependent of
the source, updating does not need to occur until (and if) the destination scrolls
back into view. Your part editor can, if desired, generally perform link updates
as a background task.

You can take the steps shown here to read the contents of a link object when
updating your link destinations.

1. Call the link object's `Lock` method. If you cannot acquire the lock for the link,
it may be momentarily in use by another object; wait and try again.

2. Retrieve your part's stored link-info structure for that link.

3. Access the link object's storage unit by calling its `GetContentStorageUnit` method. (If `GetContentStorageUnit` returns the error `kODErrNoLinkContent`, the last source update failed; do not update you destination at this time.)

Incorporate or embed the updated data into your part from the link object's contents property:

   ☐ If you are incorporating the linked data, follow the steps in "Incorporating Intrinsic Content" on page 344.

   ☐ If you are embedding the linked data as a single part, follow the steps in "Embedding a Single Part" on page 347.

   ☐ If you are translating the linked data before incorporating or embedding it, follow the steps in "Translating Before Incorporating or Embedding" on page 351. Use information you recorded when you first created the link to know which part kind to read for translation.

In any of these cases, the only differences from other data-transfer operations are that you call the `Clone` method of the link object's storage unit's draft, you specify a clone transaction of `kODCloneFromLink`, and you read from the link object's content storage unit.

You must discard any previously embedded parts and frames, replacing them with new ones cloned from the link. Also, you must connect the frames to your frame hierarchy, create facets for the currently visible ones, and change their link status by calling their `ChangeLinkStatus` method, passing the value `kODInLinkDestination`.

4. Update the link-info structure for the link with a new update ID and new change time obtained by calling the link's `GetUpdateID` and `GetChangeTime` methods.

5. Unlock the link.

6. Inspect your part's private structures to see if this change has affected the data of any link source in your part. (It can if this destination is within a source.) If so, modify the source as shown in the section "Updating a Link at the Source" (next).

7. Notify OpenDoc and your containing part that there has been a change to your part's content; see "Making Content Changes Known" on page 307.

If your part maintains the destination of a link whose source has been transferred from one part to another, the new source part might not write its data using all of the same part kinds as the original source part. Your part, therefore, might not be able to obtain updates in the format that it expects. If that situation occurs, your part should read whatever part kind it can, or else break the link.

Updating a Link at the Source

The part maintaining the source of a link can rewrite values into the link-source object as necessary to update the link. If your part is the source part, take the steps listed here to update the contents of your link source (or to write it for the first time).

The section "Automatic and Manual Updating" on page 375 describes how the user chooses whether updating should be automatic or manual. If the user has selected automatic (on-save) updating of the link source, perform this task whenever there is a change to the link-source content. If the user has selected manual updating of the link source, perform this task only on user command (see "Selection Info" on page 254).

The basic procedure for updating a link source is to first remove all content from the link source by calling its `Clear` method. By calling `Clear`, you ensure that all unneeded storage units are removed from the link, saving space in your draft.

The `Clear` method deletes the contents property of the link-source storage unit and all its data. You need to add a contents property and values back into the storage unit after calling `Clear`, just as if you were creating the link source from scratch.

In summary, follow these steps:

1. Call the link-source object's `Lock` method, and then call its `Clear` method. If you cannot acquire the lock for the link source, it may be momentarily in use by another object; wait and try again.

   □ If you are updating the link source because of content changes in your part, or if you are writing to the link source for the first time, or if this is a manual update, obtain a unique update ID and pass it to `Clear`.

   □ If you are updating the link source because of an update to a link destination within your source content, pass the link destination's existing update ID (the one that was passed to your `LinkUpdated` method) to `Clear`.

   □ If you are updating the link source because a change to an embedded frame caused your part to receive a call to its `EmbeddedFrameUpdated` method, pass the existing update ID (the one that was passed to `EmbeddedFrameUpdated`) to `Clear`.

   □ If you are just adding new part kinds to an unchanged existing link source, pass the link source's existing update ID to `Clear`. (You must update the link if a new destination has been added and if the link source does not have a complete set of promises for all part kinds that you support.)

2. Access the link-source object's storage unit, create the contents property and the appropriate values, and write your updated source data. Write either data or a promise for all part kinds that you support, including standard part kinds. Update the frame shape annotation and any other needed annotation properties.

   ☐ If the data is intrinsic content—with or without one or more embedded parts—follow the procedure given in the section "Writing Intrinsic Content" on page 341.

   ☐ If the data is a single embedded part, follow the procedure given in the section "Writing a Single Embedded Part" on page 342.

   Either way, specify a clone operation of kODCloneToLink. You are encouraged to write one or more promises instead of writing the actual data, to avoid placing unused content into the link source.

3. If you are just adding new part kinds to an unchanged existing link source, skip this step. Otherwise, after you have updated the data of the link-source object, notify it of the change, like this:

   ☐ If the content change originated in your source part, if this is the first time you are writing to the link, or if this is a manual update, call the link-source object's ContentUpdated method and pass it a new update ID (obtained from the session object's UniqueChangeID method), so that it can in turn send update notifications to all its link destinations.

   ☐ If the content change occurred in a link destination contained within your link source, call the link-source object's ContentUpdated method and pass it the link destination's existing update ID (the one that was passed to your LinkUpdated method), to avoid endless updating of circular links.

   ☐ If the content change occurred in an embedded frame and your part's EmbeddedFrameUpdated method was called, call the link-source object's ContentUpdated method and pass it the existing update ID (the one that was passed to EmbeddedFrameUpdated).

4. Unlock the link source.

In general, it is not necessary and not always desirable to perform automatic updates to link-source objects immediately in response to every content change. When content is changing rapidly, such as during text entry, it is reasonable to wait for a pause before updating any affected links.

Writing Linked Content to Storage

When your part writes itself to storage (see "Writing a Part to Storage" on page 297), or when it writes all or a portion of itself to a data-transfer object (see "Writing to a Data-Transfer Object" on page 340), it writes any linked data—whether source or destination—just as it would write any other content. In addition, however, it needs to write information for reconstructing the link objects and link-source objects involved.

Writing Links in Externalize

There is no standard way to associate a link-source object or link object with a specific region of your content; how you create that association depends on the nature of your content. However, for all links, your `Externalize` method and your methods that write to data-transfer objects need to write persistent references to the objects themselves, plus additional information. You should write the information in a format that is standard to your part kind; that way, any part editor that reads your part kind can reconstruct links from the stored data.

For the source of a link, you need to include, in addition to a persistent reference to the storage unit of the `ODLinkSource` object, the update ID associated with the linked content. (This may be different from the update ID in the link-source object itself, if the link is updated manually.)

For the destination of a link, you need to include a persistent reference to the storage unit of the `ODLink` object, plus the information in the fields of the `ODLinkInfo` structure: the part kind, creation time, modification time, update ID, and auto-update setting of the linked data. Also, if your part has translated the linked data at the destination, you need to store the original part kind of the data (the kind before you translated it).

Your part may also store extra information for convenience. For example, because your part needs to be able to draw a border around linked data, it may store link-border shapes in a private structure.

Writing Links for Data Transfer

If your part writes a single embedded frame (without surrounding intrinsic content) to the clipboard or drag-and-drop object, and if that frame is a link source or link destination, follow the procedures listed in "Writing a Single Embedded Part" on page 342. In addition, however, clone the link or link-source object into the data-transfer object's draft and add a property with the name `kODPropProxyContents` to the clipboard or drag-and-drop storage unit. In that property write a value that references the link or link-source object, as well as the link info fields and other necessary information. Any destination part that understands the proxy format can then recover the link.

If you write linked content to a data-transfer object and the destination part does not support linking, the content may be transferred, but the links will not be.

Reading Linked Content From Storage

When your part reads itself into memory, it may need to read in link-source objects and link objects as well. Likewise, when your part incorporates data that the user has pasted or dropped, your part may need to modify link sources or link destinations contained in that data.

Special care is necessary because OpenDoc can eliminate links during data transfer (see, for example, Table 8-3 on page 399). Therefore, you must perform the following two tasks when reading in data that includes links:

■ Before you attempt to read in a link-related object, you must ensure that your persistent reference to it is valid.

■ For every link-source object that you read in, you must ensure that your part is assigned as its source. The original source of the link may have been in another part, if the source content has been moved.

Reading Links in InitPartFromStorage

Here are the steps you can take to handle linked data when reading your part (in `InitPartFromStorage`). The general procedure for reading a part is described in the section "The InitPartFromStorage Method" on page 295.

1. As you encounter a persistent reference to a link object or link-source object in the content you are reading, ensure that the reference is valid. Before trying to read in the referenced storage unit, pass the persistent reference to the `IsValidStorageUnitRef` method of the storage unit containing the content you are reading.

   ☐ If `IsValidStorageUnitRef` returns true, call your draft's `AcquireLinkSource` or `AcquireLink` method to read in the object.

   ☐ If `IsValidStorageUnitRef` returns false, the link-source object or link object no longer exists, and your part should no longer consider the associated portion of its own content as linked. This is not an error situation, and you need not notify the user if it occurs.

2. For each link-source object you read, call its `SetSourcePart` method to associate it with your part. Add the link-source object to whatever private list of link sources you maintain, and associate the object with the specific content in your part that is the source of the link.

3. For each link object you read, locate the link-info structure for the link and associate the link object with the specific content in your part that is the destination of the link. Add the link object to whatever private structures you maintain for link destinations.

4. For each link object you read, be prepared to register for update notification if updating is to be automatic. Either at this point or (preferably) once the linked data becomes visible or affects visible content, pass the last-saved update ID to the link's `RegisterDependent` method.

Reading Links for Data Transfer

Here are the steps you can take to handle linked data when reading (cloning) from the clipboard or drag-and-drop object. The general procedure for reading from a data-transfer object is described in the section "Incorporating Intrinsic Content" on page 344.

1. After the clone operation completes successfully—assuming that you have followed the cloning steps listed in the section "The Cloning Sequence" on page 321 and have saved all object IDs returned by the `Clone` method—pass the ID of each cloned link object or link-source object to your draft's `IsValidID` method to determine if its object is valid.

   □ If `IsValidID` returns true, call your draft's `AcquireLinkSource` or `AcquireLink` method to read in the object.

   □ If `IsValidID` returns false, the link-source object or link object no longer exists and was not cloned. This situation occurs whenever you attempt to clone a link object or link-source object into a link destination, a configuration that OpenDoc does not permit. This is not an error condition, and you need not notify the user if it occurs. You should delete any private data you have associated with the uncloned object (but not the actual content of the link source or destination, which now simply becomes unlinked data).

2. For each link-source object you read, call its `SetSourcePart` method to associate it with your part. Add the link-source object to whatever private list of link sources you maintain, and associate the object with the specific content in your part that is the source of the link. (That information is

included in the contents property of the transferred data and is defined by the format of the part kind your editor is reading.)

3. For each link object you read, locate the link-info structure for the link and associate the link object with the specific content in your part that is the destination of the link. Add the link object to whatever private structures you maintain for link destinations. (That information is included in the contents property of the transferred data and is defined by the format of the part kind your editor is reading.)

4. If you are reading and embedding a single part that is also a link source or destination, there should be a property named `kODPropProxyContents` in the data-transfer storage unit. The property should contain a persistent reference to the link-source object or link object associated with the embedded part, plus any other needed information such as the fields of the link info structure. If you understand the format of the data in the property, read it and use it.

If you have incorporated an existing link source into your part, you may not be able to write all the data types (part kinds) to the link-source object that its previous owner did. That is not an error; simply write the part kinds that you support.

Revealing the Source of a Link

Users need to be able to navigate from the destination of a link to the source content. When the user clicks the Find Source button in the Link Destination Info dialog box (see Figure 6-5 on page 258), the destination part calls the `ShowSourceContent` method of the link object. OpenDoc in turn calls the source part's `RevealLink` method. This is its interface:

```
void RevealLink(in ODLinkSource linkSource);
```

If your part contains the source of a link, your `RevealLink` method should display the part content that corresponds to the link source, following these general steps:

1. Make your document's process the active process, if necessary. On the Mac OS platform, for example, you can call the Process Manager's `SetFrontProcess` function.

2. Using whatever part-specific method you choose, locate a display frame of the source content. If no suitable frame exists, open a part window to display the source.

3. Ensure that the frame displaying the source is visible in the window. Find its containing fame by calling its `AcquireContainingFrame` method, then call the `RevealFrame` method of the containing frame's part. (The procedure is unnecessary if your part opened a separate part window for the link source, because the display frame, being the root frame for the window, is already visible.)

4. Activate the frame, using your part's normal activation procedure (see "How Part Activation Happens" on page 198). Scroll the content in the revealed frame, if necessary, to make the link source visible.

5. Select the source content and draw a link border around it.

If your part is the part that needs to reveal an embedded frame containing a link source, you receive a call to your `RevealFrame` method. This is its interface:

```
ODBoolean RevealFrame(in ODFrame embeddedFrame,
                      in ODShape revealShape);
```

Scroll your content, if necessary, to reveal the portion of the specified embedded frame containing the specified shape. If the embedded frame is not currently visible because your containing part has scrolled your display frame out of view, call your containing part's `RevealFrame` method, passing it your own display frame and an appropriate shape (such as the shape of the embedded frame to be revealed).

Editing a Link Destination

Because OpenDoc links are unidirectional from source to destination, the OpenDoc human interface guidelines (see "Editing Links" on page 609) restrict the editing that a user can perform within the destination of a link. Basically, changing of content in a link destination should not be allowed.

It is the responsibility of the destination part to block attempts to edit its link destinations. However, the part that initially receives an editing event may be a frame embedded within, perhaps deeply embedded within, the destination part. If your part's display frame has the status `kODInLinkDestination` and the user attempts to edit content within it, your part should call the `EditInLink` method of your frame. OpenDoc in turn calls the `EditInLinkAttempted` method of the part that maintains the link destination that includes your frame.

This is the interface to `EditInLinkAttempted`:

```
ODBoolean EditInLinkAttempted(in ODFrame frame);
```

The part that maintains the link destination should, in its `EditInLinkAttempted` method, take steps similar to these:

1. It should check that it does indeed maintain a link destination involving the specified frame. If not, the method should return false and exit.

2. It should present to the user an alert box, like one at the top of Figure 14-13 on page 610, that allows the user to forego the editing, break the link, or display its source. In any case, the part should not activate itself.

    □ If the user chooses to forego editing, `EditInLinkAttempted` should simply return true.

    □ If the user chooses to display the source, `EditInLinkAttempted` should follow the instructions listed in "Revealing the Source of a Link" on page 394, calling the `ShowSourceContent` method of the link object. If `ShowSourceContent` fails, display an appropriate alert box notifying the user of the failure to find the link source, and return true from `EditInLinkAttempted`.

    □ If the user chooses to break the link, `EditInLinkAttempted` should follow the instructions listed in "Breaking and Cutting Links" (next), and return true.

If `EditInLinkAttempted` returns true, then `EditInLink` returns true to your part (the part in whose display frame the edit attempt occurred). If the user has broken the link, your part's display frame now has a different link status and you can therefore allow editing of your content.

If `EditInLinkAttempted` returns false, then `EditInLink` returns false; either OpenDoc cannot find the part that maintains the link destination or it cannot navigate to the link source. Your part should then put up its own simple alert box (shown in the center of Figure 14-13 on page 610), informing the user that editing in a link destination is not allowed.

If the user selects more than one link destination in your part and then attempts to edit the data, your part cannot even call `EditInLink`. It should then disallow editing and display a dialog box like that shown at the bottom of Figure 14-13 on page 610, suggesting that the user select a single destination.

Breaking and Cutting Links

Users can delete links in several ways, according to the guidelines presented in the section "Creating and Deleting Links" on page 606.

When you delete or cut content that includes a link source, or when you break a link at its source, your part relinquishes ownership of the link-source object, as noted in Table 8-3 on page 399. You should

- disassociate the link-source object from your part's content

- set the link's source part to null by calling the link source's `SetSourcePart` method

- save a reference to the link-source object in an undo action, rather than releasing the link source immediately

- call the `SetChangedFromPrev` method of your draft to make sure that this change is saved when the document is closed

- for a link that has been broken, change the link status of any affected frames (see "Frame Link Status" on page 377)

It is not necessary at this point to update the link source to delete its contents. If the user subsequently undoes the action, you can reverse the steps listed in the previous paragraph. You must be sure to call the link-source object's `SetSourcePart` method once again to reestablish your part as the link's source.

When you delete or cut content that includes a link destination, or when you break a link at its destination, you should

- disassociate the link object from your part's content

- save a reference to the link object in an undo action, rather than releasing the link immediately

- call the link object's `UnregisterDependent` method so that your part will no longer be notified when updates occur, if the link had been registered and if there are no remaining registered destinations of this link in your part

- call the `SetChangedFromPrev` method of your draft, to make sure that this change is saved when the document is closed

- change the link status of any affected frames (see "Frame Link Status" on page 377), if the link has been broken

Reverse all of these actions of the user undoes the break or cut.

You part should hold the references to a cut or broken link source or link until your `DisposeActionState` method is called, at which time you can release the link or link-source object.

Transfer Rules for Links and Link Sources

This section summarizes the semantics of data transfer involving link objects and link-source objects. This discussion is for informational purposes only; if you follow the procedures presented earlier in this chapter, the correct semantics will always occur.

During some data-transfer operations, OpenDoc may delete or redirect link or link-source objects. Other operations are permitted by OpenDoc but should not be supported by your part. This section lists the basic data-transfer operations, in terms of

- what happens when your part moves or copies linked data

- what happens when your part creates a link destination when pasting or dropping data that is already linked

- what configurations of links within links your part should support

The section "Moving and Copying Links" on page 614 summarizes the interface guidelines that you should follow to be consistent with these restrictions.

OpenDoc enforces the behaviors listed in Table 8-3 when existing links or link sources and their associated intrinsic content are transferred by drag and drop or with the clipboard, according to the specified kind of cloning operation.

Table 8-3   Behavior of existing links during data transfer

Operation	Data and object	Behavior
Copy (Drag-copy, or Copy followed by Paste)	Link source	Data is transferred; link source is not
	Link destination	*In same document:* Data is copied; link destination is copied also
		Across documents: Data is copied; link destination is not copied
	Source and destination of same link	Data is copied; link source and destination are both copied (but any uncopied destinations of the original source remain linked to the original source)
Move (Drag-move, or Cut followed by Paste)	Link source	*In same document:* Data is transferred; link source is transferred also
		Across documents: Data is transferred; link source is deleted (destinations within original document become unlinked)
	Link destination	*In same document:* Data is transferred; link destination is transferred also
		Across documents: Data is transferred; link destination is deleted
	Source and destination of same link	*In same document:* Data is transferred; link source and destination are both transferred
		Across documents: Data is transferred; any unmoved destinations of the link source become unlinked

Data Transfer

When pasting or accepting a drop into your part, you can incorporate or embed data that includes existing link sources or destinations and at the same time make the transferred data a link destination. In that situation, OpenDoc transfers that data and creates a link destination, but does not maintain any link sources or destinations that were included in the transferred data.

You can create links within links; OpenDoc does not prevent you from creating or pasting the source or destination of one link within the source or destination of another link. However, only some configurations make sense, as shown in Table 8-4. You can use your display frame's link status (see "Frame Link Status" on page 377), as well as private link-status information about your own intrinsic content, to decide whether to allow the creation of a link source or destination in any given situation.

Table 8-4   Creating links within links

To create a new...	Within an existing...	Recommendation
Link source	Link source	**OK.** Result is two separate link sources with partially or completely overlapping content.
Link source	Link destination	**NO.** When the destination is updated, it is generally impossible to know which changes should become part of the updated source.
Link destination	Link source	**OK.** Updates to the destination simply become part of the source.
Link destination	Link destination	**NO.** Updates to either link destination overwrite the other.

CHAPTER 9

Semantic Events and Scripting

Contents

This is the seventh of eight chapters that discuss the OpenDoc programming interface in detail. This chapter describes the scripting support provided for your parts by OpenDoc.

Before reading this chapter, you should be familiar with the concepts presented in Chapter 1, "Introduction to OpenDoc," and Chapter 2, "Development Overview." For additional concepts related to your part editor's runtime environment, see Chapter 11, "OpenDoc Runtime Features."

Scripting support is one example of the use of the OpenDoc extension interface. Extending OpenDoc through its extension interface is described in general terms in Chapter 10, "Extending OpenDoc."

This chapter first summarizes the Open Scripting Architecture and OpenDoc scripting in general. It then describes the OpenDoc semantic interface, a set of classes, utilities, and handlers you can take advantage of in implementing your support for scripting. The chapter then describes how to write and install

- semantic-event handlers
- object accessors
- object-callback functions, coercion handlers, and predispatch handlers

The chapter concludes with a discussion of how to construct object specifiers and send semantic events from your part.

All discussion in this chapter is specific to the Mac OS platform. The explanations in this chapter extend the discussions of Apple events, the Apple event object model, and the Open Scripting Architecture presented in *Inside Macintosh: Interapplication Communication*. It is assumed that you are already familiar with, or have access to, the descriptions of Mac OS scripting found in that book.

Scripting and OpenDoc

Scripting is a powerful way to automate and customize programs. By adding scripts to a program and executing them, a user can simplify and automate tasks that might otherwise require extensive and repetitive human interaction. If the program allows, a user might even be able to use scripts to change the meaning of existing commands. As a simple example, a user might customize the meaning of a "Save" command so that it updates a logging database every time a document is saved.

CHAPTER 9

Semantic Events and Scripting

OpenDoc allows for scripting of **semantic events,** distinguished from user events in that they are high-level actions understandable by the user and by the program but independent of individual user actions. Semantic events can be used to open, close, and save documents; embed parts; and manipulate part content and appearance.

OpenDoc supports your part editor's ability to receive and process semantic events through its **semantic interface,** a set of classes providing methods that you can use or override. The class `ODSemanticInterface` is a subclass of the extension class (`ODExtension`), described in Chapter 10, "Extending OpenDoc." You use a subclass of the semantic interface class and possibly one or more utility classes to set up and register semantic-event handlers and callback functions. (OpenDoc also supports your part editor's ability to create and send semantic events through another object, the **message interface,** an object of the class `ODMessageInterface`.)

Any entity that understands the semantic interface of a part can send it semantic events. Script editors can convert scripting commands to semantic events and send them to any object in any part of a document. Parts can send semantic events to their containing parts, to embedded parts, to sibling parts, to linked parts—to any parts for which they can find an address. Other types of OpenDoc components can also send semantic events; spelling checkers, for example, can use them to operate on the content of text parts.

Scripting support in OpenDoc can be pervasive; if you take full advantage of it, literally every action a user can take may invoke a script. However, a range of options exists, and you can decide what level of scripting support makes the most sense for your parts.

Your part editor supports scripting through the OpenDoc semantic interface in much the same way as a conventional application supports scripting. Your part editor must provide an interface to its content objects and operations, and it must accept semantic events. The document shell passes semantic events to OpenDoc to deliver to your parts. Event targets are described by object specifiers, which refer to objects in your parts in terms of your published content model. The document shell needs information from your part editor to resolve these specifiers so that it can determine where to deliver the events.

The Open Scripting Architecture

The scripting capability of OpenDoc is based on the Open Scripting Architecture (OSA). OSA is a powerful cross-platform messaging and scripting system that can support multiple scripting languages. OSA has three basic components: the Apple events messaging system, the Apple events object model, and one or more scripting systems. This section gives a brief summary of these components. For complete documentation of OSA, see *Inside Macintosh: Interapplication Communication*.

Apple Events

The system of semantic events at the base of the OpenDoc implementation of OSA on the Mac OS is Apple events. Apple events are described in the Apple events chapters of *Inside Macintosh: Interapplication Communication*.

Apple events are messages that applications use to request services and information from each other. The application making the request constructs and sends an Apple event to the application receiving the request. The receiving application uses an **Apple event handler** to extract pertinent data from the Apple event, perform the requested action, and possibly return a result.

Apple events constitute a standard vocabulary of actions that can be requested. Apple events are grouped into suites of related events. The *Apple Event Registry: Standard Suites* describes several commonly implemented suites. The most important suite to support for general scriptability is the **Core suite,** the suite that contains events common to many kinds of application software.

When sending an Apple event, the sending application can specify that the event apply, not to the receiving application as a whole, but to some element of the receiving application's data. For example, an application can request the data of a particular row of a particular table in a particular report. The sender constructs an **object specifier,** which it sends along with the Apple event, denoting the exact element or elements to which the event applies. The *Apple Event Registry* includes definitions of the kinds of objects recognized within each suite.

The **Apple Event Manager** is the component of system software that manages the construction, sending, and processing of Apple events. It handles Apple events in general and dispatches events for conventional applications. With OpenDoc, Apple events and the Apple Event Manager function essentially as described in *Inside Macintosh: Interapplication Communication;* however, there are some differences caused by the differences between parts and conventional applications.

■ OpenDoc does its own dispatching of Apple events, to ensure that the event is directed to the correct part and that the reply returns to the original sending part. That behavior is almost exactly the same as that provided by the Apple Event Manager, except that the sender of the event no longer has access to the event's `returnID` parameter. Because this parameter is for OpenDoc's internal use only, it is therefore missing from the `Send` method of `ODMessageInterface`.

■ OpenDoc itself implements some of the Apple Event Manager functions. For those functions, you must use the corresponding methods defined by OpenDoc instead of directly calling the Apple Event Manager. Cover methods for Apple event functions are contained in the classes `ODCPlusSemanticInterface` (for calling handlers), `ODMessageInterface` (for constructing and sending events), and `ODNameResolver` (for resolving object specifiers).You can also optionally make use of methods in the utility class `SIHelper` to install and remove handlers. Functions for which there is no corresponding OpenDoc method are available directly from the Apple Event Manager. Table 9-1 lists the Apple Event Manager functions and their equivalent OpenDoc methods.

Table 9-1   OpenDoc equivalents to Apple Event Manager functions

Apple Event Manager function (don't use)	OpenDoc method (do use)
`AEResolve`	`ODNameResolver::Resolve`
`AECallObjectAccessor`	`ODNameResolver::CallObjectAccessor`
`AECreateAppleEvent`	`ODMessageInterface::CreateEvent`
`AESend`	`ODMessageInterface::Send`
`AEInstallCoercionHandler`	`SIHelper::InstallCoercionHandler`
`AEInstallEventHandler`	`SIHelper::InstallEventHandler`
`AEInstallObjectAccessor`	`SIHelper::InstallObjectAccessor`
`AEInstallSpecialHandler`	`SIHelper::InstallSpecialHandler` (plus individual Install*Callback* methods)

continued

Table 9-1   OpenDoc equivalents to Apple Event Manager functions (continued)

Apple Event Manager function (don't use)	OpenDoc method (do use)
AEGetCoercionHandler	SIHelper::GetCoercionHandler
AEGetEventHandler	SIHelper::GetEventHandler
AEGetObjectAccessor	SIHelper::GetObjectAccessor
AEGetSpecialHandler	SIHelper::GetSpecialHandler
AERemoveCoercionHandler	SIHelper::RemoveCoercionHandler
AERemoveEventHandler	SIHelper::RemoveEventHandler
AERemoveObjectAccessor	SIHelper::RemoveObjectAccessor
AERemoveSpecialHandler	SIHelper::RemoveSpecialHandler

NOTE   The methods of the utility class SIHelper shown here have no direct equivalents in the class ODSemanticInterface. They are provided as a convenience and represent only one possible alternative to Apple Event Manager functions. If you design your own semantic interface, you can implement equivalent functionality in any manner you choose.

At run time, OpenDoc handles semantic events by accepting the events and passing them to the appropriate part editor. There is no separate dispatcher object for semantic events; the OpenDoc dispatcher that handles user events also dispatches semantic events.

Apple Event Object Model

OpenDoc relies on the Apple event **object model** to specify individual elements of a part's content. The object model defines a hierarchical arrangement of **content objects,** whose nature depends on the content model of the part. Apple events have object specifiers in their direct parameters to access individual content objects within a part. Part editors provide **object accessor** functions, used by the name resolver's Resolve method to resolve the object specifiers in Apple events that the parts receive.

The Apple event object model used by OpenDoc is slightly different from that used by conventional applications. Here are the differences:

■ The OpenDoc version of the object model has the ability to deal with multiple parts in a single document. It achieves this ability by defining a context for each Apple event. The **context** for an Apple event in OpenDoc is the equivalent of the object model's *default container;* it is the outermost object in the object hierarchy defined by the direct parameter. The default container for an Apple event is typically represented by the application that receives the event. The context for an OpenDoc Apple event, by contrast, might be the document shell or any of the parts in a document. (Before and after an event is handled, the context is always the document shell; during processing, however, the context may change multiple times.)

■ In processing an Apple event, OpenDoc reverses the Apple Event Manager's typical sequence of object resolution. OpenDoc resolves the object specifier in the direct parameter of an Apple event before calling any event handler. The direct parameter may contain a description of the destination part, and that determines the context of the event. OpenDoc therefore replaces the object specifier in the direct parameter of the Apple event with the *token* returned from the resolution (see "Returning Tokens" on page 429) before calling a part's event handler.

■ The `Resolve` method of the class `ODNameResolver`, which is a wrapper for the Apple Event Manager `AEResolve` function, has a parameter used only by OpenDoc. The parameter, of type `ODPart`, specifies the part that is the context from which to start an object resolution. Also, unlike `AEResolve`, the `Resolve` method has no `callbackFlags` parameter, because callback flags in OpenDoc are specified on a part-by-part basis; they are set when the part calls the `SetOSLSupportFlags` method of the `ODSemanticInterface` class.

■ Object resolution is possible for parts embedded within parts that do not support scripting. OpenDoc provides default object accessors and event handlers that allow a message to "pass through" a part that does not support scripting into an embedded part that does. See "The OpenDoc Semantic Interface" on page 413 for more information.

■ OpenDoc adds a noun to the *Apple Event Registry*. To represent a part (more strictly a display frame of a part), the registry defines the descriptor type `'part'`, for which you can also use the constant `cPart`.

■ OpenDoc does not support calling the `RemoveSpecialHandler` function with the keyword `keySelectProc` in order to disable object-model support. Instead, making this call throws an exception.

Your part editor should implement object accessors as if your part were a stand-alone conventional application—that is, with your part itself as the context.

Scripting Systems

A scripting system completes the OSA implementation on a platform. It is through a scripting system that the user designs, attaches, and executes code to generate the semantic events that a scriptable part receives.

Any OSA-compliant scripting system can be used with OpenDoc. On the Mac OS platform, AppleScript and UserLand Frontier are two examples. Other platforms may use these or other OSA scripting systems.

OpenDoc allows the user to employ any available scripting system and even to switch among them during execution.

Part Content Model

To fully support scripting of your parts, you must construct a content model for your parts. The model must include a full set of content objects, accessible through semantic events, that allow a complete range of operations on your user-visible content. Your part editor must provide accessor functions to resolve external references to content objects, and it must also provide semantic-event handlers that implement content operations.

Developing a content model and implementing the functions for resolving object specifiers and handling semantic events give great advantages. You increase flexibility and you provide user control over the basic functions of your part editor. For example, your parts will automatically be able to accept input from currently unavailable or unforeseen user interfaces, such as voice or pen or touch, that generate semantic events.

If you also **factor** your part editor—that is, if you separate your part editor's core data engine from its user interface—you increase its flexibility even further. Interface elements such as menus and dialog boxes, if reconstructed to invoke scripts or otherwise generate semantic events, will still be able to communicate directly with your parts. Factoring also facilitates making your parts recordable (page 412).

Content Operations

The operations of a content model should be consistent with user actions. They typically include selection, creation, deletion, insertion, setting of properties, and so on. Low-level internal functions, such as piece-table functions for efficient text insertion or matrix inversion for fast graphics processing, are probably not appropriate as content-model operations.

Your content operations correspond to the semantic events you support. You implement a semantic-event handler for each operation.

Content Objects

The objects of a content model should be consistent with the elements that the user sees and manipulates, regardless of your part editor's internal structures. Inside a text part, for example, a user may see lines, words, paragraphs, characters, and embedded parts. Those are typical content objects for such a part. Internally, your part editor might maintain run-length encoding arrays, line-end arrays, and so on. However, because they are not presented to the user, they are not part of the content model. Likewise, a graphics part might have content objects such as circles, rectangles, and lines, regardless of what internal mathematical descriptions it uses.

If a part supports embedding, embedded parts within it constitute a special class of content objects. The containing part can use content operations to manipulate the frames of embedded parts and perhaps some part-wide display properties, but it cannot in general manipulate their contents; only the parts themselves can do that.

The OpenDoc default object accessors already provide this basic ability to access the properties of, and send semantic events to, embedded frames. If your part is a container part and needs capabilities beyond this basic level, your object model can include a named type of content object that represents an embedded part to which you can pass events and from which you can extract properties.

User selections
If you want to make user selections controllable through semantic events, you must describe them with object specifiers appropriate to your part's content model. In most cases, you should allow a selection to be specified both by description ("word 1 to word 5 of 'Gettysburg Address'") and by contents ("Fourscore and seven years ago"). ◆

Resolving Object References

Object specifiers in an Apple event can refer to any content objects, including embedded parts. When it receives Apple events, your part must provide accessor functions to allow those specifiers to be resolved. The accessor functions of a part return **tokens,** descriptors that identify the content objects or properties of those objects.

As an example of object resolution, consider a document whose root part is a text part. The part contains several embedded parts, including a bar chart named "sales chart". Suppose that the user employs a script editor (or possibly a scriptable tool palette) to send a command to change the bar chart to a pie chart. A Set Data event with the part name "sales chart" as the direct parameter goes to the OpenDoc message interface, which must resolve the object specifier in the direct parameter before dispatching the event itself.

The message interface asks the document shell to identify the part named "chart part". The document shell cannot, so the message interface asks the root part. The root part's object accessor recognizes the name of the chart part and passes back a token representing the part's frame. The message interface then asks the root part to identify the "chart type" property. The root part cannot, so it returns a token that causes resolution to be passed onto the embedded part itself. The message interface asks the embedded part's object accessor to identify the "chart type" property. The accessor does and returns a token for it. The message interface inserts the token into the semantic event and dispatches the event to the embedded part's semantic-event handler. The handler then changes the chart to a pie chart.

Object accessor functions and object-specifier resolution are described in more detail in the section "Writing Object Accessors" on page 424.

Levels of Scripting Support

You can implement different levels of support for scripting in your part editor. Each successive level requires more effort, but each gives the user greater flexibility and control over the functioning of your parts.

Scriptable Parts

If you make your parts **scriptable,** they will have at least a basic level of scripting support. To do that, you must create a content model for your parts with defined content objects (available through object accessors) and content operations (represented by semantic-event handlers) that are meaningful to the user. Then your part editor publishes a description of its content objects and operations and accepts semantic events.

■ Your part editor publishes its list of content objects and operations by placing them in its **terminology resource,** a resource of type 'aete' that each scriptable part editor must provide.

■ Your part editor accepts semantic events through its semantic interface, available publicly as an OpenDoc extension object. The semantic interface includes object accessor functions as well as semantic-event handlers.

Even among scriptable parts there are different levels of support. You can allow script access to only a few content objects and operations or to many of them. For your parts to be **fully scriptable,** semantic events must be able to invoke any action a user might be able to perform.

One advantage of making your part scriptable is that you can allow it to be used by other parts, even parts that you may not have developed yourself. For example, if your part is a text part and you allow script access to all of its text-style settings, the user (or your containing part or a sibling part) can easily format any of your text for any purpose.

Recordable Parts

If you make your parts **recordable,** the user's actions can be captured as a series of semantic events, converted to scripts, and replayed at a later time to reenact the actions. A recommended way to make your parts recordable is to completely separate the user interface from the core data engine of your part editor.

If your part editor handles every user-interface event by generating, sending to itself, and handling an equivalent semantic event, it can process all semantic events through a standard bottleneck and have the Apple Event Manager record the actions. This use of a bottleneck not only allows recording but also enhances code portability.

The events that pass through the bottleneck should be just the set of actions that match your part's content model. These events need not follow exactly the inner design of your core data engine, but they should reflect the complete range of user actions.

Customizable Parts

If you make your part's interface **customizable,** the user can not only invoke all actions through scripts but can also change the nature of the actions themselves by attaching additional scripts that are invoked when the actions are executed.

To support customizable parts, you must make your parts scriptable, and you must also define content objects and operations for interface elements such as menus and buttons, or provide other ways to trigger scripts. You must provide persistent storage for any scripts that the user attaches to your part's interface elements.

Making your part fully customizable requires that you allow attachment and invocation of scripts during virtually any user action. For the highest levels of customizability, all menu commands and all editing actions should be scriptable.

Before processing any user event or semantic event, your part editor must check whether a script attached to the part wants to handle the event. If so, you allow the script to run.

If your parts are recordable, they are already almost customizable. Because for recording purposes you typically check for the presence of and invoke scripts in a semantic-event dispatching bottleneck, you can achieve full customizability with little extra effort.

The OpenDoc Semantic Interface

To help you add scripting capability to your parts, OpenDoc provides the following code interfaces and implementations:

- the semantic-interface extension protocol, defined by the abstract class `ODSemanticInterface`

- utility classes, with which you can optionally implement your semantic-interface extension

- a default semantic interface, which provides minimal capabilities for handling semantic events

This section describes how to use these three components of the OpenDoc semantic interface.

Document shell semantic interface

The document shell semantic interface is a special instantiation of a subclass of `ODSemanticInterface`, created by the document shell (or a container application) and referenced by the session object. Access to the document shell semantic interface is public, although under most circumstances there is no reason for a part to use it. The document shell semantic interface handles only those semantic events whose scope is document-wide (such as the required set of Apple events). Most semantic events sent to the document shell are passed to the root part. ◆

Scripting-Related OpenDoc Classes

Several OpenDoc classes provide the basic structure for its support of semantic events and scripting. Figure 9-1, a duplication of a portion of the OpenDoc class hierarchy (Figure 2-1 on page 77), shows the principal OpenDoc classes involved with scripting.

Figure 9-1   Inheritance hierarchy of scripting-related objects

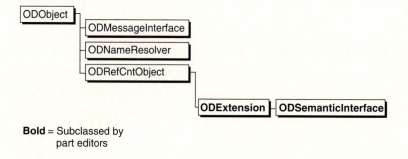

Three classes provide basic support for scripting in OpenDoc:

■ The class `ODSemanticInterface` defines the programming interface through which script editors or other sources of semantic events communicate with your part. It is a subclass of `ODExtension` and is an abstract superclass; you must subclass `ODSemanticInterface` to make your part scriptable.

You can design and implement your own subclass of ODSemanticInterface, or you can use the utility classes provided with OpenDoc; see "Scripting-Related Utility Classes" on page 416.

■ The class ODNameResolver represents the name resolver, a subclass of ODObject that is instantiated by the session object. It is used in resolving object specifiers; see "Object Resolution" on page 424.

■ The class ODMessageInterface represents the message interface, a subclass of ODObject that is instantiated by the session object. It provides an interface through which your part sends semantic events to other parts; see "Sending Semantic Events" on page 435.

(The message interface is also the object through which OpenDoc sends semantic events to your part, although your part does not make any calls to the message interface in that situation.)

OpenDoc also provides a set of scripting-related classes, shown in Figure 9-2, that are wrappers for Apple event descriptor structures. Like other OpenDoc classes, these classes descend from ODObject.

Figure 9-2   Inheritance hierarchy of the object-descriptor classes

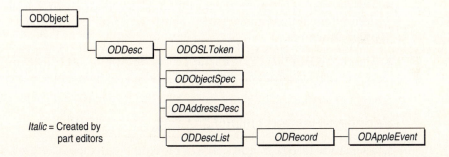

The object-descriptor classes exist so that future versions of OpenDoc can support remote callbacks. They are mostly simple wrappers for structures, although some define a few methods that you can call. Other than ODOSLToken, the structures that these objects wrap are all Apple events structures defined in the chapter "Introduction to Apple Events" in *Inside Macintosh: Interapplication Communication*.

- The class ODDesc is a general wrapper for a descriptor structure (type AEDesc), the basic structure used for building Apple event attributes and parameters. ODDesc is a direct subclass of ODObject; the other descriptor classes are all direct or indirect subclasses of ODDesc.

  ODDesc provides methods for extracting and replacing the data of the Apple event descriptor it contains.

- The class ODOSLToken is a wrapper for an OpenDoc token, described in the section "Returning Tokens" on page 429. ODOSLToken provides a method for duplicating itself.

- The class ODAddressDesc is a wrapper for an address descriptor structure (type AEAddressDesc), a descriptor structure that contains a target address.

- The class ODObjectSpec is a wrapper for an object specifier structure (type typeObjectSpecifier), a descriptor structure that describes the location of one or more Apple event objects.

- The class ODDescList is a wrapper for a descriptor list (type AEDescList), a descriptor structure that is a list of other descriptor structures.

- The class ODRecord is a wrapper for an AE structure (type AERecord), a descriptor list that can be used to construct Apple event parameters and other structures.

- The class ODAppleEvent is a wrapper for an Apple event structure (type AppleEvent), a structure that describes a full-fledged Apple event.

Scripting-Related Utility Classes

The semantic-interface utility classes provided with OpenDoc are a set of System Object Model (SOM) and C++ classes whose objects cooperate to install and provide access to your semantic-event handlers and callback functions.

Figure 9-3 shows the inheritance of the utility classes in relation to the inheritance structure of OpenDoc classes. This figure is identical to Figure 9-1 on page 414, except that the utility classes have been added.

Figure 9-3 Inheritance hierarchy of the scripting-related utility classes

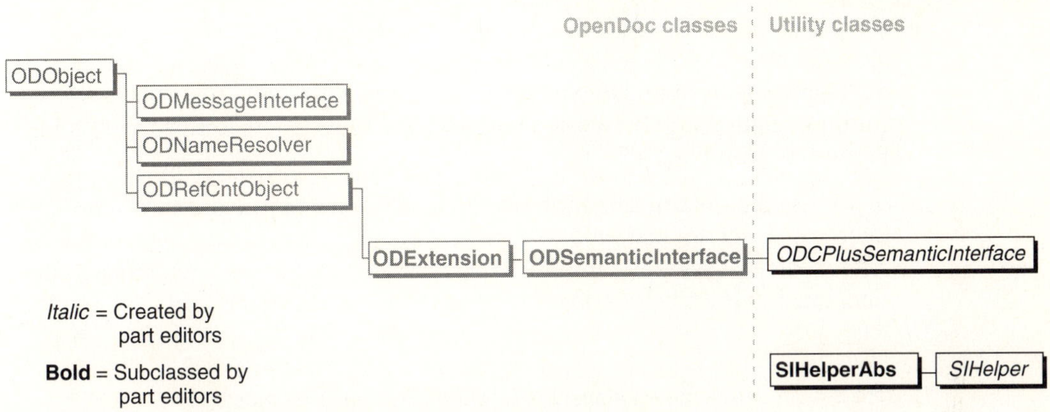

There are three scripting-related utility classes:

■ The class `ODCPlusSemanticInterface` is a subclass of `ODSemanticInterface`, although it is a utility class (defined in the SemtIntf utility library) and not strictly part of the OpenDoc class library. It is a SOM class that implements the semantic interface defined in `ODSemanticInterface`. It cannot be used alone, however; `ODCPlusSemanticInterface` must be accompanied by a subclass of the OpenDoc utility class `SIHelperAbs`.

■ The class `SIHelperAbs` is a C++ utility class (defined in the SIHlpAbs utility library). `SIHelperAbs` is an abstract superclass that specifies an interface for installing callback functions; it has no implementation. Because SOM-based classes cannot directly support remote callbacks, all of the object-callback functions supported by OpenDoc are installed and removed through method calls to subclasses of `SIHelperAbs`.

■ The class `SIHelper` (defined in the SIHelper utility library) is a subclass of `SIHelperAbs`. It is a C++ utility class that implements the semantic interface defined in `SIHelperAbs`. If you use `ODCPlusSemanticInterface`, you can either use `SIHelper` or you can replace it with your own subclass of `SIHelperAbs`.

Figure 9-4 shows some possible runtime object relationships for a part's semantic interface. (This figure uses the same conventions for showing runtime relationships as do the figures in the section "Runtime Object Relationships" on page 487.) Two arrangements are typical:

- If you do not use the default semantic interface, your part object and its semantic interface object, a subclass of `ODSemanticInterface` that you develop on your own, have mutual references. This is the fundamental runtime relationship between a part and any of its extensions, as shown in Figure 11-11 on page 499.

- If you use the default semantic interface, your part object and its semantic interface object (an instantiation of `ODCPlusSemanticInterface`) have mutual references. The semantic interface object in turn maintains a reference to the semantic-interface helper object (an instantiation of a subclass of `SIHelperAbs`).

Figure 9-4   Runtime relationships for semantic-interface objects

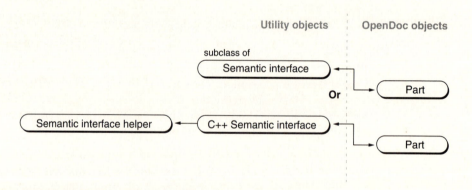

Together, the C++ semantic-interface object and the semantic-interface helper are responsible for registering and executing semantic-event handlers, coercion handlers, and object accessors, and for performing other event-manipulation functions.

The Default Semantic Interface

This section describes the semantic-event handlers, object accessors, and tokens that are provided as part of OpenDoc. They exist to make sure that script access is available to scriptable parts that are embedded within nonscriptable parts.

The default semantic interface provides basic access to the content and Info properties of embedded parts. When implementing scripting capabilities for your part editor, your can design your own handlers and accessors to build on, rather than duplicate, these capabilities.

The Default Get Data and Set Data Event Handlers

To allow senders of semantic events to access certain basic information about any part in a document—regardless of whether that part or any of its containing parts is scriptable—OpenDoc provides two default event handlers. The default handlers respond to the Get Data and Set Data Apple events; the handlers are used for any part whose own handlers do not respond to those events.

The information manipulated by these handlers is the standard set of Info properties (see Table 7-3 on page 291) attached to the part. These handlers cannot manipulate the content of any part. The event class of the handlers is `kCoreEventClass`, and their event IDs are `kAEGetData` and `kAESetData`.

You can rely on the default Get Data and Set Data handlers to provide script access to your part's standard Info properties. Such limited access does not really constitute scriptability, of course. To provide script access to your part's intrinsic content or to other Info properties of your part or of parts embedded in your part, you need to write your own handlers.

Default Object Accessors

OpenDoc provides default object accessors to give scripts access to information within parts that do not support semantic events. Even if your part editor does support scripting, you can rely on these accessors to perform the following specific tasks. You need write object accessors only for other purposes, such as accessing your intrinsic content.

■ From the null container, a default accessor can return a token representing an embedded part. If your part is not scriptable, if it does not provide such an accessor, or if its accessor does not handle this task, the name resolver's `Resolve` method uses a default accessor to return a reference to a frame embedded within your part.

The default accessor can resolve references to embedded parts specified by part name, part index, or part ID. Part ID in this case is not the part's storage-unit ID, but its **persistent object ID,** an identifying value used only for script access. A part's persistent object ID is unique within its draft and is valid across sessions. You can obtain a persistent ID for a part or a frame by calling the `GetPersistentObjectID` method of its draft; you can recreate a part or frame object by passing its persistent object ID to its draft's `AcquirePersistentObject` method.

The token returned by this default accessor has the format described in "Standard Embedded-Frame Token" on page 421.

■ From the null container, a default accessor can return a token representing a standard Info property of the part that is the current context. If you do not provide such an accessor, or if your accessor does not handle this task, the name resolver uses this default accessor to return a reference to a standard Info property of your part.

The token returned by this default accessor has a private format. See the note "Default accessors require default handlers" at the end of this section for an explanation.

■ From a container of type `cPart`, a default accessor can return a swap token (see "Returning a Swap Token" on page 430), so that the name resolver can switch the context from the current part to a more deeply embedded one. If you do not provide such an accessor, or if your accessor does not handle this task, the name resolver uses this default accessor to change the context to the appropriate part embedded within your part.

If your part editor supports scripting but you do not want to duplicate the functions of these default accessors, you can write accessors only for tasks beyond the defaults: accessing objects in your part's intrinsic content, accessing Info properties that you have defined for your own part or for parts embedded in your part, altering the ordering/indexing scheme for embedded parts, and so on.

When one of your object accessors receives a token that it does not recognize as having been created by another of your own object accessors, it can simply return the Apple event error `errAEEventNotHandled` to the name resolver. The name resolver then attempts the resolution with the default accessors.

Default accessors require default handlers

Tokens created by your object accessors contain data in a format that your semantic-event handlers can understand, whereas tokens describing Info properties created by the default accessors are in a private format. Therefore, if you allow the default accessor to return tokens for the standard Info properties, you also need to allow the default Get Data and Set Data handlers to manipulate those standard Info properties. In that case, your own Get Data and Set Data handlers need only manipulate your intrinsic content plus any custom properties you have defined for your part or for embedded parts. ◆

Standard Embedded-Frame Token

To allow access to scriptable parts embedded within parts that are not scriptable, OpenDoc provides a default embedded-part accessor, as described in the previous section. That accessor returns a token in a standard format. The token has a descriptor type `cPart`, and its `dataHandle` field contains only a frame pointer and a part pointer (of type `ODFrame*` and `ODPart*`, respectively).

If your part is a container part and is scriptable, it must be able to support the creation and reading of an embedded-frame token, either through its own object accessors or by letting the default part accessor construct the token. If you use a private format to describe an embedded-frame token, you must provide a coercion handler so that OpenDoc can coerce the token into the standard format when necessary.

Implementing Your Semantic Interface

To make your parts scriptable, your part editor must implement a semantic interface that allows it to accept semantic events, handle them, and reply to them. Either on its own or with the help of the OpenDoc utility classes and default semantic interface, your part editor must

- implement its semantic interface, either as a subclass of `ODSemanticInterface` or as a set of classes based on the utility classes `ODCPlusSemanticInterface` and `SIHelper`

- override its `AcquireExtension` and `HasExtension` methods to provide access to its semantic interface

- provide semantic-event handlers for all Apple events appropriate to its content model

- provide object accessors for its content objects

- provide other kinds of handlers (such as object-callback functions and coercion handlers) as appropriate

- make public, through a terminology resource, the events it handles and content-object types it recognizes

Writing Semantic-Event Handlers

You need to create a handler for every semantic event that your part editor recognizes. Your list of semantic-event handlers defines the content operations that your parts engage in and allow users to access.

How your semantic-event handlers manipulate the content of your parts is entirely up to you. This section discusses only the process by which your handler receives and handles a semantic event. Installing your handler is described in the section "Installation" on page 433.

A typical source of semantic events is a script engine or another part. The script engine or part generates semantic events and sends them to your document's document shell. This is how your part ends up receiving and processing a semantic event:

1. The identity of your part—the destination part—will generally have been encoded in the object specifier in the direct parameter of the Apple event. Your part can be at any level of embedding in the document, and the encoding can be either explicit or implicit. For example, your part may be the implicit target when the event explicitly requests a custom Info property of one of your embedded parts.

2. The OpenDoc document shell receives the Apple event and passes it to the message interface object by calling the message interface's `ProcessSemanticEvent` method.

3. The message interface object calls the name resolver's `Resolve` method for the event's direct parameter. Within the `Resolve` method, the object-resolution process may cycle several times (see "Resolving Object References" on page 411), until your part's semantic interface has been accessed and an object accessor of yours has returned a token that specifies an object contained within your part.

4. The message interface object calls the `CallEventHandler` method of your semantic interface to dispatch the event to your semantic-event handler. The actual implementation of your event handler could be within the body of that method, but it is more likely delegated to another class. In the default semantic interface, for example, `ODCPlusSemanticInterface::CallEventHandler` calls `SIHelper::CallEventHandler`, which in turn examines the event class and ID to determine which handler to dispatch to.

5. Your part may have an attached script for that semantic event. If so, you execute the script at this point. If not, or if the script does not handle the event, or if the script handler passes the event on after processing, you dispatch the event to the semantic-event handler.

6. Your semantic-event handler, on receiving the event, decides whether and how to resolve additional parameters. There are three general possibilities:

   □ You read data from a location the parameter points to. This is nondestructive, and you can resolve the parameter and perform the task (possibly by sending the Get Data semantic event) even if it is from another part.

   □ You overwrite data or move data to a location the parameter points to. This is a destructive action and you should perform it only on your own part. If you are acting on a list of items, for example, be sure that every item in that list represents an object in your own part before overwriting or moving data to any of them.

   □ You ignore the parameter. If you choose to ignore a parameter, do not retrieve it from the event or attempt to resolve its object specifier.

7. Your event handler carries out its operation, returning a reply Apple event if appropriate.

   You fill out reply Apple events just as conventional applications do, as described in *Inside Macintosh: Interapplication Communication*. If the semantic event was sent by another part, the message interface object generates and keeps track of the return ID for the event so that your reply can be routed back to the sender's reply-event handler.

Writing Object Accessors

Object specifiers in an Apple event can refer to any content objects. If your part is to receive Apple events, it must provide accessor functions to allow those specifiers to be resolved. Your accessor functions return tokens (see "Returning Tokens" on page 429) that your own semantic-event handlers can interpret. OpenDoc passes those tokens to your handlers when it resolves objects in the direct parameters of Apple events; your handlers themselves call the name resolver's `Resolve` method and receive the tokens for other Apple event parameters that are object specifiers.

If your scriptable part is also a container part, it must provide object accessor methods for objects that represent embedded parts, and it must be able to swap the context—that is, it must be able to hand off the object-resolution process to an embedded part (see "Returning a Swap Token" on page 430). OpenDoc includes default object accessors that provide the minimum capability for swapping context, but your part can replace or add to the capabilities of those accessors, if desired.

This section describes how your object accessor is called and which tokens it constructs and returns. The section also describes the default object accessors provided with OpenDoc so that semantic events can be sent to parts embedded within parts that do not themselves support scripting.

Object Resolution

OpenDoc resolves object specifiers for content objects within parts much as the Apple Event Manager resolves object specifiers in conventional applications. However, there are some differences, including these:

■ For semantic events sent from outside of a document, the document shell is the first handler of an object-specifier resolution. The shell does not handle events meant for any of the individual parts in the document, so in most cases it returns an error. To find the right part, OpenDoc then uses object accessor functions provided by the default semantic interface and by individual parts to obtain part-relative tokens (tokens for which the part is the context).

■ OpenDoc reads parts into memory, if necessary, when interpreting object specifiers. For example, an embedded part referred to in a specifier may not be currently visible and thus not yet read into memory. To resolve the chain of objects further, OpenDoc may have to read in the part and then access an object within it.

■ The callback flags used by the `Resolve` method (equivalent to the `callbackFlags` parameter of the Apple Event Manager `AEResolve` function) have a scope that is local to each part, rather than global to the object resolution process. Each part sets its callback flags by calling the `SetOSLSupportFlags` method of its semantic interface.

OpenDoc takes the following steps to resolve a reference to a content object. The process starts when the document shell (in the case of semantic events from outside the document) receives a semantic event and calls the message interface's `ProcessSemanticEvent` method, as described under steps 1 and 2 in "Writing Semantic-Event Handlers" on page 422.

A. Message Interface Calls Resolve

The message interface calls the `Resolve` method of the name resolver (class `ODNameResolver`), passing it the object specifier in the direct parameter of the Apple event (steps 1 and 2 of Figure 9-5).

If the direct parameter does not exist, there may be a subject attribute in the event that takes the place of a direct parameter. A **subject attribute** is an object specifier that refers to the target part by its persistent object ID (see "Default Object Accessors" on page 419). All events sent through AppleScript include a subject attribute, and all events sent through the `Send` method of the message interface include a subject attribute (unless the `toFrame` parameter of `Send` is null). The presence of a subject attribute allows a scripting system to record an event's targets even if it has no direct parameter.

If there is no direct parameter or subject attribute, or if the direct parameter is not an object specifier, `Resolve` is not called and the event goes to the document shell (and then to the root part if the shell does not handle it).

B. Resolve Locates the Proper Object

Not shown in Figure 9-5 is the fact that the `Resolve` method first accesses the document shell's semantic interface and gives it a chance to resolve the object specifier. If, as is typical, the event is targeted to a part rather than to the document shell itself, the default semantic interface passes resolution to the root part. The `Resolve` method then takes the following steps, first with the root part and then with the appropriate embedded parts until the specifier is finally resolved.

(Because Apple event objects exist in a hierarchy of containers, the `Resolve` method may make several cycles through the following steps, encountering several context swaps, before identifying the specific object within a hierarchy.)

1. Starting with the default container (this part's context), the `Resolve` method calls the `AcquireExtension` method of this part to get its semantic interface and thence the list of its object accessors. The `Resolve` method finds the accessor for the specified property or element and calls it (step 3 of Figure 9-5).

2. The object accessor returns a token to the `Resolve` method, following the steps listed in the section "Returning Tokens" on page 429.

   ☐ If the object is not an embedded part, the accessor puts into the token whatever information is needed to map the token to the right content object. Then it returns the token to the `Resolve` method.

   ☐ If the content object represents an embedded frame as a whole, the accessor creates and returns a token that specifies the embedded frame.

   ☐ OpenDoc provides a default accessor that performs this task if this part's object accessor does not, or if this part is not scriptable. See "Default Object Accessors" on page 419.

   ☐ If the content object represents a directly accessible property of an embedded part—either a standard Info property such as the embedded part's modification date, or a custom property that this part may have defined, such as "is-selected"—the accessor creates and returns a token that specifies the requested property.

☐ OpenDoc provides a default accessor that performs this task (for the standard Info properties only) if this part's object accessor does not, or if this part is not scriptable. See "Default Object Accessors" on page 419.

☐ If the content object represents an object within an embedded part, or a property of the embedded part that this part cannot access, the accessor returns a special token (see "Returning a Swap Token" on page 430). At the next pass, the embedded part's list of accessors is used instead (step 4 of Figure 9-5).

OpenDoc provides a default accessor that performs this swap if this part's object accessor does not, or if this part is not scriptable. See "Default Object Accessors" on page 419.

3. The `Resolve` method finds the object accessor for the next property or element in the hierarchy of the object specifier and passes the returned token as the container to that accessor. That accessor, in turn, returns another token. This cycle continues, with context swaps occurring when appropriate, until the innermost element of the object specifier has been converted to a token and passed back to `Resolve` (steps 5 and 6 of Figure 9-5).

C. OpenDoc Calls the Correct Event Handler

After resolving the object specifier, `Resolve` returns the final token to the message interface object (step 7 of Figure 9-5). OpenDoc then passes that final token to the proper part's semantic-event handler, as the direct parameter of the Apple event (step 8 of Figure 9-5).

(If the Apple event has a subject attribute but no direct parameter, OpenDoc calls the proper part's semantic-event handler but discards the token.)

Figure 9-5   Resolving an object specifier involving an embedded part

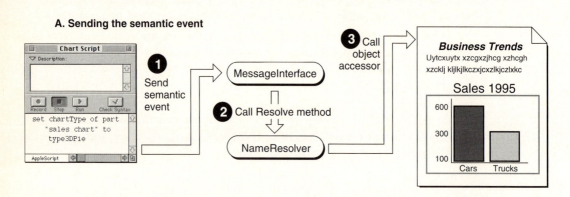

A. Sending the semantic event

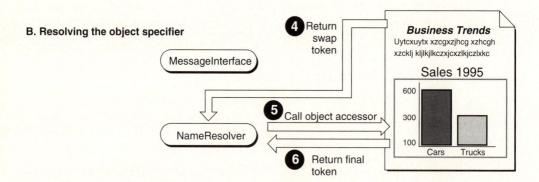

B. Resolving the object specifier

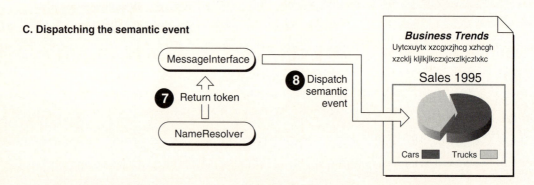

C. Dispatching the semantic event

Returning Tokens

In the OpenDoc version of Apple events, a token is a special descriptor structure, implemented as an OpenDoc object of type `ODOSLToken`, that a part uses to identify one or more content objects within itself. Your object accessor functions return tokens when they successfully resolve object specifiers. The structure of a token is not public, but it contains an OpenDoc object (of type `ODDesc`) that parts can access in order to extract or insert Apple event descriptor data.

OpenDoc hides the structure of the `ODOSLToken` object; you cannot manipulate its fields directly. This privacy allows OpenDoc to store extra information that it needs inside a token; it also ensures that OpenDoc's scripting support will be compatible with future distributed-object models.

When your object accessor needs to return a token, it modifies the `ODOSLToken` object that was passed to it by modifying the `ODDesc` descriptor object it contains. Your accessor can perform this task with a utility function or with methods of `ODDesc` itself.

1. The accessor calls the `GetUserToken` method of the name resolver to access the OpenDoc descriptor object (of type `ODDesc`) contained within the token that was passed to the accessor.

2. The accessor can optionally create a descriptor of type `AEDesc` and set its `descriptorType` and `dataHandle` fields to store the information needed.

3. The accessor assigns the data to the descriptor object:

   □ If it has created an Apple events (`AEDesc`) descriptor, the accessor can assign the `AEDesc` descriptor to the `ODDesc` object by using the utility function `AEDescToODDesc` (from the ODDesUtl utility library provided with OpenDoc). The accessor then disposes of the `AEDesc`.

   □ If it has not explicitly created an Apple events descriptor, the accessor can assign the descriptor data to the descriptor object directly by calling its `SetRawData` and `SetDescType` methods.

The ODDesUtl utility library also provides the function `ODDescToAEDesc`, which allows you to extract (for inspection or modification) the `AEDesc` descriptor structure from an `ODDesc` object. The class `ODDesc` itself includes the methods `GetRawData` and `GetDescType`, which allow you to extract the descriptor data.

Your object accessors can verify the tokens passed to them by calling the name resolver's `IsODToken` method. The name resolver also provides the `GetContextFromToken` method, which allows your accessor to determine, for example, which display frame of its part contains the target of the event.

Returning a Swap Token

Sometimes your object accessor function is asked to access a content object (or a property that your part cannot directly access) from an object whose class is `cPart`—meaning that the requested item is something within a frame embedded in your part. In this case, the accessor must pass back a special token, called a **swap token,** to inform the name resolver of its inability to furnish the required token. Your accessor creates this token by calling the `CreateSwapToken` method of the name resolver to initialize the swap token, passing it a pointer to the embedded frame and a pointer to the part in the embedded frame. Your accessor then should simply return a value of `noErr`, taking no further action.

Upon receipt of the swap token, the name resolver changes the current context from your part to the embedded part and once more tries to access the object in that context.

If your part is a container part and is scriptable, it must support such context switches with swap tokens, either through its own object accessors or by letting a default accessor (see "Default Object Accessors" on page 419) perform the swap.

Note
OpenDoc reserves the descriptor types `'swap'`, `'part'`, and `'tokn'` for its own use. Do not use these values in the `descriptorType` field of your own tokens. ◆

Other Considerations

When you write an object accessor, note that, in interpreting object specifiers, "part X of doc Y" implies "part X of <current draft> of doc Y".

Your part can provide object accessors for document-wide user-interface elements, to be used when it is the root part of a document. For example, as root part it can provide accessors for window scroll bars or for document characteristics such as page size.

If your object accessor needs to know the frame through which your part was accessed—the frame that displays the part that is the current context—it can call the `GetContextFromToken` method of the name resolver. The value returned represents the most recent frame passed to `CreateSwapToken`.

Writing Other Kinds of Handlers

In addition to semantic-event handlers and object accessors, you can write
other special-purpose functions and install them for use in interpreting
semantic events. This section discusses OpenDoc issues related to object-
callback functions, coercion handlers, and other kinds of handlers.

Object-Callback Functions

Your part can provide **object-callback functions** for the `Resolve` method to call
when your part needs to provide extra information before object resolution can
occur. You can use these functions, also called *special handlers*, for a variety
of purposes:

- You can provide an object-counting function (CountProc) so that, when the
  object specifier involves a test, `Resolve` can determine how many elements it
  must examine in performing the test. You must provide this function if you
  want the Apple Event Manager to perform *whose tests*, that is, to resolve
  object specifier records of key form `formTest` without your part itself having
  to parse the whose clause and perform the counting test.

- You can provide an object-comparison function (CompareProc), which
  determines whether one element or descriptor structure is equal to another.
  You must provide this function if you want the Apple Event Manager to
  perform whose tests without your part itself having to parse the whose
  clause and perform the comparison.

- You can provide a token-disposal function (DisposeTokenProc)—which
  overrides the Apple Event Manager's `AEDisposeDesc` function—in case you
  need to do any extra processing when your tokens are disposed of.

- You can provide an error-callback function (GetErrDescProc), which
  provides a descriptor into which the Apple Event Manager can write
  information about resolution failures.

- You can provide three kinds of marking-callback functions, which allow
  your part to use its own marking scheme to identify sets of objects.

  □ A marking function (MarkProc) marks a set of objects.

  □ An unmarking function (AdjustMarksProc) removes marks from
    previously marked object sets.

  □ A marker-token function (GetMarkTokenProc) returns a token that can be
    used to mark a set of objects.

All callback functions in OpenDoc function exactly as they do with conventional applications, except for these minor changes:

- Each has an additional parameter, of type ODPart, to allow access to your part object from the callback function.

- Some parameters have different types from their conventional equivalents. For example, parameters of type AEDesc in conventional callbacks are of type ODDesc or ODOSLToken in OpenDoc callbacks.

- OpenDoc callback functions return an error type of ODErr instead of the OSErr type returned by callback functions in conventional applications.

You install object callbacks as described in the section "Installing Handlers, Accessors, and Callbacks" on page 434.

Object-callback functions (and whose tests) are described in more detail in the chapter "Resolving and Creating Object Specifier Records" in *Inside Macintosh: Interapplication Communication.*

Coercion Handlers

Coercion handlers are functions that convert data of one descriptor type into data of another descriptor type. Coercion handlers are common in Apple events. Some are provided by the Apple Event Manager; others may be provided by your part editor. Any coercion handlers installed by your part editor are called only when your part is the context for the Apple event. Normally, the document shell is the context, but there are two situations in which your part can become the context:

- when an object accessor installed by your part must be called during the resolution of an object specifier

- when your part's semantic-event handler is called

Coercion handlers are not chained by OpenDoc. That is, an embedded part does not inherit the coercion handlers of its containing part, and a root part does not inherit the coercion handlers of the shell.

Coercion handlers are described in more detail in the chapter "Responding to Apple Events" in *Inside Macintosh: Interapplication Communication.*

Predispatch Handlers and Recording

A **predispatch handler** is a function that it is called whenever your document receives any Apple event, before any part's handler for that Apple event is called. OpenDoc allows you to install predispatch handlers and to specify whether or not you are currently using a given predispatch handler.

For example, if your part is recordable, you can install a predispatch handler to intercept the Start Recording and Stop Recording Apple events that are sent to the document shell. (OpenDoc does not automatically forward those events to each part in a document.) Even so, your part may be read into memory and initialized after the user has turned recording on, in which case your predispatch handler won't receive the Start Recording Apple event. Therefore, when your part initializes itself, it should also check with the Apple Event Manager to see if recording is on. If so, it can record its actions.

Predispatch handlers are described in more detail along with the `keyPreDispatch` constant in the chapters "Responding to Apple Events" and "Creating and Sending Apple Events" of *Inside Macintosh: Interapplication Communication.*

Installation

Once you have implemented your semantic interface, you need to install its components as described in this section.

Making Your Semantic-Interface Extension Available

Your semantic interface is an extension class plus related classes. You can either provide your own subclass of `ODSemanticInterface`, or you can implement both `ODCPlusSemanticInterface` and `SIHelper`. Either way, you must override the (inherited) part methods `HasExtension` and `AcquireExtension` so that they return the semantic interface object. The `ODType` constant that names the semantic-interface extension is `kODExtSemanticInterface`; the constant is passed by callers of your `HasExtension` and `AcquireExtension` methods.

In implementing and interacting with your semantic-interface extensions, follow the rules for using OpenDoc extensions, as described in "The OpenDoc Extension Interface" on page 441.

Installing Handlers, Accessors, and Callbacks

Your part editor's semantic interface is mainly a table of handlers that OpenDoc uses when processing a semantic event. If you use the OpenDoc scripting-related utility classes, you call methods of `SIHelper` to install and remove event handlers, object accessors, and other special callback functions; you use methods of `ODCPlusSemanticInterface` to call them.

- You install semantic-event handlers by calling the `InstallEventHandler` method of `SIHelper`.

- You install object accessors by calling the `InstallObjectAccessor` method of `SIHelper`.

- You install coercion handlers by calling the `InstallCoercionHandler` method of `SIHelper`.

- You install object callback functions in either of two ways. You can call the `InstallSpecialHandler` method of `SIHelper` and pass it a parameter specifying the kind of function to install, or you can call function-specific methods such as `InstallCountProc` and `InstallMarkProc`. Constants for the parameter you pass to `InstallSpecialHandler` are defined by the Apple Event Manager and have names such as `keyAECompareProc`.

- You install a predispatch handler either by calling the `InstallSpecialHandler` method of `SIHelper`, passing it a parameter whose value is `keyPreDispatch`, or by calling the `UsingPreDispatchProc` method of your subclass of `ODSemanticInterface`.

Other methods of `SIHelper` allow access to and removal of these handlers, accessors, and callbacks.

You use the `SetOSLSupportFlags` method of your subclass of `ODSemanticInterface` to set flags that, during the resolution process, notify the name resolver's `Resolve` method of the kinds of object-callback support that your part editor can provide for resolution of object specifiers.

Installing System-Level Handlers

To install system-level semantic-event handlers, coercion handlers, object accessors, and object-callback functions, you can use the standard Apple Event Manager installation functions and set the `isSysHandler` parameter to `TRUE`.

In general, installing system-level handlers is discouraged because of the difficulty of ensuring your part's availability to handle calls to them. If you do install them, be sure that you don't leave them installed after your part has closed. You should remove any installed system-level handlers in your part's `ReleaseAll` method or possibly in your part's `Release` method when the reference count goes to 0.

Making Your Terminology Resource Available

When a scripting system first compiles a script that targets an OpenDoc document, it needs access to the terminology ('`aete`') resources associated with that document. The scripting system gains this access by sending a Get AETE Apple event to OpenDoc, which converts it to an OpenDoc Get AETE Apple event (class ID `kAEOpenDocSuite`, event ID `kGetAETE`) and sends it to the document shell.

The document shell handles the OpenDoc Get AETE Apple event by returning the terminology resource in its reply event's result parameter. (If you create a container application, it must handle the OpenDoc Get AETE event if it is to be scriptable.)

Your part editor should include a terminology resource in its shared library. OpenDoc caches this resource, along with the terminology resources of all other installed part editors on the user's system, for use by the scripting system. Because the scripting system merges all terminology resources into a single composite resource for all parts and all documents, it is extremely important that your part editor avoid terminology conflicts with other part editors. As a minimum, be sure to avoid conflicts with any terminologies defined in the current suites of Apple events.

Also, because the only available terminologies are those in the system-wide merged '`aete`' resource, your part editor cannot make its terminologies known dynamically; it cannot itself handle the Get AETE event, and it cannot make use of a scripting-size ('`scsz`') resource.

Sending Semantic Events

Although the ability to send semantic events is not required for scriptability, OpenDoc provides support for it. This section discusses the OpenDoc-specific aspects of sending semantic events; for more information, see the chapter "Creating and Sending Apple Events" in *Inside Macintosh: Interapplication Communication.*

The OpenDoc message interface object (ODMessageInterface) is responsible for constructing Apple events, getting and setting event attributes, parsing events, and sending events. This section describes how your part uses the message interface and the Apple Event Manager to send a semantic event.

To construct the Apple event, you call the CreateEvent method of the message interface object to create an ODAppleEvent object. You can then construct additional parameters and add them to the Apple event by calling the Apple Event Manager AEPutParamPtr or AEPutParamDesc function.

Constructing Object Specifiers

To send an Apple event to an OpenDoc part, the sender must use an object specifier that identifies the target part. The object specifier is typically in the direct parameter of the Apple event, although for events without direct parameters, OpenDoc places it in a subject attribute.

Conventional applications using the Apple Event Manager to send events to a part in an OpenDoc document construct the appropriate object specifier themselves. If your part sends a semantic event, you can use the methods described in this section to construct an object specifier. If you send a semantic event to your own part (as when recording), you follow the same procedures as when sending an event to another part.

Using CreatePartObjSpec

If your part sends a semantic event to another part, you can use the CreatePartObjSpec method of the message interface to construct an object specifier for the direct parameter of the event. You must also call the CreatePartAddrDesc method of the message interface to create an address descriptor that identifies the process (OpenDoc document) in which the destination part resides.

If you use CreatePartObjSpec, OpenDoc dispatches to the specified part directly, without calling the Resolve method of the name resolver. This dispatching is efficient and fast. However, you cannot inspect the contents of the object specifier constructed by CreatePartObjSpec or use it for recording, and you cannot use it as a component of another object specifier that you construct.

Using EmbeddedFrameSpec

You can also use the `EmbeddedFrameSpec` method of `ODPart` to help construct an object specifier. You can inspect the resulting specifier, you can use it for recording, and you can use it as the direct parameter or as another parameter in an Apple event. Object specifiers created through `EmbeddedFrameSpec` have forms such as "embedded frame 2 of embedded frame 1 of the root frame".

To construct an object specifier in this way, you call the `EmbeddedFrameSpec` method of the part containing the frame that is the target for the event. Here is the interface to `EmbeddedFrameSpec`:

```
void EmbeddedFrameSpec(in ODFrame embeddedFrame,
                       in ODObjectSpec spec);
```

A part receiving this method call should first call the `EmbeddedFrameSpec` method of its own containing part. It should then create an object specifier for the supplied embedded frame (using index number or any other appropriate identifying characteristic) and add it to the return value from its own call to `EmbeddedFrameSpec`. The final object specifier returned to the original caller thus describes the target frame in the context of its document.

A root part receiving this call should return a null object specifier.

Constructing object specifiers with `EmbeddedFrameSpec` is most useful for situations in which a target part's position in the embedding hierarchy is more important than its specific identity. However, `EmbeddedFrameSpec` fails if any part in the embedding hierarchy from the target frame to the root frame is not scriptable or has not implemented the `EmbeddedFrameSpec` method. Also, an object specifier constructed by this method becomes incorrect if the identifying characteristic of any frame in the hierarchy changes.

Using Persistent Object ID

The most reliable method for constructing an object specifier for a part is by using its persistent object ID. Use the persistent ID if you are constructing an object specifier and your call to `EmbeddedFrameSpec` fails, if you are sending an Apple event to a part with no display frames, or any time you need an object specifier that will be valid for a part regardless of its position in the embedding hierarchy.

Call the `GetPersistentObjectID` method of the target frame's or part's draft and use the return value in the object specifier. If your own frame is the target, as when recording, call your own draft's `GetPersistentObjectID` method and pass it your own display frame.

Sending the Event

To send the Apple event, you call the `Send` method of the message interface object. The message interface adds a subject attribute representing the target part (your part if you are sending the event to yourself) to the event. The message interface also generates and keeps track of the return ID for the event so that the reply can be routed back to your part editor's reply event handler.

CHAPTER 10

Extending OpenDoc

Contents

10

This is the last of eight chapters that discuss the OpenDoc programming interface in detail. This chapter describes how you can use or alter portions of the OpenDoc class library to enhance the capabilities of your part editors.

Before reading this chapter, you should be familiar with the concepts presented in Chapter 1, "Introduction to OpenDoc," and Chapter 2, "Development Overview." For additional concepts related to your part editor's runtime environment, see Chapter 11, "OpenDoc Runtime Features."

This chapter discusses the following ways in which you can extend OpenDoc:

■ By creating OpenDoc extension objects for your part editor, you can add programming interfaces to your parts for any purpose. The semantic interface support in OpenDoc, described in Chapter 9, "Semantic Events and Scripting," is an example of the use of extension objects.

■ By creating a settings extension, you can give users access to editor-specific settings through the Part Info dialog box.

■ By creating specialized dispatch modules, you can define new kinds of user events that your parts can respond to.

■ By creating specialized focus modules, you can define new categories of foci (shared resources) that your parts can acquire and exchange.

■ By creating a subclass of `ODTransform`, you can extend the ways in which your part transforms the images it draws.

■ By creating a shell plug-in, a modification of the functions of the document shell, you can add additional document-wide capabilities to OpenDoc.

■ By patching (replacing) specific OpenDoc objects, you can modify some of the fundamental capabilities of OpenDoc.

The OpenDoc Extension Interface

You can greatly extend the capabilities of your parts, in terms of fast processing of information or communication with other parts, if you use the interface-extension capabilities of OpenDoc. The extension protocol allows parts or other OpenDoc objects to increase their capabilities by extending their programming interfaces. By using extension interfaces, your parts can communicate with other parts or other kinds of OpenDoc components in ways not possible with the standard OpenDoc programming interface.

The semantic interface extension to OpenDoc, described in Chapter 9, "Semantic Events and Scripting," is an example of the use of extensions to support scripting. Other kinds of extension interfaces can be especially valuable in those situations where scripting cannot provide enough integration or bandwidth.

You design, create, and attach such an extension to your part editor. At runtime, other parts can then access and use the extension interface by passing its extension name to method calls to your parts.

Extension Objects

All subclasses of ODObject, including shapes, facets, documents, windows, frames, and parts, can be extended. An extension is itself an object, an instantiation of a subclass of ODExtension. Each extension object is related to its **base object**—the object whose interface it extends—by its extension name, an ISO string. A caller accesses a base object's extension through that extension name. (*Base object* in this sense has nothing to do with inheritance; this book uses the term *superclass* to describe an ancestor in the class hierarchy.) For example, the extension name for the semantic interface extension to a part is kODExtSemanticInterface.

Extensible objects create and delete their own extensions and manage the extensions' storage. If desired, a base object can share an extension object among multiple clients (callers), perhaps using a reference-counting scheme to decide when to delete the extensions. A caller can query an extensible object to see if it supports a specified extension.

The ODExtension class itself has minimal functionality. It is a superclass for subclasses that implement actual extension interfaces. Every extension object knows what base object it is an extension of.

Using an Extension

To access the extension interface of an extensible part, a client, or caller, takes these steps:

1. It calls the part's override of its inherited HasExtension method to see if the extension is supported, passing the part (the base object) an extension name.

2. If the part has such an extension, the client then calls the part's (override of its inherited) AcquireExtension method to get a reference to the extension

object. The part either creates the extension object or increases its reference count (if the object already exists) and passes the reference back to the client.

3. The client makes extension-interface calls directly to the extension object.

When the client has finished using the services of the extension object, it takes these steps:

1. The client calls the extension's (override of its inherited) `Release` method, to let the extension know that the client no longer needs it.

2. The extension in turn calls the (override of its inherited) `ReleaseExtension` method of its part (its base object) if its reference count has dropped to 0. The base object can then delete the extension.

   However, if the extension's base object has already been deleted and has called the extension's `BaseRemoved` method (see "Closing Your Part" on page 308), the extension cannot call its base's `ReleaseExtension` method.

Implementing Extensions

Your part editors can implement any kinds of desired extension interfaces through this mechanism. The capabilities gained through extensions can be in almost any area. Examples include extensions to handle text search, spell checking, linking, specialized text formatting, database access, and specialized graphics processing. In general, extension objects are best suited for tasks requiring high bandwidth or tight integration, for which scripting is not appropriate.

If you implement an extension object for your part, the extension should include a System Object Model (SOM) constructor (`somInit`), a SOM destructor (`somUninit`), and an initialization (`InitExtension`) method. The extension could also support a `GetBase` method, through which a client can obtain a reference to the extension's base object. (The `ODExtension` class provides a default implementation for `GetBase`.)

Your part is the factory for its extensions, which are reference-counted objects. You must follow the procedures described in the section "Factory Methods" on page 463 when creating, managing, and deleting extensions. Also, if your part's document is closed while it has extensions remaining in memory, your part's `ReleaseAll` method must call the extensions' `BaseRemoved` method.

An extension object must always be valid (attached to its base object) to be used. If a client tries to access an invalid extension, a `kODErrInvalidExtension` exception is generated. Any time after your part, as base object, calls its extension's `BaseRemoved` method, the extension is invalid. If you want to provide your own validation scheme for extensions, you need to override the `ODExtension` methods `CheckValid`, `IsValid`, and `BaseRemoved`.

Your extension interfaces can be private to your parts, or you can establish or follow public standards. CI Labs is the agency responsible for coordinating standard extension interfaces for parts. For information on existing extension interfaces, or to propose new interfaces, please contact CI Labs at the address shown in the section "Cross-Platform Consistency and CI Labs" on page 71.

The Settings Extension

The Part Info dialog box (see "Selection Info" on page 254) is accessed by the user from the Edit menu and displayed by the Info object (`ODInfo` class). The information that OpenDoc displays in a part's Part Info dialog box consists of the part's Info properties. **Info properties** are those properties in a part's storage unit, separate from the part's contents property, that are intended to be visible to the user. They include properties such as creation date and modification date (which cannot be changed by the user) as well as name and part kind (which can be changed by the user).

The Part Info dialog box provides access to only the standard Info properties that all OpenDoc parts have. To define and allow access to Info properties specific to your part editor, you can create a **settings extension** to display your own Settings dialog box.

If you implement a settings extension, a button with the title "Settings…" appears in the lower-left corner of the Part Info dialog box. When the user clicks this button, OpenDoc calls your settings extension's `ShowSettings` method. This call gives you a chance to display your Settings dialog box so that the user can edit your editor-specific settings.

Your settings extension should be implemented as a subclass of the `ODSettingsExtension` class. `ODSettingsExtension` is itself a subclass of `ODExtension`.

Custom Event Types

You can extend OpenDoc's event-dispatching architecture to include new kinds of events by creating your own dispatch module.

Creating a Dispatch Module

The class `ODDispatchModule` is an abstract superclass. OpenDoc uses instances of a subclass of `ODDispatchModule` to dispatch certain types of events (such as keystroke events) to part editors. For normal program execution, you do not need to subclass `ODDispatchModule` or even access the existing dispatch module objects directly. Your interaction with OpenDoc regarding event dispatching is mainly through the dispatcher.

You can, however, provide for dispatching of new types of events or messages to your part editor by subclassing `ODDispatchModule`. For example, you could create a dispatch module to handle events from an exotic input device such as a 3D glove for a virtual reality game.

Patching the dispatcher
It is possible to use custom dispatch modules to patch the functioning of the dispatcher in relation to all event types, although that practice is in general not recommended. In most cases there is no need for such drastic alteration of OpenDoc functionality. ◆

At runtime, the dispatcher maintains a dictionary of installed dispatch modules, keyed by event type. When the dispatcher's `Dispatch` method is called, it looks up the dispatch module for the supplied event type and calls the `Dispatch` method of that module.

When the standard OpenDoc dispatch module transforms an event of one type (such as a mouse-down event in the menu bar) into an event of another type (such as an OpenDoc menu event), it passes the event back to the dispatcher for redispatching, by calling the dispatcher's `Redispatch` method. This redispatching allows your custom dispatch module to patch out or monitor the standard dispatch module for just those transformed events.

If you subclass `ODDispatchModule`, you need to implement a SOM constructor (`somInit`), a SOM destructor (`somUninit`), and an initialization method. Your initialization method should call (but not override) the `InitDispatchModule` method of `ODDispatchModule`.

Your dispatch module is responsible for actually dispatching events. The dispatcher calls your module's override of the `Dispatch` method, passing it the event information.

You install the dispatch module by calling the `AddDispatchModule` method of the dispatcher; you remove a dispatch module by calling the `RemoveDispatchModule` method of the dispatcher. The installation might occur during the initialization of your part (or shell plug-in, if you create one).

Using a Dispatch Module as a Monitor

You can also install a dispatch module as a **monitor.** In this case, the dispatch module is notified of events of its kinds but does not have to dispatch them. You might use a monitor in a debugging tool, for example, to capture all events and display a log of the events in a window.

You install a monitor with the dispatcher's `AddMonitor` method. For a given event, the dispatcher calls the `Dispatch` method for all installed monitors (of that event type) before calling the `Dispatch` method of the regular dispatch module for that event type. The dispatcher ignores the Boolean function result of the `Dispatch` method of all monitors; therefore, unlike with normal use of a dispatch module, you can have more than one monitor for a single event type.

Custom Focus Types

You can extend OpenDoc's model for shared-resource arbitration by creating your own focus module, allowing your parts to recognize and negotiate ownership of new kinds of focus.

Creating a Focus Module

The class `ODFocusModule` is an abstract superclass. OpenDoc uses instances of a subclass of `ODFocusModule` to assign ownership of specific types of focus to part editors. For normal program execution, you do not need to subclass

`ODFocusModule` or even access the existing focus module objects directly. Your interaction with OpenDoc regarding focus ownership is mainly through the arbitrator.

You can, however, subclass `ODFocusModule` for new types of focus ownership, perhaps related to new types of peripheral devices or new classes of shared resources. For example, if you provide an exotic input device such as a 3D glove for a virtual reality game, you could create a focus module that tracked the ownership of input from the glove.

You define a new kind of focus to be handled by that focus module by creating an ISO string that is the name of the focus. As an example, the ISO string that defines the scrolling focus is "Scrolling." Currently defined foci are listed in Table 5-4 on page 208.

Patching the arbitrator
It is possible to use custom focus modules to patch the functioning of the arbitrator in relation to all types of focus, although that practice is in general not recommended. In most cases there is no need for such drastic alteration of OpenDoc functionality. ◆

If you subclass `ODFocusModule`, you need to implement a SOM constructor (`somInit`), a SOM destructor (`somUninit`), and an initialization method. Your initialization method should call (but not override) the `InitFocusModule` method of `ODFocusModule`.

Your focus module is responsible for maintaining the identities of the individual frames that own the foci managed by your focus module. You must implement the methods `AcquireFocusOwner`, `SetFocusOwnership`, `UnsetFocusOwnership`, and `TransferFocusOwnership`, all called by the arbitrator to request or change the owner of a focus.

You must also implement the methods `BeginRelinquishFocus`, `CommitRelinquishFocus`, and `AbortRelinquishFocus`, which your focus module uses in the two-stage process of relinquishing the ownership of a focus. The arbitrator calls these methods, and your focus module in turn calls the equivalent methods of the part that currently owns the focus.

You install a focus module by calling the `RegisterFocus` method of the arbitrator; you remove it by calling the `UnregisterFocus` method of the arbitrator.

Extending OpenDoc

The simple way

You can create a default focus module for any exclusive focus without having to subclass `ODFocusModule`. You simply pass the name of the focus and a value of `kODNull` (for the focus module object reference) to `RegisterFocus`. The arbitrator then creates and returns a focus module for your focus that has properties equivalent to those of the existing OpenDoc focus modules. ◆

Focus Modules for Nonexclusive Foci

The arbitrator and focus modules allow foci to be **nonexclusive,** meaning that a given focus can have more than one owner. For instance, if video input is provided, a focus module for video focus might track the part or parts that are currently receiving video input.

If you create a focus module for nonexclusive foci, you must implement methods for testing exclusivity (`IsFocusExclusive`) and for allowing a caller to iterate over the owners of a focus (`CreateOwnerIterator`).

Custom Transform Objects

OpenDoc transform objects provide powerful transformational capabilities that are sufficient for most two-dimensional drawing. With transforms, you not only can position your graphical objects, but you also easily can scale, rotate, and skew them. You can combine the operations of frames' internal transforms with those of facets' external transforms to achieve sophisticated effects with a minimum of code.

If you need to extend the power of transform objects even further, you can obtain the extra capability most efficiently by creating your own transform subclass. If you need to provide for nonlinear transformations (such as curved projections or sophisticated perspective effects), you can implement them as new methods and as overrides to the methods of `ODBaseTransform`, the superclass of `ODTransform`.

448   Custom Transform Objects

If you subclass `ODBaseTransform`, you must override at least the following methods:

Copy	InvertPoint	Reset
CopyFrom	InvertShape	TransformPoint
GetMatrix	PostCompose	TransformShape
HasMatrix	PreCompose	WriteTo
Invert	ReadFrom	

Your `GetMatrix` method must throw the exception `ODErrTransformErr`. Your `HasMatrix` method must return `kODFalse`. Other methods should perform tasks appropriate to your transform.

For more information on matrices and transformations in two-dimensional drawing, you can consult any standard computer-graphics textbook, such as *Computer Graphics Principles and Practice*, 2nd ed., by Foley, vanDam, Feiner, and Hughes (Addison-Wesley, 1990).

Shell Plug-Ins

You can extend the capabilities of the document shell or add session-wide functionality to OpenDoc by implementing shell plug-ins. Shell plug-ins are shared libraries rather than subclasses of `ODExtension`. A shell plug-in is not associated with any particular part object. Your shell plug-in must be installed on the user's machine when a document first opens, if it is to be used with that document.

You can create shell plug-ins for any of several purposes, including these:

■ to install a dispatch module or focus module that will be available to all parts in the document

■ to install an object (such as a spelling checker) into a name space, allowing it to be accessed as a service by all parts in the document

■ to replace parts of OpenDoc with your own capabilities, from individual objects (see "Patching OpenDoc," next) to entire subsystems (see "Runtime Object Relationships" on page 487)

A shell plug-in has a single exported entry point to OpenDoc: its installation function. Your plug-in library needs to implement only that function, with this interface:

```
OSErr ODShellPluginInstall(Environment* ev,
                           ODDraft* draft,
                           ODShellPluginActionCodes* action );
```

The installation function must have exactly the specified name as well as the specified parameters and return value. You must ensure that the function name `ODShellPluginInstall` appears in your library's list of exported symbols.

The `draft` parameter specifies the document draft that is being opened. Use the `action` parameter to return a value specifying whether the document shell should maintain a connection to your shell plug-in library after the installation function completes.

The installation function must always return `noErr`, unless it cannot execute. For any `ODShellPluginInstall` function that returns an error, OpenDoc displays a dialog box to the user requesting that the shell plug-in be removed from the user's system.

Your shell plug-in must follow the conventions for shared libraries. On the Mac OS platform, it should have the file type `'shlb'` so that the Code Fragment Manager can recognize it as an import library, and it can optionally have the initialization and termination entry points available to import libraries. (Its expected `main` entry point is replaced by the `ODShellPluginInstall` function.) For more information on shared library structure, see *Inside Macintosh: PowerPC System Software.*

Execution of a shell plug-in happens like this:

1. Whenever the user opens an OpenDoc document, OpenDoc launches the document shell. The document shell initializes itself and the session object, and gains access to the document's current draft.

2. The document shell then accesses each plug-in library and calls its `ODShellPluginInstall` function. The `ODShellPluginInstall` function performs the functions the plug-in is designed for: it installs custom focus modules or dispatch modules, it patches session-level objects, or it otherwise modifies shell functionality. `ODShellPluginInstall` then returns the appropriate `OSErr` value and exits.

3. After all plug-ins have executed, the root part of the OpenDoc document opens the document window.

If it is to be executed, your shell plug-in file must be located in the OpenDoc Shell Plug-Ins folder on the user's system. See Appendix C, "Installing OpenDoc Software and Parts" on page 633, for more information.

Patching OpenDoc

You can enhance or alter the functioning of OpenDoc in ways even more fundamental than implementing extension interfaces, dispatch modules, and focus modules. Because OpenDoc is modular and object-oriented, you can directly replace certain of its objects with your own versions.

OpenDoc allows you to patch any of its session-level objects. The session-level objects are those directly referenced by the session object, as shown in Figure 11-4 on page 488. They are represented by these OpenDoc classes:

`ODArbitrator`	`ODInfo`	`ODSemanticInterface` subclass[*]
`ODBinding`	`ODLinkManager`	`ODStorageSystem`
`ODClipboard`	`ODMessageInterface`	`ODTranslation`
`ODDispatcher`	`ODNameResolver`	`ODUndo`
`ODDragAndDrop`	`ODNameSpaceManager`	`ODWindowState`

[*] The document shell's semantic interface

This section discusses the mechanics of writing a patch to a session-level object, although it does not discuss the capabilities of the individual objects or the reasons for patching them. Before patching any object, be sure you are very familiar with its purpose and its interface. Read the appropriate parts of this book and the *OpenDoc Class Reference for the Mac OS* for more information.

Writing a Patch

Because your OpenDoc patch replaces a specific object with a known public interface, you should write it as a subclass of the class of object you are patching. You must override every method, and your overrides (other than `somInit` and `somUninit`) should not call their inherited versions. If you want only partial replacement of OpenDoc's functionality, delegate to the patched-out object (the one you have replaced) those methods that you do not wish to change.

Immediately after creating your replacement object, your patch installer (see "Installing a Patch," next) should call the object's initialization method (Init*ClassName*). For example, if you are replacing the drag-and-drop object, you would call your replacement object's InitDragAndDrop method immediately after calling new to create it.

Your replacement object's initialization method should call the Get*ClassName* method of the session object to get a reference to the current object and then store that reference in a field. For the drag-and-drop example, your InitDragAndDrop method would call the session object's GetDragAndDrop method and store the returned reference in a field such as fOldDragAndDrop.

At the end of initialization, your Init*ClassName* method should assign the replacement object as the current object. It should call the Set*ClassName* method of the session object and pass itself (somSelf) as the new object reference. For example, if you were replacing the drag-and-drop object, you would make this call:

```
theSession->SetDragAndDrop(ev, somSelf);
```

Your destructor method (somUninit) should delete the patched-out object (the one referenced in the fOldDragAndDrop field, for example) before calling the inherited somUninit.

If the object you are replacing has additional entry points besides those based on the session object's reference to it, you need to patch those also. For example, on the Mac OS platform the drag-and-drop object registers callbacks with the Mac OS Drag Manager; your replacement object would have to reregister those callbacks to point to itself.

Installing a Patch

Once you have written your patch, you need to install it so that OpenDoc uses it in place of the original object. Depending on what your patching needs are, you can place your patch installer in either of two places.

- If the scope of your patch needs to be global (applied to all OpenDoc documents), make your patch installer a shell plug-in (see "Shell Plug-Ins" on page 449). Install the patch within your plug-in's Install function.

■ If the scope of your patch is confined to the document containing your part, you can use your part editor's `Open` method to install the patch. Only the root part of a document can install an OpenDoc patch.

When called, your installer instantiates and initializes the patch object.

Potential Patch Conflicts

Every time it opens a document, the document shell installs, in order, all shell plug-ins, and then the root part opens its window. This installation sequence can lead to patching conflicts. Because you do not control the order in which shell plug-ins are installed, you cannot ensure that your patch will not itself be patched out by a subsequently installed patch.

You can minimize the potential for conflicts by writing your patch correctly. Properly written patch objects always delegate everything but their specific functionality to the object that was previously in place. Consistently following this convention ensures the proper chaining of patch functionality.

Ultimately, the root part controls which patches remain, because it has the final opportunity to install its own patches.

OpenDoc Runtime Features

Contents

This chapter concludes the programming portion of this book by discussing several aspects of the OpenDoc runtime environment that are of interest to you as a part-editor developer. The topics in this chapter are different from the programming-interface topics discussed in the previous eight chapters. Nevertheless, they are important to understanding how your parts function at runtime with OpenDoc.

- "The Runtime Environment" describes in general the runtime architecture of OpenDoc and its effect on part development.

- "Creating and Releasing Objects" describes how your part editor creates and releases objects (including how to be efficient about it), how it manages multiple references to objects, and when it should purge memory.

- "Accessing Objects Through Iterators" describes how your part can use iterators to access collections of objects.

- "Binding" describes how your part editor is bound to a part at runtime according to the kinds of data stored in the part and the kinds and categories of data supported by your editor.

- "Runtime Object Relationships" summarizes and illustrates how OpenDoc objects in a document interact with each other for specific purposes.

- "The Document Shell" describes how the OpenDoc document shell performs its functions and how its functioning relates to your part editor's responsibilities.

The Runtime Environment

The runtime model for the execution of part editors in the OpenDoc environment is different from that of conventional applications. This section discusses those differences in terms of the runtime process model, System Object Model runtime issues, and the part wrapper object. It also discusses name spaces, a runtime service provided by OpenDoc.

The OpenDoc Runtime Process

The OpenDoc document-centered approach requires a runtime process model significantly different from the classic application-centered process model. On personal-computer platforms, each process is usually owned by an application. This process provides the address space in which the application code executes as well as the memory for every document opened by that application. The operating system assigns a document to a process based on the document's type, an indication of which application created it.

In OpenDoc, a document no longer has a single type but is instead composed of many parts that may be of different types. Thus, the document, not any application, is the owner of the process. The document manages standard tasks such as handling the event loop, managing files, printing, and interacting with system menus, dialog boxes, and so on. In OpenDoc, some of this behavior is provided by a shared library called the document shell. The fact that individual parts in a document share this code is one reason why part editors can be significantly smaller than conventional applications.

The document shell has the following basic responsibilities:

- It creates and initializes the session object, which in turn creates and initializes the other session-wide OpenDoc objects, as shown in Figure 11-4 on page 488.

- It opens the document chosen by the user.

- It accepts events and passes them to the OpenDoc dispatcher.

- It handles certain document-wide menu commands.

The executable code of part editors is stored and accessed as shared libraries, independent of any process. (Note that part-editor code must be reentrant on the Mac OS because several instances of a part in a single document may use the same editor.) What the process provides is an address space for the contents of a particular document, along with any additional memory needed by the individual part editors. All state information used by any part editor is, with some minor exceptions, maintained in the processes of those documents that contain parts manipulated by the editor.

Multiprocess runtime model

The single-process-per-document model is not the only runtime model possible with OpenDoc. On platforms that provide fast process switching and efficient interprocess dispatch, the document shell process can run each part in a separate process. ◆

CFM and the System Object Model

Two cornerstones of the OpenDoc runtime environment are dynamic linking, which allows compound documents to be assembled at runtime, and a language-neutral object model, which facilitates runtime compatibility of parts and minimizes the recompilation required by changes to OpenDoc or to part editors.

Dynamic linking on the Mac OS platform is provided by the Code Fragment Manager (CFM). The object model used by OpenDoc is the System Object Model (SOM). This section introduces some runtime aspects of CFM and SOM that are of interest to part-editor developers. (The particulars of writing SOM-based code are discussed in the section "Developing With SOM and IDL" on page 83.) For more information, see the SOM appendix of the *OpenDoc Cookbook for the Mac OS*.

Dynamic Linking

OpenDoc depends on dynamic linking to allow the appropriate executable code to be added to the runtime environment of a document. Before a document is opened, there is no way of knowing what part editors may be needed to manipulate its contents. The dynamic linking used by OpenDoc on the Mac OS relies on the **Code Fragment Manager (CFM)** to manipulate code fragments. The dynamic linking provided by CFM has the following capabilities:

■ It allows an executable module to be loaded into memory once and then shared by multiple processes.

■ It allows dynamically linked code to call code contained in another dynamically linked library.

■ It gives dynamically linked code access to global variables.

SOM and Distributed Dispatching

System Object Model (SOM) objects are CORBA-compliant, meaning that they follow the language-neutral distributed standards of the **Common Object Request Broker Architecture (CORBA),** established by the **Object Management Group (OMG),** an industry consortium. Compliance with these standards mean that objects compiled in different languages or with different compilers can communicate with each other.

More than that, SOM objects running on different machines can communicate with each other. This distributed dispatching may be a future capability of OpenDoc and is therefore supported in these basic architectural features:

- Almost all objects are instantiated by factory objects rather than by constructors called by your part. See Table 11-1 on page 464 for a list of the factory objects.

- The OpenDoc support for scripting is designed to allow for remote callback functions; see "Scripting-Related OpenDoc Classes" on page 414.

- To enhance performance, OpenDoc minimizes the frequency of interpart and interlibrary method calls, except in cases—such as layout support—where frequent calls cannot be avoided.

SOM Exception Handling

OpenDoc objects are SOM objects, and as such they follow the CORBA rules for handling exceptions. Every method call made to an OpenDoc object (including your part, as a subclass of `ODPart`) must therefore include an environment parameter (`ev`), a pointer to a value that can describe an error. For example, the `CreateLinkSource` method of `ODDraft` has the following prototype (in IDL):

```
ODLinkSource CreateLinkSource(in ODPart part);
```

The method takes a single parameter, of type `ODPart`. To use this method, however, a caller in C++ must supply two parameters:

```
MyLinkSource = MyDraft->CreateLinkSource(ev, somSelf);
```

If execution of the method results in an error condition, the receiver of the call (the draft object in this case) must place an exception code in the value pointed to by `ev` and return. The caller must therefore examine the `ev` parameter after every call to a SOM object to see if an exception has been raised.

All OpenDoc methods that you call, as well as all public methods of your part editor that you write, must return errors this way. These are the implications for your exception handling:

■ You must supply an environment variable with all method calls to OpenDoc objects.

■ You must check the environment variable after the call returns.

The environment variable is passed along through a sequence of calls and can be used in calls to both SOM and C++ objects. Here is how you can use it correctly:

■ If your SOM method calls another SOM method, it can simply pass on the environment parameter it has received. This is the usual case, since your part editor executes only in response to calls to its SOM interface, and thus should always have received a value for the environment variable.

■ If your SOM method calls a C++ method that may in turn call a SOM method, your SOM method can pass the environment parameter on to the C++ method (if the C++ method was designed to accept it; see next bullet).

■ If your C++ method is called by a SOM method and in turn makes calls to SOM methods, it is best to design it to accept an environment parameter that it can then pass on.

■ If your C++ method does not itself receive an environment parameter but it does call a SOM method, it can use a function provided by SOM (`somGetGlobalEnvironment`) to obtain a value for the environment variable.

For more information on the environment parameter and exceptions, see *SOMObjects Developer Toolkit Users Guide* and *SOMObjects Developer Toolkit Programmers Reference Manual* from IBM.

Any exception-handling scheme that you use must support this method of passing exceptions. An OpenDoc utility library (Except), described in the *OpenDoc Cookbook for the Mac OS,* helps you check the environment variable after each method call.

The Part-Wrapper Object

Your part first initializes itself when OpenDoc calls its `InitPart` or `InitPartFromStorage` method, as described in "Initializing and Reading a Part From Storage" on page 294. At that time, OpenDoc passes your part an object reference in the `partWrapper` parameter of `InitPart` or `InitPartFromStorage`.

That reference is to a **part-wrapper object,** a private object that OpenDoc creates and uses to represent your part.

The part wrapper keeps other parts of OpenDoc from having direct pointers to your part object; its only function is to delegate methods of `ODPart` to your part. Using a part wrapper gives OpenDoc more flexibility in manipulating parts. For example, use of a part wrapper allows OpenDoc to switch editors for a part without having to close and reopen the part's document.

You must use your part-wrapper reference in all calls to the OpenDoc interface that require you to pass a reference to yourself—for example, when registering your part for idle time. (Typically, if your part object keeps a field such as `fSelf` to hold a reference to itself, that field should contain the part-wrapper reference.) Specifically, you should never pass `somSelf` as a parameter to any OpenDoc method except when accessing objects such as extensions and embedded-frame iterators for which your part itself is the factory.

Part-wrapper methods
The interface to `ODPart` includes three part-wrapper methods—`IsRealPart`, `GetRealPart`, and `ReleaseRealPart`—that are intended for the part-wrapper object only. OpenDoc calls these methods when associating your part with or disassociating it from its part wrapper. When you subclass `ODPart` to create your part editor, do not override these methods. ◆

Name Spaces

Each OpenDoc session provides a runtime service allowing you to define name spaces. A **name space** is an object that maps data types to values. It consists of a set of string–value pairs that associate the string (an ISO string) with the value (a 4-byte unsigned value, which could be a pointer to code).

For example, OpenDoc uses name spaces to represent the preferences of the user for binding parts (whose part kinds are represented by ISO strings) to part editors (represented by pointers to editor IDs).

Name spaces are a general-purpose runtime registry mechanism. You can use them to define global spaces in which to share information with other parts. You can define as many name spaces as you wish; the OpenDoc **name-space manager** keeps a list (which is itself a name space) of all currently defined name spaces.

For example, you can use a name space to create palettes or other controls to be shared among several parts. Use an ISO string to identify the name space itself and ISO strings to identify each of the controls it encompasses. You then can get pointers to the controls (if the name space has already been instantiated) or instantiate the name space and provide pointers to the controls (if your part is the first in the session to use the name space).

If you publish the ISO strings that define your name space and its contents, the name space can be used publicly. If you do not publish the names, you can still use the name space for your own private global variables.

Creating and Releasing Objects

This section discusses how your part editor allocates and releases OpenDoc objects, and how it should release unneeded memory when requested to do so by OpenDoc.

Factory Methods

Any OpenDoc object that you create must be instantiated by a **factory method,** a method of one class used to create an instance of another class. You should never use the C++ `new` operator, for example, to create an object of an OpenDoc class (except for subclasses, such as `ODExtension`, through which you extend OpenDoc and for which your part is the factory).

Table 11-1 lists the factory methods you should use to instantiate any of the OpenDoc classes whose objects your part editor might ever need to create. The table lists methods that create new objects as well as those that return previously created objects, whether currently in memory or stored persistently. Note that your own part editor has the factory methods for the classes `ODEmbeddedFramesIterator` and any of its own extension objects, including `ODSemanticInterface`. Note also that `ODDraft` has the factory method for `ODPart` and any of its subclasses, including your part.

Table 11-1   Factory methods for OpenDoc classes

Object to be created	Class and factory method
ODCanvas	ODFacet::CreateCanvas ODWindowState::CreateCanvas
ODContainer	ODStorageSystem::CreateContainer ODStorageSystem::AcquireContainer
ODDesc	ODNameResolver::GetUserToken
ODDocument	ODContainer::AcquireDocument
ODDraft	ODDocument::CreateDraft ODDocument::AcquireDraft ODDocument::AcquireBaseDraft
ODEmbeddedFramesIterator (subclass)	ODPart::CreateEmbeddedFramesIterator
ODExtension (subclass)	ODObject (subclass)::AcquireExtension (usu. ODPart (subclass)::AcquireExtension)
ODFacet	ODFacet::CreateEmbeddedFacet ODWindowState::CreateFacet
ODFacetIterator	ODFacet::CreateFacetIterator
ODFocusOwnerIterator	ODArbitrator::CreateOwnerIterator
ODFocusSet	ODArbitrator::CreateFocusSet
ODFocusSetIterator	ODFocusSet::CreateIterator
ODFrame	ODDraft::CreateFrame ODDraft::AcquireFrame
ODFrameFacetIterator	ODFrame::CreateFacetIterator
ODLink	ODDraft::AcquireLink
ODLinkSource	ODDraft::CreateLinkSource ODDraft::AcquireLinkSource
ODLinkSpec	ODDraft::CreateLinkSpec
ODMenuBar	ODMenuBar::Copy ODWindowState::CopyBaseMenuBar

continued

Table 11-1   Factory methods for OpenDoc classes (continued)

Object to be created	Class and factory method
`ODNameSpace`	`ODNameSpaceManager::CreateNameSpace` `ODNameSpaceManager::HasNameSpace`
`ODObjectIterator`	`ODObjectNameSpace::CreateIterator`
`ODOSLToken`	`ODOSLToken::DuplicateODOSLToken`
`ODPart` (subclass)	`ODDraft::CreatePart` `ODDraft::AcquirePart`
`ODPlatformTypeList`	`ODStorageSystem::` `CreatePlatformTypeList`
`ODPlatformTypeListIterator`	`ODPlatformTypeList::` `CreatePlatformTypeListIterator`
`ODSemanticInterface` (subclass)	`ODPart::AcquireExtension`
`ODSettingsExtension`	`ODPart::AcquireExtension`

`ODShape`	`ODShape::Copy`
	`ODShape::NewShape`
	`ODFrame::CreateShape`
	`ODFacet::CreateShape`

`ODStorageUnit`	`ODDraft::CreateStorageUnit` `ODDraft::AcquireStorageUnit`
`ODStorageUnitCursor`	`ODStorageUnit::CreateCursor`

`ODStorageUnitRefIterator`	`ODStorageUnit::`
	`CreateStorageUnitRefIterator`
	
	`ODStorageUnitView::`
	`CreateStorageUnitRefIterator`

`ODStorageUnitView`	`ODStorageUnit::CreateView`

`ODTransform`	`ODTransform::Copy`
	`ODTransform::NewTransform`
	`ODFrame::CreateTransform`
	`ODFacet::CreateTransform`

`ODTypeList`	`ODStorageSystem::CreateTypeList`

continued

Table 11-1   Factory methods for OpenDoc classes (continued)

Object to be created	Class and factory method
`ODTypeListIterator`	`ODTypeList::CreateTypeListIterator`
`ODValueIterator`	`ODValueNameSpace::CreateIterator`
`ODWindow`	`ODWindowState::RegisterWindow`
	`ODWindowState::RegisterWindowForFrame`
`ODWindowIterator`	`ODWindowState::CreateWindowIterator`

Reference-Counted Objects

The use of reference-counted objects is part of the OpenDoc memory-management scheme. **Reference-counted objects** maintain a count of the current number of references to them; that is, they are shared objects that are aware of how many other objects are making use of them at any one time.

During an OpenDoc session, many objects are created. Because the relationship among objects can be very complex, it may be difficult for a part or for OpenDoc to determine when it is safe to delete an object from memory. Reference counting is a way to determine when runtime objects can be deleted and valuable memory space reclaimed.

A reference count is 0 or a positive integer. A value greater than 0 means that at least one reference to the object currently exists, and thus the object must not be removed from memory. All descendants of `ODRefCntObject` (including frames, links, link sources, and parts) are reference-counted.

Each reference-counted object is created through a call to its factory method, the method (usually in another class) responsible for creating that object and initializing its reference count. For example, a draft object is created by calling the `CreateDraft` or `AcquireDraft` method of a document object. Likewise, a frame object is created by calling the `CreateFrame` or `AcquireFrame` method of a draft object. See Table 11-1 on page 464 for a list of factory methods.

These are the reference-counted OpenDoc objects:

ODContainer	ODLinkSource	ODSettingsExtension
ODDocument	ODMenuBar	ODShape
ODDraft	ODPart	ODStorageUnit
ODExtension	ODPersistentObject	ODTransform
ODFrame	ODRefCntObject	ODWindow
ODLink	ODSemanticInterface	

When it is first created by its factory object, a reference-counted object has a reference count of 1. Thus, the frame object returned by a draft's CreateFrame method always has a reference count of 1, because that method always creates a new object. The frame object returned by a draft's AcquireFrame method, however, may have a reference count greater than 1, because that method may return a new reference to a pre-existing frame.

Calling the Release method of a reference-counted object decrements its reference count; calling its Acquire method increments its reference count. Calling the Release method of a reference-counted object when its reference count is 1 causes its new reference count to be set to 0 and may result in the object being deleted from memory. It is an error to attempt to access an object whose reference count is 0.

Each reference-counted object stores its own reference count and returns it to callers of its GetRefCount method. When the object's reference count goes to 0, the object is responsible for notifying its factory object so that the factory object can delete it from memory. The factory object can choose to delete it immediately, or, for efficiency, keep it in memory until OpenDoc calls its Purge method when memory is needed.

Whenever your part editor writes a reference to a reference-counted object into a data structure, it should increment that object's reference count by calling its Acquire method. When your part editor is finished working with that object, it should call the object's Release method.

Because shape and transform objects are reference-counted and are widely used, it is important to remember always to release them instead of deleting them. Any method call with which you acquire a shape or transform must be balanced by a subsequent call to `Release`.

```
clipShape = facet->AcquireClipShape(ev, biasCanvas);
...
clipShape->Release(ev);
clipShape = kODNULL;
```

Likewise, any method call that assigns a reference-counted object to another object increases its reference count. Therefore, you can immediately release your own reference to it.

```
newShape = facet->CreateShape(ev);
...
facet->ChangeGeometry(ev, newShape, transform, biasCanvas);
newShape->Release(ev);
newShape = kODNULL;
```

Acquire versus Get

Methods whose names begin with *Acquire* increment the reference counts of the objects they return; methods whose names begin with *Get* do not. Therefore, every call to `ODDraft::AcquireFrame`, for example, must be balanced with a call to `ODFrame::Release`. A call to `Facet::GetCanvas`, on the other hand, requires no corresponding call to decrement reference count. ◆

As a reference-counted object, your part is responsible for implementing an override of the `Release` method and for calling the `ReleasePart` method of its draft object when your part's reference count goes to 0. Your part does not need to release all of its references or do any other shutting down or deallocation at that point. The `ReleasePart` method calls your part's destructor, which takes care of deallocation. However, your part could get rid of unneeded structures or services before calling `ReleasePart`. For example, a communications part editor may choose to close its driver as soon as its reference count reaches 0.

If your part has a reference count of 0, but calling your draft's `ReleasePart` method has not resulted in your part's destruction (perhaps because no purge has been performed), the draft object can retrieve and reuse your part. In that case, any structures or services you deallocated when the reference count went to 0 must be reallocated. Your `IncrementRefCount` method can perform those tasks for the case in which the reference count goes from 0 to 1.

Note that your part is destroyed after its `ReleaseAll` method is called, regardless of its current reference count, when its draft closes. See "Closing Your Part" on page 308 for more information.

Testing objects for equality

If you need to compare two existing OpenDoc objects for equality, don't simply compare their pointers. Instead, call the `IsEqualTo` method (defined in `ODObject`) of either object. `IsEqualTo` always gives the correct result, even in a distributed environment when comparing pointers may fail. However, be sure never to call the `IsEqualTo` method of a null object reference. ◆

Handling Byte Arrays and Other Parameters

Many parameters to OpenDoc methods consist of references to objects or to other data that needs special attention in terms of allocating and releasing the storage associated with it. This section discusses parameter handling for byte arrays, strings, and objects.

To make the OpenDoc programming interface CORBA-compliant and capable of distributed execution, OpenDoc requires you to use a certain format when passing method parameters that point to buffers containing variable-length data.

OpenDoc defines the `ODByteArray` structure as a sequence of octets (unsigned 8-bit values). It consists of a buffer size field, a data length field, and a pointer to the buffer associated with the structure. All variable-length data is passed to or from OpenDoc with byte arrays. For example, the storage-unit methods `GetValue` and `SetValue` use byte arrays for the data being passed.

The caller of a method that takes variable-length data must place the data in a buffer pointed to by a byte array; the receiver of the data then retrieves the data from the buffer and uses it. Both sender and receiver must understand the underlying type of the data. For example, if your part calls `SetValue`, your part passes a structure of type `ODByteArray`, but the method understands the implied type of the contents of the buffer (a storage-unit value).

If you are the caller of a method that uses a byte array as a parameter, follow these rules for allocating and releasing the array:

■ You as caller are responsible for allocating and releasing the storage of the byte array structure itself. You can allocate the byte array either on the stack or in the heap.

■ If the byte array is an `in` parameter, you as caller allocate the storage for the data buffer to which the byte array points, and you also release that storage after the method returns and you no longer need the data. (If the method needs to retain the data in the data buffer, it makes a copy.)

■ If the byte array is an `out` parameter or a function result, the method allocates the storage for the data buffer to which the byte array points; you as caller release that storage when you no longer need it.

All data passed by means of a byte array must be self-contained; for example, it can't contain pointers to data outside of itself.

If you are the caller of a method that uses a parameter that is a string (type `ODISOString` or one of its equivalents, such as `ODValueType`) or an OpenDoc object, similar rules apply:

■ If the string or object is an `in` parameter, you are responsible for both allocating and releasing its storage.

■ If the string or object is an `out` parameter or a function result, the method allocates the storage, and you must release the string or object when you no longer need it.

Purging

The OpenDoc document shell manages OpenDoc memory usage within the process in which it executes. When the document shell needs more memory, it can ask other objects in its process to voluntarily surrender noncritical memory that they have been using.

Every subclass of `ODObject`, including your part, must implement an override of the `Purge` method. When the document shell calls your part's `Purge` method, your part should free any caches or other noncritical buffers or objects, freeing up to the amount of memory requested in the `Purge` call. If necessary, your part can first write any data it desires to persistent storage.

Purging is the appropriate way to get rid of frames that you have created through lazy internalization (next).

Lazy Internalization

Your part does not necessarily have to maintain frame objects in memory at all times for all of its embedded frames and display frames. You may have many display frames or embedded frames, only a few of which are visible at any one time. In such a case, you might want to reduce memory use by creating frame objects only for those frames that are currently visible. Then, as the user scrolls through your part, resizes your display frame, or brings other display frames of your part into view, you can create frame objects for frames that appear and release frame objects of frames that disappear. This process, which could be called **lazy internalization,** works like this:

- At initialization, your part can create frame objects for just the visible frames of its embedded parts, as described in the section "Storing and Retrieving Embedded Frames" on page 302.

- As each additional frame becomes visible through scrolling, resizing, or removal of obscuring content, you create the frame object by calling your draft's `AcquireFrame` method. OpenDoc then calls the `DisplayFrameConnected` method of the part (either your part or the embedded part) displayed in the frame.

- As each previously visible embedded frame becomes invisible, you can simply leave it in memory but marked as purgeable, or you can call the frame's `Release` method.

- Maintain connections to your released frames by saving their storage-unit IDs. If a previously released frame becomes visible again, you can create it once again by calling `AcquireFrame`. OpenDoc in turn calls the part's `DisplayFrameConnected` method once again, if necessary.

Accessing Objects Through Iterators

The OpenDoc class library implements over ten iterator classes, which you can use to access collections of OpenDoc objects such as facets, windows, and drag items. In addition, OpenDoc defines the interface for an iterator that you must subclass in all cases (`ODEmbeddedFramesIterator`), and one that you must subclass only if you create a focus module for a nonexclusive focus (`ODFocusOwnerIterator`).

All OpenDoc iterator classes share certain characteristics, and you can use them all in a similar fashion. The iterators that you implement should also function in the same manner. For example, all iterators have at least these three methods:

First   Begins the iteration: sets your position to the first element in the collection and returns the element at that position.

Next   Advances your position in the collection by 1 and returns the element at your new position.

IsNotComplete   Returns kODTrue if the element at your current position is valid; returns kODFalse if your current position is beyond the last element in the collection.

Some iterators also have these methods:

Last   Returns the final element in the collection.

Previous   Returns the element in the collection prior to the one at your current position.

For most iterators, the First and Next methods return their collection items as function results; for some, the collection items are returned in output parameters.

Some iterators allow you to traverse the collection in either direction (beginning to end or end to beginning). For those iterators, the direction is an invariant; once the iteration has begun, you can't change direction. If you are traversing the collection from the beginning to the end, you call First followed by a series of calls to Next; in this case you cannot call Previous. If you are traversing the collection from the end to the beginning, you call Last followed by a series of calls to Previous; in this case you cannot call Next.

You can set up an iteration in several ways. A common method is to set up a for loop that uses the IsNotComplete method to test for completion.

```
ODFrameFacetIterator* iter = frame->CreateFacetIterator(ev);
for (ODFacet* facet = iter->First(ev); iter->IsNotComplete(ev);
        facet = iter->Next(ev))
{
    //...perform the task of the iteration
}
```

Alternatively, you can use a `while` statement to test for completion.

```
ODFrameFacetIterator* iter = frame->CreateFacetIterator(ev);
ODFacet* facet = iter->First()
while (iter->IsNotComplete())
{
    //...perform the task of the iteration
    facet = iter->Next(ev);
}
```

A third possibility—if the `Next` method returns its item as a function result and if it consistently returns a null value for a nonexistent element—is to use that method itself to test for completion.

```
ODFrameFacetIterator* iter = frame->CreateFacetIterator(ev);
while ((facet = iter->Next(ev)) != kODNULL)
{
    //...perform the task of the iteration
}
```

OpenDoc iterators follow these conventions:

■ You can call `Next` without first calling `First`. If you do, your first call to `Next` is the same as a call to `First`.

■ You must call either `First` or `Next` before calling `IsNotComplete`. If you do not, `IsNotComplete` generates the exception `kODErrIteratorNotInitialized`.

■ For an empty collection, `First` and `Next` return `kODNULL` (if that type of iteration returns its information in the function result), and `IsNotComplete` returns `kODFalse`.

■ If `IsNotComplete` returns `kODTrue`, the last item obtained is valid.

■ If `IsNotComplete` returns `kODFalse` (at the end of the iteration), a subsequent call to `Next` returns `kODNULL` (if that type of iteration can return null values).

■ If the collection is modified while an iteration is in progress, calling any of these iterator methods generates the exception `kODErrIteratorOutOfSync`.

11

OpenDoc Runtime Features

Accessing Objects Through Iterators   473

Binding

Binding is the runtime process of assigning executable code to instance data. For parts, binding is the assignment of the correct part editor to a given part. For example, when the stored data of a part is to be brought into memory, OpenDoc binds a specific part editor to that data, loads the editor (if it has not already been loaded), and transfers control to the editor so that it can read in the data of the part. The resulting combination of part editor bound to part data constitutes the part object in memory, including both state and behavior.

On opening a document, OpenDoc binds editors to all parts that need to be displayed. During execution, OpenDoc binds part editors to part data when a part is read in or when its editor is changed. OpenDoc may unload part editors at various times, especially if memory is low. Also, when a part needs more memory, the document shell can unload the part editors used by inactive parts. Thus, a given part editor may need to be bound and loaded more than once in a session.

The interface to the binding process is not entirely public. OpenDoc accomplishes it with the help of the **binding object** (class ODBinding). The binding object considers part-kind and part-category information provided by part editors, part-kind information stored with parts, and preferences specified by users when choosing an editor for each part.

Information Used for Binding

This section describes the information your part editor must provide to make binding work correctly. On the Mac OS platform, you provide most of that information in a **name-mapping resource** (type 'nmap').

Part Kinds Supported by an Editor

For binding of parts to editors, these two kinds of information need to be available to OpenDoc:

- Your part editor must include certain structures containing information about the data formats it handles. OpenDoc uses those structures to construct name space objects that it uses to bind part editors to parts.

- Your stored parts must include information about the data formats in them.

OpenDoc decides which editor to bind to a given part based on the part kind and part category of the data. **Part kind** is a typing scheme, analogous to file type, that can include specifications of data type, creator application, and even version. Part kinds are ISO strings such as "text", "SurfDraw:Bitmap", or "AcmeDB:Kind:FlatDatabase". Part-editor developers define the part kinds that their editors use; each kind is a specific data format that the editor understands.

Tokenized strings

At runtime, OpenDoc and by part editors often manipulate ISO strings as **tokens** (short, regularized representations of the strings). Before passing ISO strings to OpenDoc, you therefore may need to convert them to tokens with the `Tokenize` method of the session object. ◆

The fact that part editors can store multiple representations of their parts also means that they are not necessarily confined to reading and editing a single part kind. Your SurfWriter 3.01 Pro editor, for example, may be capable of reading and writing data of SurfWriter 1.0 ("SurfWriter:Kind:StyledText") and plain text ("text") format, as well as its own preferred format ("SurfWriter:Kind:IntlText").

At a minimum, your part editor needs to store only your own preferred part kind. A better alternative is to store your preferred kind plus one common standard public format. Beyond that, you should probably store additional formats only on user instruction, to keep your stored parts from being too large.

The method for defining the part kinds your editor supports differs among platforms. On the Mac OS, your part editor's name-mapping resource needs to include a table that lists, in fidelity order, the part kinds your editor can read and write. That information is converted at runtime into a name space object that the document shell can access.

Part Kinds Stored in a Part

Your part editor stores each of its parts in a format, or part kind, that your editor recognizes. But your part is not limited to one part kind per part; it can store multiple representations of its data in a single part. You store different representations in the `kODPropContents` property of your part's storage unit, as values with different part kinds, arranged in order of fidelity.

Fidelity refers to the faithfulness of a given representation to a part editor's native, or preferred, part kind. For example, assume that you store a part created with your SurfWriter 3.01 Pro part editor as three separate representations with the following part kinds: "SurfWriter:IntlText", "SurfWriter:StyledText", and "text". The highest-fidelity representation is "SurfWriter:IntlText", which represents the native format of your part editor; the "SurfWriter:StyledText" representation is an older, simpler format that lacks some of the latest SurfWriter features; and the "text" representation is plain, unformatted ASCII text.

Storing part representations in order of fidelity is crucial to ensuring that the best available editor is bound to a part.

Standard part kinds

To increase the chances that your parts will be readable in all situations, you should if possible store at least one widely readable part kind, in addition to your editor's preferred part kind, every time you write your part to storage. On the Mac OS, certain common formats (such as `'TEXT'` and `'PICT'`), expressed as file-type signatures rather than ISO strings, are defined as standard part kinds. (See "Mac OS Binding Information" on page 479 for information on how to support those standard kinds.) Other standards, for Mac OS as well as for other platforms, may be defined by CI Labs. ◆

Part Categories Supported by an Editor

Part category is a typing scheme similar to part kind, except that it defines only a broad classification of the data manipulated by a part editor. Like part kinds, part categories are ISO strings; they have designations such as "plain text", "3D graphics", "time", or "sound". (The full ISO string for the styled-text category, for example, is the OpenDoc ISO-string prefix followed by "OpenDoc:Category:Text:Styled".)

Your part editor must specify the part categories corresponding to the part kinds it supports. On the Mac OS platform, your editor's name-mapping resource needs to include a table that lists, for each part kind that your editor can read and write, the part category or categories that that part kind belongs to. (A part kind can correspond to more than one part category; for instance, an unstyled text part could belong to both "plain text" and "styled text" part categories.)

Table 11-2 lists the part categories that OpenDoc currently recognizes and briefly explains the general kind of stored data each represents.

Table 11-2   Part categories

Part category	Explanation
kODCategoryPlainText	Plain ASCII text
kODCategoryStyledText	Styled text
kODCategoryDrawing	Object-based graphics
kODCategory3DGraphic	3D object-based graphics
kODCategoryPainting	Pixel-based graphics
kODCategoryMovie	Movies or animations
kODCategorySampledSound	Simple sampled sounds
kODCategoryStructuredSound	Sampled sounds with additional information
kODCategoryChart	Chart data
kODCategoryFormula	Formula or equation data
kODCategorySpreadsheet	Spreadsheet data
kODCategoryTable	Tabular data
kODCategoryDatabase	Database information
kODCategoryQuery	Stored database queries
kODCategoryConnection	Network-connection information
kODCategoryScript	User scripts
kODCategoryOutline	Outlines created by an outliner program
kODCategoryPageLayout	Page layouts
kODCategoryPresentation	Slide shows or other presentations
kODCategoryCalendar	Calendar data
kODCategoryForm	Forms created by a forms generator
kODCategoryExecutable	Stored executable code
kODCategoryCompressed	Compressed data

continued

Table 11-2   Part categories (continued)

Part category	Explanation
kODCategoryControlPanel	Data stored by a control panel
kODCategoryControl	Data stored by a control, such as a button
kODCategoryPersonalInfo	Data stored by a personal information manager
kODCategorySpace	Stored server, disk, or subdirectory (folder) data
kODCategoryProject	Project-management data
kODCategorySignature	Digital signatures
kODCategoryKey	Passwords or keys
kODCategoryUtility	Data stored by a utility function
kODCategoryMailingLabel	Mailing labels
kODCategoryLocator	Locators or addresses, such as URLs
kODCategoryPrinter	Stored printer data
kODCategoryTime	Stored clock data

Part category is not included in the information stored with a part; only part editors store information about the categories of the part kinds they manipulate. OpenDoc uses that information at runtime to help the user define a default editor for each category.

User Strings

OpenDoc manipulates editor names, part kinds, and part categories as tokenized ISO strings. However, as noted in the following sections, there are several points at which the user can intervene in the binding process, and ISO strings are not appropriate for user display. OpenDoc requires that user-readable text be in the form of international strings that can be in any script or language.

Therefore, your part editor needs to provide, in its name-mapping resource, international strings for its editor name, part kinds, and part categories so that OpenDoc can display them to the user at the appropriate times.

The user-readable name of your part editor (in English) might typically be close to, but not exactly the same as, its ISO string name and the kinds of parts it creates. For example, "SurfWriter 3.0" might be the user-readable name of a part editor whose editor ID (ISO string name) is "SurfCorp:SurfWriter3.0" and whose native part kind is "SurfCorp:SurfWriter:IntlText".

Mac OS Binding Information

On the Mac OS platform, your name-mapping resource must provide at least one more table. The table defines a Mac OS file type for each OpenDoc kind that your editor can edit. The Mac OS Operating System uses that information to provide the proper icon for each of your parts.

An additional Mac OS–specific table is necessary in some cases. If your part editor can edit any of the standard Mac OS file types (such as `TEXT` and `PICT`), you must provide a table that lists all the standard file types and standard clipboard data types that you support. The table must also give a user-visible string and category designation for each type. This table is completely separate from the table of OpenDoc kinds supported by your editor, as described in "Part Kinds Supported by an Editor" on page 474; you should not put any standard Mac OS kinds into that table.

Note
If your part editor supports *only* standard Mac OS file types, then it should include this table but *not* include the tables that specify other part kinds and categories and the user strings for them. ◆

Apple Guide Support

On the Mac OS platform, if your part editor is to provide Apple Guide help to the user, you have two responsibilities.

■ You must write the appropriate guide files and install them in the Editors folder on the user's system. For installation instructions, see Appendix C, "Installing OpenDoc Software and Parts." For information on writing guide files, see *Apple Guide Complete*.

■ You must include a name-mapping resource that specifies the name (or names) of the guide files to be used by your editor.

Binding Information for Part Viewers

Part viewers must provide one additional table, to notify OpenDoc that they are viewers and not full editors. This table consists of an editor ID and a designation of the type of viewer it represents. Version 1.0 of OpenDoc recognizes only one viewer type, kODSimpleViewer.

The Binding Process

This section describes when binding occurs and how OpenDoc decides which editor to bind to a part, depending on which editors are available on the user's machine.

When Binding Occurs

Part binding occurs whenever your part is instantiated, typically when OpenDoc or another part calls the CreatePart or AcquirePart method of your draft. For example, binding can occur in the following situations:

- When a draft opens, OpenDoc binds a part editor to each visible part.

- As the user adds parts to an open document, OpenDoc binds part editors to the new parts.

- Drawing a part requires part binding if OpenDoc has not already bound an editor to the part.

- For a part to accept semantic events, OpenDoc must first bind its editor to it.

- When translation occurs, OpenDoc binds a part editor to the translated part.

Binding can thus occur in many different situations, not just when a part's document first opens. Your part editor needs to be able to function with any part to which it has just been bound, including a part that it has never edited before.

Binding to Preferred Editor

The most obvious binding for a part is to the editor that created it. A stored part may have, in its storage unit, a property of type kODPropPreferredEditor that specifies the editor that last edited the part. That editor is considered the **preferred editor** of the part. It may be the editor that originally created the part, or it may be an editor that was later bound to it. Every time a new editor is bound to a part, that editor becomes the part's preferred editor and remains so until a different editor is bound to the part.

When OpenDoc searches for an editor to bind to a part, it looks first for the preferred editor. If the preferred editor is present, OpenDoc binds it to the part.

If the preferred editor is not present on the user's system, or if there is no property of type kODPropPreferredEditor in the part, OpenDoc examines in order each of the part kinds in the stored part, seeking to match that part kind with a part kind supported by an editor on the user's system. OpenDoc first examines the part's preferred kind (if the kODPropPreferredKind property exists) and then searches the remaining part kinds from highest fidelity to lowest (that is, from first to last in the contents property).

For each part kind under consideration, OpenDoc attempts to find an editor in this priority order:

- default editor for kind

- default editor for category

- any available editor for that kind

The following sections describe each of these steps.

Binding to Default Editor for Kind

After the preferred editor, the highest-priority binding for a part is to the **default editor for kind**, the user's chosen default editor for all parts of the part kind under consideration. For every part editor installed on a user's system, OpenDoc maintains a table that specifies the part kinds for which that editor is the default editor.

By setting the default, the user chooses, for example, a single favorite text editor for processing any text part of a given part kind (when the part's preferred editor is not available). Figure 11-1 shows the Editor Setup dialog box, which displays all the default editors chosen by the user.

OpenDoc Runtime Features

11

Figure 11-1   Editor Setup dialog box

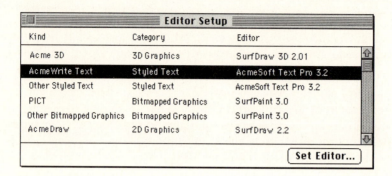

Through the Set Editor button in the Editor Setup dialog box, the user can change the defaults. Figure 11-2 shows a Set Editor dialog box in which the user has specified the SurfWriter 3.01 Pro editor as the default editor for all text whose part kind (expressed as a user-visible string) is "AcmeWrite Text". Only editors that can handle the part kind being considered appear in the dialog box.

Figure 11-2   The Set Editor dialog box

If, for the part kind under consideration, OpenDoc finds its default editor for kind, OpenDoc binds that editor to the part.

Binding to Default Editor for Category

If, for the part kind under consideration, there is no specified default editor for kind, OpenDoc looks for the **default editor for category** for the part category (or categories) of that part kind. As with the default editor for kind, OpenDoc maintains a list of the user's choice for default editor for each part category. By setting this default, the user chooses, for example, a single favorite graphics editor for editing any kind of bitmap (when its preferred editor and the default editor for its kind are not defined or not available).

In the Editor Setup dialog box shown in Figure 11-1 on page 482, note the "Other Styled Text" item, which shows that the user has selected "AcmeSoft Text Pro 3.2" as the default editor for the category of styled text. (In the Set Editor dialog box, only editors that support a given category appear when that category is displayed.) In this case, if the user opens a styled-text part with a part kind of "SurfWriter 3.0", and only the AcmeSoft Text Pro 3.2 and MacWrite II Text 5.0 text editors are available, OpenDoc will bind the AcmeSoft Text Pro 3.2 to the part (if the editor can read SurfWriter 3.0 text), because it is the default editor for that category.

Binding to Any Available Editor for That Kind

If there is no default editor for the category of the part kind under consideration, OpenDoc then searches for any editor in the system that can read that part kind. If it finds such an editor, OpenDoc binds the editor to the part.

In the previous example, if the AcmeSoft Text Pro 3.2 editor cannot read SurfWriter 3.0 text, OpenDoc then looks for an editor that can. If it turns out that MacWrite II Text 5.0 can read SurfWriter 3.0 text, OpenDoc binds it to the part.

If this attempt fails, OpenDoc repeats the entire process for each of the remaining (lower-fidelity) part kinds in the part. It looks first for the default editor for that kind, then the default editor for its category, and finally any editor that can read it.

Returning to the same example, suppose that the part has also stored a plain text version of its data. On the second round, OpenDoc locates the default editor for the plain text (AcmeSoft Text Pro 3.2) and binds it to the part. In this case, style information is lost, but the user is still able to read and edit the part.

This example illustrates the obvious advantage of having multiple stored representations of your part. The user has a better chance of being able to open and use some form of your part, even when your part editor is not available.

Default editors exist only to allow the user to express a preference for an individual editor when a part's preferred editor is not present.

Binding to Editor of Last Resort

If there is no part editor on the user's machine that can read any of the part kinds stored in a part, the part remains unviewable and uneditable. However, OpenDoc still binds an editor to the part so that the part's document can be opened. This is the **editor of last resort;** it is always available, and it displays an icon view of the part within the area of the part's frame.

On viewing the icon displayed by the editor of last resort, the user can select it and display the Part Info dialog box. In that dialog box, OpenDoc displays the part kind of the highest-fidelity version of the part. The user can use that information to determine what editor to purchase in order to read the part.

If the user attempts to open the part, OpenDoc displays a dialog box in which the user can specify a translation of the part to a part kind that can be read by an available editor, if such a translation is possible. See "Binding With Translation" (next).

The editor of last resort never modifies the part it displays; it does not change the part kinds or their storage order in the part's storage unit.

Binding With Translation

If the user's machine has no part editor that can handle any of the part kinds in a stored part, it can still be possible to find an editor—if any of the part's kinds can be translated into a part kind for which an editor does exist.

OpenDoc uses the translation object to give the user the opportunity to convert a part from a part kind that cannot be used to one that an existing part editor can read and edit.

Part editors initiate translation during data transfer (see "Translation" on page 333). OpenDoc initiates translation in the following situations:

- if the user specifies it after attempting to open a part displayed by the editor of last resort

- if the user specifies it after attempting to open a document whose root part has no available editor

- if the user specifies, in the Document Info dialog box, a part kind for the root part that requires translation (see the section "The Document Shell and the Document Menu" on page 503 for more information)

- if the user specifies, in the Save a Copy dialog box, a part kind for the root part that requires translation (see the section "The Document Shell and the Document Menu" on page 503 for more information)

To set up a translation that will allow the user to open a part or document for which there is no editor, OpenDoc displays the translation dialog box (Figure 11-3). The dialog box contains pop-up menus from which the user selects a part kind to translate to and a specific editor to use with the translated part.

Figure 11-3   The translation dialog box

```
┌─────────────────────────────────────────┐
│  Translate this part to:                 │
│                                          │
│    Kind: [ SurfWriter Text    ▼ ]        │
│  Editor: [ SurfWriter 1.3     ▼ ]        │
│                                          │
│          [ Cancel ]    [  OK  ]          │
└─────────────────────────────────────────┘
```

OpenDoc sets up the pop-up menu of part kinds in the translation dialog box (and in the Document Info and Save a Copy dialog boxes) as described in the section "Translation" on page 333. Once the user picks a translated part kind, OpenDoc calls the translation object to perform the translation. Then OpenDoc binds the translated data to its new part editor and opens the part or document.

Consequences of Changing Part Editor or Part Kind

As a result of the binding process, your part editor can be bound to a part that it hasn't previously edited. (Binding to your editor is especially likely if the user has specified your editor as the preferred editor of that part's kind or category.) This binding may occur in these situations:

- The part's document opens on a machine that does not have the part's previous editor, and your part editor can read its part kind or else the user translates the part to a kind that your editor can read.

- The user, using the Paste As command, pastes a part into a document and either specifies your part editor as the preferred editor or specifies that the part be translated to a part kind readable by your part editor.

- The user, in a part's Part Info dialog box or a document's Document Info dialog box, specifies your part editor as the preferred editor or changes the part's kind (perhaps through translation) to a part kind readable by your part editor.

- The user makes a copy of a document with the Document menu's Save a Copy command and specifies a part kind for the root part (perhaps requiring translation) that is readable by your part editor.

In each of these situations, once the binding occurs, the part's storage unit contains at least one part kind that your editor can read. However, the stored data in the part may not necessarily have exactly the same part kinds, in exactly the same order, that your editor would normally write into a part's storage unit. In this case, OpenDoc calls your part's `ChangeKind` method, passing it the new part kind.

OpenDoc can also call your part's `ChangeKind` method at times other than when your part editor is bound to a part. If your part editor supports more than one part kind and the user has specified (for example, in the Part Info dialog box or Document Info dialog box) that your current part's kind be changed to another kind that your part editor can read, OpenDoc calls your part's `ChangeKind` method and passes it the new part kind. This is the interface to `ChangeKind`:

```
void ChangeKind(in ODType kind);
```

Your part editor needs to start manipulating the part's data in the new format. Your `ChangeKind` method must store the data in an order that reflects your own fidelities. It should also make sure that the new part kind is specified in the part's `kODPropPreferredKind` property.

For example, suppose that your SurfWriter 1.1 part editor supports only "SurfWriter:StyledText" and "text" formats. Suppose further that your editor is bound to a part whose highest-fidelity part kind is "SurfWriter:IntlText" (perhaps originally created with the SurfWriter 3.0 editor) but that also contains a "SurfWriter:StyledText" representation. In this case, you need to make sure that "SurfWriter:StyledText" is specified as the preferred kind when you subsequently write the part. You could also include a "text" representation, which must be stored *after* the preferred kind. (If your part editor supports it, you can optionally write a higher-fidelity version than the preferred kind; if you do, you must place it *before* the preferred kind in your storage unit.)

Note
These modifications do not occur if the editor of last resort is bound to a part. It never modifies the part it "displays"; it does not change the part kinds of the values, or their fidelity ordering, in the part's storage unit. ◆

Runtime Object Relationships

The runtime state of an OpenDoc document involves relationships among a variety of objects instantiated from the OpenDoc classes (see Figure 2-1 on page 77 and Figure 2-2 on page 78). Taken together, the diagrams in this section show the principal runtime relationships among the major OpenDoc objects for a single document. The details of the interactions among the objects are explained elsewhere in this book.

The objects are instantiated from groups of classes in individual shared libraries called **subsystems.** OpenDoc is distributed as a set of subsystems. Platform developers, in providing OpenDoc on a given platform, can implement or replace individual subsystems. Part-editor developers generally need not be concerned with the characteristics of specific subsystems. For information purposes, however, subsystem boundaries are shown on the runtime object diagrams presented in this section.

The Session Object

When an OpenDoc document is open, the session object occupies a central place in the relationships among the objects that constitute, support, and manipulate the document. Figure 11-4 shows the uppermost levels of that relationship.

Figure 11-4   Runtime relationships of the session object

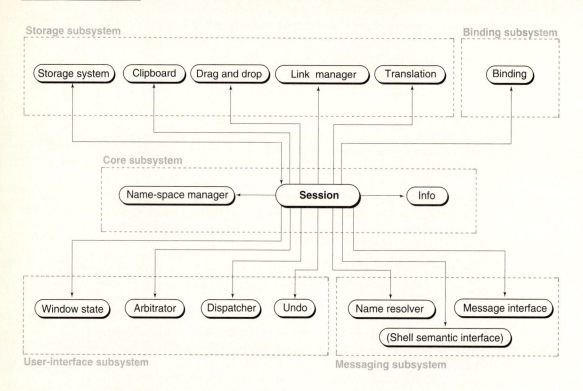

All figures in this book that illustrate runtime object relationships use the following conventions:

- Individual objects are represented as labeled oval boxes.

- Arrows between the boxes show object references (equivalent to pointers in C++), as defined primarily by the availability of accessor functions for them in the public interface to OpenDoc. The references as shown here may not strictly mirror the actual (private) references that exist between OpenDoc objects.

  (Various shades or patterns used on the arrows are for visual distinction only; they do not imply different kinds of object references.)

- A mutual reference between a pair of objects is represented by an arrow with a head on each end.

- A one-to-many relationship, in which one object can simultaneously reference more than one other object of a given kind, is represented by an arrow with a double head on one end.

- In diagrams that show an embedding hierarchy (such as Figure 11-6 on page 493), objects lower in the diagram are embedded more deeply than the objects above them. Objects at the same height are at the same level of embedding.

As Figure 11-4 shows, the session object maintains many (mostly one-way) relationships with other objects, allowing your part to gain access to many objects through the session object. The objects are grouped into categories according to the kinds of tasks they perform together; the following subsections discuss and expand upon the object relationships in terms of those categories. Note also that Figure 11-4 is incomplete; Figure 11-5 on page 492 and Figure 11-9 on page 497 continue the object-reference hierarchy.

Session-Level Objects

As Figure 11-4 shows, the session object instantiates and maintains direct references to the following objects, accessible globally to all parts in a document.

- OpenDoc uses the binding object to pick the proper part editor for each part in a document, both when the document is opened and whenever a new part is added to it. Binding is further discussed in the section "Binding" on page 474.

- Both OpenDoc and part editors use the translation object, a wrapper for available platform-specific data translation services. If no editor is available that can manipulate the data of a part, or if the user wants the data in a different format, OpenDoc or a part editor can translate the data of a part into a part kind for which a specific translator exists. See "Translation" on page 333 and "Binding With Translation" on page 484 for more information.

- The name-space manager keeps track of all name space objects, which themselves contain tables of information needed for registration purposes. See "Name Spaces" on page 462 for more information.

- The window state object is a list of all the open windows in which OpenDoc parts are displayed. The window state object references each open window; see Figure 11-5 on page 492. (The window state object also appears in Figure 11-8 on page 496, in relation to other objects of the user-interface subsystem.)

- The storage system object controls persistent storage for the session. The storage system references one or more container suites; see Figure 11-9 on page 497.

- The clipboard object is a session-wide object that represents the clipboard. It references a storage unit that represents the data held on the clipboard.

- The drag-and-drop object is also a single session-wide object. It references a storage unit that represents the data to be transferred by a drag operation.

- The dispatcher accepts user events from the underlying operating system through the document shell and dispatches them to part editors. It references dispatch modules, as shown in Figure 11-8 on page 496.

- The arbitrator negotiates temporary ownership of a focus, the designation of a shared resource such as the menu bar, keystroke stream, and so on. It references focus modules, as shown in Figure 11-8 on page 496.

- The undo object stores command histories for all parts in the document. It allows parts to reverse or restore the effects of multiple previous user commands. There is a single, session-wide undo object used by all parts in a document.

- The name resolver resolves object specifiers into particular objects on which semantic events can operate.

- The message interface transfers semantic events into and out of parts. If a part editor needs to send (rather than receive) semantic events, it uses the message interface. Other objects related to semantic events are shown in Figure 11-11 on page 499.

- The Info object represents the Part Info dialog box, an extensible dialog box used by part editors. Other objects related to extensions are shown in Figure 11-11 on page 499.

- The link manager keeps track of cross-document links, facilitating the transfer of information between the source and destination parts. The link manager is used only by the document shell and container applications; parts need never access to it. The link manager is built on platform-specific facilities; on the Mac OS platform, for example, it uses the Edition Manager. Other objects related to linking are shown in Figure 11-10 on page 498.

■ The shell semantic interface is an instance of a subclass of
`ODSemanticInterface` that represents the scripting support built into the
document shell. See the note "Document shell semantic interface" on
page 414 for more information.

If your part needs to access any one of these session-level objects, first obtain a
reference to the session object by calling the `GetSession` method of your part's
storage unit. Then call the specific method of the session object (such as
`GetClipboard`) that returns a reference to the needed object. To facilitate
repeated access to the session object, you might store the results of `GetSession`
in a part field with a name such as `fSession`.

Drawing-Related Objects

The objects that make up the OpenDoc drawing capability provide a set of
platform-independent protocols for embedding (placing embedded frames
within the content of a part), layout (manipulating the sizes and locations of
embedded frames), and imaging (making part content and frames visible in a
window). They describe part geometry in a document and provide wrapper
objects for certain platform-specific imaging structures, whether for printing or
for screen display.

The Window State and Windows

Figure 11-5 is a simplification of the runtime object relationships among the
objects involved with a document window. It is a continuation of one branch of
Figure 11-4 on page 488 and shows the upper-level relationships between a
window and the parts it contains.

Figure 11-5   Window-related object relationships

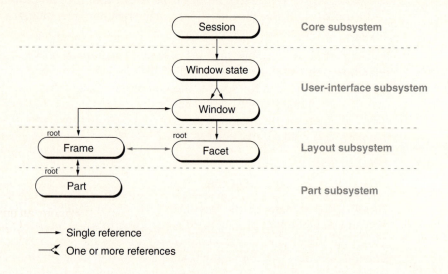

The window state object, referenced by the session object, references one or more window objects, which are wrappers for platform-specific window structures.

Each window object references a single facet object (the *root facet*), the visible representation of the frame object (the *root frame*) that is the display frame of the outermost part (the *root part*) in the document displayed in the window. The root frame in turn references the root part, which controls some of the basic behavior (such as printing) of the document. The root frame and root facet fill the content region of the window.

This relationship of window to root facet, root frame, and root part applies whether the window is a document window or a part window opened from an embedded frame.

The embedding relationships among facets, frames, and parts shown in Figure 11-5 is not complete; it continues down through all parts in the document. The root facet references its embedded facets, and the root part references its embedded frames, as shown in the next section.

Embedding

Figure 11-6 shows the relationships among facet, frame, and part objects at any level of embedding in a document. It is a direct continuation of Figure 11-5 but also applies at any level of embedding. In this and all other object diagrams that show embedding relationships, objects lower in the diagram are embedded more deeply than the objects above them.

The first thing to note from Figure 11-6 is that embedding is represented by two separate but basically parallel structures.

■ On the left side of the figure, each part references one or more display frames (the frames in which the part's contents are displayed) and zero or more embedded frames. Those embedded frames, in turn, reference the parts for which they are the display frames. The document embedding structure is thus a frame-to-part, frame-to-part sequence in which each part only indirectly references its embedded parts. Furthermore, an embedded frame does not directly reference its containing part; instead, it references its **containing frame,** a display frame of its containing part.

Figure 11-6   General embedding object relationships

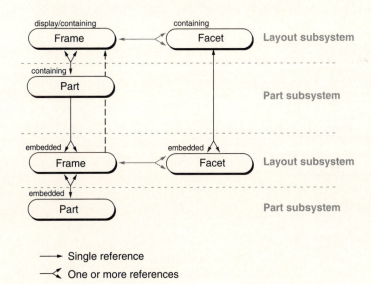

■ On the right side of Figure 11-6, the facets for the frames form their own, simpler hierarchy. Each containing facet directly references its embedded facets, and each embedded facet directly references its containing facet. This more direct imaging hierarchy allows for fast event dispatching by OpenDoc.

Connecting the two hierarchies are the frame-to-facet references. Each frame that is visible references the facet or facets that correspond to it. (A frame can have more than one facet.) Each facet likewise references its frame. Note that facets need not exist unless their frames need to be drawn.

For a specific example of this embedding-object relationship in a given document, see Figure 3-1 on page 104.

Layout and Imaging

The frame and facet objects shown in Figure 11-6 have additional references besides those shown. A part's display frame (or frames) and facet (or facets) use several other OpenDoc objects when laying themselves out and preparing to draw the content of their part. Figure 11-7 shows these additional relationships for a given frame-facet pair at any level of embedding.

Figure 11-7   Layout and imaging object relationships

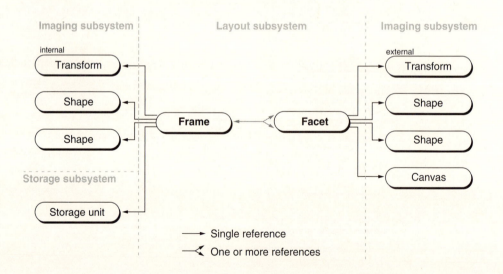

Each display frame object for the part being drawn can include references to these objects:

- a transform object (the internal transform) that defines the geometric offset or transformation of the part within its frame

- a shape object (the frame shape) that defines the basic shape of the frame

- another shape object (the used shape) that defines the portion of the frame shape that is actually drawn into

- a storage unit, for storing the state of the frame into its document (unless it's a nonpersistent frame)

Each of the facet objects for the part being drawn represents an area within a window (or printer image) that corresponds to a visible display frame (or part of a frame) of the part. The facet can include references to these other objects, which hold platform-specific drawing information:

- a canvas object that describes a platform-specific drawing context or structure

- a transform object (the external transform) that defines an external geometric offset or transformation for the facet within the containing part

- a shape object that defines the clip shape for the facet (what portion of the frame shape is drawn)

- another shape object that defines the active shape for the facet (what portion of the frame shape accepts events)

During the layout and imaging process, a part editor is typically asked to draw the contents of a particular facet. The part editor gets the clipping, transformation, and layout information from the facet and its frame, and then makes platform-specific graphics calls to perform the actual drawing.

For a more complete description of the relationships among frames, facets, and parts, see Chapter 3, "Frames and Facets." For a more complete description of the drawing process, see Chapter 4, "Drawing."

User-Interface Objects

Runtime relationships in the user-interface subsystem include some objects not directly referenced by the session object. Figure 11-8 extends a portion of Figure 11-4 on page 488 to show these additional objects:

■ The window state object references (in addition to all window objects) the menu bar object, which represents the base menu bar created by OpenDoc. Your part copies and adds to this menu bar to create its menus.

■ The dispatcher references one or more dispatch modules, which control which frame or part handles each event. The dispatching system is modular; you can extend it to handle new classes of events by adding dispatch module objects.

■ The arbitrator references one or more focus modules, which allocate temporary ownership of shared software or hardware resources. Like the dispatcher, the arbitrator is modular; through addition of focus modules, you can extend it to handle new classes of shared resources.

Figure 11-8   User-interface object relationships

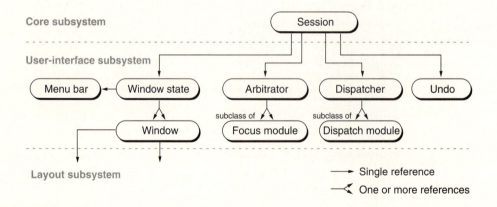

Storage Objects

The storage capabilities of OpenDoc include both document storage and data transfer. As Figure 11-4 on page 488 shows, five objects directly referenced by the session object are involved with storage issues.

Document Storage

OpenDoc manages persistent storage for parts and other objects in documents. Storage in OpenDoc consists of structured storage elements that can contain many data streams. Figure 11-9 shows the main storage-related objects and their runtime relationships. It is a continuation of one branch of Figure 11-4 on page 488.

Figure 11-9   Storage-container-document relationships

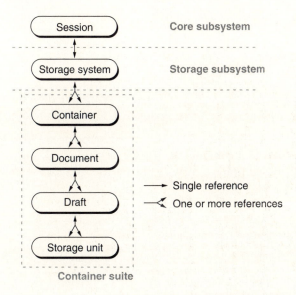

These objects combine to make up a **container suite,** a specific implementation of the OpenDoc storage architecture. Container suites can be implemented in different ways on different platforms and need not be limited to file-based systems. Here is how the objects relate to each other:

■ The storage system object, referenced by the session object, instantiates and maintains a list of container objects. Each container may contain one (or possibly more, depending on the capabilities of the container suite) document objects, each of which represents an OpenDoc document.

■ Each document contains one or more draft objects. Each draft is unique and represents a snapshot of the document's state at a particular moment.

■ Each draft contains a number of storage-unit objects. Each storage unit can contain several different data streams, all of which provide information about the object to which the storage unit applies. The data streams, or values, in a storage unit are identified by property name (the kind of information contained) and value type (the data type of that information). A storage unit can hold more than one property, and a property can hold streams of more than one value type.

Besides being referenced by its draft, each storage unit is also referenced by the object whose data it stores. As Figure 11-10 shows, for example, a part has a reference to its main storage unit.

Storage units and the storage system are described in more detail in Chapter 7, "Storage."

Part Storage

Figure 11-10 shows additional object references maintained by the part object, beyond those shown in Figure 11-6 on page 493, that facilitate data transfer.

■ A part object that contains the source of a link references a link-source object, created by the part that contains the source data. The link source references (a) a storage unit that holds a copy of the source data for the link and (b) one or more link objects.

Figure 11-10   Part-storage relationships

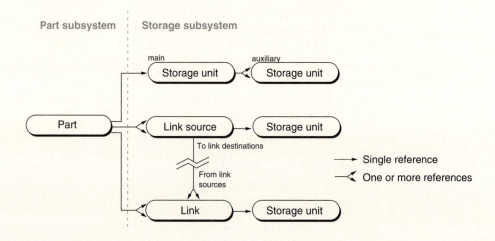

■ A part object that contains the destination of a link references a link object. The link object references a storage unit that holds a copy of the source data for the link. (Links and link sources for an intradocument link share the same storage unit.)

Figure 11-10 also shows how a part must organize the storage of its content. To store its data in its draft, the part references its one main storage unit, which in turn can reference other auxiliary storage units.

Storage for data transfer and other data-transfer issues are described in more detail in Chapter 7, "Storage."

Extension Objects and Semantic Events

OpenDoc provides a flexible method for extending its capabilities through an extension interface. Extensions to objects such as parts provide interfaces through which callers can access additional functionality.

Figure 11-11 shows additional object references that a part object can maintain, over and above those shown in Figure 11-10 on page 498 and Figure 11-6 on page 493.

■ Part editors expose their extended interfaces to other parts through an extension object (a subclass of ODExtension). A part can define an extension for any purpose.

Figure 11-11   Part-extension relationships

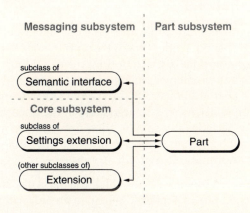

- If a part supports semantic events (scripting), it references its semantic-interface object, a subclass of `ODSemanticInterface`, itself a subclass of `ODExtension` and provided as part of OpenDoc.

- If it provides a custom dialog box, callable from the Part Info dialog box, to allow users to change part settings, the part includes a reference to its subclass of the settings extension object. The settings extension is also a subclass of `ODExtension`.

The Document Shell

The document shell is the OpenDoc object responsible for handling document-wide and draft-wide operations. It is the closest OpenDoc runtime equivalent to a conventional application, although the same document shell handles all kinds of OpenDoc parts and documents. One of its main responsibilities is to accept events from the operating system and pass them on to OpenDoc for dispatching. Another is to handle certain menu items.

This section summarizes the runtime operations and responsibilities of the document shell and its relationship to part editors. It also describes how the document shell handles commands from the Document menu.

The discussion in this section is largely for informational purposes; your part editor never has to call the document shell.

Document Shell Operations

In OpenDoc, the document—not any application—is the owner of the process in which the document is opened. Under OpenDoc on the Mac OS platform, the document manages standard tasks like handling the event loop, managing files, and interacting with system menus, dialog boxes, and so on. This behavior is provided by a shared library called the OpenDoc **document shell.** Individual part editors implicitly use this shared code in the document. For this reason, part editors can be significantly smaller than conventional applications. However, part editors must cooperate with each other in ways that conventional applications normally do not.

The document shell represents the process in which the parts of a single OpenDoc document execute. It is instantiated when an OpenDoc document is launched, and it is released when the document is closed. The document shell's basic responsibilities are the following:

- It creates and initializes the session object.

- It opens a document (as instructed by the user) from storage.

- It accepts user and semantic events and passes them to the OpenDoc dispatcher.

- It handles most items on the Document menu.

Opening a Document

When the user opens a document, OpenDoc generates a new process that instantiates the document shell. The document shell instantiates the session object, which in turn instantiates the globally available OpenDoc objects, such as the arbitrator and the window-state object. The document shell then opens the document file and reads the document object and its most recent draft object into memory. The document shell then reads in the draft's window-state object to reconstruct the document's windows. For each window, the window state reads in the root frame.

The root frame for the window reads in the root part. The root part creates and registers the window, determines which of its embedded frames are visible, reads them in, and constructs facets for them by calling the root facet's CreateEmbeddedFacet method. The embedded frames read their own parts. Those parts in turn read in their embedded frames and create facets for them, and so on, until all visible frames, parts, and facets have been read from storage.

Once all of the necessary objects are read in, OpenDoc asks each facet to draw itself; the part editor of the facet's frame draws the part content that is visible in the facet.

Saving and Reverting a Document

When the user saves a document, the draft object asks each part in the document to write itself to the document file. Each part writes its data and references to its embedded frames. The document shell then writes the window state to the document file.

When a document is saved, its data is saved in the context of the current draft. (Each draft of a document includes its own window state, allowing the user to open earlier drafts for viewing at any time.)

If the user specifies that a document is to be saved as stationery, the document shell sets a flag in the document file to notify the operating system that a document is stationery instead of an ordinary OpenDoc document.

Reverting a draft means throwing away any changes that have been made since the last save. The document shell releases the existing window state and restores the window state from the previously saved draft. As a result of reverting a draft, the active part and thus the selection and user-interface elements may change.

Closing a Document

The document shell closes a document when its last document window closes. As a result of this closing, some other OpenDoc document window may become active, with its own active frame and selection.

If changes are to be saved when the document closes, the document shell follows the procedures described in the previous section. If the user closes a document without saving changes to the current draft, the document shell releases the window state, leaving the document in its state as of the last save.

Handling User Events

The document shell receives all user events directly and ensures that events intended for individual parts get to the proper part editor.

The document shell passes all events to the dispatcher for dispatching to the appropriate part, without first classifying them. The dispatcher rejects events it can't identify, returning them to the shell to handle.

To dispatch an event, the dispatcher locates the appropriate dispatch module for the event and asks it to dispatch the event. The dispatch module actually distributes the event to the appropriate part or document, in cooperation with the window state and the arbitrator, using the facet hierarchy. (See Chapter 5, "User Events," for more information.)

Part of the document shell's event-handling job is to provide information to part editors about mouse tracking. The document shell also supplies the basic menu bar used by OpenDoc documents and parts.

The document shell can handle standard Mac OS window events, such as a click in the close box, although the dispatcher gives the root part of the window a chance to handle such events first. See "Handling Window Events" on page 232 for more information.

Menu events go first to the document shell; the shell handles most Document menu commands and passes others (see "The Document Menu" on page 248) to the dispatcher for sending to the appropriate part.

Handling Semantic Events

Semantic events sent to a part in a document are received first by the document shell and then passed to the dispatcher to be distributed in the same manner as user events. See "Writing Semantic-Event Handlers" on page 422 for more information.

The document shell has its own semantic interface, through which it handles the required set of Apple events. See the note "Document shell semantic interface" on page 414 for more information.

The Document Shell and the Document Menu

Figure 11-12 shows the standard OpenDoc Document menu on the Mac OS platform. The OpenDoc document shell creates the standard Document menu and handles most items in it. Items not handled by the document shell are handled by the root part or the active part, as described in the section "The Document Menu" on page 248. See also "Document Menu" on page 539 for a discussion of the user-interface considerations related to the Document menu and its items.

Figure 11-12   The Document menu

Here is how the document shell handles each item in the menu:

■ **New.** The document shell creates a new, blank document whose root part is of the same part kind as the root part of the active window (which may be either a document window or a part window). The shell then opens the document in a separate document window. When a document containing your part opens, your part receives several method calls, as described in "Opening a Document" on page 501 and "Initializing and Reading a Part From Storage" on page 294.

■ **Open Selection.** (Handled by the active part; see "The Document Menu" on page 248.)

■ **Open Document.** The document shell displays a file-navigation dialog box, through which the user selects a document to open. The document opens in its own document window.

■ **Insert.** (Handled by the active part; see "The Document Menu" on page 248.)

■ **Close** *Window.* The document shell closes the frontmost window. When a document containing your part closes because its last open document window closes, your part receives several method calls, as described in "Closing Your Part" on page 308.

■ **Delete** *Document.* The document shell saves the currently open document and then moves it to the Trash.

■ **Save** *Document.* The document shell saves the current document (the document containing the currently active part). If this is the first save of the document, the document shell displays a standard-file dialog box to allow the user to choose a document name and location.

■ **Save a Copy.** The document shell saves a copy of the current draft into a new file. The document shell displays a file-navigation dialog box (Figure 11-13) to allow the user to specify the name and choose a location. The current document remains open.

Figure 11-13   Save a Copy dialog box

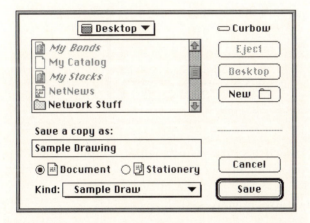

The Save a Copy dialog box also allows the user to specify a part kind for the root part. If your part is saved through this command, your part editor receives a call to its `ExternalizeKinds` method; see "The ExternalizeKinds Method" on page 300 for an explanation.

■ **Revert to Saved.** The document shell reopens the last saved version of the current document, replacing the presently open version of it.

■ **Drafts.** The document shell displays the draft history of the current document in a movable modal dialog box. The user can use the dialog box to create new drafts of the document and select previous drafts for editing. An example of the Drafts dialog box is shown in Figure 1-16 on page 62.

■ **Document Info.** The document shell brings up the Document Info dialog box, shown in Figure 11-14.

Figure 11-14   Document Info dialog box

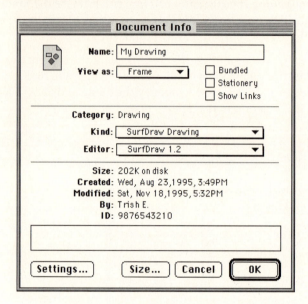

The user can then perform several actions, including changing the view type, part kind, and editor for the root part as well as the heap size for the document.

The dialog box also contains these three checkboxes:

- Bundled. The user checks this box to make the root part bundled. The document shell sets the bundled state of the root frame to true.

- Stationery. The user checks this box to make this document a stationery pad.

- Show Links. When the user checks this box, all part editors should display all link borders in all windows displaying the document. Because the user can check this box at any time, your part editor should check whether it needs to display link borders each time it draws its contents. See "Link Borders" on page 380 for more information.

The user can also access the root part editor's Settings dialog box through the Settings button in the Document Info dialog box. For more information on settings, see "The Settings Extension" on page 444.

- **Page Setup.** (Handled by the root part; see "The Document Menu" on page 248.)

- **Print.** (Handled by the root part; see "The Document Menu" on page 248.)

Human Interface Guidelines

Basic Interface Elements

12

Contents

This chapter leads off the presentation of the OpenDoc human interface guidelines for the Mac OS platform by describing the basic appearances of the following fundamental elements of the OpenDoc human interface:

- icons

- borders

- controls

- pointers

- menus

Further instructions for displaying and handling these items and more complex elements, such as windows, selections, content items, and data transfers, are found in the next two chapters: Chapter 13, "Guidelines for Part Display," and Chapter 14, "Guidelines for Content Manipulation." See also Appendix B, "HI Checklist," for a quick summary of all guidelines.

About the OpenDoc Human Interface

In OpenDoc, users focus primarily on creating *content*. Because OpenDoc is document centered rather than application centered, users interact far more with your parts than with your part editor. They manipulate your parts' content, in the context of other related parts, to achieve a task. Because the software that manipulates the document is mostly hidden from the user, users do not explicitly launch or switch applications as they edit separate parts. The OpenDoc human interface guidelines are designed to facilitate that focus on parts and content. By following them, you will enhance the consistency and smoothness the user experiences while editing multiple parts of a compound document.

Key to the OpenDoc human interface is that it embraces a wide range of concepts in what constitutes a part. OpenDoc does not limit users to creating content commonly found in paper documents. Many OpenDoc documents do not resemble paper documents at all. An OpenDoc document can contain many kinds of media (text, graphics, movies, sounds, animations), and it can also represent very different kinds of functionality (file access, database access, Internet access, telephony, spreadsheet manipulation, and so on).

View Type

In a document window, most parts draw themselves in framed areas displaying their content. However, a part can also display itself as one of three types of icons. As shown in Figure 12-1, there are four view types: large icon, small icon, thumbnail, and frame.

Figure 12-1   OpenDoc view types

Large icon   Small icon   Thumbnail   Frame

Programmatically, every part is displayed in a frame, regardless of its view type. However, for the purposes of this book and the human interface with which the user interacts (via the View As menu in the Part Info dialog box), the term *frame* is used to mean the view type in which all of a part's content is visible and manipulable. A single part can, of course, display its content in more than one frame, and each frame can show a different view type. Also, regardless of the view type of a part, it can be selected or inactive. (Only parts displayed in frame view type can be active.)

All parts must support all view types, at least to the extent appropriate to their content model. A sound part, for example, might have thumbnail and frame view types whose appearances are not very different from its icon appearance, because its content and its ability to play sound or be embedded in another part are unrelated to its visual form.

Preferred View Type for Embedded Parts

By convention, most parts displayed in an open document have a frame view type, and most parts on the desktop or in desktop folders have an icon view type. Parts in icon view that are dragged from the Finder and dropped onto an open document should change to frame view; parts in frame view dragged to the desktop or desktop folders should change to icon view.

Despite these conventions, the containing part controls the view types of its embedded parts. An embedded part should initially appear in whatever view type its containing part sets when it creates the embedded part's frame. The user can subsequently change the view type of the embedded part by using the Part Info dialog box or a View menu, if the containing part provides one.

Icons

This section discusses the icons that represent the software entities that you create: parts, stationery, part editors, and part viewers.

Part Icons

This section describes the icons that you provide for parts. You need to provide part icons in three sizes (large, small, and thumbnail), and three bit depths (1 bit, 4 bit, and 8 bit, for display on monitors of different capabilities).

Large Icon

The large icon size for a part is 32-by-32 pixels. The default part icon is shaped like the outline of a page with a turned-down right corner.

The part icon represents the content of a part. It can represent a document or one part of a document. This icon is the same shape as document icons created by conventional applications, reinforcing the idea that OpenDoc parts are similar to other documents with which the user is familiar. You should provide this icon in three bit depths, 1 bit, 4 bit, and 8 bit, to be displayed on mono-chrome and color monitors. Figure 12-2 shows an example of a generic 32-by-32-pixel icon in grayscale.

Figure 12-2   A 32-by-32-pixel part icon

You can customize your large part icon by adding graphic elements to the document page. These graphics may relate to the kind of content that your part editor creates, or to your part-editor icon (see "Part-Editor Icons" on page 519). You should develop your icons as a family according to the guidelines in the chapter "Icons" of *Macintosh Human Interface Guidelines*. Figure 12-3 shows some examples of part icons customized for different parts. Color Plate 4 at the front of this book shows an example of a custom large part icon in three bit depths.

Figure 12-3   Custom part icons

SurfWriter   SurfPaint   SurfDB

Use the shape of the document icon unless the content your part editor creates is fundamentally different from that of most documents. For example, QuickTime documents look like film, and database icons usually have an image that resembles the traditional storage medium for large amounts of data (stacked disks).

Small Icon

Small icons are 16-by-16 pixels. A small icon should have the same content as a 32-by-32-pixel icon, but you can optimize it for this size. See the chapter "Icons" of *Macintosh Human Interface Guidelines* for instructions on designing and customizing small icons. Don't eliminate significant elements of the icon design, or the smaller version may look significantly different from the larger version. You also need to provide this icon in the three bit depths, 1 bit, 4 bit, and 8 bit. Figure 12-4 shows a generic example of the small part icon in grayscale.

Figure 12-4   A 16-by-16-pixel part icon

You can customize this icon just as you do the large icon. Figure 12-5 shows some examples of custom small icons. Color Plate 4 at the front of this book shows an example of a custom small part icon in three bit depths.

Figure 12-5   Custom 16-by-16-pixel part icons

SurfWriter   SurfPaint   SurfDB

Thumbnail

Larger than the other part icons, the thumbnail icon shows a miniature representation of the first image of a part's content. For example, a thumbnail for a page-oriented document would show a representation of the content of one of the pages. The thumbnail icon is 64-by-64 pixels.

Because of its size, the thumbnail icon can make its part more recognizable than a large or small icon can, because some of the part's content is shown (although scaled down). When parts are viewed as icons in documents, the thumbnail icon provides additional feedback about the part's content. The thumbnail icon can also appear in some dialog boxes. You should provide this icon in three bit depths, 1 bit, 4 bit, and 8 bit, to be displayed on monochrome and color monitors. OpenDoc does not provide a resource for this icon. Your part editor creates the thumbnail at runtime.

The image on the thumbnail icon is called a poster page. The first page of the part is usually set as the default poster page. Your part editor can allow the user to determine which page of the document appears as the poster page. You should regenerate the thumbnail for a document each time the document is saved.

The thumbnail icon takes up a 64-by-64-pixel square, not all of which may be needed to display the poster page. You can set the size or orientation of the poster page as appropriate within the square to show a reasonable approximation of the part's content. You can add additional content outside of the poster page, but within the square, if it represents the actual content of the part more faithfully. Figure 12-6 shows two typical thumbnail shapes within the 64-by-64-pixel square.

Figure 12-6   Dimensions of the thumbnail icon

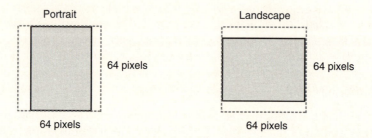

Figure 12-7 shows sample thumbnail icons for different kinds of parts. Each thumbnail icon will appear unique, displaying a representation of its content. Therefore, you shouldn't attempt to provide a default thumbnail icon for your part.

Figure 12-7   Sample thumbnail icons

Text
document

Graphics
document

Movie
document

Stationery Icons

A stationery pad is a template with which the user can create a document or embed a part in a document. Stationery pads may have extensive content, such as a form, or they may have no content at all. Users can create stationery from existing parts or documents by clicking the Stationery checkbox in the Document Info dialog box.

Because users most commonly generate new parts and documents through stationery, you should in general deliver stationery pads with your editor and should consider them the principal tool for creating parts of your part kind. Stationery serves as an inexhaustible source of new parts, and it is difficult to change or destroy it accidentally. You may choose to include several stationery pads as examples. Users can drag a stationery pad into a document to open a new frame onto a part represented by the stationery.

The stationery icon shows the outline of a page, similar to the page in the document icon, but with the lower-right corner turned up and a second page visible in the background. Figure 12-8 shows a generic stationery icon in grayscale in two sizes. Color Plate 1 at the front of this book shows the same pair of default stationery icons in three bit depths.

Figure 12-8   Stationery pad icons

You can customize your stationery icon by adding graphic elements to the stationery document page. This icon should relate visually to the part icon and the part-editor icon. Figure 12-9 shows some examples of custom stationery pad icons in gray scale. Color Plate 4 at the front of this book shows an example of custom stationery icons in three bit depths.

Figure 12-9   Custom stationery icons

SurfWriter   SurfPaint   SurfDB

The name of the stationery pad you create should indicate its purpose. For example, a stationery pad that creates a medical form might be called Medical Form. For stationery pads that have no initial content, use the name of the category or the product. For example, a graphics part stationery pad might be called Drawing. Don't use the word stationery in the name.

When the user employs a stationery pad to create a document or a part, the part initially has the name of the stationery pad plus a unique number (such as "Medical Form 1"). The user can assign the document or part a name by opening the Document Info dialog box (Figure 11-14 on page 506) or the Part Info dialog box (Figure 6-3 on page 256).

Part-Editor Icons

A part editor is software that manipulates and displays a part's content and provides the user interface for that part. The user interface of a part editor usually includes menus, tool palettes, rulers, dialog boxes, and alert boxes.

The part-editor icon is a square shape with grayscale shading to give the illusion of three dimensions. Its resemblance to the OpenDoc logo makes it easily recognizable to users as a part-editor icon. You should provide this icon in the large and small icon sizes and in three bit depths, 1 bit, 4 bit, and 8 bit. Figure 12-10 shows the default part editor icon in grayscale. Color Plate 2 at the front of this book shows the same pair of default part-editor icons in three bit depths.

Figure 12-10   Part-editor icons

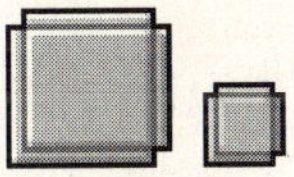

You should customize your part-editor icon with an image that provides continuity between the part-editor icon and its corresponding part icon. Make the image extend to the outline of the icon space. Don't add pixels to the outline of the part-editor icon or outside of its shape. Create the icons to take full advantage of each size, making sure that they maintain the critical visual elements so as to appear as different sizes of the same icon.

Because your part icons are displayed far more often than your part-editor icons, you should probably design your part icons first. Then, adapt their basic graphic elements to your large part-editor icons, and finally simplify them for the small icons. Use the icon resource templates provided with OpenDoc to create icons that conform to these guidelines. Figure 12-11 shows examples of custom part-editor icons in grayscale. Color Plate 4 at the front of this book shows an example of custom part-editor icons in three bit depths.

Figure 12-11   Custom part-editor icons

SurfWriter   SurfPaint   SurfDB

Because they normally deal only with parts, users will rarely see the part-editor icon. It appears in some dialog boxes in small icon size.

Part-editor icons in alert boxes
In most circumstances, when a conventional application displays an alert box it draws one of the standard Note, Caution, or Stop icons in the box, as described in *Macintosh Human Interface Guidelines*. However, because OpenDoc editors are less visible to the user than conventional applications, you should display your part-editor icon in the alert box in place of one of the standard icons if your part editor is reporting an error about itself—for example, if it cannot acquire enough memory or if some expected file is missing. ◆

Part-Viewer Icons

A part viewer is a part editor that allows a user to view or print parts but not to modify or save part data. Part viewers facilitate the effective distribution of documents to people who do not all share the same set of part editors. People receiving a part viewer along with a document can read the viewer's parts in the document but cannot change them. Developing a part viewer and distributing it widely protect your investment in your part editor, because the use of a part viewer allows users to share information created with your editor without illegally giving it away. Wide distribution of a part viewer can also increase the demand for your editor, as more and more users read your parts and want to edit them.

Basic Interface Elements

The part-viewer icon is related to the part-editor icon. It has the same square shape but with a recessed center area with reflective streaks that suggest a monitor view. You should provide this icon in the large and small icon sizes and in three bit depths, 1 bit, 4 bit, and 8 bit. Figure 12-12 shows the default part-viewer icon in grayscale. Color Plate 3 at the front of this book shows the same pair of default part-viewer icons in three bit depths.

Figure 12-12   Part-viewer icons

You should customize your part-viewer icon so that there is continuity of design between the part-viewer icon and its corresponding part-editor icon. To distinguish this icon from the part-editor icon, keep the visual elements inside of the monitor space, rather than extending them to the icon's outline. It's a good idea to start designing your part-viewer icons by using the resource templates provided with OpenDoc. Because of its limited area and its visibility in the interface, you should keep the small icon in mind when designing the large size. Figure 12-13 shows some custom part-viewer icons in grayscale in two sizes. Color Plate 4 at the front of this book shows an example of custom part-viewer icons in three bit depths.

Figure 12-13   Custom part-viewer icons

SurfWriter   SurfPaint   SurfDB

Selected Icon Appearance

The user can select a part represented in any of the icon view types. The selection procedure is the same as for icons in the Mac OS Finder. The user positions the pointer over the icon and presses and then releases the mouse button to select the icon. The containing part then displays the highlighted

Icons

appearance of the icon, which may vary according to the selection model of the containing part. If the containing part displays selections with color highlighting or inverse video, the selected icon should appear darker (as in the Mac OS Finder). If the containing part instead marks selections with borders and resize handles, the selected icon should show this border and four resize handles (in contrast to the usual number of eight, because of the small size of the icon). The icon within the border can have either its normal appearance or a darker (selected) appearance.

When an active window containing a selected icon becomes inactive, the containing part displays a single-pixel black outline around the icon to show a background selection appearance. Figure 12-14 shows selected icons and an icon with a background selection appearance. Color Plate 5 at the front of this book shows these selected appearances in color.

Figure 12-14   Selected appearance of icons

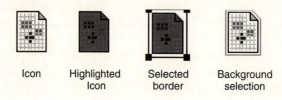

Icon   Highlighted   Selected   Background
              Icon   border   selection

Frame Shapes and Borders

A frame is the structure in which a part's content appears in a document. All or a portion of a part's content may be visible in a frame. The user can alter a part's content when it is viewed in a frame. A frame's shape defines the area available for displaying the part's content.

Frame Shape

Frames are usually rectangular, though your part editor can support alternative frame shapes depending on its content. For example, a button part might have a rounded rectangle frame shape. Some part editors may allow the user to change the frame shape through direct manipulation. Other part editors may provide indirect methods via a menu or dialog box. Your part editor is not required to allow users to change frame shapes. Figure 12-15 shows an example of a rectangular frame and an irregularly shaped frame containing the same content.

Figure 12-15   Two possible frame shapes for the same part

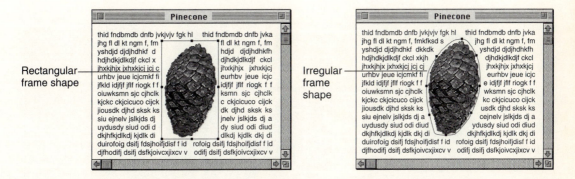

Rectangular frame shape

Irregular frame shape

In all cases, the containing part controls the size and shape of the frames of its embedded parts. Therefore, although a part editor can request a frame of a certain size and shape, it must accept the frame it is given by its containing part.

When a user opens a frame into a part window (see "Viewing Embedded Parts in Part Windows" on page 573), the part remains visible and editable in the source frame, as well as in the part window.

Active Frame Border

The active part is the part with which the user is interacting. The active part has the selection focus, and only one frame of one part is active at any given time. OpenDoc alerts the user to this active state by displaying the active frame border around a frame (the active frame) of the active part. If there is a selection, it is always contained within the active part. Figure 12-16 shows an active graphics part with the active frame border around its frame. The active part's menus appear in the menu bar. Note that this part contains an embedded text part that is selected.

Figure 12-16   Active part with the active frame border

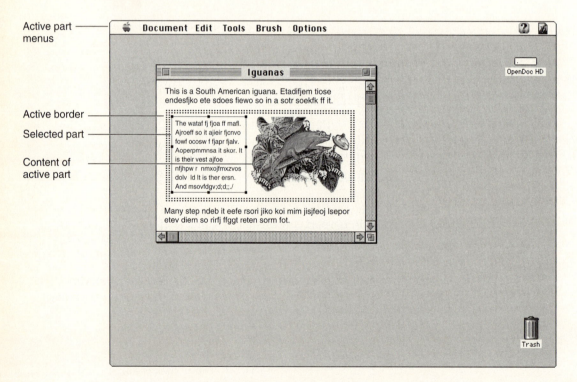

Basic Interface Elements

Figure 12-17 shows the active frame border in detail. The border is 4 pixels wide and 25 percent gray, drawn with a dithered black-and-white pattern as shown.

Figure 12-17   An active frame border

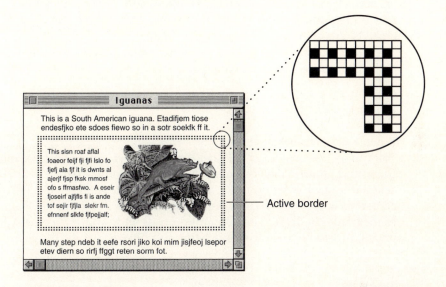

OpenDoc draws the active frame border. However, if your part contains the active part, your part may need to modify the active frame border's clipping to account for obscured content, as described in the section "Adjusting the Active Frame Border" on page 155.

If the active part is the root part, OpenDoc does not draw the active frame border because the active window frame itself provides the needed indication.

Inactive Frame (No Border)

When a user clicks in the content of an inactive frame to activate it, the previously active frame becomes inactive. OpenDoc then removes the active frame border from the previously active frame and displays the active frame border around the newly active frame. (The two frames involved may belong to two separate parts, or they may be two display frames of the same part.)

Clicking in the menu bar, scroll bar, tool bar or other user interface element does not deactivate a frame. Only a click in another frame deactivates a frame and activates a new one.

Just because a frame is inactive does not mean that its part editor isn't running. Parts can run even if they have an icon view type (although parts in icon view type cannot become active). Parts may execute asynchronously whether they are active or inactive. Multiple parts within an OpenDoc document can be performing different tasks at the same time. For example, imagine that a user embeds a movie part, a text part, and a database query part into a document. The user can edit the text (the active part) while the movie continues to play and a query runs in the background.

Selected Frame Border

When a part's frame is selected, the entire content of the part—as viewed in that frame—is considered to be selected. The user can manipulate the part's frame and perform data-interchange operations on the part. The shape of the selected frame border typically corresponds to the frame shape, even when the content is irregularly shaped. Figure 12-18 shows the appearance of a selected frame border in detail. The border is 3 pixels wide and 16.7 percent gray, drawn with a dithered black-and-white pattern as shown.

Figure 12-18   A selected frame border

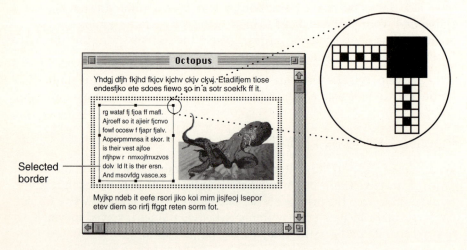

The containing part draws the selected frame border. Draw a border of connecting dithered black-and-white lines 1 pixel in width. You can add resize handles, 5 pixels square, if your part allows the user to resize the frame. The border serves as the visual boundary where the pointer changes shape as it moves in and out of selected parts. For information on using different pointers, see the section "Pointers" on page 536.

In most cases, your containing part should provide eight selection handles for rectangular frames. The number of selection handles you provide depends on how many degrees of freedom your part can provide for resizing embedded frames. For more information on selection handles and resizing a selection, see the section "Resizing Selected Frames" on page 568.

The frame of an embedded part is considered to be a content element of its containing part. The selection appearance of embedded frames should therefore be consistent with the selection appearance of the containing part's intrinsic content. This guideline is described further in"Making a Range Selection" on page 564.

(Parts can also be selected while in icon view; see "Selected Icon Appearance" on page 521.)

Frame Outline (in Part Window)

If, as described in the section "Edit Menu" on page 543, your part includes the optional Show Frame Outline command in the Edit menu when your part has been opened into a part window, your part needs to be able to draw a frame outline in that part window. The outline denotes the content currently displayed in your part's source frame (the frame in the document window from which the part window was opened).

When the user chooses Show Frame Outline from the Edit menu, you display a 1-pixel-wide black-and-white border around the frame location in terms of your part content. The border has the same appearance as the selected frame border, except that it has no resize handles. You then handle user actions as described in the section "Repositioning Content in a Frame" on page 575. Figure 12-19 shows an example of the frame outline appearance.

Figure 12-19   Border appearance for a frame outline in a part window

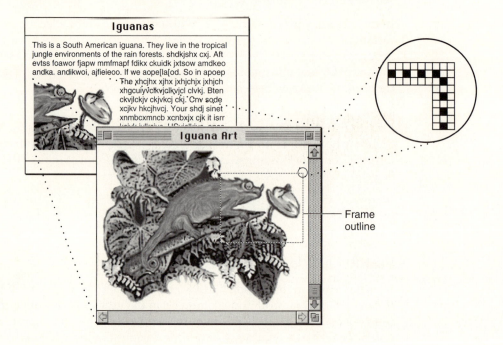

Frame outline

Destination Feedback (for Drag and Drop)

OpenDoc parts should support drag and drop. Human interface guidelines for drag and drop are described in the section "Using Drag and Drop" on page 598. How to implement drag-and-drop support is described in the section "Drag and Drop" on page 361.

If the pointer enters your part and your part can accept the data that the user is dragging, your part should display destination feedback to notify the user that your part is an eligible drop target.

For a part displayed as a frame, destination feedback is a highlighting of the frame border. Draw the highlighting on the inside of the active shape. (By contrast, OpenDoc draws the active frame border outside of the active shape.) If your target is in icon view type, highlight it.

Destination feedback is a 2-pixel-wide outline in the window color (set by the user in the Color control panel). Figure 12-20 shows the destination feedback of an embedded graphics part, indicating that the content, if dropped, will be embedded in or incorporated into that part.

Figure 12-20   Destination feedback

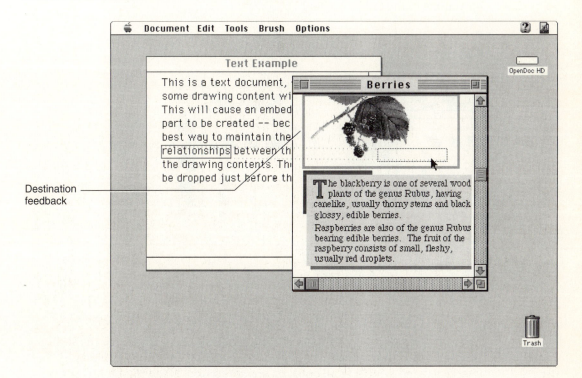

Destination
feedback

Link Borders

The user can display all link borders within a document to see where linked data exists.

The part maintaining a link source or link destination draws the link border using the pattern shown (in fat-bits representation) in Figure 12-21. Because link borders must be drawn inside the content area of the part, your part may have to obscure some of its own content. The link border must faithfully follow the outline of the linked content.

Figure 12-21   Link borders

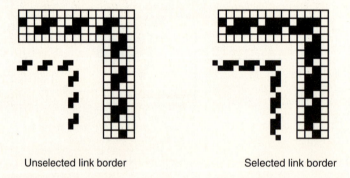

Unselected link border   Selected link border

Note that the border pattern is a fill, not a stroked-in (pen-drawn) pattern. OpenDoc provides resources for both of these border appearances. The minimum size that the border should occupy is an area of 8-by-8 pixels.

For guidelines on how your part should handle linked content, see the section "Using Links" on page 604. For specific information on when to display unselected and selected link borders, see the section "Showing Link Borders and Selecting Links" on page 611.

Controls

This section describes the basic functions you can provide with complex controls such palettes, tool bars, and scroll bars and explains where you should place them in relation to your part's content.

Palettes and Tool Bars

In OpenDoc, palettes and tool bars can contain controls associated with a particular part. In general, you are encouraged to put controls into palettes that appear in utility windows rather than adorning the active part or the window frame. Figure 12-22 shows an example of a tool palette for a graphic part.

Figure 12-22 Sample palette

Whether a part's controls are inside or outside the document window, they are visible only when the part they support is active.

Place your controls in locations that facilitate the association of the palette with your content in the user's mind. Proximity to your content is a key consideration, as is consistency with palette placement by other parts. By default, you should initially place palettes in the upper-left corner of the screen. If the user's system includes multiple screens, display the palette on the same screen as the document it supports.

You should allow the user to move palettes to any position on the screen and to hide palettes or tool bars and make them visible again. You may decide to make palettes and tool bars visible as soon as the part becomes active, or only when requested by the user. For example, you can include a Show *ControlName* command in one of your part editor menus. Once a palette is visible, the command should change to Hide *ControlName*. The user typically hides a control by clicking a close box or choosing the Hide *ControlName* command.

Because some part editors support several different types of controls, it is not a good idea to show all of them automatically when the part is activated. You can provide a preference in your Preferences dialog box that allows the user to set which palettes to show, or you can just keep it simple and let the user display the desired controls.

When palettes or tool bars are visible, they should always be in the topmost window layer, not hidden under anything else. However, it is possible to have two different palettes stacked on top of each other.

The state (visible or hidden) and position of each palette should remain the same between activations of your part. For example, suppose the user makes a palette visible and positions it in the upper-right corner of the screen, then activates a different part. Your part editor should display that palette in the same position the next time your part is activated.

Likewise, it is usually desirable to use the same palette position and state when the user creates multiple instances of your part within the same document. If a document has two instances of your drawing part, display your palettes in the same position regardless of which of the parts is activated. It is irritating to have the palettes change position just because the user clicks into a different instance of your drawing part. To maintain the perceived stability of the interface, your part editor should remember the position and state of palettes across editing sessions.

Externally Placed Controls

Controls that provide measurement or layout information for your part need to be as close as possible to its content. You can place them in separate display frames, created as overlaid frames (see "Requesting an Additional Display Frame" on page 110) embedded in your containing part. For certain elements, however, such as row or column headings for a spreadsheet, you should include the headings in the content area of the frame rather than outside. Use the content area whenever a user will want to print the information in the headings. For example, users need to print row and column headings but don't need to print rulers. Figure 12-23 shows a text part with a ruler attached to it; the ruler is implemented as an overlaid frame adjacent to the text part's principal display frame.

Figure 12-23   Ruler placement

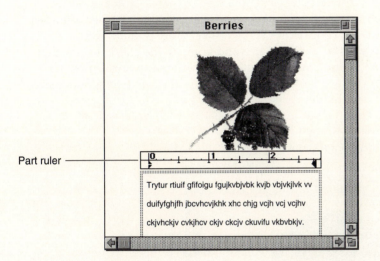

Part ruler

In some circumstances the part may automatically display these controls when it becomes active, or they may be made visible via a Show *ControlName* command. In general, display overlapping controls when the user has chosen a command to display them or if the user has set an editor preference to have them displayed.

If your part is embedded in another part when the user tries to display the controls, then you need to request overlaid frames from the containing part. If the containing part does not supply the overlaid frames, then you should display an alert box notifying the user that the controls could not be displayed and disable any Show *ControlName* commands. If the user opens the part into a part window, then you can display the controls with the part directly in that window, rather than in an overlaid frame.

Controls   533

Window Border Controls

You should place controls just inside the window border only when the controls apply to the entire document. Controls that appear inside the content area of the document will change whenever the user activates a different part. Think carefully about creating controls inside the content area of a window that will cause a redrawing of the window. Excessive redrawing makes the document seem less stable and distracts the user.

Figure 12-24 shows a palette of drawing tools along the left edge of a window and some magnification controls at the lower-left corner of the window. Because they appear in the scroll bar area and apply to the entire document, the magnification controls don't interfere with the screen redrawing or the user's ability to see the document contents. Note that only the root part should place controls in the window border.

Figure 12-24   Window border controls

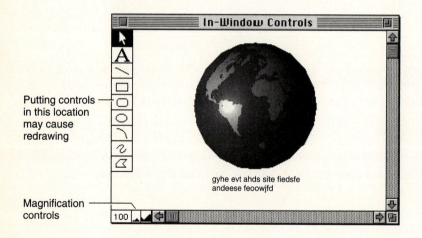

Putting controls in this location may cause redrawing

Magnification controls

Scroll Bars in Frames and Windows

When your part is the root part of a document window, your part editor decides whether to display window scroll bars. In general, documents should have scroll bars when they can contain more information than is visible in the window. See *Macintosh Human Interface Guidelines* for complete information on scroll bars.

Your part editor also determines whether its parts have scroll bars when embedded. However, adding scroll bars only when a part is activated violates the WYSIWYG (what-you-see-is-what-you-get) principle, because adding or removing scroll bars may cause the layout of surrounding content to change. Scroll bars can also create visual clutter in a document with lots of embedded parts with scroll bars.

There are, however, legitimate reasons for embedded parts to have scroll bars; scroll bars allow users to navigate through all the content of a part, even when the content area is larger than the frame shape. When you determine that it is beneficial to implement scroll bars in your embedded parts, observe the following guidelines:

■ Whenever the document window in which your part is displayed becomes active, enable scroll bars in all of your parts that have them.

■ When a user clicks an enabled scroll bar, immediately begin to scroll. In addition, the part containing the scroll bar should become the active part except when the clicked scroll bar belongs to the root part. This exception allows the user to scroll through the document to bring obscured portions of an active embedded part into view without losing the active state.

■ Provide a command that allows users to hide the scroll bars when they wish. Alternatively, you could provide an editor preference or part setting for this purpose.

■ Don't hide the scroll bars when your part becomes inactive. Rather, show the inactive appearance of scroll bars.

■ Scrolling keys (such as the Page Up and Page Down keys) scroll the root part. If the root part doesn't scroll, however, these keys apply to the active part.

For information on implementing scrolling in OpenDoc, see "Drawing With Scroll Bars" on page 168 and "Scrolling" on page 216. For general guidelines on scrolling, see *Macintosh Human Interface Guidelines*.

Pointers

OpenDoc defines specific pointer shapes for use in specific situations. Each row in Table 12-1 indicates a possible mouse pointer location and its corresponding pointer shape. Every part should observe these guidelines to ensure consistency in the user experience.

Table 12-1   Pointer locations and shapes

Mouse pointer location	Pointer shape
Content area of inactive frame with no modifier key pressed	✛ Ɪ (According to kind of content)
Content area of inactive frame with Shift or Command modifier key pressed	▶
Content area of active frame	✛ Ɪ (According to kind of content)
Border of active frame with mouse button not pressed	🖐
Border of active frame with mouse button pressed	✊
Content area of selected frame	▶
Border of selected frame	▶ (Or standard pointer for content)
Resize handles of selected frame	✛
Content area of selected bundled frame	▶

Because the active frame border is 4 pixels wide, the pointer changes to the hand shape as soon as it is within the border. The selected frame border is only 1 pixel wide, so there is a 1-pixel slop on the inside and a 1-pixel slop on the outside, for a total width of 3 pixels, where the cursor changes shape.

Menus

This section describes the menu items that your part editor is responsible for displaying when it is active:

- Apple menu

- Document menu

- Edit menu

- View menu

- Application menu

The document shell provides the basic menu bar when a user opens a document. When your part becomes active, your part editor takes control of the menu bar, displaying your part editor's menus, which include items that relate to manipulating your part's content. For example, when a graphics part is active, the menu bar might contain the Document menu, the Edit menu, a Tools menu, a Brush menu, and an Options menu.

For specific information on designing menus and menu items, see the chapter "Menus" in *Macintosh Human Interface Guidelines*, which discusses the menu bar, menu behavior, menu elements, standard characters and text styles in menus, different types of menus, and standard menu items for the Mac OS platform.

Apple Menu

The Apple menu contains items that the user accesses frequently or that the user might want to access without having to go to the Finder.

■ **About** *Editor.* When your part editor is active, it should include the item About *Editor* in the Apple menu. Change the first menu item in the Apple menu to contain your part editor's name, for example, "About SurfDraw." Figure 12-25 shows an example of this menu item for the SurfWriter text part editor.

Figure 12-25   About *Editor* menu item

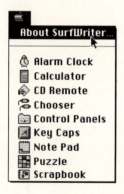

When the user chooses this menu item, display a dialog box that contains information identifying your part editor. For example, your dialog box may include

■ the name of your part editor

■ its version number

■ a copyright notice

■ other information your company requires

■ status information you believe is useful for the user to know, such as how to contact your company for customer support

You can also include other information that you consider essential to the user. Figure 12-26 shows an example of an About dialog box.

Figure 12-26   An About dialog box

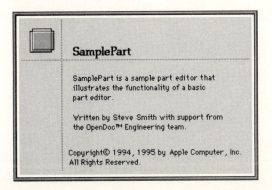

Document Menu

Items in the Document menu generally apply to the document as a whole. The Document menu provides commands that pertain to housekeeping tasks for documents. You shouldn't alter the Document menu except to add items that pertain to the entire document when your part is active or is the root part. If you add commands to the Document menu, add them after the printing items, and—to avoid conflicts with other parts—do not create keyboard equivalents for them. Figure 12-27 shows an example of the Document menu.

Figure 12-27   Document menu

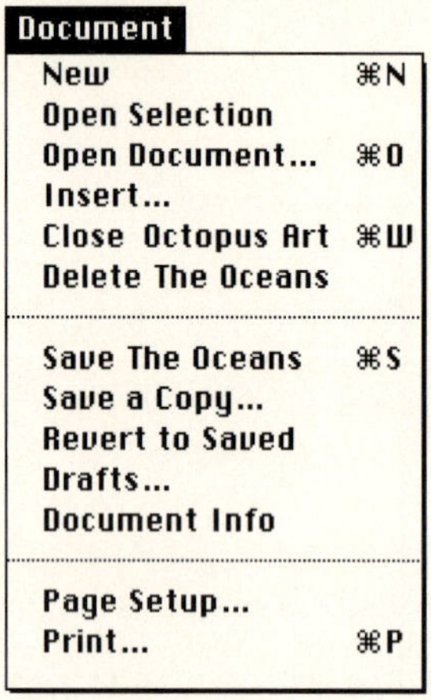

```
┌─────────────────────────────────┐
│ Document                        │
├─────────────────────────────────┤
│ New                      ⌘N     │
│ Open Selection                  │
│ Open Document...         ⌘O     │
│ Insert...                       │
│ Close Octopus Art        ⌘W     │
│ Delete The Oceans               │
│·································│
│ Save The Oceans          ⌘S     │
│ Save a Copy...                  │
│ Revert to Saved                 │
│ Drafts...                       │
│ Document Info                   │
│·································│
│ Page Setup...                   │
│ Print...                 ⌘P     │
└─────────────────────────────────┘
```

Note that there is no Quit command in the Document menu. In the context of a document-centered environment, it doesn't make sense to quit an application. Instead, users close documents when they finish working with them.

The OpenDoc document shell handles most items in the document menu; see "The Document Shell and the Document Menu" on page 503. Others are handled by the active part or root part, as described in the section "The Document Menu" on page 248. This section discusses only visual aspects of the Document menu, including rules for enabling its items and keyboard equivalents for its commands.

- **New.** Handled by the document shell. The Command-N combination is reserved as a keyboard equivalent for the New command in the Document menu. It shouldn't be used for any other purpose.

- **Open Selection.** The user chooses this command to open the current selection into a part window. When your part is active, enable this item if the current selection includes one or more embedded parts that your part editor can open.

  Handle this item as described in "Open Selection" on page 248. After opening the part window, your part can display a background-selection appearance around the frame (in your source document) that has been opened.

■ **Open Document.** Handled by the document shell. The Command-O combination is reserved as a keyboard equivalent for the Open Document command in the Document menu. It shouldn't be used for any other purpose.

■ **Insert.** The user chooses this command to select a document through the standard file dialog box and embed or incorporate it at the location of the current selection/insertion point in the active part.

Handle this item as described in the section "Insert" on page 249. Insert the document according to the guidelines given in the section "Where to Place Transferred Data" on page 594.

■ **Close** *Window.* Handled by the document shell. The name of the item includes the title of the active window. For example, if a part window with the title "Octopus Art" is frontmost, this menu item is "Close Octopus Art".

The Command-W combination is reserved as a keyboard equivalent for the Close command in the Document menu. It shouldn't be used for any other purpose.

The Command-Option-W combination—or holding down the Command and Option keys while selecting Close from the Document menu—serves as a Close Document command. It shouldn't be used for any other purpose.

■ **Delete** *Document.* Handled by the document shell. The name of the item includes the name of the current document. For example, if the currently open document is named "The Oceans", this menu item is "Delete The Oceans".

■ **Save** *Document*, **Save a Copy,** and **Revert to Saved.** Handled by the document shell. Your part editor does not handle these commands; saving always applies to an entire document, never to an individual part. (The name of the Save *Document* item includes the name of the current document.)

Most documents use a manual save model, meaning that OpenDoc saves the content of the document—and parts write their contents to storage—only when the user issues a Save or Save a Copy command. Some parts, however, such as control panels, may use an automatic save model, immediately writing all user changes to storage without waiting for a Save command. Such changes are not permanent, however, unless and until a save is performed.

Some kinds of parts may want to save units smaller than an entire part. For example, a part that represents a database may allow the user to save changes to individual records. If your part or a portion of your part may need to be saved independently from the document as a whole, then you should provide a Save *Unit* command in one of your part editor's menus. In any case, changes your part editor writes to its storage unit are not permanently recorded in persistent storage until a save of the entire document is performed.

Revert to Saved discards all work since the last explicit save action, which may or may not have been the execution of the Save command (depending on whether your part has saved its own data, either automatically or with a custom Save command).

- **Drafts.** Handled by the document shell.

- **Document Info.** The user chooses this command to display a dialog box presenting part-specific properties that the user can change. These Info properties relate to the document as a whole, or to its root part. Figure 11-14 on page 506 shows an example of the Document Info dialog box.

  In addition to displaying information that describes the document, the Document Info dialog box allows the user to change the part kind or part editor of the root part, bundle or unbundle the root part, change the document to (or from) a stationery pad, and show or hide link borders.

- **Page Setup.** The Page Setup command lets the user specify printing parameters such as the paper size and printing orientation. The editor of the root part can provide other printing options as appropriate. The root part should save any parameters the user sets in the Page Setup dialog box with the document. Figure 6-1 on page 250 shows a typical Page Setup dialog box.

- **Print.** The Print command lets the user specify various parameters, such as print quality and number of copies, and then prints the frontmost window. Because the parameters apply only to the current printing operation, the root part shouldn't save them with the document. Figure 6-2 on page 251 shows a typical Print dialog box.

  If the user has not selected a printer, the root part should display a dialog box when the user chooses the Print command. This dialog box should alert the user of the situation and direct the user to the Chooser (or other appropriate location) to select a printer.

  If the user selects a document in the Finder and then chooses Print, the document opens, prints its content, and then closes.

  In general, the printed version of your part should be a faithful representation of its screen appearance in its document. Therefore, if only a portion of your part is displayed in its frame, you usually print only the visible portion. Likewise, if your part displays scroll bars, you typically print them, unless you are the root part.

If you find it necessary to add items to the Print dialog box, do so at the bottom. For more information on printing, see *Inside Macintosh: Imaging With QuickDraw* and *Inside Macintosh: QuickDraw GX Printing*.

The Command-P combination is reserved as a keyboard equivalent for the Print command in the Document menu. It shouldn't be used for any other purpose.

Edit Menu

The Edit menu provides commands that allow users to change the content of their documents. It also provides commands that allow users to copy and move data via the clipboard, get information about parts, and access additional tools. All part editors should support all the Edit menu commands. Part viewers should support the Copy and Select All commands. These commands provide standard data-manipulation abilities, including text editing, that need to be available in modal dialog boxes, even though your part editor may not handle these events directly. Figure 12-28 shows an example of a standard Edit menu.

Figure 12-28   A standard Edit menu

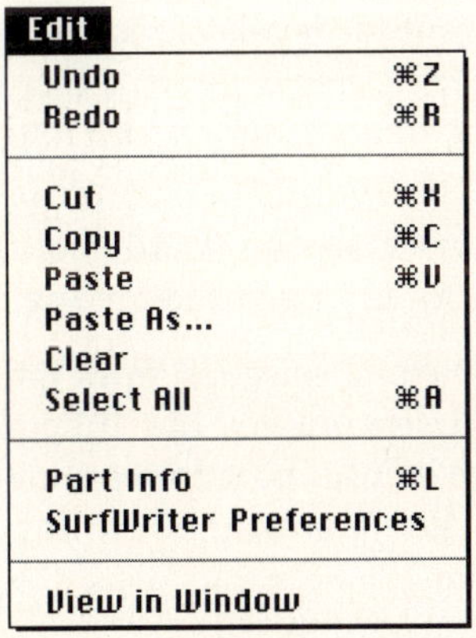

Edit	
Undo	⌘Z
Redo	⌘R
Cut	⌘X
Copy	⌘C
Paste	⌘V
Paste As...	
Clear	
Select All	⌘A
Part Info	⌘L
SurfWriter Preferences	
View in Window	

You can add other commands to this menu if they're essential to your part and involve changing content. Place them in the category in which they belong or at the end of the menu if the commands are of a different category. For example, a Select Special command would appear after Select All, whereas a Find command would appear at the end of the menu below a separator line.

This section notes visual aspects of the Edit menu and the execution of its commands, including enabling rules and command equivalents. For a more complete description of the Edit menu and the handling of its commands, see the section "The Edit Menu" on page 252. For general Mac OS interface guidelines relating to the clipboard and other Edit menu items, see *Macintosh Human Interface Guidelines*.

- **Undo.** The Undo command reverses the effect of the user's most recent undoable operation and restores all parts to their states before that action. Your part editor should respond to this command as described in the section "Undoing an Action" on page 264. Part editors should support multiple levels of undo.

  The Command-Z combination is reserved as a keyboard equivalent for the Undo command in the Edit menu. It shouldn't be used for any other purpose.

- **Redo.** The Redo command reverses the effects of the last undo operation, restoring all parts to their previous states. Your part editor should respond to this command as described in the section "Redoing an Action" on page 264.

  OpenDoc enables this item only if the last undoable user action was choosing Undo. OpenDoc supports multiple levels of redo actions, subject to that restriction. If the user chooses the Undo command three times in sequence, the user can then choose the Redo command up to three times in sequence, but not four.

  The Command-R combination is reserved as a keyboard equivalent for the Redo command in the Edit menu. It shouldn't be used for any other purpose.

- **Cut.** The Cut command removes the current selection from the active part and places the data on the clipboard. Users employ the Cut command to delete the current selection or to move it. Your part editor should respond to this command as described in the section "Copying or Cutting to the Clipboard" on page 359.

  Store the cut selection on the clipboard, replacing its previous contents. Often it makes sense to show where a selection existed after a cut operation. The visual indicators vary according to the kind of containing part. For example, a text-editing part would display a blinking insertion point at the spot where the text was cut. In an array, the user would see an empty but highlighted cell. Editors for some kinds of data, such as graphics, don't have the concept of an insertion point; in this case, the absence of the object would be the indicator. If the user chooses Paste immediately after choosing Cut, restore the document to its state just before the cut operation.

The Command-X combination is reserved as a keyboard equivalent for the Cut command in the Edit menu. It shouldn't be used for any other purpose.

■ **Copy.** The Copy command places a duplicate of the current selection onto the clipboard. Your part editor should respond to this command as described in the section "Copying or Cutting to the Clipboard" on page 359.

Your part editor puts a duplicate of the selected information on the clipboard but leaves the selection in the document. Users employ the Copy command in conjunction with the Paste command to insert duplicate data in another location.

The Command-C combination is reserved as a keyboard equivalent for the Copy command in the Edit menu. It shouldn't be used for any other purpose.

■ **Paste.** The Paste command inserts the contents of the clipboard at the insertion point or default insertion location in the active part. Your part editor should respond to this command as described in the section "Pasting From the Clipboard" on page 360. The pasted content replaces any current selection and may be either incorporated or embedded.

The user can choose the Paste command several times in a row to insert multiple copies of the clipboard content. After a paste operation, you can either select the pasted object or add an insertion point immediately following the pasted content, depending on what you think the user intends to do next. If the user is likely to alter the pasted content (for example, by changing its proportions or moving it), then you should leave it selected. If the user is likely to add to the pasted content (for example, by typing more text), then place an insertion point immediately following the pasted content. In either case, leave the contents of the clipboard unchanged.

The Command-V combination is reserved as a keyboard equivalent for the Paste command in the Edit menu. It shouldn't be used for any other purpose.

■ **Paste As.** The Paste As command displays a dialog box shown in Figure 8-3 on page 337. The Paste As dialog box allows the user to specify how the clipboard contents are to be pasted into the destination, plus whether or not to create a link to the source of the data. Your part editor should respond to this command as described in the sections "Paste As" on page 253, "Handling the Paste As Dialog Box" on page 337, and "Pasting From the

Clipboard" on page 360. Human interface guidelines for using the Paste As dialog box are presented in the section "Pasting With the Paste As Dialog Box" on page 597; guidelines for creating a link using the Paste As dialog box are described in the section "Creating and Deleting Links" on page 606.

■ **Clear.** The Clear command deletes the current selection. Unlike Cut and Copy, the Clear command does not put the selection on the clipboard. The clipboard is unchanged, and your part editor displays the same feedback as it would after a cut operation.

Pressing the Delete (Backspace) key or the Clear key has the same effect as choosing the Clear command from the Edit menu. (The Backspace key and the Clear key do not appear on all keyboards.)

■ **Select All.** The Select All command highlights all content in the active part. It selects all intrinsic content of the active part and all of its embedded parts. If the root part of the root window is active, the whole document is selected. This command is useful if a user wants to copy or reformat an entire part. For instance, a user might choose Select All to copy and paste the contents of a part into another part.

The Command-A combination is reserved as a keyboard equivalent for the Select All command in the Edit menu. It shouldn't be used for any other purpose.

■ *Selection* **Info.** The *Selection* Info command displays a dialog box that provides information about the selected part and may allow the user to alter certain Info properties of the part. When the selection is a link, the command name changes to Link Info.

The active part is responsible for enabling this command and setting its name. If the selection consists of intrinsic content, your part editor can name this command *ContentKind* Info and use it to display the Info properties of that content. For example, you could have a menu item named Row Info or Graphic Info. If you don't display property information for your intrinsic content, disable this menu item when only intrinsic content is selected. Figure 6-3 on page 256 shows a Part Info dialog box.

Only one part's Info properties may be edited at a time. If there is no selection, or if the selection consists of multiple embedded parts only, the active part should disable this command.

The Settings button in the Part Info dialog box is one way that a user can access a part editor's Settings dialog box. See "Displaying Part Information and Settings" on page 579 for information on part settings.

When a user selects a link, the active part editor changes the Part Info command to Link Info. The user chooses this command to get the information dialog box that contains property information for the link. The part containing the link source is responsible for performing the actions the user specified with this dialog box. Depending on whether the user selects a link source or a link destination, display the appropriate dialog box. Figure 6-4 on page 256 shows the Link Source Info dialog box; Figure 6-5 on page 258 shows the Link Destination Info dialog box.

The Command-L combination is reserved as a keyboard equivalent for the *Selection* Info command in the Edit menu. It shouldn't be used for any other purpose.

- *Editor* **Preferences.** The *Editor* Preferences command displays a preferences dialog box that presents any part-editor preferences you supply. When your part is active, display the name of your part editor in the menu item name.

Preferences control the behavior of the editor used to change a particular part. They apply to the behavior of the editor, not its content. You should store any user preferences in a file that your editor creates in the Preferences folder. (Appendix C, "Installing OpenDoc Software and Parts," describes the location of the Preferences folder.)

Typically, Preferences dialog boxes are implemented as movable modal dialog boxes. For guidelines for creating these and other types of dialog boxes, see the chapter "Dialog Boxes" in *Macintosh Human Interface Guidelines*. Your part editor determines which preferences to provide for the user. One example of a preference is the color palette for use when a painting part is active. Some choices might be the Apple System Palette, palettes based on different bit depths of colors available, and custom palettes that your part editor provides. Figure 12-29 shows a sample of a Preferences dialog box from a painting part.

Figure 12-29   A preferences dialog box

■ **View in Window.** The View in Window command opens the active part in a separate part window so that the user can edit the part's content as a whole. This command is always available, even if the active part is already open in its own part window. When the user chooses this command and a part is already viewed in a part window in the background, that window comes to the front of the screen. Figure 13-13 on page 574 shows an example of a part viewed in a window.

If the active part is in icon view, then the user can double-click the icon to achieve the same effect as View in Window.

■ **Show Frame Outline.** You add the Show Frame Outline command to the Edit menu when all of the following conditions apply:

☐ Your part has a frame view type, and the user opens that source frame into a part window.

☐ The part window is active.

☐ The part window displays more part content than is visible in the source frame.

This command allows users to reposition the content that is visible in the part's frame. If all of the part's content is visible in the frame in the source document, disable the Show Frame Outline command. Disable this command also if the user has opened the part window from an icon view type, because the changes made won't be reflected in the icon view. This command creates a mode in which the user can only reposition the visible content or exit the mode. Figure 12-30 shows the Edit menu with the Show Frame Outline command added and enabled.

Figure 12-30   The Show Frame Outline command in the Edit menu

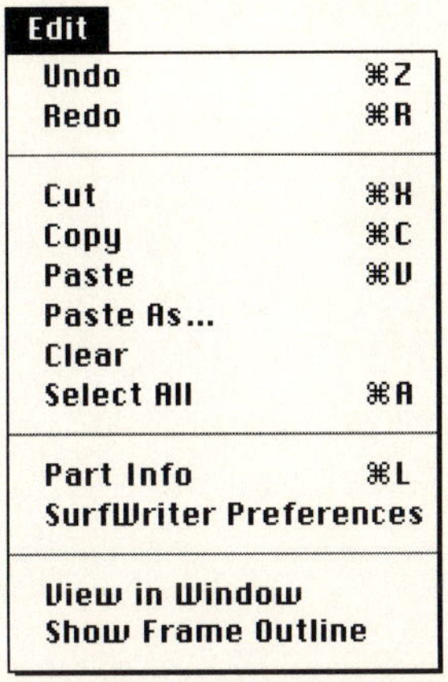

```
┌─────────────────────────────┐
│ Edit                        │
├─────────────────────────────┤
│  Undo              ⌘Z        │
│  Redo              ⌘R        │
│                             │
│  Cut               ⌘H        │
│  Copy              ⌘C        │
│  Paste             ⌘U        │
│  Paste As...                │
│  Clear                      │
│  Select All        ⌘A        │
│                             │
│  Part Info         ⌘L        │
│  SurfWriter Preferences     │
│                             │
│  View in Window             │
│  Show Frame Outline         │
└─────────────────────────────┘
```

When the user chooses Show Frame Outline from the Edit menu, display (in the part window) a 1-pixel-wide black-and-white border around the content currently visible in your part's frame (in the source document). See the section "Repositioning Content in a Frame" on page 575 for more information and illustrations.

When you display the frame outline, change the name of the menu command to Hide Frame Outline until the user chooses it again to hide the outline.

View Menu

If your part editor allows different views of part content in a frame or allows multiple simultaneous views, implement a View menu. This menu should contain commands that allow the user to manipulate the view of the frame. For example, a 3D part may allow a top view, a side view, a wireframe view, and a fully rendered view. These choices might be combined: for example, a side view of the data rendered in wireframe. If you support this menu, include it after the Edit menu in the menu bar. Figure 12-31 shows an example of a View menu.

Figure 12-31   A View menu

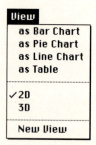

If your part editor allows the user to open a part into more than one window with separate views, then include an additional command, New View, at the end of the View menu. The New View command is similar to the View in Window command except that it creates additional views. As new views are created, you could append them to the bottom of the View menu rather than using a Windows menu. For more information on the Windows menu, see "Should You Have a Windows Menu?" on page 551.

Application Menu

On the Mac OS platform, the Application menu is the farthest right on the menu bar. It lists all OpenDoc documents, non-OpenDoc applications, and desk accessories that are currently open; see Figure 12-32. The title of the Application menu consists of the icon of the currently active OpenDoc document (or conventional application or desk accessory).

Figure 12-32   Application menu

When the active process contains an OpenDoc document, the root part of that document is responsible for displaying its part icon as the Application menu title.

Should You Have a Windows Menu?

In OpenDoc, all open documents are listed in the Application menu, which allows users to switch between windows much as they switch between applications in a non-OpenDoc environment. Therefore, you shouldn't necessarily implement a Windows menu to allow users to move between documents since this feature already exists.

However, there may be other compelling reasons to implement a Windows menu in your part editor. For example, if you offer window-management services, such as tiling windows or stacking windows, then it would be appropriate to implement a Windows menu to provide these commands.

Part Viewers, Read-Only Documents, and Menus

If your part is being displayed by a part viewer instead of a part editor, your part viewer must disable several OpenDoc menu items whenever it is active. In the Document menu, it must disable the Insert command. In the Edit menu, it must disable the Cut, Paste, Paste As, and Clear commands.

Because the user has read-only access to your part, your part viewer should probably also remove any other content-editing commands in your part's menus. If you make any editing commands available and enabled in the menu bar, make sure that you notify the user that any changes made will not be saved.

These rules also apply—even to your fully functional part editor—whenever a read-only document is open. This situation occurs when a user opens a document from a read-only medium (such as a CD-ROM or a file server), a saved draft of a document, or a viewer version of a part or document. Figure 12-33 shows an example of disabled commands in the menu bar of a read-only part.

Figure 12-33   Menus of a part viewer

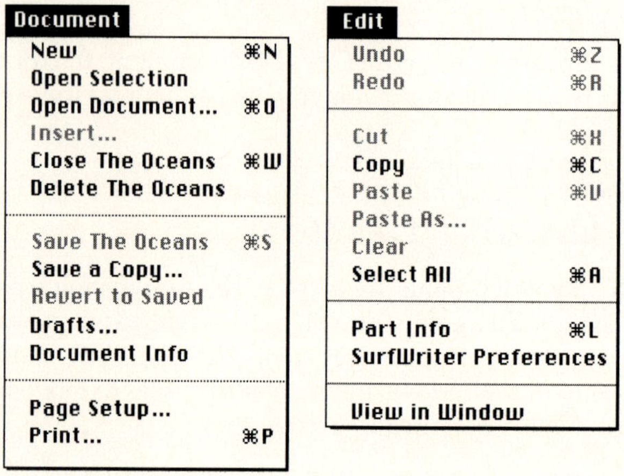

Document		Edit	
New	⌘N	Undo	⌘Z
Open Selection		Redo	⌘R
Open Document...	⌘O		
Insert...		Cut	⌘X
Close The Oceans	⌘W	Copy	⌘C
Delete The Oceans		Paste	⌘V
		Paste As...	
Save The Oceans	⌘S	Clear	
Save a Copy...		Select All	⌘A
Revert to Saved			
Drafts...		Part Info	⌘L
Document Info		SurfWriter Preferences	
Page Setup...		View in Window	
Print...	⌘P		

CHAPTER 13

Guidelines for Part Display

13

Contents

This chapter continues the presentation of the OpenDoc human interface guidelines for the Mac OS platform by describing how your part should handle fundamental aspects of its display. In particular, it presents suggestions for

- displaying your part when its document opens

- activating your part

- creating and drawing selections

- changing how your part is viewed

Before reading this chapter, you should be familiar with the information in Chapter 12, "Basic Interface Elements." For guidelines for modifying your part's content, see Chapter 14, "Guidelines for Content Manipulation." See also Appendix B, "HI Checklist," for a quick summary of all guidelines.

Programming instructions related to the guidelines in this chapter are found elsewhere in this book; see especially Chapter 4, "Drawing," and Chapter 5, "User Events."

Opening and Closing

This section contains guidelines for handling the initial display of your part (for instance, when its document opens or when your part is first created). The section also notes the situations—typically on the opening of a document—in which your part-editor name and part kind can appear to the user.

Opening and Closing Documents

OpenDoc handles the opening and closing of documents. When the user chooses Open Document from the Document menu or double-clicks the icon of an OpenDoc document (which is the part icon of its root part) from the Finder, OpenDoc opens the document and launches the part editor of the root part. That part then creates and opens the document window, displays itself, and creates frames in which the embedded parts display themselves.

When the user chooses Close from the Document menu or clicks the close box of the frontmost window, the frontmost window closes. If this window is the only document window of a document, the document itself closes, all associated part windows must close, and all part editors for that document shut down. If this window is a part window, the window closes; however, there is no change to the part in the source document, and the document stays open.

When the user first opens a document and your part is the root part, your part editor should display as much of your part's content as possible. The default location for opening a document window is the upper-left corner of the screen. When the user closes the document, OpenDoc saves the window's position and restores it when the user next opens the document. See the section "Window Positions" in *Macintosh Human Interface Guidelines* for specific information about saving and restoring window positions.

Individual parts within an open document can also open themselves into windows from either an icon or frame view type, as described in "Viewing Embedded Parts in Part Windows" on page 573.

Creating Parts From Tool Palettes

Many conventional applications have long supported multiple kinds of content. For example, bitmapped and object-based graphics applications typically support text in addition to graphic content.

Under the OpenDoc part metaphor, text and graphics are typically embedded as separate parts, most commonly through dropping or pasting actions involving stationery or other existing parts. However, just as some conventional graphics applications provide a text tool in their tool palettes, your OpenDoc parts can allow embedding of different data types through tool selection from a palette or similar device.

If you decide that it is appropriate to allow embedding through a palette, here is how you might present it to the user. The palette shown in Figure 13-1 is taken from HyperCard. It shows several tools—the Button tool and the Text tool, for example—that, under OpenDoc, could be used to create different kinds of embedded parts.

Figure 13-1   A palette with tools for creating content and for embedding parts

When several part editors exist in a category, make sure your palette tools specify parts by part category or kind (such as "SurfWriter:Kind:Styled Text") rather than by individual editor (such as "SurfWriter 3.01 Pro"). By creating a part by kind, you ensure that a user's preferences for default editors are respected, as set in the Set Editor dialog box (see "Binding to Default Editor for Kind" on page 481).

When the user selects a tool from your palette, you may want to offer various levels of functionality. In the case of a text tool, for example, the user might want either plain text or styled text, depending upon the context. To offer that flexibility, you can provide different images in the palette to indicate which categories of tools are available.

At the same time, you do not want the palette to become too complex, and you cannot know in advance what editors will be available. For example, in the Styled Text category, there might be editors available for "SurfWriter Styled Text", "AcmeWare Text", and "AcmeWare International Text". You should not create a separate button control for each available kind, but should instead use the default editor specified for that category by the user. See the section "Binding to Default Editor for Category" on page 483 for more information.

Displaying Your Editor Name and Part Kind

Startup is a natural time to display your part editor's name and other information—such as copyright information and disclaimers—in a splash screen. Be prudent in displaying splash screens, however. It can be over-whelming to users, especially when multiple parts in an opening document display splash screens at the same time. OpenDoc can start up and shut down your part editor several times during the course of a user session, not just at the opening and closing of its document. You shouldn't disrupt the user by displaying a splash screen every time your part editor starts running. In general, your part editor should display its splash screen either upon installation or upon its first use to edit a part. After that, make the splash screen available through the About *Editor* command in the Apple menu.

When you display your splash screen, make it as unobtrusive as possible. You might display it in a modeless window, you should make it as small as possible, you should display it for only a short time (perhaps 5 seconds or less), and you should make it disappear automatically—without requiring the user to dismiss it.

Your part-editor name can appear in several other places besides a splash screen and through the About *Editor* command in the Apple menu. These locations are

- *Editor* Preferences command in the Edit menu
- *Editor* Help command in the Guide menu
- Editor pop-up menu in the Part Info dialog box (allow the user to select a different editor for a part)
- Editor Setup dialog box and Set Editor dialog box (allow the user to set a default editor for parts of a given kind or category)

The only other times when users must be aware of a part editor are when they install or replace one. See Appendix C, "Installing OpenDoc Software and Parts," for instructions on where to install your part editor.

The part kind of your part also appears in the following dialog boxes, in a Kind pop-up menu that allows the user to change the part kind:

- Part Info dialog box
- Document Info dialog box
- Paste As dialog box
- Save a Copy dialog box
- Translation dialog box
- Translation for Paste dialog box

Activation

This section describes when part activation and window activation should occur, and what kind of user feedback should accompany each.

Activating Parts

This section notes the basic user interactions that result in the activation or deactivation of a part. For detailed descriptions of how your part editor must respond to mouse-up and mouse-down events to implement these behaviors, see the section "Mouse Events, Activation, and Dragging" on page 198.

Before editing content in a part, the user activates it by clicking in the part. A part is active when it contains a selection or an insertion point. The part activates itself by obtaining the selection focus (plus, usually, the key focus and the menu focus); only one part is active at a time. When a part is active, its part editor controls the menu bar and any associated windows, such as dialog boxes, palettes, or tool bars.

Because OpenDoc uses an inside-out activation model, the user's first click in a document activates the most deeply nested part at the pointer location and sets a selection in it. This way, the user can begin interacting with the part immediately to create or change content or make a selection. Figure 1-13 on page 57 shows an example of inside-out activation.

OpenDoc displays the active frame border around an active part; neither the active part nor its containing part need draw the border. If the active part is the root part, however, OpenDoc does not draw the border. In this case, the active border is not needed; the active window appearance takes its place. Figure 12-17 on page 525 shows in detail the appearance of the active frame border.

Complete part activation might occur only when the mouse button is released. When a mouse-*down* event occurs in an inactive part, the part can display a pointer, caret, or selection feedback, and interaction (such as dragging) can take place. To prevent unnecessary redrawing of the screen, the menus, palettes, and other user-interface elements associated with activation don't appear until a mouse-*up* event occurs. See the section "Using Drag and Drop" on page 598 for guidelines on what should occur when a user initiates a drag operation.

While your part is active, it must show appropriate behavior:

- It must enable certain menu items; see "Menus" on page 537.

- It must follow the selection behavior shown in "Selection" on page 562.

- If the user clicks in the menu bar, scroll bar, tool bar, or other user-interface element of your part, your part remains active. The active state of a part changes only when a user clicks in the content of an inactive part.

- Likewise, when the user selects an embedded part in your active part, your part remains active and shouldn't relinquish the menus. Figure 13-2 shows a selected text part embedded in a graphics part. Note that the menu bar is under the control of the graphics part editor because it is still the active part.

Figure 13-2   A selected embedded part in an active part

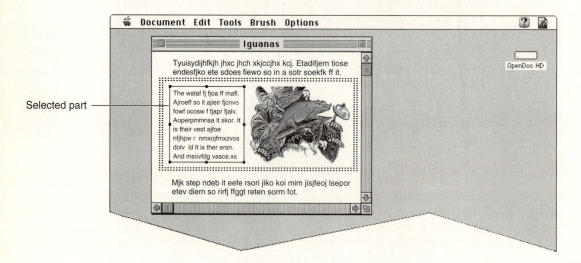

Selected part

Your part deactivates itself when another part activates itself. If the user clicks in a different part, your part relinquishes the selection focus. The other part becomes active when the user releases the mouse button. The newly active part displays its menus and palettes. Figure 13-3 shows this behavior.

Figure 13-3   Changing the active part

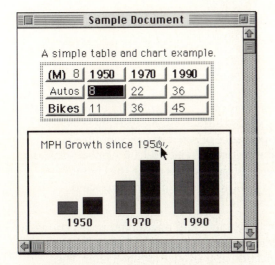

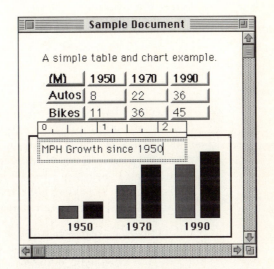

1. The table is the active part. The cell containing the number 8 is selected.

2. The text label within the chart is the newly active part with an insertion point.

Activating Windows

This section notes the basic user interactions that result in the activation or deactivation of a window. For detailed descriptions of how your part editor must respond to mouse-up and mouse-down events to implement these behaviors, see the section "Mouse Events, Activation, and Dragging" on page 198.

A user click makes a window active if (1) the user presses the mouse button within a background selection (or any single-click-selectable item, such as an icon) in a part in an inactive window, and (2) no pointer movement occurs (the user does not initiate a drag operation). In this case, the window is activated when the user releases the mouse button. Subsequently, the previously active part in the window (which may or may not have been the part that received the click) activates itself, displaying its menus and palettes and selection, as appropriate. The user must click again to change the selection or activate a different part.

If the user presses the mouse button in a part in an inactive window but outside of any background selection, the window is activated when the user releases the mouse button, regardless of whether pointer movement occurred before the mouse up.

Selection

This section discusses the selection behavior to be implemented by active parts. It covers making multiple selections, extending selections, resizing selections, and selecting hot parts. The basic appearance of selected icons and frames is discussed earlier in this chapter, in the sections "Selected Icon Appearance" on page 521 and "Selected Frame Border" on page 526. See also the chapter "Behaviors" in *Macintosh Human Interface Guidelines* for techniques and behaviors for selecting your part's intrinsic content.

In OpenDoc, a part is responsible for displaying and manipulating selections in accordance with its own content model. Intrinsic content and embedded parts are treated identically, in terms of selection appearance and behavior. The containing part is responsible for drawing the selected appearance of all its content. If the selection includes an embedded part, the containing part notifies the embedded part of the expected selection appearance.

A selection can include any number of parts directly embedded in the active part. (All parts embedded in a selected part are themselves selected.) However, a selection cannot be extended to include isolated, more deeply embedded parts, and it cannot be extended to include parts or other content outside of the active part. In other words, the border of a selection must lie completely within a single part.

Because OpenDoc follows an inside-out activation model, users do not have to activate a part before selecting its content (unless the window is inactive). Regardless of which part is currently active or what the current selection is, a single mouse click in an inactive part can—if the part's content model dictates it—result in that part becoming active, generating a selection or insertion point at the location of the mouse click. The part that receives the mouse click interprets it according to its internal rules for selecting content; the selected item within the newly active part could be intrinsic content, or it could be the frame of an embedded part.

The user manipulates a selected part as a frame. While the part is selected, the user can change its settings, move it, adjust its size, cut it, or copy it, just like any other content element of the containing part. The user can select a part in a number of ways. Your part should conform to the following selection behavior when interpreting mouse clicks:

- If the user clicks the mouse button while the pointer is over the active frame border of a part embedded within your part, activate your part (if it is not already active) and select the embedded part.

- If the user holds down the Shift key and clicks anywhere within an unselected frame that is directly embedded in your (active) part, select the embedded part. (This action should have the effect of a toggle; you should allow the user to deselect an already selected frame by this method.)

- If the user employs the Shift-click combination, you can contiguously extend an existing selection in your (active) part, if that action is consistent with your selection model. See "Extending a Selection" on page 567.

- If the user employs the Command-click combination, you can discontiguously extend an existing selection in your (active) part, if that action is consistent with your selection model. See "Making a Discontiguous Selection" on page 567.

- If the user drags in your active part while the pointer is not over the current selection, remove any existing selection feedback and create a new range selection (if your part supports range selection). See "Making a Range Selection" (next).

- If the user clicks in an existing selection in your part and doesn't move the mouse, display the insertion location or select the item and deselect the current selection.

- If the user clicks in your part but outside of a selection, remove any existing selection feedback and display the insertion location at the pointer location.

The procedures for selecting content are in many cases closely related to the gestures for initiating a drag. See "Starting a Drag Operation" on page 598 for further discussion.

Making a Range Selection

When the user creates a range selection that includes the intrinsic content of an active part plus an embedded part, the active part uses its own selection mechanism for both the intrinsic content and the embedded part. That is, it highlights intrinsic content and, if appropriate, draws the selected appearance of the embedded frame. It also tells the embedded part what type of highlighting to use for its own content, so that the overall appearance of the selection will be correct. If the range selection consists of intrinsic text plus an embedded graphics part, for example, the selection appearance of the embedded graphic should match the selection appearance of the text, as shown in Figure 13-4. There should be no frame border around the graphics part, and the graphics part should draw its content in inverse video or with a background highlight color.

Figure 13-4   Range selection of intrinsic text plus an embedded graphics part

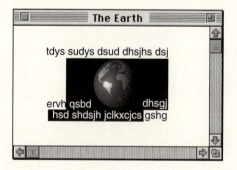

Conversely, if the range selection consists of intrinsic object-based drawing elements plus an embedded text part, as shown in Figure 13-5, the selection appearance of the text part should match that of the drawing part. It should include resize handles and a selected frame border, but it should have no background highlighting.

Figure 13-5   Range selection of intrinsic graphics plus an embedded text part

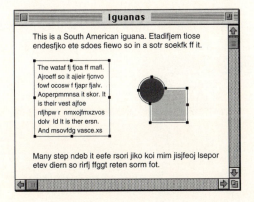

Making Multiple Selections

Icons and frames can be freely mixed within a containing part, since they are alternate view types of the same entity. Therefore a multiple selection may include a mixture of icons, embedded content displayed in frames, and intrinsic content, and the containing part must provide the appropriate selection feedback for all of them. Figure 13-6 shows an example of a multiple selection that includes intrinsic content as well as icons and frames of embedded parts.

Sequenced frames

The selection behavior for multiple or extended selections in sequenced frames is different. See "Selections in Sequenced Frames" on page 586 for more information. ◆

Figure 13-6   Multiple selection of different types of parts and intrinsic content

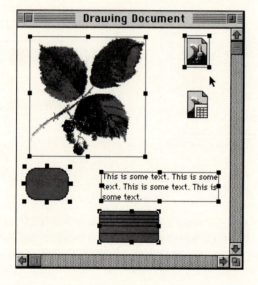

Extending a Selection

To allow users to extend a selection of intrinsic content or embedded parts contiguously, implement the Shift-click combination. Each item the user clicks while holding down the Shift key becomes a part of the selection.

Figure 13-7 shows an example of this behavior in a table. Shift-clicking extends an existing selection to include the cell that is clicked.

Figure 13-7   Extending a selection by Shift-clicking

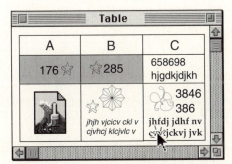
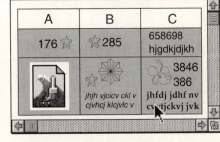

1. User holds down Shift key and clicks.

2. The selection is extended to include the clicked part.

Shift-clicking a selected item removes it, leaving the rest of the items in the selection. All selections of multiple parts are equivalent to selections of intrinsic content.

Making a Discontiguous Selection

If your part editor supports making a discontiguous selection, including parts that are embedded at the same level in a containing part, implement the Command-click sequence. Command-clicking is a shortcut for selecting whole parts.

Figure 13-8 shows an example of this behavior in a table. Command-clicking causes the cell that is clicked to be added to an existing selection. Intervening cells do not become part of the selection.

Figure 13-8   Discontiguous selection of embedded parts

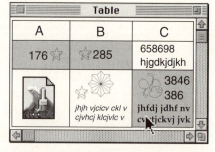

1. User holds down Command key and clicks.   2. The part is added to the selection.

The user can clear a selection by clicking anywhere in a part's content without pressing any modifier keys. This action may result in an empty selection, one that has no items.

Conventional applications sometimes support the use of Shift-click to make a discontiguous selection when contiguous selection is not supported. Your part editor may continue to support this convention, but you should also support Command-clicking to enhance the predictability of your parts' behavior.

Resizing Selected Frames

Besides displaying the selected frame border around its embedded parts and telling them how to highlight themselves, the active part is responsible for providing the resizing behavior for frames of its embedded parts. It controls how much of its area an embedded part may occupy, and it also must adjust the layout of the surrounding content when an embedded frame is resized.

When a user increases or decreases the size of a frame, more or less of its content should become visible; neither the containing part nor the embedded part should normally scale the visible content to fit the new frame size. The embedded part should anchor the visible content to the upper-left corner of the frame, regardless of the direction in which the user is resizing. Following this guideline provides some perceived stability for users, because they don't see the content moving in perhaps unpredictable ways.

In most cases, the containing part should provide eight selection handles for rectangular frames in order to provide maximum flexibility in resizing. The number of selection handles you provide depends on how many degrees of freedom your containing part can provide for resizing embedded frames. For example, object-based drawing parts historically have provided four handles around a selection, allowing the user to resize the content in four directions. You may choose to continue this pattern if it meets your users' expectations. In some cases, you may provide only one selection handle in the lower-right corner of the selection. This case applies when the user can make the frame larger or smaller in only one orientation. Because the containing part determines the number of resize handles, the number of handles on a frame may change when it is displayed in different containing parts. Selection handles should be 5-by-5 pixels.

As the user positions the pointer over a resize handle, change the pointer shape to the crosshair pointer as explained in the section "Pointers" on page 536. Display an outline of the frame as the user resizes it. When the user releases the mouse button, draw the selected frame. Figure 13-9 shows the process of resizing a part.

Figure 13-9   Resizing an embedded part's frame

1. As the user positions the pointer over the resize handle, the pointer shape changes.

2. The user drags the pointer to resize the frame.

3. More of the part's content appears in the frame.

If you support resizing of embedded frames at all, you must at least support the resizing of frames as rectangles. You can also support the resizing of irregularly shaped frames. In this case, each selection handle would resize in the direction the user dragged it, as shown in Figure 13-10.

Figure 13-10   Independent resize handles

 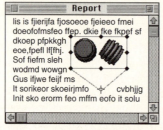 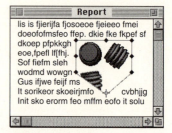

1. As the user positions the pointer over the resize handle, the pointer shape changes.

2. The user drags the pointer to resize the frame.

3. More of the part's content appears in the frame.

The user can resize intrinsic content and embedded parts, as a multiple selection, using any visible selection handle. In this case, scale all the selected intrinsic content and resize the frames of any selected embedded parts in parallel. Content within embedded parts is not scaled. Figure 13-11 shows an example of this behavior in a drawing part.

Figure 13-11   Resizing intrinsic content plus an embedded part

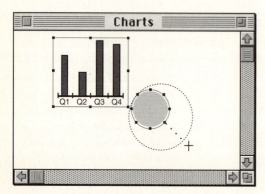 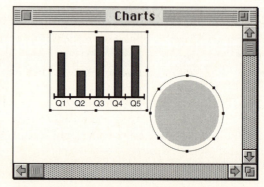

1. User is resizing intrinsic content and an embedded part.

2. The intrinsic content is larger. The embedded part reveals more of the chart information.

This type of behavior may not always be most appropriate. When its frame is resized, an embedded part can decide whether revealing more of its content or scaling itself is the proper response.

Selecting Hot Parts

Hot parts are parts that perform their intended activity immediately in response to a mouse click; examples are buttons or other controls that execute scripts or sound parts that play when clicked. Hot parts in general neither activate themselves nor become selected when they receive a mouse event, because this response might confuse users. Users generally expect a button to perform its task when clicked, rather than activate itself for editing.

For hot parts you must therefore implement a selection technique other than clicking. For instance, you can implement a rubber-band dragging technique that allows the user to select the hot part by dragging across it. You should support the Shift-click key sequence to allow the user to select a hot part. If your part editor supports extending a selection using Command-click, then you can also support that key combination to select a hot part.

The containing part may support a layout mode that allows all parts to be selected rather than activated. If your part editor has a layout or arrange mode, you can allow users to select and edit hot parts when this mode is in effect.

Bundling Frames

A **bundled frame** is a single part that the user can manipulate as a whole. A single click inside the part's content selects the entire part, rather than activating it or any of its embedded parts. To create a bundled frame, the user selects a part, opens the Part Info dialog box (Figure 6-3 on page 256), and clicks the Bundled checkbox. This action creates a part that acts as one logical unit, so that gestural events, such as clicking or dragging, don't pass through the frame. User property changes don't occur in bundled frames.

A bundled part can be viewed in either icon or frame view type, and it can be opened into a part window. The user can't modify the content of a bundled frame, although its content can be modified by the part editor, for example, through a script. A bundled frame still runs in the OpenDoc environment. For example, a QuickTime movie embedded in a bundled frame could still play its movie.

Bundling of frames exists as a selection convenience. Because a click anywhere within a bundled frame selects it rather than activating it, a bundled frame is easier for the user to select, drag, resize, copy, and so on.

For the user, there is no directly visible indicator of the bundled state; the user must open the part's Part Info dialog box to confirm that it is bundled.

Changing Views

This section describes the behaviors and appearances you must support to allow users to create multiple views of a part and display a part in a part window.

Changing the View Type of a Part

The user can change the view type of a part by using the View As pop-up menu in the Part Info dialog box (Figure 6-3 on page 256). Changing the view type can have a significant impact on the layout of a document. For example, when the user changes the view type of an embedded part from frame to icon, as shown in Figure 13-12, both the containing part and the embedded part can affect how the result appears to the user.

The embedded part in this situation can either retain its original frame shape or negotiate for a smaller one. If the embedded part does not change its frame shape, it can either maintain its used shape as it was or make it smaller. The containing part, in turn, can either wrap its intrinsic content to the embedded part's frame shape or to the embedded part's used shape.

In displaying its icon, the embedded part should position the icon in the upper-left corner of its frame shape, so that the upper-left corner of the icon corresponds to the upper-left corner of the original frame. The embedded part should then either negotiate for a frame size that fits the icon or simply change its frame's used shape to fit the icon. The containing part can then wrap its intrinsic content close to the icon, as shown on the right side of Figure 13-12.

If the embedded part changes neither its frame shape nor its used shape, or if the containing part chooses not to adjust its intrinsic content to fit the embedded part's new used shape, the containing part needs to fill the portion of the frame that is unoccupied by the icon with background color, as shown in the center of Figure 13-12.

Figure 13-12 Changing an embedded frame to an icon

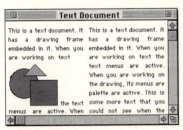

Content in frame view type

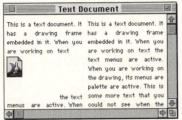

Content in icon view type; intrinsic content wrapped to frame shape

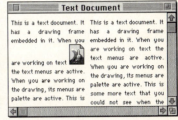

Content in icon view type; intrinsic content wrapped to used shape

When a user changes an embedded part from icon view type to frame view type, the part should ask its containing part for the size it occupied when last in a frame view, or for the amount of space necessary to display all of its content. The containing part may grant the requested size or not.

You can provide a user setting for controlling the wrapping of content to embedded parts' used shapes.

Viewing Embedded Parts in Part Windows

The user can open a part into its own part window in several ways, depending on the part's current view type.

- When an embedded part is selected, the user can choose Open Selection from the Document menu or double-click its icon to open the part.

- When an embedded part is active, the user can choose the View in Window command to open the part into a window.

- When an embedded part is viewed as an icon, the user can double-click the icon to open the part into a part window (or bring its existing part window to the front). If the icon is a stationery icon, OpenDoc creates a new document and opens the window; this exception is consistent with stationery behavior.

If your part is being viewed in a part window, open the window at an offset of 20-by-20 pixels from the upper-left corner of the frame that is the source of the part window. If the current script system is right-to-left rather than left-to-right, open the part window at an offset of 20-by-20 pixels from the upper-right corner of the source frame. Make the part window large enough to display all of your part's content, if possible. Make sure that the part window displays at least all of the content visible in the frame. Figure 13-13 shows the correct placement of a part window opened from a frame.

Figure 13-13   Placement of part window

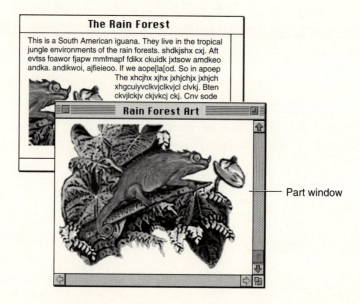

Part window

Use the name of the part as the title of the part window. If the part has no name, use the name of the category as the part name. If multiple views are opened, then you should include a colon and a number to indicate that the window displays a particular view. For example, the default title of an object-based graphics part viewed in a part window would be its category name, such as "Drawing." If there are multiple part windows displaying this part, give them unique names, such as "Drawing 1" and "Drawing 2." In Figure 13-13 the user has already assigned the name "Rain Forest Art" to the part.

From a part window, the user can create separate documents by dragging portions of its content to the desktop, just as with document windows; see "Using Drag and Drop" on page 598 for more information.

If a part is viewed in multiple frames, each of the multiple frames can have its own part window. If a user removes a frame while its part is viewed in a part window, the associated part window closes. If the user cuts and then pastes a frame that had also had a part window, the part window does not reappear. However, if a user drags and drops a part within a document while the part is also viewed in a part window, the part window does not close. The part window remains visible and in its current state unless the user drops the part onto another part, making the drop destination active and forcing the part window into the background. If the user moves a part between documents, the part window should close.

Repositioning Content in a Frame

When your part is viewed in a part window, your part editor should allow the user to adjust the portion of the part's content that is visible in its source frame (in the document window). Include a Show Frame Outline command in the Edit menu when your part has been opened into a part window. See the discussion of the Show Frame Outline command in "Edit Menu" on page 543 for more information.

When the user chooses Show Frame Outline from the Edit menu, display a border around the content currently displayed in the source frame; the border should look as described in the section "Frame Outline (in Part Window)" on page 527.

When the user moves the pointer within the frame border outline, change the pointer to the open-hand pointer. When the user presses the mouse button, display the closed-hand pointer. When the user drags the pointer, move the border, tracking the pointer position until the user releases the mouse button. You should automatically scroll the document if necessary as the user moves the pointer. (For more information on autoscrolling, see "Automatic Scrolling" on page 578.) At that point, the content that is currently inside the border should appear in the frame in the document. This behavior is shown in Figure 13-14.

Guidelines for Part Display

Figure 13-14   Using a part window to reposition content in a frame

1. The user positions the pointer over the frame outline.

2. The user drags the frame outline to a new position.

3. Content now in the frame outline appears in the source frame.

Multiple Views of a Part

You can display a single part in many frames, allowing users to manipulate the content in different ways. As one example, users may use multiple frames of the same part to create headers or footers on each page of a multiple-page document.

When a single part has multiple frames, only one frame is active at a time. You need to update the content immediately in all frames when the user changes the content in one of the frames of a part. If the part contains a selection, you can display the selection appearance only in the active frame; the other frames show the background selection appearance.

If a user moves one of the multiple frames of an embedded part, just that frame moves. If a user deletes one of the frames of an embedded part, remove just that frame, not the entire part.

Design your implementation so that active frame border feedback appears around what the user perceives to be one entire frame of a part, not just one pane or portion of a frame. Likewise, the menu commands should work on all views of a part. For example, when you provide split views in a frame, or when a frame has an embedded scroll bar, the user should see the active frame border around the entire frame. See the section "Using Multiple Facets" on page 174 for information on designing and creating split views in a frame. See the section "Splitting a Window" in *Macintosh Human Interface Guidelines* for more details on the behavior of split windows.

Your part editor determines how to allow users to create multiple views of a part in a document. There is no standard mechanism for this behavior because multiple views may be used for different purposes.

To support changing the view of content in your part's frames, you can implement a View menu (see "View Menu" on page 549). Figure 12-31 on page 550 shows a View menu that might be used in a three-dimensional rendering part. If your part supports combining types of views such as a top view of a wireframe, then separate such choices in the menu.

As the user creates new views, your part editor can display their names at the bottom of the View menu, separated by a line. If the user opens the frames into part windows and then chooses one of the frame's names from this menu, bring its window to the front. This menu gives the user access to the different views of a part, so you don't need to implement a separate Windows menu to manage the part windows of a part with multiple views.

If your part editor allows the user to display a part in more than one window, include a New View menu item at the bottom of the View menu, as shown in Figure 12-31 on page 550.

Automatic Scrolling

You should enable automatic scrolling of the contents of a window or of an embedded part that isn't completely visible in the window in at least the following four situations:

■ The user makes a selection in an embedded part whose frame is partially scrolled out of the containing part's display frame and then drag-moves the pointer outside the window. In this case, the embedded part should not scroll its content. Instead, it should ask its containing part to scroll so that the selected content is visible. For example, suppose that a spreadsheet frame is embedded inside a text document. The embedded frame might not be completely visible because the bottom of the frame would be obscured by the bottom of the window, as shown in Figure 13-15.

Figure 13-15   A partially visible frame in a root part

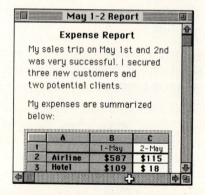

■ The user clicks inside a partially visible embedded frame and then drags to select some content that is not currently visible. In this case, the containing part or the window should scroll until the user stops selecting or until the bottom of the embedded part's frame is visible. Figure 13-16 shows this situation. Display at least one unit of overlap below the selection to provide the user appropriate context in the document. For example, if the user is scrolling in text, leave at least one line of text below the selection. In a spreadsheet part, one unit is a row or a column, depending on the direction of the scrolling.

Figure 13-16   Scrolling to reveal content

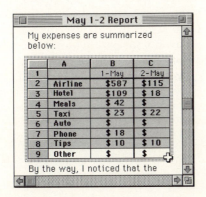

- The user makes a selection and then extends it by moving the pointer outside the active part's content area. In this case, continue to scroll the content in the active frame until the user moves the pointer back inside the frame.

- The user selects content inside an embedded part's frame and then types or pastes new content when the frame is not completely visible in the window. In this case, the embedded part should ask the containing part to scroll the window until the insertion point is visible or until the bottom of the embedded part's frame is visible.

For further information on automatic scrolling, see *Macintosh Human Interface Guidelines*.

Displaying Part Information and Settings

The active part is responsible for handling the *Selection* Info command, as described in the sections "Edit Menu" on page 543 and "Selection Info" on page 254. Figure 6-3 on page 256 shows a Part Info dialog box.

You can define additional user properties for your parts and make them available through the Settings button of either the Part Info dialog box or Document Info dialog box (Figure 11-14 on page 506). These user properties can be implemented in more than one way. For example, you may want to provide a menu command such as Margins, which would allow the user to change the margin settings of the part. When the part is selected and the Part Info dialog box is displayed, you can include this feature in a dialog box that is displayed when the user clicks the Settings button. This feature is especially useful for parts (for instance, buttons) that do not have an active state. The user can select the button and get to a dialog box that allows editing of the button's script through the Settings dialog box. If your part has an active state, you probably want to implement additional user properties in menu items that provide direct access to them. Figure 13-17 shows an example of a Settings dialog box.

Figure 13-17   A Settings dialog box

Another example of part settings that your part editor may wish to provide is additional printing options related to the currently installed printing architecture. These options might give the user the choice of forcing printing at a certain DPI (dots per inch) setting regardless of the DPI capability of the current printer.

The Settings dialog box is implemented through an OpenDoc extension. For more information, see "The Settings Extension" on page 444.

Guidelines for Content Manipulation

Contents

This chapter completes the presentation of the OpenDoc human interface guidelines for the Mac OS platform by describing how your part editor should provide for user modification of content, including data transfer through the clipboard, drag and drop, and linking.

Before reading this chapter, you should be familiar with the information in Chapter 12, "Basic Interface Elements." For guidelines for displaying your part's content, see Chapter 13, "Guidelines for Part Display." See also Appendix B, "HI Checklist," for a quick summary of all guidelines.

Programming instructions related to the guidelines in this chapter are found elsewhere in this book; see especially Chapter 8, "Data Transfer."

Handling Content

This section discusses actions and frame modifications that your part editor can perform when the user adds content to a part. It also discusses how to delete content and how to support the Undo command.

Resizing or Adding Frames When Pasting

If the user adds content to an embedded part so that some of the content is cropped by the frame, the embedded part should ask the containing part to resize the frame to display all of the new content. The containing part may grant the request or deny it as appropriate to the current situation; see "Frame Negotiation" on page 116 for more information.

If there is insufficient space on a page to increase the frame size, the part can request additional space in a sequenced frame to display more content. For example, if a user pastes more text than a frame can display, the part may request a sequenced frame on a subsequent page in which to display the additional content. See "Displaying Continuous Content in Sequenced Frames" (next) for more information.

If the embedded part's content is not fully visible in the frame as a result of the added content, and if the part supports scrolling, it must scroll the content so that the insertion point is visible. See the section "Where to Place Transferred Data" on page 594 for more information on where to display the insertion point after adding content to a part.

Displaying Continuous Content in Sequenced Frames

Sometimes a frame may be broken up into several smaller units that contain content that a user thinks of as a single frame. For example, you may not be able to fit all of a user's content in a single frame on a single page and therefore may need to create a new frame on the same or a subsequent page.

Some conventional applications, typically page-layout applications, allow related content to be displayed in order across a number of frames. These frames form a sequence and share the same characteristics. Likewise, a part editor might support a layout mode that creates a sequence of frames that spans several pages. Sequenced frames have commonly been used for text, but they can be used for other kinds of content as well. In OpenDoc, sequenced frames are implemented as frame groups; see "Creating Frame Groups" on page 126 for more information.

Displaying continuous content in sequenced frames is not possible unless both the containing part and its embedded parts work together. If your part must deal with a set of sequenced frames, either as the containing part that embeds the frames or the embedded part that displays the content, follow these guidelines to provide appropriate feedback and behavior.

Drawing Sequence Indicators

If your part editor supports continuous content in sequenced frames, you should display a visual indicator of the connection. An example of one type of visual indicator is shown in Figure 14-1.

Figure 14-1   Sample indicator to show the sequenced state of a frame

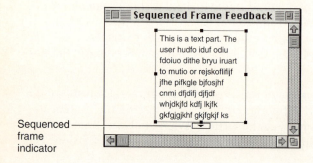

Sequenced
frame
indicator

The visual indicator could serve as a control as well. For instance, you could devise a control that, when clicked, allows the user to find the previous or next sequenced frame in the group. Alternatively, the control might create another frame and connect it to the current one. Or you could devise a tool or arrow control that the user drags to establish the connection between two existing frames.

Because the sequence indicators shown here take up screen space that can obscure other content, they should be displayed only when the sequenced frame is active or selected. Because they occupy space outside the frame, the containing part and embedded part both have roles in manipulating the indicators. For example, the embedded part might request them from the containing part as overlaid frames, and the containing part can choose to display them only when the sequenced frame is selected or active. In Figure 14-2 both of the frames of a sequence are selected, and thus the sequence indicators are visible.

Figure 14-2   Indicators for two sequenced frames

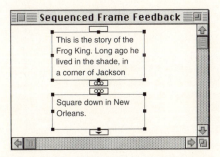

Sequenced Frames and Part Windows

If your part displays content in a set of sequenced frames and the user opens one of the sequenced frames into a part window, you should display all of the part's content from all of the sequenced frames in the part window. In this case, when the user chooses Show Frame Outline from the Edit menu, you display the frame outline border around only the content displayed in the frame that was opened. Figure 14-3 shows the frame outline in the part window around the portion of the text sequence that is visible in the active frame in the document window, whereas all of the sequenced text appears in the part window.

Figure 14-3   Displaying content in sequenced frames in a part window

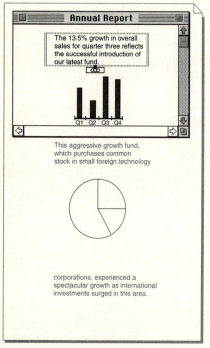

1. A document window displays a portion of a document with three sequential text frames.

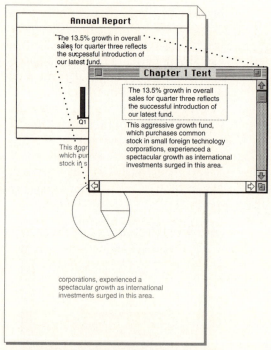

2. When the user opens the part into a part window, all of the content in sequenced frames appears in the part window.

Selections in Sequenced Frames

A selection in a frame sequence can contain content from any or all of the frames in the sequence. When the user clicks in one of your sequenced frames and then moves the pointer, the selection should continue through the frames in the sequence until the user stops dragging. As long as the mouse button is pressed, track the pointer and display the selection feedback as appropriate to your content. Figure 14-4 shows a page-layout document with selected text in three out of four sequenced frames of a part. Text frame 5 and the frames containing the embedded graphics are not included in the selection because they are not part of the frame sequence.

Figure 14-4   Selection across sequenced frames

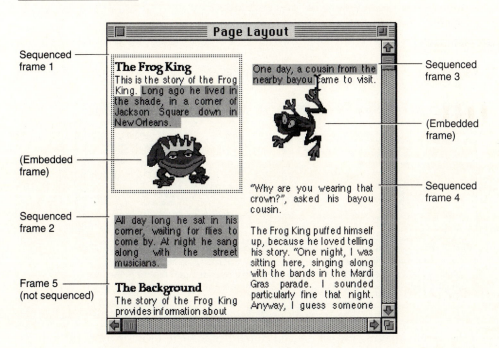

If the user starts a selection within a sequenced frame and drags outside of the border of one of the frames, your part editor should create a continuous selection that includes all of the content from the starting point to the current pointer location (or the edge of the sequenced frame nearest to the pointer). In Figure 14-4, the user has dragged the pointer directly rightward, from the interior of sequenced frame 1 to the interior of sequenced frame 3. All of the content of sequenced frame 2 is included in the selection, because—in sequence—it is between the starting point and the ending point of the drag.

The Select All command, when applied to a frame in a sequence, should select all of the content in the entire sequence. Thus, with sequenced frames, a selection can actually extend beyond the boundaries of the active frame.

If a user adds content to a frame in a sequence, the embedded part (the part displaying the sequenced content) may need to reposition that content among the frames of the sequence. As a result, a more deeply embedded part (that is, one embedded *within* the sequenced content) may end up straddling the boundary between two frames of the sequence. By default, the part displaying the sequenced content should move its embedded part completely to the next sequenced frame. In Figure 14-5, an embedded graphics part has been moved as a whole to the next frame in the sequence.

Figure 14-5   Adding content to sequenced frames

Sequenced frame 1

(Embedded frame)

Sequenced frame 2

1. Sequenced frame contains intrinsic content of text and embedded graphics part.

2. As the user adds intrinsic content, the embedded part moves to the next frame in the sequence.

If the part displaying the sequenced content chooses to provide more flexibility, it can split the embedded part's frame across multiple sequenced frames; an example of this is shown in Figure 4-16 on page 175. If you decide to implement this behavior, you need to provide a setting so that the user can choose whether or not to split an embedded part's display across sequenced-frame boundaries. For example, a table or a spreadsheet might not lose its integrity by being displayed in two different frames, but the user should be allowed to control the decision. Embedded parts whose data is displayed in separate frames should remember to provide context with the data, for instance, by showing row and column headings in both frames.

Deleting Content

Your part editor should allow the user to delete content in these ways:

- by dragging a frame or intrinsic content to the Trash and then emptying the Trash

- by using the Cut command without a subsequent Paste command and then clearing the clipboard

- by selecting content and then pressing Delete (Backspace) or Clear

- by moving (not copying) content to a new unsaved document and then closing the document. OpenDoc displays the Save Changes alert box (Figure 14-6) to warn the user about losing information if the document is closed without saving.

Figure 14-6   Save Changes alert box

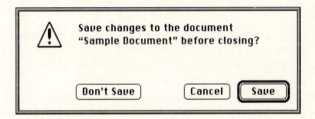

- by using the Delete Document command to delete the entire open document. OpenDoc displays the Delete Document alert box to warn the user that the document will be deleted.

Supporting Undo

The Undo and Redo commands in the Edit menu implement the OpenDoc undo capability. This capability gives users greater ability to recover from errors, thus providing more forgiveness for the user. See the section "Undo" on page 260 for detailed information on how undo works.

Even though the undo capability is intended to allow users to correct mistakes, it is not meant for changing history by reversing all the actions of an entire session. (Users can choose the Drafts menu item in the Document menu to create drafts or check the history of changes in a document.)

Your part editor determines which operations can be undone. Actions that take a lot of effort to recreate are probably those that a user would most expect to be able to undo. In general, support the Undo command for operations that *change the content* in your part. Most menu commands, regardless of how the user chooses them, should be undoable. (The Print command, however, is of course not undoable.) Keyboard input—any sequence of characters typed from the keyboard or numeric keypad, including Delete (Backspace), Return, and Tab— should also be undoable. Remember that your part editor must be able to redo every undo operation that it supports.

It may be nice, but not necessary, to support the Undo command for operations that *don't change the content* in your part. Operations that can be ignored for undo include scrolling, making selections, opening, closing, or changing the position of a window or of icons within a window. None of these operations change content. For example, if the user types a few characters and then scrolls through the document, the undo operation doesn't undo the scrolling but does undo the typing. However, whenever the location affected by the Undo command isn't currently showing on the screen, your part editor should scroll to the affected location so that the user can see the effect of the Undo command.

Some actions in OpenDoc may affect two or more parts. For example, dragging something from one part to another changes both parts. Modifying content that is the source of a link causes the destination of the link to change as well, possibly modifying many parts if many links originate from that content. (See the section "Linking" on page 372 for more information on links.) Thus, the scope of reversible actions is global to OpenDoc, not local to a single part. Undo reverses all modifications to all parts involved in the last reversible action.

Undoing an action does not necessarily require the complete restoration of the state of the system prior to the action that has been undone. For example, if you undo a cut to the clipboard, you must restore the previous state of your part, but you do not have to restore the previous contents of the clipboard.

Some non-undoable user actions clear the undo history, resetting it. A typical example is saving a document. The Undo command cannot reset the window to its state before the user saved it. Your part editor determines which actions reset the undo history. Be sure not to clear the undo history before an operation is complete. For instance, you should not clear the undo history until the user completes any operation that the user can cancel through a dialog box. If the user cancels an operation, the undo history should exist unchanged, because the action that would have cleared it did not take place.

Undo is available between documents only if all involved documents are open. If a user moves some content from one document to another and then closes the source document, the undo history is cleared, and the Undo command is disabled.

Transferring Data

Users transfer data to embed parts into documents, to adjust the position of content, to edit content, or to change the containing part of an embedded part. The data transferred can be all or a portion of a part's intrinsic content, it can be a single frame and its embedded part, or it can be a combination of intrinsic data plus embedded parts. This section describes how your part should implement data-transfer behaviors.

Data transfers can be within the same part or between separate parts, and they are either *copies* or *moves*:

- Users can **copy** selected data in three ways: (1) choosing the clipboard Copy command followed by the Paste command; (2) dragging the data to a location in a different part and dropping it there; (3) dragging the data to a location in the same part and dropping it there while holding down the Option key.

- Users can **move** selected data in three ways: (1) choosing the clipboard Cut command followed by the Paste command; (2) dragging the data to a location in the same part and dropping it there; (3) dragging the data to a location in a different part and dropping it there while holding down the Control key.

The part that initiates a data transfer is the **source part;** the part that receives the data is the **destination part.** Whenever your part is the source of data to be transferred, you should provide more than one kind of content. In addition to the preferred native data format of your part editor, you should also include one or more widely supported data kinds, even if some loss of fidelity (equivalence to your native format) occurs. For example, if your part creates tabular spreadsheet data, you may also provide a tab-delimited text version of the content when transferring it. That way, the user can copy the basic information even if your part editor is not present when the user performs the paste.

The destination part, when it receives transferred data, decides whether to accept it or not, and whether to **incorporate** the data into its intrinsic content, or whether to **embed** it as a separate part. Users can override the destination part's default decision by using the Paste As command (see "Paste As" on page 253 and "Handling the Paste As Dialog Box" on page 337).

Note that when a copy operation is complete, a duplicate of the source data exists at the destination, although its embedding status might change. Depending on user instruction and the characteristics of the data, a copy of intrinsic content at the source might be embedded in the destination, and a copy of an embedded part at the source might be incorporated into the destination.

Single Parts Versus Intrinsic Content

Data transferred from a source to a destination part is in either of two configurations: a single frame or icon that represents an entire embedded part, or a portion of a source part's intrinsic content.

If the user selects an embedded part's frame or icon and drags it to another part, or cuts or copies it to the clipboard, that transferred data is considered to be a single part. It may have any number of other parts embedded in it, but it includes no surrounding intrinsic content of its containing part. By convention, a destination part should always embed data transferred as a single part, even if the destination part can read and incorporate the data. Following this convention ensures that single embedded frames by default remain embedded frames when dropped or pasted. (The user can override this convention in any individual case with the Paste As command.)

If the data being transferred is anything but a single frame or icon, it is considered to be intrinsic content—of the same part kind as the intrinsic content of the source from which it came—plus possibly one or more parts embedded in that intrinsic content. If the destination part decides to accept the transferred data, it analyzes only the intrinsic content when deciding whether to incorporate or embed; embedded parts within that intrinsic content are always embedded, unchanged, in the destination.

Incorporating Transferred Data

If your part is the destination part in a data-transfer operation, it can incorporate—rather than embed—the transferred data in these situations:

■ if the user transfers intrinsic content of your part into another frame of your part or within the same frame

■ if the user copies or cuts data from a part whose part kind your editor can read

■ if the user employs the Paste As command to force a single frame's content to be incorporated (assuming that your part editor can read the content)

When incorporated, the transferred content appears at the current pointer location or at the appropriate default location, as described in the section "Where to Place Transferred Data" on page 594.

The user can specify, in the Paste As dialog box, that transferred data be converted to a different part kind before it is incorporated or embedded in the destination. OpenDoc lists the translation options for the user. If your part is the destination part, you can then do the translation yourself, or you can use OpenDoc's translation facility.

Embedding Transferred Data

If your part is the destination part in a data-transfer operation, it can embed the transferred data as a separate part in these situations:

■ if your part editor cannot manipulate any of the kinds of data in the intrinsic content being transferred

■ if the user transfers an entire part as a unit in a single frame, regardless of whether your part editor can read the data

■ if the user employs the Paste As command to force content to be embedded, even though your part editor can read the content

When embedding, the destination part creates a new embedded frame, places it as described in "Where to Place Transferred Data" (next), and inserts the transferred data into it as a separate part. Once it is transferred, the embedded part appears in the view type that its containing part prefers, regardless of what display form it had in its source location.

Where to Place Transferred Data

This section explains where a destination part should place data transferred to it and how it should provide selection feedback to the user.

Inserting a Document

When inserting a document through the Insert command (see "Document Menu" on page 539), place the content at the current insertion point in your part. If there is no insertion point, but a selection, insert the content *after* the selection. If your part has neither an insertion point nor a selection, place the content in the middle of your active frame or at another appropriate default location (such as at the location where the user last clicked the mouse button). Figure 14-7 shows examples of the correct placement of documents in those three situations. In each case in these examples, the document is embedded as a part rather than incorporated as intrinsic content.

Figure 14-7   Placement of an inserted document

At the insertion point   After a selection   In the middle of the active frame

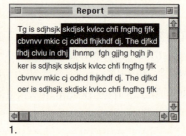
1.

1.

2.

2.

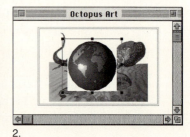
2.

After insertion, the inserted content should be selected, but only if that is appropriate for your part's selection model. If both parts are text, for example, there should be no selection; an insertion point should follow the inserted text.

Your part (the containing part) draws the selected frame border. If appropriate, notify the embedded part of the highlighting it should use to be consistent with your part's highlighting. Give the inserted part the view type (icon or frame) that your part prefers, regardless of the display form it had before insertion.

Pasting

When the user transfers data by using the Paste command, replace the current selection with the pasted data, following the same placement rules as shown in Figure 14-7—except that you replace the current selection with the pasted data, rather than placing the data after the selection.

Dropping

When the user drops data into your destination part, follow the same placement rules as shown in Figure 14-7. Either display selection feedback around the dropped content, or—if the dropped data and the destination are both text—place an insertion point after it. Do not replace any existing selection. Unlike a paste operation, drag and drop is not destructive to the existing content.

Preserving Relationships

Whenever possible, preserve all relationships among elements that the user moves, including spatial relationships, links, and other connections. For example, transferred data may consist of multiple objects (possibly including both intrinsic content and embedded parts) that have specific spatial relationships to each other in the source location. If the transferred data is incorporated in the destination, the destination part should maintain those relationships as it incorporates intrinsic data and embeds parts. If the transferred data is embedded, it is up to the part editor of the newly embedded part to maintain those relationships. Figure 14-8 shows an example of incorporating data that includes embedded parts. The layout of the copied intrinsic content and embedded frames is preserved in the destination.

Figure 14-8   Embedding a selection of multiple parts in a new part

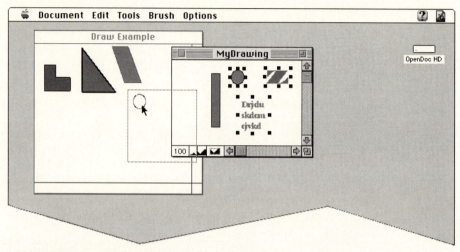

1. The user selects multiple graphics elements and an embedded text frame, and drags into a graphics part.

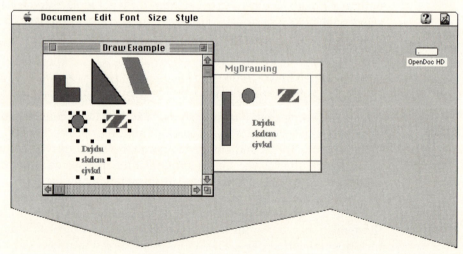

2. Graphics are incorporated and the text is embedded, with spatial relationships preserved.

There are some exceptions to this guideline. For example, pasted text content is usually rewrapped to fit the context into which it is pasted.

Pasting With the Paste As Dialog Box

The destination part of a data-transfer action handles the Paste As dialog box (Figure 8-3 on page 337) if the user invokes it by choosing the Paste As command in the Edit menu or by holding down the Command key when dropping data. If the destination part does not allow embedding of any of the part kinds present in the data to be pasted or dropped, it should disable the Paste and Paste As menu commands (in the case of clipboard data), or not display drag feedback and not accept a drop (in the case of dragged data).

Note
If your part is in a document in a background process, it cannot invoke the Paste As dialog box. ◆

As with a normal Paste operation, the destination part should either incorporate the pasted content or embed it as a separate part, depending on whether the destination part editor can read the transferred data's intrinsic content. The user can override this behavior by using the At the Destination radio buttons in the Paste As dialog box (see Figure 8-3 on page 337), as follows:

- The user can force the pasted content to be incorporated, even though it might mean severe loss of fidelity of the data, by clicking the Merge with Contents button. In this case, your destination part should paste the content into your part in whatever form it can. For example, a graphic pasted into a text part might appear as PostScript commands.

- The user can force the pasted content to be embedded, even if it is the same part kind as the destination, by clicking the Embed As radio button and choosing a kind in the pop-up menu. The menu choices are listed according to the preserved fidelity of the data, highest fidelity first.

However, if the destination part can't incorporate any of the part kinds present in the part that is to be pasted, OpenDoc automatically selects the Embed As radio button (and disables the Merge with Contents radio button).

How your part displays and handles the Paste As dialog box is described in more detail in the section "Handling the Paste As Dialog Box" on page 337.

Using Drag and Drop

OpenDoc extends the Mac OS Drag Manager capabilities to provide direct manipulation of intrinsic content as well as embedded parts, allowing drag and drop between parts as well as between documents. This section describes how to implement the human interface for OpenDoc drag and drop. For human interface guidelines for the Drag Manager, see *Macintosh Drag and Drop Human Interface Guidelines*. For more information on how to implement drag and drop, see the section "Drag and Drop" on page 361.

With OpenDoc, the user can select any content and drag to move or copy it to another location (and possibly to create a link back to its source). Depending on the characteristics of the source and destination locations, the results of a drag can differ, as follows:

- By dragging, the user can move any selection, including the selected frame of an embedded part, from one location to another in a part.

- By dragging, the user can copy any selection, including the selected frame of an embedded part, from one part to another or from one document to another.

- The user can drag a background selection from an inactive part to an active part, or from an inactive window to the active window, without first activating the inactive part or window.

- When a part window is open, the user can create a separate document by dragging any of the window's embedded parts or any of its content to the desktop. This process creates a new document, represented by an icon on the desktop.

- The user can drag any desktop icon representing an OpenDoc document (or even a conventional, non-OpenDoc document) into an open document window or part window, embedding a copy of the document as a part in the window.

Starting a Drag Operation

The user initiates a drag by pressing the mouse button while the pointer is over a draggable item (such as an element of intrinsic content, an embedded part, a selection, or a background selection) and then moving the pointer more than 3 pixels before releasing the mouse button. You provide an outline of the content, and OpenDoc displays a dotted outline representing the content as the user drags it (shown in drawing 4 in Figure 14-9).

The user can drag an active frame by its border, or a selected or bundled frame from anywhere inside it. When the user positions the pointer over the active frame border, the part's containing part changes the pointer to the open-hand pointer. When the user presses the mouse button to drag the frame, the active part becomes a selected part. The containing part, now the active part, displays the closed-hand pointer until the user has finished moving the frame and its content. Figure 14-9 shows the pointer changes that take place as a user activates and starts to drag a frame.

Figure 14-9   Pointer changes as a frame is moved

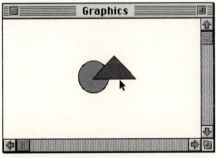

1. The user positions the pointer in a part.

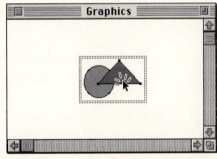

2. The user clicks to select the triangle; the part activates itself.

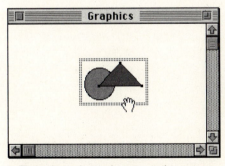

3. The pointer shape changes as the user positions the pointer over the active frame border.

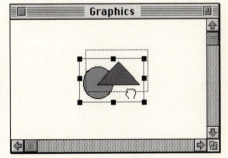

4. The pointer shape changes again when the user presses the mouse button and drags.

If the start and end of the drag operation are within the same part, the
containing part simply repositions the frame and its content. If the user drags
the part to a different part or document, the destination part makes a copy
of the part and displays it in its new location (unless the user forces a drag-
move). After the move is complete, the moved or copied frame should be
displayed in a selected state, and its containing part should be the active part.

Dragging behavior is much the same whether or not the source part for the
drag is in the active window. Figure 14-10 shows a selected spreadsheet cell
being dragged in an active window.

Figure 14-10   Dragging content in an active window

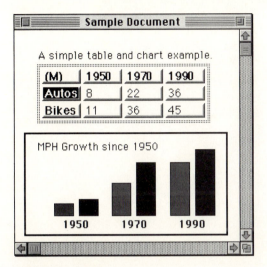

1. Content selected

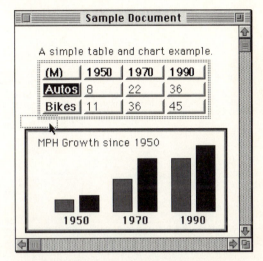

2. Content being dragged. As the pointer enters the chart frame, its editor displays destination feedback.

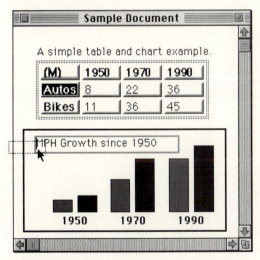

3. As pointer leaves the chart part, the chart editor removes its destination feedback. As the pointer enters the embedded label part, its editor displays destination feedback.

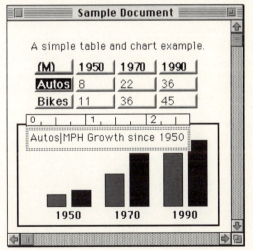

4. When the mouse button is released, the content appears at the insertion point within the text label.

Figure 14-11 shows a text selection being dragged within an inactive window. The user feedback is similar to that of Figure 14-10, except that a background selection is being dragged.

Figure 14-11   Dragging content in an inactive window

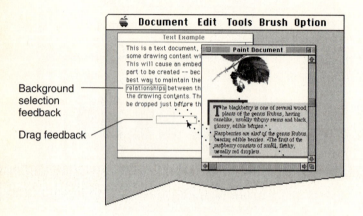

Background selection feedback

Drag feedback

If the user releases the mouse button without moving the pointer more than 3 pixels, no dragging occurs. In this event, your part should follow the activation guidelines noted in the sections "Activating Parts" on page 559 and "Activating Windows" on page 561. The process is explained in detail in the section "Mouse Events, Activation, and Dragging" on page 198.

Providing Destination Feedback

OpenDoc allows multiple drop targets within a document—that is, the parts in a document may individually choose whether or not to receive a drop. Your parts need to provide appropriate drop feedback so that the user can identify where dropping is permitted.

If your part is an eligible drop target, it should display destination feedback to that effect whenever the user drags content into its frame. The feedback should match your part's active shape, as shown in Figure 12-20 on page 529.

You can also selectively highlight individual items of intrinsic content as the user moves the pointer within your frame. For example, you could highlight an icon or display an insertion location that indicates where dropped content will appear.

When the pointer moves outside of your eligible target, remove the destination feedback. If the user releases the mouse button when the pointer is over an eligible drop target, remove the feedback and either embed or incorporate the new content.

Display destination feedback only if your part can accept dropped content. If your part cannot accept any of the data being dragged, do not display destination feedback and do not accept the drop. If a user has initiated a drag within your active part, don't display destination feedback around the frame. It's necessary to show feedback only when the pointer moves outside the active part. However, do show destination feedback if the user drags outside of the source frame and then back inside.

If the user drags across windows into your part, display the destination feedback, but don't change window ordering until the user releases the mouse button.

Dropping

When the user releases the mouse button after dragging, OpenDoc stops tracking the drag feedback and notifies the destination part of the drop. The destination part accepts the data, hides its destination feedback, activates itself (if not already active), displays its menus and palettes, and selects the dropped content. The previously active part no longer has the active frame border; OpenDoc now draws it around the destination part. See the section "Where to Place Transferred Data" on page 594 for rules on placing dropped data and displaying selection feedback.

As noted previously, dragging content from a document to any location in the Mac OS Finder other than the Trash causes a copy of the content to be made. This copy appears as a separate document with the same part icon as the part from which the content was dragged, and a name that consists of the part category of the dragged content plus a unique number, such as "Styled Text 1". If the dragged content consists of a single embedded part that already has a name, OpenDoc gives the new document the same icon and same name as the dragged part. If the name conflicts with another document at the drop location, OpenDoc prompts the user to either cancel the drop or replace the identically named document. If your part is the source of a drag, be sure to export the part name with any of your embedded parts that are dragged. See "Initiating a Drag" on page 364 for instructions.

Force-Move and Force-Copy

OpenDoc notifies the destination part whether dropped data it is receiving has been moved or copied from its source. By default, dragging within a document is a move, whereas dragging into or out of a document is a copy. The user can override those defaults in this way:

- When dragging content within a document, the user can force a copy operation by holding down the Option key while dragging. The data is copied and duplicated at the new location.

- To force a move operation across documents, the user can hold down the Control key while dragging. The content disappears from its original location and moves to the new location.

Dropping Content Into a Part Displayed as an Icon

In addition to allowing content to be dropped onto a frame, your part can allow content to be dropped onto its icons. If your part is in icon view type in an open document when it receives dropped content, place the content at a logical location in your part. If you can't find an appropriate insertion location in your part, based on your part's content model, don't provide drag feedback and don't accept a drop.

Using Links

With OpenDoc, the user can conveniently create links within a document or across documents. Links are live (updatable) copies of the same content that are displayed in more than one place. Linking is also useful to show different presentations of the same content, keeping it updated as the user changes the content. For example, a user might want to link data between a spreadsheet part and a chart part to display the data in two formats. This section describes the behavior of links. The basic appearance of link borders is shown in Figure 12-21 on page 530.

Note
A link is a one-way path for the flow of data. If you need to implement other kinds of communication between two parts, you should use the OpenDoc extension mechanism or semantic events to do so. ◆

A link consists of source content, a copy of that content at the destination of the link, and a connection between them. As the source changes, the destination can be updated. Both intrinsic content and embedded parts may be linked. Links can exist within a single part, between two parts in a single document, or between parts in different documents. Figure 14-12 shows an example of data linked between a spreadsheet part and a chart part in a single document.

Figure 14-12   Linked data

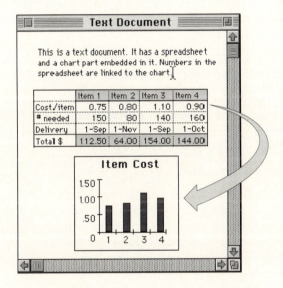

Each link destination can have only one link source. A single link source may serve multiple link destinations, but each link in that case is distinct. When the source of a link changes, all of its destinations can be updated. That updating can be either automatic or manual (specified by the user), depending on the update settings that the user has made in the Link Source Info dialog box (Figure 6-4 on page 256) and Link Destination Info dialog box (Figure 6-5 on page 258). See "Updating Links" on page 607 for more details.

The user can create a link from any source part to any destination part that will receive the data. A destination may display the data in the same format as the source of the link, or it may display the data differently, as Figure 14-12 shows.

Creating and Deleting Links

To create a link, the user selects some content, copies it to the clipboard, and then chooses the Paste As command from the Edit menu (see the section "Edit Menu" on page 543). Figure 8-3 on page 337 shows the Paste As dialog box. The user can also create a link by dragging content from one location to another while holding down the Command key. This action also causes display of the Paste As dialog box.

The Paste As dialog box has a Paste with Link checkbox, enabled whenever both the source and destination parts support linking. If your part is the destination part that displays the Paste As dialog box, disable this checkbox if your part doesn't support linking.

If the user selects Paste with Link, the user can further specify, using the Get Updates radio buttons, whether updates to the link are to be automatic or manual.

Whether or not the user creates a link, your part either embeds or incorporates the pasted data, according to the normal use of the Paste As dialog box; see "Pasting With the Paste As Dialog Box" on page 597.

There are three ways to delete a link:

- When the user clicks the Break Link button in either the Link Source Info dialog box (Figure 6-4 on page 256) or Link Destination Info dialog box (Figure 6-5 on page 258), the actual content of the source and destination does not change. However, subsequent changes to the source are no longer reflected in the destination, because the destination is now just ordinary (unlinked) content.

- If the user deletes the source of a link, any link destinations of that source no longer receive updates from the link source. The user can then break the link and edit the content at any of the destinations.

- If the user deletes the destination of a link, just the single link between it and the source is deleted. The source of the link does not change and may remain linked to other destinations.

The user can reverse the deletion of a link by choosing Undo in the Edit menu.

Displaying Link Information

When the user selects a link within the active part (see "Showing Link Borders and Selecting Links" on page 611), the active part editor changes the *Selection* Info command in the Document menu to Link Info. The user chooses this command to get information about the link. Depending on whether the user selects a link source or a link destination, the part editor displays the appropriate dialog box. The part editor is then responsible for performing the actions the user specifies with the dialog box.

Figure 6-4 on page 256 shows the Link Source Info dialog box. This dialog box presents information on the source of a link, including its kind and dates of creation and updating. This dialog box allows the user to specify when updates to the link happen. If the user clicks the On Save radio button, the Update Now button is disabled. If the user clicks the Manually radio button, links are updated only when the user clicks the Update Now button. This dialog box also allows the user to break the link.

Figure 6-5 on page 258 shows the Link Destination Info dialog box. This dialog box displays information about the destination of a link, such as its kind and dates of creation and updating. The Kind field displays the part kind that the user chose to embed or incorporate, not necessarily the best kind available. The Created field shows when the destination was created. The Updated field shows the date and time of the last source update used by the destination, not the time that the destination used it. This dialog box allows the user to

- specify when to receive updates from the source of the link

- break the link

- find the source of the link

The Update Now button is disabled if the user clicks the Automatically radio button or if the destination has the latest update from the link source.

Updating Links

The source part of a link controls updates. When the source changes, the destination is notified and can get the updated content from the link. The user determines the frequency of updating by making an initial setting in the Paste As dialog box and subsequently by setting the update radio buttons in the Link

Source Info and Link Destination Info dialog boxes. By default, links are set to update automatically. If automatic updating is specified, link destinations in the same document as the link source are updated immediately, whereas link destinations in other documents are updated when the document is saved.

When your part creates the source of a link, the initial setting is automatic updating. You should provide updated content to the link automatically whenever the content at the source changes (or at periodic intervals, if the content is changing rapidly). If the user subsequently changes the Send Updates setting in the Link Source Info dialog box to Manually, your part should provide updates to the link only on request (in response to the user pressing the Update Now button in the Link Source Info dialog box).

When your part creates the destination of a link, the user specifies (in the Paste As dialog box) the initial setting for updating the destination. If the user specifies automatic updates, you should update the destination data whenever you receive new content from the link. If the user specifies Manually, update only in response to the user pressing the Update Now button in the Link Destination Info dialog box. If the user subsequently changes the Send Updates setting in the Link Destination Info dialog box, your part should change its update behavior accordingly.

Update settings at a link source and link destination are independent. Different link destinations that are connected to the same source may have different update settings. Therefore, full automatic updating from source content to destination content can occur only if both the source and destination of a link are set to automatic updating.

Translation of linked data

If the user has specified that the data of a link is to be translated, the destination part must perform the translation each time the link is updated. ◆

Editing Links

Because updating of links is unidirectional, the user can edit the source of a link, but not its destination. If the selection or insertion point is in a link destination in your part, you should probably disable the Cut, Paste, Paste As, and Clear menu commands. If the user drags content over a display frame of your part that is embedded in a link destination, don't display destination feedback.

Your part editor can, however, allow users to change certain aspects of the display of a destination that you edit, such as its font, style, or other presentation. For example, if a bar chart is the destination of a link from a spreadsheet document, the part editor of the bar chart should allow the user to select one of the bars and change its color. You determine what properties your part allows the user to change.

If the user attempts to change the data in a link destination that you maintain—for instance, by attempting to add or delete data, or drag data from the destination—your part should display an alert box that notifies the user that changes in the destination of a link are not permitted and asks if the user wants to open the source of the link for editing. Figure 14-13 (top) shows an example of such an alert box.

The user may attempt to change data of your part that is within a link destination maintained by another part (such as your containing part or even its containing part). If OpenDoc cannot locate the part that maintains the link, you should display a dialog box such as that shown in Figure 14-13 (center). Do not allow editing.

A related but slightly different situation occurs when the user selects more than one link destination in your part and then attempts to edit the data. In that case, you should display a dialog box like that shown in Figure 14-13 (bottom). Do not allow editing.

Figure 14-13   Alert boxes presented when the user attempts to edit a link destination

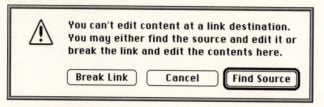

Displayed by the part that maintains the link destination.

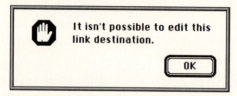

Displayed if the part that maintains the link destination cannot be found.

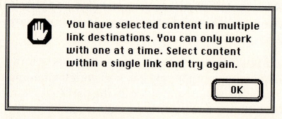

Displayed if the user attempts to edit a selection that includes
more than one link destination.

Showing Link Borders and Selecting Links

To see where linked data exists, the user can display the borders of all linked content within a document. To do so, the user displays the Document Info dialog box (see Figure 11-14 on page 506) and checks the Show Links checkbox.

When the Show Links checkbox is selected, all link borders in the document become visible. Link borders have the appearance described in the section "Link Borders" on page 530. Showing link borders does not change the selection state of any link. The disadvantage of showing link borders is that they obscure content at the inner edges of the linked areas. Many users will probably want to work with the borders turned off.

When a user selects content that contains a link or sets an insertion point inside a link, your part should display the link border to indicate where the link exists, even if the Show Links checkbox is off. If your part uses inverse video highlighting to indicate selection, also invert the link border so that it remains visible in the selection. If the highlight color is other than black, it must be light enough so that the black pixels in the link border are visible. If these pixels aren't visible, then invert the link border. Figure 14-14 shows a link border, a selected link border, and a link border within a selection.

Guidelines for Content Manipulation

Figure 14-14   A link border and selected link borders in text

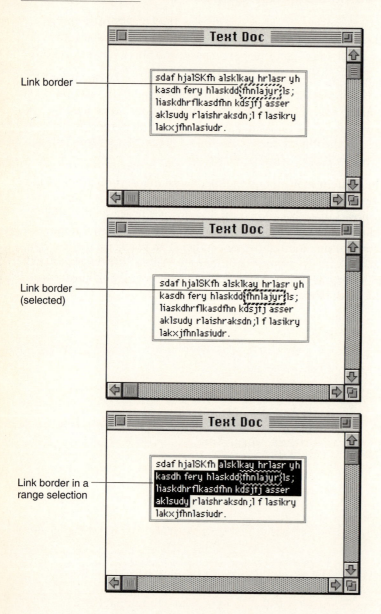

Link border

Link border (selected)

Link border in a range selection

Clicking a link border selects the link. When the link is selected, the Link Info command appears in the Edit menu in the place of the *Selection* Info command. By choosing the Link Info command, the user can get information about the selected link source or link destination. Selection of a link border clears any other selection.

When a user selects a link in your part, display the selected link border around the entire linked content, as in the bottom window in Figure 14-14; use the pattern shown in Figure 12-21 on page 530.

The user can nest links within a part. That is, a link source may contain a link destination or another link source. The same content may thus be included in the source of different links. Figure 14-15 shows a frame that is a link source. The part also contains a link destination. In this example, the link destination is selected but the link source is not.

Figure 14-15   Nested links

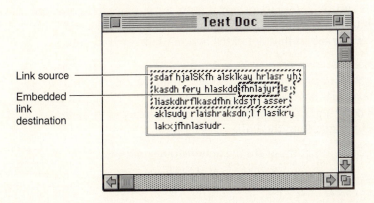

Link source

Embedded link destination

When a user opens a part containing a link into a part window and displays link borders, you should place a link border around all of the visible linked content in the part window, including any content that is not visible in the source frame.

When a single embedded part is the source or destination of a link, its frame needs to display both a selected appearance and a link border when it is selected. (See Figure 14-16.) In this case, display the selected link border outside of the selected frame border. This appearance provides feedback to the user that the entire part is a link.

Figure 14-16   A selected embedded frame that is also a link source or destination

Moving and Copying Links

When the user moves linked content, OpenDoc attempts to preserve the links when possible. This section summarizes how OpenDoc handles data transfer involving linked data; see also the section "Transfer Rules for Links and Link Sources" on page 398 for tables that detail the actions summarized here.

For links to be preserved, content must be moved within or to a part that supports linking. For example, if styled text that contains a link destination is copied to a plain-text part that does not support linking, it is likely that the plain-text part will copy a plain-text version of the transferred data to the destination but will not maintain the link.

For parts that support linking, these are the actions that can occur:

- If the user moves the source or destination of a link within a document, OpenDoc preserves the link.

- If the user moves the source and destination of a link together, OpenDoc preserves the link. (However, if the move is to a different document, the link is broken for any other destinations of the moved source that remain in the original document.)

- If the user moves only the source or the destination of a link to a different document, OpenDoc breaks the link.

- When the user cuts content that includes the source or destination of a link, OpenDoc places the link content on the clipboard. If the user then pastes the content, OpenDoc attempts to reconnect the link. If the user chooses to embed or merge a lower-fidelity representation of the data, the links are lost.

- Copying the source of a link does not alter the source or its links; they remain unchanged. The new copy initially has no links from it. The user can subsequently create links from the new copy, but these are independent of the original source and its links.

- The user can copy to the clipboard a link destination or a link source/link destination pair, but not a link source. It makes no sense to have multiple sources for a link.

- Copying both the source and destination of a link creates an entirely new link between the copy of the source and the copy of the destination. This link has no relationship to the original source or destination or any of their links.

- The user can create multiple links to the same link source in two ways:

  - Copy the destination of a link to another location.
  - Copy the source of a link, and use the Paste As command (specifying Paste with Link) to create a destination at another location. Since the Paste As command gives the user control over the kind, embedding, and appearance of the new link at the new destination, the same link source may appear quite differently at the different destinations.

Supporting Scripting

You are strongly encouraged to provide support for scripting in your parts. Scripting allows customization of your part's user interface. It is likely that most users will experience scripting indirectly, by using documents created from stationery that contains scripts to provide extra functionality to the user. For example, a user might create a new medical form for a patient and be unaware that data validation is performed by a script.

Attaching Scripts

You can attach scripts either to your part as a whole or to some portion of its intrinsic content. Scripts might be attached to text fields, menu commands, buttons, checkboxes or radio buttons, pop-up menus, other controls, or even graphic objects or other content items.

Any part can have a script property associated with it, as an annotation to its storage unit. The script property contains a value whose type defines it as an OSA script. Through the script, the user or another part can customize the part's behavior.

Support provided by a part for its script might be implemented in different ways. For example, the editor for a button part might provide a user interface to edit the script. In contrast, a HyperCard-like container part might only support attaching existing scripts to embedded parts.

If a part editor supports attaching scripts to its intrinsic content, such scripts are stored within the part's content rather than as a separate script property. In that case, the user interface should be similar to that used for attaching scripts to embedded parts.

Script-Editing Interface

There can be different interfaces for editing a part's script. For example, a part editor may allow access to the script through a Settings dialog box accessed through the Part Info dialog box. In addition, it may implement a menu command that invokes a dialog box for editing the script. Some parts, such as buttons, do not have an active state and therefore cannot have a menu command. In this case, the Settings dialog box is the only recommended option.

Some part editors may support editing the scripts attached to their embedded parts. For example, a HyperCard-like container part might have menu commands that provide a user interface for editing the script in an embedded part's script property. The recommended keyboard equivalent for this command is Command-Option-click (as in HyperCard). You can, however, support other keyboard equivalents, such as Option–Double-click.

Dropping Scripts on a Part

You may wish to give your part the ability to accept scripts dropped onto it. For example, if the user drags an OSA script file onto a button part, the button's part editor should highlight the button appropriately to indicate that it can accept a drop. When the user releases the mouse button, the button part editor should copy the contents into the script property.

Drag and drop is intended only as an alternative method for attaching scripts. Therefore, you must also provide a primary mechanism that is easily discoverable, such as the use of a Settings dialog box.

Appendixes

Embedding Checklist

This appendix summarizes the capabilities that your part editor must have if it is to support embedding. If you want your parts to be container parts, you must implement these features in your code.

Keep in mind that handling embedded parts usually means handling embedded *frames;* in most cases, your part directly interacts only with the frames of the parts embedded in it. Those embedded frames in turn interact with the parts displayed in them, and the embedded parts interact with their own embedded frames, and so on, down through the embedding hierarchy.

This checklist is meant for quick reference only. The items in the list are discussed in greater detail elsewhere in this book.

Content Model and Storage

☐ Add embedding to your part's content model. Create a content element that you can track and manipulate to represent an embedded frame. You might create a proxy object that can represent a frame in both its stored and in-memory state.

☐ Maintain a list of the frames embedded in your part. Implement an iterator (a subclass of `ODEmbeddedFramesIterator`) to allow callers access to the frame objects in the list. Implement your part's `CreateEmbeddedFramesIterator` method, through which callers instantiate the class.

☐ When you write your part to storage, write persistent references to your embedded frames into your part's content stream. (Do not write them into a separate property.) When you read your part from storage, reconstruct your embedded frames from the stored persistent references in your content.

For efficiency, you can use lazy creation for this purpose. Create a frame object for each embedded frame only when you need to display it. Purge unneeded frames when requested.

Embedded-Frame Management

☐ You control the sizes and locations of your embedded frames. Support frame negotiation, if appropriate, in your `RequestFrameShape` method.

☐ Be prepared to receive requests for additional frames from an embedded part. Implement your `RequestEmbeddedFrame` method, and handle calls to it as appropriate for your content model.

If you add a requested frame, use the requested shape for both sizing and relative positioning of the frame, if your content model allows it. Normalize the frame shape that you return. Give the frame an appropriate group ID and sequence number.

If you grant requests for additional embedded frames, implement your part's `RemoveEmbeddedFrame` method so that embedded parts can have you delete those frames when they are no longer needed.

☐ If you create an embedded frame that displays the same content in the same presentation as another embedded frame, use `AttachSourceFrame` to have the embedded part attach the new frame to the original (source) frame, so that updates in one will be reflected in the other.

☐ When you no longer need an embedded frame, permanently remove it by removing all of its facets, setting its containing frame to null, and calling its `Release` or `Remove` method, as appropriate.

☐ Another part may request that you scroll your part's content to reveal an embedded frame. You may have to accomplish this by scrolling your own content, or by requesting that your containing part scroll its content. Implement your part's `RevealFrame` method to fulfill this request.

☐ Support undo of all embedded-frame manipulations.

Depending on your part's content model and features, you may also want to add support for these capabilities:

☐ If you support sequenced frames, use frame groups to define sets of sequentially ordered embedded frames. Assign sequence numbers so that the embedded part can know in what order to fill its frames with content.

☐ If your content model suggests that you should make any of your content properties (such as, for example, text font or style) available for adoption by embedded parts, implement your `AcquireContainingPartProperties` method so that embedded parts can call it. Likewise, call your embedded parts' `ContainingPartPropertiesUpdated` method whenever you change any of your adoptable content properties.

☐ Whether or not you support linking, implement your part's `LinkStatusChanged` method, so that you can call your embedded frames' `ChangeLinkStatus` methods and communicate changes in your own display frame's link status.

Drawing

☐ Define the initial view type (icon or frame) that embedded parts should have. By convention, most embedded parts should have frame view type.

☐ Create facets for all of your visible embedded frames. Add facets as frames become visible; remove facets or mark them as purgeable when frames are no longer visible.

☐ When a frame embedded in your part is the active frame, you need to clip whatever content the active frame border obscures, and you also need to clip the active frame border where your content obscures it. Implement your part's `AdjustBorderShape` method for this purpose.

☐ Support selection of your embedded frames. Highlight a selected embedded frame by drawing the selected frame border (and resize handles, if you support resizing of embedded frames) on the embedded frame's frame shape, not its used shape.

☐ When a range selection includes an embedded frame, give the embedded part's facet the highlight style the embedded part should adopt to be consistent with your highlighting model.

☐ When your part is displayed in thumbnail view type, you are responsible for integrating miniature representations of any visible embedded parts into the thumbnail.

Depending on your part's content model and features, you may also want to add support for these capabilities:

☐ If you support overlapping of embedded frames and intrinsic content, maintain the proper clip shapes for all of your embedded frames' facets. Maintain a z-ordered list of your embedded facets, and use it to account for overlaps with other embedded frames and with your part's content elements.

☐ If you wrap your content to the used shape of your embedded parts, implement your part's `UsedShapeChanged` method, so that embedded parts can notify you when that used shape changes.

- [ ] If you create offscreen canvases, implement your part's `CanvasUpdated` method so that you can transfer your embedded parts' asynchronous drawing to your parent canvas.

- [ ] If you support split-frame views of embedded parts, provide multiple facets for your embedded frames.

Event Handling

- [ ] Handle these events that occur within and on the borders of an embedded frame's facet: `kODEvtMouseDownEmbedded`, `kODEvtMouseUpEmbedded`, `kODEvtMouseDownBorder`, `kODEvtMouseUpBorder`, and `kODEvtBGMouseDownEmbedded`. Use these events to initiate a drag of the embedded frame, to select the embedded frame, or to activate your own part.

- [ ] Enable and respond to these items in the Document menu:

  - [ ] Open Selection: open a selected embedded frame into a window. (Also support double-clicking on a selected icon to open it.)

  - [ ] Insert: embed a user-chosen part into your part. Handle as described under "Data Transfer" in this checklist.

- [ ] Enable and respond to these items in the Edit menu:

  - [ ] Undo, Redo: include embedded frames in the actions that you save and restore.

  - [ ] Cut, Copy, Paste, Paste As: include embedded frames in the data you manipulate. Handle as described under "Data Transfer" in this checklist.

  - [ ] *Selection* Info: Display a selected embedded frame's Part Info dialog box.

Depending on your part's content model and features, you may also want to add support for these capabilities:

- [ ] If you want to receive events sent to an embedded frame that its part chooses not to handle, set the event-propagating flag of the frame when you create it.

- [ ] If you support resizing of embedded frames, use mouse-down events in resize handles of selected embedded frames to initiate resize operations.

Data Transfer

General

☐ Modify your basic routines for writing and reading data to account for embedded parts. This includes transfers involving the clipboard, the drag-and-drop object, link-source objects, link objects, other parts (as per the Insert command), and fulfilled promises.

   ☐ Do all reading and writing in the context of cloning. In addition to reading and writing intrinsic data, clone embedded frames (and other referenced objects) to or from the storage units involved.

   ☐ If you write a single embedded part, you should also write its frame as an annotation to the storage unit. If you read a single embedded part, use that annotated frame as the frame of the part you read.

   ☐ Modify your part's `CloneInto` method to add cloning of your part's embedded parts.

☐ Follow the conventions for receiving transferred data. Incorporate the data if your part editor can read it; otherwise, embed it as a separate part.

☐ Modify your handling of the Paste As dialog box: allow the user to select the Embed As button.

Cutting Data

☐ If you cut (or drag-move) data from your part that includes embedded frames, keep these cautions in mind:

   ☐ Don't assume that removing one embedded frame removes a part entirely; other frames of the part may still be embedded in your part.

   ☐ Be sure to set the containing frame of each removed frame to null, since it is no longer embedded in your part.

   ☐ Use your own display facet's embedded facet iterator to delete the facets of each frame that was removed.

   ☐ Be sure to remove or release, rather than delete, each cut frame object. To support undo, do that only when your part's `DisposeActionState` method is called.

Embedding Checklist

Linking

☐ Implement your part's `EditInLinkAttempted` method, so that embedded parts can notify you when the user attempts to edit their data when it is part of a link destination that you maintain.

☐ Call the `ChangeLinkStatus` method of any embedded frame that becomes part of, or ceases to be part of, a link source or destination that you maintain.

☐ Implement your part's `EmbeddedFrameUpdated` method, so that embedded frames can notify your part when their content has changed and your part can in turn update any link sources involving that embedded content.

For Scripting Support

☐ In your content model, create a content object that represents an embedded frame. Create an object accessor for embedded frames, if you want access to any custom information about your embedded frames. (OpenDoc provides a default accessor that can access an embedded frame or any of its standard user properties.)

☐ Write a semantic-event handler that can manipulate any of an embedded frame's properties that you define, such as its position or its selection state. (Semantic events involving standard user properties of the embedded frame's part will be passed to the part itself.)

☐ Implement your part's `EmbeddedFrameSpec` method, to create an object accessor for your embedded frame.

HI Checklist

This checklist contains questions about the OpenDoc human interface that you can ask yourself while reviewing the part-editor software you create. These questions will help bring to mind the particulars of the guidelines.

You must be able to answer every question "yes" to ensure conformity with the guidelines. However, to provide the most usable interface sometimes you need to make tradeoffs in your application. Remember to maintain the spirit of the guidelines when reviewing your product.

Splash Screen

☐ Do you automatically display a splash screen only once, either upon software installation or first software use?

☐ Is the splash screen unobtrusive, and does it disappear automatically (without user interaction)?

Icons

☐ Do all document, stationery, part-editor, and part-viewer icons conform to the standard shapes?

☐ Do you provide the following part icons?

    ☐ Large (32-by-32 pixels) in bit depths of 1 bit, 4 bit, and 8 bit?
    ☐ Small (16-by-16 pixels) in bit depths of 1 bit, 4 bit, and 8 bit?

☐ Do you provide the following stationery icons?

    ☐ Large (32-by-32 pixels) in bit depths of 1 bit, 4 bit, and 8 bit?
    ☐ Small (16-by-16 pixels) in bit depths of 1 bit, 4 bit, and 8 bit?

☐ Do you provide the following part-editor icons?

    ☐ Large (32-by-32 pixels) in bit depths of 1 bit, 4 bit, and 8 bit?
    ☐ Small (16-by-16 pixels) in bit depths of 1 bit, 4 bit, and 8 bit?

☐ If you provide a part viewer, do you provide the following part-viewer icons?

   ☐ Large (32-by-32 pixels) in bit depths of 1 bit, 4 bit, and 8 bit?

   ☐ Small (16-by-16 pixels) in bit depths of 1 bit, 4 bit, and 8 bit?

☐ Do thumbnail icons accurately represent the selected part's contents?

☐ Do all icons relate visually as an icon family?

Menus

Apple Menu

☐ Does the Apple menu start with a menu item that reads "About *Part Editor*" or "About *Part Viewer*"? Does this item display a dialog box containing information about the editor or viewer of the active part?

Document Menu

☐ Have you maintained the standard Document menu except to add items that apply to the active document?

☐ If enabled, does the Insert command display the standard file dialog box? If a user selects a document using that dialog box, is the content of that document embedded or incorporated into the active part? After the insert operation, is the inserted content selected correctly?

☐ Does the Page Setup command display a Page Setup dialog box?

☐ Does the Print command display a Print dialog box to print the frontmost window? Is Command-P the keyboard equivalent?

Edit Menu

☐ Have you maintained the standard Edit menu except to add items that involve changing part content?

☐ Does the Undo command reverse the effects of the last undoable user action and restore all parts to their states before that action? Is Command-Z the keyboard equivalent?

☐ Does the Redo command reverse the effects of the last undo action and restore all parts to their states before that undo? Is Command-R the keyboard equivalent?

☐ Does the Cut command remove the selection and place it on the Clipboard? Is Command-X the keyboard equivalent?

☐ Does the Copy command copy the selection to the Clipboard? Is Command-C the keyboard equivalent?

☐ Does the Paste command place the contents of the Clipboard at the insertion point? Is Command-V the keyboard equivalent?

☐ Does the Paste As command display the Paste As dialog box?

☐ Does the Clear command remove the selection? Does pressing the Delete (Backspace) or Clear key have the same effect?

☐ Does the Select All command select all the contents of the active part? Is Command-A the keyboard equivalent?

☐ Is the Part Info command enabled in the Edit menu when the user has selected part content? Does the Part Info command display the standard Part Info dialog box? Is Command-L the keyboard equivalent?

☐ Is the Link Info command displayed in the Edit menu instead of Part Info whenever the user selects a link? Does the Link Info command display the standard Link Source Info or Link Destination Info dialog box? Is Command-L the keyboard equivalent?

☐ Do you support the *ContentKind* Info command? Is the *ContentKind* Info command displayed in the Edit menu instead of Part Info or Link Info when the user selects content within a part other than a link? Does the *ContentKind* Info command display a *ContentKind* Info dialog box? Is Command-L the keyboard equivalent?

☐ Does the *Editor* Preferences command (or, if appropriate, *Viewer* Preferences) display a dialog box for controlling behavior of the editor (or viewer) of the active part?

☐ Does the View in Window command open the active part into a part window? Does double-clicking a part's icon also open it into a window? If the icon or active part is already opened into a window, does the View in Window command bring that window to the front?

☐ Does the Show Frame Outline command appear in the Edit menu only when a frame is opened into a window (through "View in Window") that is frontmost? Does the Show Frame Outline command display an outline of the frame in the window to show the portion of a part's contents that is visible in the frame? Can the user drag this outline to adjust the visible region of the part within the frame?

☐ Does the Hide Frame Outline command appear in the Edit menu instead of Show Frame Outline after a user has chosen Show Frame Outline? Does the Hide Frame Outline command remove the display of the outline of the frame in the part window?

View Menu

☐ If there is a View menu, does it appear to the right of the Edit menu? Does it contain only items that allow a user to manipulate the view of the selected frame or create new views?

Part Info Dialog Box

☐ Does the Part Info dialog box show that your part correctly supports the following properties?

    ☐ Category, stating the type of data in a part

    ☐ Kind, the data format of the part's contents

    ☐ Editor, a pointer to the editor being used to edit the part's contents

    ☐ Name, a text string identifying the part

Frames

Resizing Frames

☐ Can users resize a frame by selecting it and dragging any selection handle on the frame's border?

☐ Are selection handles 5-by-5 pixels?

☐ Do you provide cursor feedback when the user resizes a frame?

Sequenced Frames

☐ If your part supports sequenced frames, does all of the content in the frames appear in a part window when the user opens one of the sequenced frames?

Changing View Types

☐ When the user selects a part icon, chooses Frame from the View As pop-up menu in the Part Info dialog box, and clicks OK, does the part appear as content displayed in a frame?

☐ When a user selects a frame, chooses one of the icon representations from the View As pop-up menu in the Part Info dialog box, and clicks OK, does the part's frame change into an icon?

☐ If your part receives a message about the view type its containing part prefers it to have, do you draw your part accordingly?

Selections

Selecting a Part Viewed as a Frame

☐ Does an active part become selected after a user clicks on its border?

☐ Does a bundled, unselected part become selected after a user clicks anywhere within its frame?

☐ Does your active part display the specified selected frame border around embedded parts?

Selecting Multiple Parts

☐ Can users select multiple embedded parts within your active part by holding down the Shift key and clicking on multiple icons or frames? Does a click on an already selected part during this sequence remove the part from the selection?

☐ Can users select multiple embedded parts within an active part by holding down the Command key and clicking on multiple icons or frames? Does a click on an already selected part during this sequence remove the part from the selection?

☐ If your part supports dragging to select, can users select multiple parts within an active part by dragging across the parts? If the user drags across parts while holding down the Shift key, are previously selected parts removed from the selection and unselected parts added to the selection?

Scrolling Behavior

☐ When a user starts to make a selection in an embedded part partly obscured by the window border and extends the selection by moving the pointer outside the window in the direction of the obscured portion, does the window scroll to reveal the content? Does the window stop scrolling when the user moves the pointer back inside the frame or when the border of the embedded part's frame becomes visible?

☐ If you support scroll bars for your part, can users hide them to see the document as it will print?

☐ Does clicking in an enabled scroll bar in your part cause its content to scroll immediately?

Drag and Drop

☐ Can users drag a selected item after placing the cursor anywhere within the item (or on the item's border if the item is a part frame)?

☐ When a user selects an item and drags it to a new location *within* your document, does the item appear in the new location?

☐ When a user selects an item and drags it to another document, is the item copied into the document?

☐ When a user selects an item and drags it to the desktop, does a copy of the item, displayed as a large icon, appear on the desktop?

☐ When a user selects a part icon on the desktop and drags it into a document, do you make a copy of the item in the document?

☐ When a user drags your stationery icon into a destination whose preferred view type for embedded parts is frame, do you create a new part in the document?

☐ Does holding down the Control key during a drag operation force a move operation?

☐ Does holding down the Option key during a drag operation force a copy operation?

☐ If the user holds down the Command key while dragging part content or a part, do you display the Paste As dialog box, enabling the creation of a link?

☐ Do you correctly incorporate or embed content as a result of drag-and-drop operations?

Linking

☐ When the user chooses the Paste As dialog box, do you allow a link destination to be created in your part?

☐ When a user checks the Show Links checkbox in the Document Info dialog box and clicks OK, do your parts display link borders?

☐ When the user unchecks the Show Links checkbox in the Document Info dialog box and clicks OK, do you remove its link borders?

☐ Do you display the correct selected and nonselected link borders in your parts?

☐ When the user selects within a link in your part, do you display the link border around the linked content? If the user clicks outside of the link, do you remove the link border?

☐ When the user selects content that contains a link, do you display the link border?

☐ When the user clicks on the border of a link, do you select the link and remove any content selection?

☐ When the user clicks the Find Source button in the Link Destination Info dialog box, does the source of that link appear?

☐ Can users use the Cut and Paste menu items to move a link?

☐ Can users use the Copy and Paste menu items to copy a link?

☐ If the user tries to change the content of a link destination that will be destroyed when the destination receives an update from the link source, do you display an alert box to warn the user?

☐ When a user selects the Break Link button in either the Link Destination Info dialog box or the Link Source Info dialog box, do you remove the link?

☐ Do you delete links after a user selects the source and/or destination of a link and chooses the Cut menu item or presses the Delete (or Clear) key?

☐ Do you update an automatic link in the same document when the source content changes?

☐ Do you update a manual link when the user chooses Update Now in the Link Source Info dialog box?

☐ Do you update an automatic link in a different document when the source document is saved, when both source and destination specify automatic updating?

☐ Do you update a manual link when the user chooses Update Now in the Link Destination Info dialog box?

Installing OpenDoc Software and Parts

This appendix describes where on users' computer systems you should install the OpenDoc software that you create.

OpenDoc creates two folders on the user's hard disk. These are the Editors and Stationery folders. In general you should use the Installer software (available as a software developer's kit) to install all the pieces of OpenDoc software that you distribute, including stationery pads, part editors, part viewers, and online documentation. Installation software simplifies the installation task for users who choose to do a standard installation. It also helps users to focus on the document-centered aspect of OpenDoc because they don't have to deal with several pieces of software.

Install part editors and part viewers in the Editors folder, which can be either in the System Folder on the user's startup volume or on the root of any mounted volume. If you provide multiple editors or viewers, you can place them in your own part-editors folder within the Editors folder.

If you plan to distribute additional files with your part editor, such as extensions, create a separate folder in your part-editors folder in which to store these additional files. If you create shell plug-ins, install them in the OpenDoc Shell Plug-Ins folder within the Editors folder. Figure C-1 shows an example of the Editors folder structure for several installed part editors.

Localization of folder names
The names of the Editors folder, the OpenDoc folder, and the Stationery folder may be different on different localized systems, but their relative positions will not. Your installation procedures should not rely on these specific folder names. ◆

Figure C-1   Sample Editors folder structure

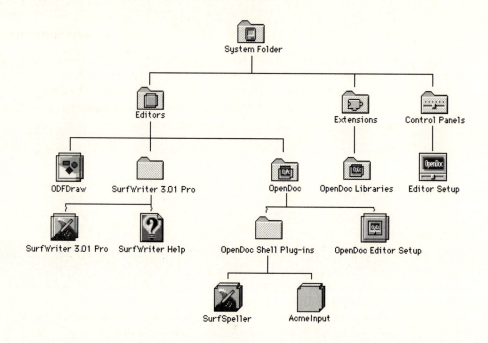

Install any stationery pads that you distribute with your part in your own
folder within the Stationery folder. Users can move the location of this folder or
store stationery documents elsewhere if they wish to do so. Figure C-2 shows
an example of the Stationery folder with stationery pads installed.

Figure C-2   Sample Stationery folder structure

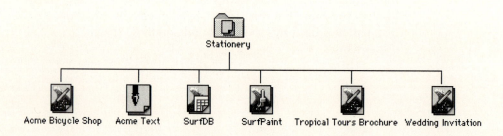

Installing OpenDoc Software and Parts

If you distribute any electronic documents, such as ReadMe files, that describe your parts, install them in the Stationery folder. When you place a document in your folder, you must choose a name that relates to your parts or part editors. For example, you could create a document with the name SurfWriter ReadMe.

OpenDoc creates a Documents folder either on the root level of the user's hard disk or on the desktop. Because users can store their documents anywhere, this folder is optional. It exists to encourage users to store the documents they create separately from the stationery and the part editors.

Glossary

abstract class A class used only to derive other classes. An abstract class is never instantiated. Compare **concrete class.**

action data Information stored in the undo object's action history that allows a part to reverse the effects of an undoable action.

action history The cumulative set of reversible actions available at any one time, maintained by the undo object.

action subhistory A subset of action data added to the undo object's action history by a part in a modal state. The part can then remove the subhistory from the action history without affecting earlier actions.

action type A constant that defines whether an undoable action is a single-stage action (such as a cut) or part of a multistage action (such as a drag-move).

activate (1) For a part, to acquire the selection focus; a part activates itself when a mouse-up event occurs within its frame. (2) For a Mac OS window, to bring it to the front.

active frame The frame that has the selection focus. Editing takes place in the active frame; it displays the selection or insertion point. The active frame usually has the keystroke and menu foci also.

active part The part displayed in the active frame. The active part controls the part-specific palettes and menus, and its content contains the selection or insertion point. The active part can be displayed in one or more frames, only one of which is the active frame.

active shape A shape that describes the portion of a facet within which a part expects to receive geometry-based user events. If, for example, an embedded part's used shape and active shape are identical, the containing part both draws and accepts events within the unused areas of the embedded part's frame.

ancestor See **superclass.**

annotation A property in a part's storage unit that is separate from the part's contents.

Apple event The platform-specific message that underlies a semantic event on the Mac OS platform.

Apple event handler See **semantic-event handler.**

Apple Event Manager The component of Mac OS system software that manages the construction, sending, and processing of Apple events.

application See **conventional application.**

Application menu A standard menu on the Mac OS platform through which the user can activate any of the currently open OpenDoc documents or conventional applications.

637

arbitrator   An OpenDoc object that manages negotiation among parts about ownership of **shared resources.** Examples of such resources are the menu focus, the selection focus, the keystroke focus, and the serial ports.

automatic updating   The updating of a link whenever the source content changes. Compare **manual updating.**

auxiliary storage unit   An extra storage unit that a part uses to store its contents. Compare **main storage unit.**

base class   See **superclass.**

base draft   The original draft of a document. Every OpenDoc document has a base draft, from which all subsequent drafts are ultimately derived. See also **current draft.**

base frame   An existing embedded frame, associated with a newly created embedded frame, that defines certain characteristics of the new frame.

base menu bar   The menu bar that contains the menus shared by all parts in a document. The document shell installs the base menu bar; parts copy it and add their own menus and items.

base object   The object whose interface is extended by an extension object.

beginning action   An action type that specifies the beginning of a multistage undo transaction. Compare **ending action.**

Bento   A compound-document storage technology that underlies OpenDoc storage on the Mac OS and some other platforms.

Bento container suite   A container suite for OpenDoc that is based on Bento.

bias transform   A transform that is applied to measurements in a part's coordinate system to change them into **platform-normal coordinates.**

binding   (1) The process of selecting an executable code module based on type information. (2) In SOM, a file that allows a compiler to match a method implementation with its declaration. Also called a header file.

border   See **frame border.**

bundled frame   A frame whose contents do not respond to user events. A mouse click within a bundled frame selects the frame's part but does not activate it.

CALib   See **container application library.**

canvas   The platform-specific drawing environment on which frames are laid out. Each window or printing device has one drawing canvas. See also **static canvas** and **dynamic canvas.**

canvas coordinate space   The coordinate space of the canvas upon which a part's content is drawn. It may or may not be equal to **window coordinate space.**

category   See **part category.**

CFM   See **Code Fragment Manager.**

child class   See **subclass.**

CI Labs   See **Component Integration Laboratories.**

circular link   A configuration of links in which changes to a link's destination indirectly affect its source.

class   A programming entity comprising data structures and methods, from which objects that are instances of the class are created.

class hierarchy   The structure by which classes are related through inheritance.

clean   Unchanged since last saved to persistent storage. Compare **dirty.**

clipboard   A system-maintained buffer that provides a facility for transferring data within and across documents.

clipboard focus   A designation of ownership of access to the clipboard. The part with the clipboard focus can read from and write to the clipboard.

clip shape   A shape that defines the limits of drawing within a facet.

clone   To copy an object and all its referenced objects. When you clone an object, that object plus all other objects to which there is a **strong persistent reference** in the cloned object are copied.

close   For a frame, to remove from memory but not from storage. A closed frame is not permanently removed from its document. Compare **remove.**

Code Fragment Manager (CFM)   On the Mac OS platform, the portion of system software that manages the runtime loading and dynamic linking of code modules.

coercion handler   In the Open Scripting Architecture, a function that converts data from one descriptor type into another.

command ID   A position-independent identifier for a menu command. See also **synthetic command ID.**

Common Object Request Broker Architecture (CORBA)   A standard promulgated by the Object Management Group industry consortium for defining interactions among objects.

component   A software product that functions in the OpenDoc environment. Part editors and part viewers are examples of OpenDoc components.

Component Integration Laboratories (CI Labs)   A consortium of platform and application vendors that oversees the development and distribution of OpenDoc technology.

compound document   A single document containing multiple heterogeneous data types, each presented and edited by its own software. A compound document is made up of **parts.**

concrete class   A class designed to be instantiated. Compare **abstract class.**

connect or **reconnect**   For a frame object, to reestablish its connection to the part its displays. Reconnecting a frame may involve recreating it from storage.

container   (1) A holder of persistent data (documents), part of an OpenDoc **container suite.** (2) See **container part, container application.**

container application   An application program that has been modified to support embedding of OpenDoc parts. A container application functions as both document shell and part editor for the root part. Same as **embedding application.**

container application library (CALib) A library that facilitates the creation of container applications.

container part A part that can embed other parts within its content. Compare **noncontainer part.** See also **container application.**

container property A visual or behavioral characteristic of a containing part, such as its text font, that it makes available for embedded parts to adopt. Embedded parts can adopt the container properties of their containing parts, thus giving a more uniform appearance to a set of parts. Compare **property, Info property.**

container suite A document storage architecture, built on top of a platform's native file system, that allows for the creation, storage, and retrieval of compound documents. A container suite is implemented as a set of OpenDoc classes: containers, documents, drafts, and storage units. See also **Bento.**

containing frame The display frame of an embedded frame's containing part. Each embedded frame has one containing frame; each containing frame has one or more embedded frames.

containing part A part in which a frame is embedded. Each embedded frame has one containing part; each containing part has one or more embedded frames.

content See **part content.**

content area The potentially visible area of a part as viewed in a frame or window. If the content area is greater than the area of the frame or window, only a portion of the part can be viewed at a time.

content coordinate space The coordinate space defined by applying the internal transform of a frame to a point in **frame coordinate space.**

content element A user-visible data item presented by a part's content model. Content elements can be manipulated through the graphic or scripting interface to a part.

content extent The vertical dimension of the content area of a part in a frame. Content extent is used to calculate **bias transforms.**

content model The specification of a part's contents (the data types of its content elements) and its content operations (the actions that can be performed on it and the interactions among its content elements).

content object A content element that can be represented as an object and thus accessed and manipulated through semantic events.

content operation A user action that manipulates a content element.

content storage unit The storage unit of a data-transfer object (clipboard, drag-and-drop, link-source, or link) that holds the data being transferred.

content transform The composite transform that converts from a part's content coordinates to its canvas coordinates.

content view type See **frame view type.**

context The outermost object in the object hierarchy defined by the direct parameter of an Apple event. It is the OpenDoc equivalent of the Apple event object model's default container.

conventional application   An application that directly handles events, opens documents, and takes full responsibility for manipulating, storing, and retrieving all of the data in its documents. Compare **component.**

coordinate bias   The difference between a given coordinate system and **platform-normal coordinates.** Coordinate bias typically involves both a change in axis polarity and an offset.

copy   A data-transfer operation in which the transferred data remains in its original source location while a copy of it is inserted at the destination. Compare **move.**

CORBA   See **Common Object Request Broker Architecture.**

Core suite   The set of Apple events that any scriptable part is expected to support on the Mac OS platform.

current draft   The most recent draft of an OpenDoc document. Only the current draft can be edited.

current frame   During drawing, the frame that is being drawn or within which editing is occurring.

customizable   A level of scripting support of a part. A customizable part defines content objects and operations for interface elements such as menus and buttons; it allows the user to change its behavior during virtually any user action. Compare **scriptable, recordable.**

default editor for category   A user-specified choice of part editor to use with parts whose **preferred editor** and **default editor for kind** are both not present.

default editor for kind   A user-specified choice of part editor to use with parts whose **preferred editor** is not present.

default object accessors   Object accessors provided by OpenDoc that can be used to resolve content objects or properties of parts that do not themselves support scripting. Default accessors can return tokens representing an embedded frame, a standard Info property of a part, or a context switch (swap token).

delegation   A relationship between objects in which the objects cooperate to perform a task but do not necessarily have related types or methods. Compare **inheritance.**

derived class   See **subclass.**

descendant   See **subclass.**

destination content   The content at the destination of a link. It is a copy of the **source content.**

destination part   For a link, the part that displays the information copied from the source of the link. Compare **source part.**

dirty   Changed since last saved to persistent storage. Compare **clean.**

dispatcher   The OpenDoc object that directs user events and semantic events to the correct part.

dispatch module   An OpenDoc object used by the dispatcher to dispatch events of a certain type to part editors.

display form   See **view type.**

display frame   A frame in which a part is displayed. A part's display frames are created by and embedded in its containing part. Compare **embedded frame**.

document   In OpenDoc, a user-organized collection of parts, all stored together.

document part   See **part**.

document process   A thread of execution that runs the document shell program. The document process provides the interface between the operating system and part editors: it accepts events from the operating system, provides the address space into which parts are read, and provides access to the window system and other features.

document shell   A shared library that provides an environment for all the parts in a document. The shell maintains the major document global structures: storage, window state, arbitrator, and dispatcher. This code also provides basic document behavior, such as document creation, opening, saving, printing, and closing. OpenDoc provides a document shell for each platform.

document window   A window that displays an OpenDoc document. The edges of the content area of the window represent the frame border of the document's root part. The OpenDoc document shell manages the opening and closing of document windows. Compare **part window**.

draft   A configuration of a document, defined at a certain point in time by the user. A document is made up of a set of drafts.

draft key   A number that identifies a specific cloning transaction.

draft permissions   A specification of the class of read/write access that a part editor has to a draft.

drag and drop   A facility of OpenDoc that allows users to move or copy data through direct manipulation.

drag-copy   A drag-and-drop operation in which the dragged data remains at the source, and a copy is inserted at the destination.

drag-move   A drag-and-drop operation in which the dragged data is deleted from the source and inserted at the destination.

drawing canvas   See **canvas**.

DSOM   Distributed System Object Model, a version of System Object Model (SOM) that works transparently over a network. See **system object model**.

dynamic canvas   A drawing canvas that can potentially be changed, such as a window that can be scrolled or paged to display different portions of a part's data. Compare **static canvas**.

edit-in-place   See **in-place editing**.

editor   See **part editor**.

editor ID   The SOM class ID of a part editor.

editor of last resort   The part editor that displays any part for which there is no available part editor on the system. The editor of last resort typically displays a gray rectangle representing the part's frame.

editor preferences   A dialog box, accessed through the Edit menu, in which the user can view and change preferences for the part editor of the currently active part.

embed   To display one part in a frame within another part. The embedded part retains its identity as a separate part from the containing part. Compare **incorporate.**

embedded content   Content displayed in an embedded frame. A containing part editor does not directly manipulate embedded content. Compare **intrinsic content.**

embedded frame   A frame that displays an embedded part. The embedded frame itself is considered intrinsic content of the containing part; the part displayed within the frame is not.

embedded-frames list   A containing part's private list of all the frames embedded in it.

embedded part   A part displayed in an embedded frame. The data for an embedded part is stored within the same draft as its containing part. An embedded part is copied during a duplication of its containing part. An embedded part may itself be a containing part, unless it is a **noncontainer** part.

embedding application   See **container application.**

embedding part   See **container part.**

ending action   An action type that specifies the completion of a multistage undo transaction. Compare **beginning action.**

environment parameter   A parameter used by all methods of System Object Model (SOM) objects to pass exceptions.

event   See **user event.** Compare **semantic event.**

event handler   (1) A routine that executes in response to receiving a user event. (2) See **semantic-event handler.**

event-info structure   A data structure that carries information about an OpenDoc user event in addition to that provided by the event structure.

event structure   A platform-specific data structure that carries information about an OpenDoc user event. On the Mac OS platform, it is a Mac OS event record.

exception   An execution error or abnormal condition detected by the runtime facilities of the system.

exclusive focus   A focus that can be owned by only one frame at a time. The selection focus, for example, is exclusive; the user can edit within only one frame at a time. Compare **nonexclusive focus.**

extension   An OpenDoc object that extends the programming interface of another OpenDoc object. Part editors, for example, can provide additional interfaces through extensions.

externalize   See **write.**

external transform   A transform that is applied to a facet to position, scale, or otherwise transform the facet and the image drawn within it. The external transform locates the facet in the coordinate space of its frame's containing part. Compare **internal transform.**

extracted draft   A draft that is extracted from a document into a new document.

facet   An object that describes where a frame is displayed on a canvas.

factoring   Separating the code that controls a part editor's user interface from the code that performs the part editor's basic functions. Factoring facilitates making parts **recordable.**

factory method   A method in one class that creates an instance of another class.

fidelity   The faithfulness of translation attained (or attainable) between data of different part kinds. For a given part kind, other part kinds are ranked in fidelity by the level at which their editors can translate its data without loss.

focus   A designation of ownership of a shared resource such as menus, selection, keystrokes, and serial ports. The part that owns a focus has use of that shared resource.

focus context   The scope of data access that results from focusing a storage unit. The focus context can be the entire storage unit, the entire contents of a particular property, or just a particular value of a particular property.

FocusLib   An OpenDoc utility library that helps a part to set up a QuickDraw graphics port properly for drawing.

focus module   An OpenDoc object used by the arbitrator to assign an owner or owners to a given focus type.

focus set   A group of foci requested as a unit.

frame   A bounded portion of the content area of a part, defining the location of an embedded part. The edge of a frame marks the boundary between intrinsic content and embedded content. A frame can be a rectangle or any other, even irregular, shape.

frame border   A visual indication of the boundary of a frame. The appearance of the frame border indicates the state of the frame (active, inactive, or selected). The frame border is drawn and manipulated by the containing part or by OpenDoc, not by the part within the frame.

frame coordinate space   The coordinate space in which a part's frame shape, used shape, active shape, and clip shape are defined. Compare **content coordinate space.** See also **window coordinate space, canvas coordinate space.**

frame group   A set of embedded frames that a containing part designates as related, for purposes such as flowing content in sequence from one frame to another. Each frame group has its own **group ID;** frames within a frame group have a **frame sequence.**

frame negotiation   The process of adjusting the size and shape of an embedded frame. Embedded parts can request changes to their frames, but the containing parts control the changes that occur.

frame sequence   The order of frames in a frame group.

frame shape   A shape that defines a frame and its border, expressed in terms of the frame's local coordinate space.

frame transform   The composite transform that converts from a part's frame coordinates to its canvas coordinates.

frame view type   A view type in which all or a portion of a part's content is displayed in a frame, the border of which is visible when the part is active or selected. Other possible view types for displaying a part include large icon, small icon, and thumbnail. Frame view type is sometimes called *content view type*.

fulfill   To replace a promise written to a data-transfer object with the actual data it represents.

fully scriptable   Characteristic of a scriptable part in which semantic events can invoke any action a user might be able to perform.

graphics system   A specific drawing architecture. Some graphics systems (such as Display PostScript) are available on more than one platform; some platforms support more than one graphics system (such as QuickDraw and QuickDraw GX on the Mac OS).

group ID   A number that identifies a frame group, assigned by the group's containing part.

Guide menu   A standard Mac OS menu through which the user can access Apple Guide or other kinds of help files.

Help menu   See **Guide menu.**

hot part   A part, such as a control, that performs an action (such as running a script) rather than activating itself when it receives a mouse click.

icon   A small, type-specific picture with a name. Three of the possible view types for a part consist of icons: **large icon, small icon,** and **thumbnail.**

identity transform   A transform that has no effect on points to which it is applied.

implementation binding   See **private header file.**

inactive frame   A frame that does not have the selection focus.

inactive part   A part that has no active display frames.

incorporate   To merge the data from one part into the contents of another part so that the merged data retains no separate identity as a part. Compare **embed.**

Info property   One of a set of user-accessible characteristics of a part or its frame. The user can modify some Info properties, such as the name of a part; the user cannot modify some other Info properties, such as part category. Most standard Info properties defined by OpenDoc are stored as distinct **properties** in the storage unit of the part or its frame. Part developers can assign additional, custom Info properties to their own parts or to embedded parts. Also compare **container property.**

inheritance   A relationship between classes wherein one class (the subclass) shares the type and methods of another class (the superclass).

in-limbo flag   A flag, maintained by every frame object, that specifies whether any part currently owns the frame.

in-place editing   User manipulation of data in an embedded part without leaving the context of the document in which the part is displayed—without, for example, opening a new window for the part.

inside-out activation   A mode of user interaction in which a mouse click anywhere in a document activates the smallest possible enclosing frame and performs the appropriate selection action on the content element at the click location. OpenDoc uses inside-out selection. Compare **outside-in activation.**

instance   See **object.**

instantiate   To create an object of a class in memory at runtime.

Interface Definition Language (IDL)   A syntax created by IBM to describe the interface of classes that can be compiled by the System Object Model (SOM) compiler.

internalize   See **read.**

internal transform   A transform that positions, scales, or otherwise transforms the image of a part drawn within a frame. Compare **external transform.**

interoperability   Access to an OpenDoc part or document from different platforms or with different software systems.

intrinsic content   The content elements native to a particular part, as opposed to the content of parts embedded within it. Compare **embedded content.**

invalidate   To mark an area of a canvas (or facet, or frame) as in need of redrawing.

invalid shape   The area of a frame, facet, or canvas that needs redrawing. Update events cause redrawing of the invalid area.

invariant   An aspect of the internal state of an object that must be maintained for the object to behave properly according to its design.

ISO string   A null-terminated 7-bit ASCII string.

iterator   A class or object that provides sequential access to a collection of objects of another class. A part's embedded-frames iterator, for example, provides access to all of the part's embedded frames.

keystroke focus   A designation of ownership of keystroke events. The part whose frame has the keystroke focus receives keystroke events. See also **selection focus.**

keystroke focus frame   The frame to which keystroke events are to be sent.

kind   See **part kind.**

large icon view type   A view type in which a part is represented by a 32-by-32-pixel bitmap image. Other possible view types for displaying a part include small icon, thumbnail, and frame.

layout   The process of arranging frames and content elements in a document for drawing.

lazy internalization   The process of creating objects (such as embedded frames) in memory only when they are needed for display, such as when the user scrolls them into view. Lazy internalization can help minimize the memory requirements of your parts.

leaf part   See **noncontainer part.**

link   (1) A persistent reference to a part or to a set of content elements of a part. (2) An OpenDoc object that represents a link destination.

link destination   The portion of a part's content area that represents the destination of a link.

link key   A number that identifies a specific transaction to access a link object or link-source object.

link manager   An OpenDoc object that coordinates cross-document links.

link source   The portion of a part's content area that represents the source of a link.

link specification   An object, placed on the clipboard or in a drag-and-drop object, from which the source part (the part that placed the data) can construct a link if necessary.

link status   The link-related state (in a link source, in a link destination, or not in a link) of a frame.

lock   To acquire exclusive access to. A part must lock a link source object or link object before accessing its data.

main storage unit   The storage unit that holds the contents property (`kODPropContents`) of a part. A part's main storage unit, plus possibly other **auxiliary storage units** referenced from it, holds all of a part's content.

manual updating   The updating of a link only on explicit request by the user. Compare **automatic updating.**

member function   See **method.**

message   See **semantic event.**

message interface   An OpenDoc object that provides an interface to allow parts to send messages (semantic events) to other parts, in the same document or in other documents.

method   An function that manipulates the data of a particular class of objects.

modal focus   A designation of ownership of the right to display modal dialog boxes. A part displaying a modal dialog box must first acquire the modal focus, so that other parts cannot do the same until the first part has finished.

monitor   A dispatch module that is installed in order to be notified of events, without necessarily dispatching them.

monolithic application   See **conventional application.**

monolithic part   See **noncontainer part.**

mouse region   An area (by default a size of 1 pixel square) within which the user can move the mouse pointer without triggering an event.

move   A data-transfer operation in which the transferred data is deleted from the source location and inserted at the destination. Compare **copy.**

name-mapping resource   A Mac OS resource, of type `'nmap'`, that contains information used for part binding.

name resolver   An OpenDoc object that determines the proper recipient of a semantic event. The name resolver can resolve **object specifiers,** permitting semantic events to be sent to individual objects within a part.

name space   An object consisting of a set of text strings used to identify kinds of objects or classes of behavior, for registration purposes. For example, OpenDoc uses name spaces to identify part kinds and categories for binding.

name-space manager   An OpenDoc object that creates and deletes name spaces.

noncontainer part   A part that cannot itself contain embedded parts. Compare **container part.**

nonembedding part   See **noncontainer part.**

nonexclusive focus   A focus that can be owned by more than one frame at a time. OpenDoc supports the use of nonexclusive foci. Compare **exclusive focus.**

nonpersistent frame   A frame that exists as an object in memory but has no storage unit and is not stored persistently.

normalize   For a frame shape, to strip relative-positioning information from it. The origin of a normalized shape is at (0, 0).

object   A programming entity, existing in memory at runtime, that is an individual specimen of a particular **class.**

object accessor   A function called by the name resolver to resolve semantic-event object specifiers.

object-callback function   A function called by the name resolver to allow your part to provide extra information needed for semantic-event object resolution.

Object Management Group (OMG)   An industry consortium that promulgates standards for object programming.

object model   A feature of Apple events that allows a part to define a hierarchical arrangement of content objects to represent the elements of the part's content.

object resolution   The process of converting object specifiers into tokens that represent objects manipulated by a part's semantic-event handlers.

object specifier   A designation of a content object within a part, used to determine the target of a semantic event. Object specifiers can be names ("blue rectangle") or logical designations ("word 1 of line 2 of embedded frame 3").

offscreen canvas   A canvas used for offscreen drawing.

OLE   Object Linking and Embedding, Microsoft Corporation's compound document architecture.

OLE interoperability   A technology that enables seamless interoperability between OpenDoc and Microsoft Corporation's Object Linking and Embedding (OLE) technology for interapplication communication. This technology allows OLE objects to function automatically as parts in OpenDoc documents, and OpenDoc parts to function automatically as OLE objects in OLE containers.

OpenDoc   A multiplatform technology, implemented as a set of shared libraries, that uses component software to facilitate the construction and sharing of compound documents.

OpenDoc Development Framework (ODF) A part-editor framework that facilitates creation of OpenDoc parts and permits simultaneous development for both the Mac OS and Windows platforms.

Open Scripting Architecture (OSA) An architecture of messages (semantic events) and handlers that allows users to control parts by means of scripts. Any scripting language that supports the OSA can be used with OpenDoc parts.

outside-in activation A mode of user interaction in which a mouse click anywhere in a document activates the largest possible enclosing frame that is not already active. Compare **inside-out activation.**

overlaid frame An embedded frame that floats above the content (including other embedded frames) of its containing part and thus need not engage in frame negotiation with the containing part.

override To replace a method belonging to a superclass with a method of the same name in a subclass, in order to modify its behavior.

owner For a canvas, the part that created the canvas and attached it to a facet. The owner is responsible for transferring the results of drawing on the canvas to its parent canvas.

parent canvas The canvas closest above a canvas in the facet hierarchy. If, for example, there is a single offscreen canvas attached to an embedded facet in a window, the window canvas (attached to the root facet) is the parent of the offscreen canvas.

parent class See **superclass.**

part A portion of a compound document; it consists of document content, plus—at runtime—a part editor that manipulates that content. The content is data of a given structure or type, such as text, graphics, or video; the code is a part editor. In programming terms, a part is an object, an instantiation of a subclass of the class `ODPart`. To a user, a part is a single set of information displayed and manipulated in one or more frames or windows. Same as **document part.**

part category A general classification of the format of data handled by a part editor. Categories are broad classes of data format, meaningful to end users, such as "text", "graphics", or "table". Compare **part kind.**

part content The portion of a part that describes its data. In programming terms, the part content is represented by the instance variables of the part object; it is the state of the part, the portion of it that is stored persistently. See also **intrinsic content, embedded content.** Compare **part editor, part.**

part editor An OpenDoc component that can display and change the data of a part. It is the executable code that provides the behavior for the part. Compare **part viewer.**

part ID An identifier that uniquely names a part within the context of a document. This ID represents a storage unit ID within a particular draft of a document.

part info (1) Part-specific data, of any type or size, used by a part editor to identify what should be displayed in a particular frame or facet and how it should be displayed. (2) User-visible information about a given part, displayed in the Part Info dialog box.

part kind   A specific classification of the format of data handled by a part editor. A kind specifies the specific data format handled by a part editor. Kinds are meaningful to end users, and have designations such as such as "MacWrite 2.0" or "QuickTime 1.0". Compare **part category.**

part viewer   A part editor that can display and print, but not change, the data of a part. Compare **part editor.**

part window   A window that displays an embedded part by itself, for easier viewing or editing. Any part that is embedded in another part can be opened in its own part window. The part window is separate from the **document window** displaying the entire document in which the part is embedded.

part-wrapper object   A private OpenDoc object that is used to reference a part.

persistence   The quality of an object that allows it to span separate document launches and be transported to different computers. For example, a part written to persistent storage is typically written to a hard disk.

persistent object   An object (of a subclass of `ODPersistentObject`) whose data can be stored persistently.

persistent object ID   A persistent identifying value for a part or frame, used only for script access.

persistent reference   A number, stored somewhere within a storage unit, that refers to another storage unit in the same document. Persistent references permit complex runtime object relationships to be stored externally, and later reconstructed.

platform   A hardware/software operating environment. For example, OpenDoc is implemented on the Mac OS, Windows, and OS/2 platforms.

platform-normal coordinates   The native coordinate system for a particular platform. OpenDoc performs all layout and drawing in platform-normal coordinates; to convert from another coordinate system to platform-normal coordinates requires application of a **bias transform.**

plug-in   See **shell plug-in.**

position code   A parameter (to a storage unit's `Focus` method) with which you specify the desired property or value to access.

predispatch handler   In the Open Scripting Architecture, a function that has the opportunity to handle any semantic event sent to a document, before the event is dispatched to its target part.

Preferences dialog box   A dialog box that displays information specific to a particular part editor.

preferred editor   The part editor that last edited a part, or for whom the part's data was just translated. If a part's preferred editor is not present, OpenDoc attempts to bind the part to the user's **default editor for kind** or **default editor for category.**

preferred kind   The part kind that a part specifies as its highest-fidelity, preferred format for editing. It is the part kind stored as the first value in the contents property of the part's storage unit, unless the storage unit also contains a property of type `kODPropPreferredKind` specifying another value as the preferred kind.

presentation   A particular style of display for a part's contents—for example, outline or expanded for text, or wireframe or solid for graphic objects. A part can have multiple presentations, each with its own rendering, layout, and user-interface behavior. Compare **view type.**

private header file   A generated file containing macros that provide access to instance variables and invoke superclass methods of a System Object Model (SOM) class.

promise   A specification of data to be transferred at a future time. If a data transfer involves a very large amount of data, the source part can choose to write a promise instead of actually writing the data to a storage unit.

property   In the OpenDoc storage system, an element of a storage unit. A property defines a kind of information (such as "name" or "contents") and contains one or more data streams, called **values,** that consist of information of that kind. Properties in a stored part are accessible without the assistance of a part editor. Compare **container property, Info property.**

property name   An ISO string that identifies a particular property in a storage unit. Compare **value type.**

protocol   The programming interface through which a specific task or set of related tasks is performed. The drag-and-drop protocol, for example, is the set of calls that a part editor makes (and responds to) to support the dragging of items into or out of its content.

proxy content   Data, associated with a single embedded frame written to the clipboard (or drag-and-drop object or link-source object), that the frame's original containing part wanted associated with the frame, such as a drop shadow or other visual adornment. Proxy content is absent if intrinsic content as well as an embedded frame was written.

public header file   A generated file containing the client interface of a System Object Model (SOM) class.

purge   To free noncritical memory, usually by writing or releasing cached data. In low-memory situations, OpenDoc can ask a part editor or other objects to purge memory.

read   For a part or other OpenDoc object, to transform its persistent form in a storage unit into an appropriate in-memory representation. Same as **internalize;** compare **write.**

recordable   A level of scripting support of a part. A recordable part allows the user to automatically convert user actions into scripts attached to the part. Compare **scriptable, customizable.**

recursive link   A configuration of links contained within links, in which changes to a link's destination directly affect its source.

reference   A pointer to (or other representation of) an object, used to gain access to the object when needed.

reference count   The number of references to an object. Objects that are reference-counted, such as windows and parts, cannot be deleted from memory unless their reference counts are zero.

reference-counted object   An object that maintains a reference count. All classes descended from `ODRefCntObject` are reference-counted.

release   To delete a reference to an object. For a reference-counted object, releasing it decrements its reference count.

remove   To delete an object (such as a frame) permanently from its draft, as well as from memory. Compare **close.**

resolve   See **object resolution.**

revert   To return a draft to the state it had just after its last save.

root facet   The facet that displays the root frame in a document window.

root frame   The frame in which the root part of a window is displayed. The root frame shape is the same as the content area of the window.

root part   The part that forms the base of a document and establishes its basic editing, embedding, and printing behavior. A document has only one root part, which can contain content elements and perhaps other, embedded parts. Any part can be a root part.

root storage unit   See **content storage unit.**

root window   See **document window.**

save   To write all the data of all parts of a document (draft) to persistent storage.

scope   The range of a cloning operation, limiting which objects are to be copied. Scope is expressed in terms of a frame object or its storage unit.

script   A sequence of written instructions that, when executed by a script interpreter, are converted to semantic events that manipulate parts.

scriptable   A level of scripting support of a part. A scriptable part is able to accept semantic events for its publicly published content objects and operations. Compare **customizable, recordable.**

select   To designate as the locus of subsequent editing operations. If the user selects an embedded part, that part's frame border takes on an appearance that designates it as selected. The embedded part itself is not activated at this stage.

selection focus   A designation of ownership of editing activity. The part whose frame has the selection focus is the active part and has the selection or insertion point. See also **keystroke focus.**

semantic event   A message sent to a part or one of its content elements. Semantic events pertain directly to the part's content model and can have meaning independent of the part's display context. For example, semantic events could direct a part to get, set, or delete data. Compare **user event.** See also **Open Scripting Architecture.**

semantic-event handler   A routine that executes in response to receiving a specific semantic event.

semantic interface   A set of OpenDoc objects that provides an interface to allow parts to receive messages (semantic events) from other parts, in the same document or in other documents.

sequence number   A number that defines the position of a frame in its **frame group.**

service   An OpenDoc component that, unlike a part editor, is not primarily concerned with editing and displaying parts. Instead, it provides a service to parts or documents, using the OpenDoc extension mechanism. Spelling checkers or database-access tools, for example, can be implemented as services.

Settings dialog box   A dialog box, accessible through the Part Info dialog box, that displays part-specific, custom Info properties.

settings extension   An OpenDoc extension class that you can use to implement a Settings dialog box.

shape   A description of a geometric area of a drawing canvas.

shared resource   A facility used by multiple parts. Examples of shared resources are the menu bar, keystrokes, serial ports, and selection focus. See also **arbitrator.**

shell plug-in   A shared library that modifies or extends the functions of the document shell.

sibling   A frame or facet at the same level of embedding as another frame or facet within the same containing frame or facet. Sibling frames and facets are **z-ordered** to allow for overlapping.

signature   (1) A Mac OS resource defined by a four-character sequence (such as `'odtm'`) that identifies an application to the Finder. (2) The aspect of a method defined by its return type and parameter list.

small icon view type   A view type in which a part is represented by a 16-by-16-pixel bitmap image. Other possible view types for displaying a part include large icon, thumbnail, and frame.

SOM   See **System Object Model.**

SOM class ID   An ISO string of a particular format that identifies a System Object Model (SOM) object, such as a part editor.

SOM object   An object or class created according to the System Object Model.

source content   The content at the source of a link. It is copied into the link and then into the **destination content.**

source frame   (1) An embedded frame whose part has been opened up into its own **part window.** (2) The frame to which other **synchronized frames** are attached.

source part   (1) In data transfer, the part that provides the data that is transferred. (2) For a link, the part that contains the original information that is copied and displayed at the destination of the link. Compare **destination part.**

split-frame view   A display technique for windows or frames, in which two or more facets of a frame display different scrolled portions of a part's content.

static canvas   A drawing canvas that cannot be changed once it has been rendered, such as a printer page. Compare **dynamic canvas.**

stationery   A part that opens by copying itself and opening the copy into a window, leaving the original stationery part unchanged.

storage system   The OpenDoc mechanism for providing persistent storage for documents and parts. The storage system object must provide unique identifiers for parts as well as cross-document links. It stores parts as a set of standard properties plus type-specific content data.

storage unit   In the OpenDoc storage system, an object that represents the basic unit of persistent storage. Each storage unit has a list of properties, and each property contains one or more data streams called values.

storage-unit cursor   A preset storage unit/ property/value designation, created to allow swift focusing on frequently accessed data.

storage-unit ID   A unique runtime identifier of a storage unit within a draft.

storage-unit view   A storage unit prefocused on a given property and value. A storage-unit view provides thread-safe access to a storage unit.

strong persistent reference   A persistent reference that, when the storage unit containing the reference is cloned, causes the referenced storage unit to be copied also. Compare **weak persistent reference.**

subclass   A class derived from another class (its **superclass**), from which it inherits type and behavior. Also called *derived class* or *descendant*.

subframe   A frame that is both an embedded frame in, and a display frame of, a part. A part can create an embedded frame, make it a subframe of its own display frame, and then display itself in that subframe.

subject attribute   An object specifier, attached to a semantic event, that refers to the target part by its persistent object ID.

subsystem   A broad subdivision of the interface and capabilities of OpenDoc, divided along shared-library boundaries. The OpenDoc subsystems include shell, storage, layout, imaging, user events, and semantic events. Individual OpenDoc subsystems are replaceable.

superclass   A class from which another class (its **subclass**) is derived. Also called *ancestor, base class,* or *parent class.* See also **inheritance.**

swap token   A special Apple event token that signals OpenDoc of an object accessor's failure furnish a required token. Passing a swap token causes a switch in the **context** of object resolution.

synchronized frames   Separate frames that display the same representation of the same part, and should therefore be updated together. In general, if an embedded part has two or more editable display frames of the same presentation, those frames (and all their embedded frames) should be synchronized.

synthetic command ID   A command ID created by OpenDoc for a menu command that had not previously been registered with the menu bar object.

System Object Model (SOM)   A technology from International Business Machines, Inc., that provides language- and platform-independent means of defining programmatic objects and handling method dispatching dynamically at runtime.

terminology resource   A Mac OS resource (of type `'aete'`) that is required for scriptability.

thread-safe   Said of an activity, or access to data, that can be safely undertaken in a multitasking environment.

thumbnail view type   A view type in which a part is represented by a large (64-by-64 pixels) bitmap image that is typically a miniature representation of the layout of the part content. Other possible view types for displaying a part include large icon, small icon, and frame.

token   (1) A short, codified representation of a string. The session object creates tokens for ISO strings. (2) In Apple events for OpenDoc, a special descriptor structure that a part uses to identify one or more content objects within itself.

transform   A geometric transformation that can be applied to a graphic object when it is rendered, such as moving, scaling, or rotation. Different platforms and different graphics systems have transforms with different capabilities.

translation   The conversion of one type of data to another type of data. Specifically, the conversion of data of one part kind to data of another part kind. The translation object is an OpenDoc wrapper for platform-specific translation capabilities. Note that translation can involve loss of **fidelity.**

translator   A software utility, independent of OpenDoc, that converts data from one format to another. A translator may, for example, convert text in the format used by one word processor into a format readable by a different one. The translation capability of OpenDoc relies on the availability of translators.

undo   To rescind a command, negating its results. The undo object holds command history information to support the undo capability of OpenDoc.

update ID   (1) A number used to identify a particular instance of clipboard contents. (2) A number used to identify a particular instance of link-source data.

usage binding   See **public header file.**

used shape   A shape that describes the portion of a frame that a part actually uses for drawing; that is, the part of the frame that the containing part should not draw over.

user event   A message, sent to a part by the dispatcher, that pertains only to the state of the part's user interface, not directly to its contents. User events include mouse clicks and keystrokes; they deliver information about window locations, scroll-bar positions, editing actions, and the like. Compare **semantic event.**

user-interface part　A part without content elements, representing a unit of a document's user interface. Buttons and dialog boxes, for example, can be user-interface parts.

validate　To mark a portion of a canvas (or facet, or frame) as no longer in need of redrawing. Compare **invalidate.**

value　In the OpenDoc storage system, a data stream associated with a property in a storage unit. Each property has a set of values, and there can be only one value of a given data type for each property.

value type　An ISO string that specifies the format of a particular value in a property. Compare **property name.**

viewer　See **part viewer.**

view type　The basic visual representation of a part. Supported view types are large icon, small icon, thumbnail, and frame.

weak persistent reference　A persistent reference that, when the storage unit containing the reference is cloned, is ignored; the referenced storage unit is not copied. Compare **strong persistent reference.**

window　An area of a computer display in which information is presented to users in a graphic user interface. Windows typically contain one or more content areas and controls, such as scroll bars, that allow the user to manipulate the display. Window systems are platform-specific.

window canvas　The canvas attached to the root facet of a window. Every window has a window canvas.

window-content transform　The composite transform that converts from a part's content coordinates to its window coordinates.

window coordinate space　The coordinate space of the window in which a part's content is drawn. It may or may not be equal to **canvas coordinate space.**

window-frame transform　The composite transform that converts from a part's frame coordinates to its window coordinates.

window state　An object that lists the set of windows that are open at a given time. Part editors can alter the window state, and the window state can be persistently stored.

wrapper　An object (or class) that exists to provide an object-oriented interface to a non-object-oriented or system-specific structure. The OpenDoc class `ODWindow`, for example, is a wrapper for a system-specific window structure.

write　For a part or other OpenDoc object, to transform its in-memory representation into a persistent form in a storage unit. Same as **externalize;** compare **read.**

z-ordering　The front-to-back ordering of sibling frames used to determine clipping and event handling when frames overlap.

Index

A

AbortClone method 325
AbortCurrentTransaction method 265
AbortRelinquishFocus method (ODPart) 91, 210, 211, 447
About *Editor* (menu command) 538, 557–558
abstract superclasses 81
AcquireActiveShape method 150
AcquireAggregateClipShape method 163
AcquireBaseDraft method 249, 292, 464
AcquireClipShape method 151
AcquireContainer method 249, 464
AcquireContainingFrame method 395
AcquireContainingPartProperties method (ODPart) 90, 115, 128
AcquireContentTransform method 141, 163, 169
AcquireDocument method 292, 464
AcquireDraft method 249, 464
AcquireDraftProperties method 249
AcquireExtension method 92, 442, 464
 for scripting 433, 465
AcquireFocusOwner method 447
AcquireFrame method 464
 for data transfer 346, 350
 for embedded frames 303
 in lazy internalization 471
 when embedding 305
AcquireFrameShape method 148
AcquireFrameTransform method 141, 169
AcquireInternalTransform method 145
AcquireLink method 383, 385, 464
 when reading linked data 392, 393
AcquireLinkSource method 392, 393, 464
Acquire method 91, 467
AcquirePart method 248, 295, 305, 350
 as a factory method 465
AcquirePersistentObject method 420

AcquireStorageUnit method 301, 465
AcquireUsedShape method 111, 149
Acquire versus *Get* methods 468
AcquireWindowAggregateClipShape method 171
AcquireWindowContentTransform method 141, 171
AcquireWindowFrameTransform method 141, 171
AcquireWindow method
 when handling a dialog box 237, 238
 when opening a window 231, 259
 and window ID 228
acquiring foci. *See* focus, RequestFocus, RequestFocusSet
action data 262
ActionDone method 357, 358, 360, 361
action history 260, 262–264, 265
ActionRedone method 359
action subhistory 264
action types 263
ActionUndone method 358
activate events 195
ActivateFrontWindows method 236
activation
 See also focus
 and drag and drop 600–602
 inside-out vs. outside-in 57, 559
 of parts 54–58, 198–207, 213–214, 559–561
 and scroll bars 535
 of windows 205–207, 214, 561–562
activation protocol 87
active frame border
 adjusting 152, 155–157
 defined 48
 illustrated 55, 524–525
 and root part 559
 suppressing 157
active part 48, 54, 56, 150

657

B

F

H

`HandleEvent` method (`ODPart`) 91, 192, 197, 234, 356
handles. *See* resize handles
`HasExtension` method 92, 433, 442
`HasMatrix` method 449
`HasNameSpace` method 465
`HasPlatformPrintJob` method 184
Help menu. *See* Guide menu
Help. *See* Apple Guide
Hide Frame Outline (menu command) 549
`Hide` method 233, 241
`HighlightChanged` method (`ODPart`) 90, 161
highlighting. *See* selections
hit-testing 142, 215–216
Home key (on keyboard) 194
hot parts 168, 571

I, J

icons 513–522
    in alert boxes 520
    large 513–514
    for part editors 519, 520
    for parts 513–518
    for part viewers 520–521
    selected appearance of 521–522
    small 515
    stationery 517–518
    thumbnail 515–517
idle time 196
IDL. *See* Interface Definition Language
imaging 494–495
    See also drawing; layout; printing
imaging protocol 87
implemented classes 81–82
inactive frame appearance 525–526
inactive part 55, 56
incorporating
    guidelines for 593
    and translation 593
    vs. embedding 43–44, 336, 592

`IncrementRefCount` method 469
Info dialog box (part-specific) 258
Info object 82, 255, 444, 490
Info properties 255, 291–292, 444
`InitDispatchModule` method 446
`InitExtension` method 443
`InitFocusModule` method 447
initialization. *See* `InitPart` method;
        `InitPartFromStorage` method; reading
        a part
`InitPartFromStorage` method (`ODPart`) 91,
        295–297, 392–393, 461
`InitPart` method (`ODPart`) 91, 294–295, 461
`InitPersistentObject` method 295, 296
in-limbo flag 265–266
inline input 221–222
in-place editing 51
Insert (menu command) 249, 541, 594–595
insertion point 594
`InsertValue` method 277
inside-out activation 57, 559
installation 633–635
    localized folder names and 633
`InstallCoercionHandler` utility method 406,
        434
`InstallCountProc` utility method 434
`InstallEventHandler` utility method 406, 434
`InstallMarkProc` utility method 434
`InstallObjectAccessor` utility method 406,
        434
`InstallSpecialHandler` utility method 406,
        434
interchange. *See* data transfer
Interface Definition Language (IDL) 75, 83–85
    and C++ 84–85
    directional attributes in 84
internalization 293
internal transform 495
    coordinate conversion with 137
    defined 48
    for scrolling 144–146
international strings 478–479
international text handling 221–222
intrinsic content 41
`InvalidateFacetUnderMouse` method 220

`Resolve` method 407, 408
  as Apple Event Manager replacement 406
  called by message interface 422, 425
  called by semantic-event handlers 424
resolving object specifiers 411, 424–430
`returnID` parameter (Apple events) 406
`RevealFrame` method (`ODPart`) 90, 395
`RevealLink` method (`ODPart`) 91, 394–395
reverting (a draft) 502, 505
Revert to Saved (menu command) 505, 541
root facet 227, 492
root frame 227, 492
root part 39, 154, 492
root window 227
runtime object relationships 487–499
runtime process model 458–459

S

Save a Copy (menu command) 505, 541
Save a Copy dialog box
  Kind pop-up menu in 558
Save Changes alert box 589
Save *Document* (menu command) 505, 541
scaling content 569
scope (for cloning) 325–327
scriptability levels
  customizable 413
  recordable 412
  scriptable 411–412
scripting 68–69, 403–438, 499
  classes related to 82, 414–416
  and recording 433
  systems for 409
scroll bars
  and activation 535
  in embedded frames 168–170, 217–218, 535
  in windows 535
scrolling
  automatic 578–579
  of embedded-part contents 165–166
  event handling and 216–218, 535
  to insertion point when pasting 583

and internal transform 144–145
and scroll-bar placement 168–170
with scroll bars in a separate frame 170, 218
with scroll bars inside your frame 168–169, 217–218
of window contents 164–165
scrolling focus 208
Select All (menu command) 254, 546, 587
selected frame border 55, 526–527
selected link border 611–613
selected part 55, 148
selection focus 54, 208
selection handles 527, 568–571
Selection Info (menu command) 254–258, 546, 607
  disabling 255, 258
selections 54–58, 218–219, 562–572
  background 522
  clearing 568
  click-selectable content 200
  extending
    contiguously 567
    discontiguously 567–568
  of hot parts 571
  of icons 521–522
  of links 611–613
  multiple 565–568, 570–571
  and part activation 562
  range 564–565
  in sequenced frames 586–588
  user actions to create 563, 571
`Select` method 228
semantic-event handlers 422–423, 434
  system-level 434
semantic events 68, 404, 499
  See also Apple events
  classes for 82, 414–416
  and document shell 503
  sending 69, 435–438
semantic-events protocol 89
semantic interface 404, 421–435
  default 413–421
  of the document shell 414, 491
  installing 433–435
semantic interface object 80, 500
SemtIntf utility library 417

W, X, Y,

Z

This Apple manual was written, edited, and composed on a desktop publishing system using Apple Macintosh computers and FrameMaker software. Proof pages were created on an Apple LaserWriter Pro printer. Final page negatives were output directly from text files on an AGFA Large Format Imagesetter. Line art was created using Adobe™ Illustrator and Adobe Photoshop. PostScript™, the page-description language for the LaserWriter, was developed by Adobe Systems Incorporated.

Text type is Palatino® and display type is Helvetica®. Bullets are ITC Zapf Dingbats®. Some elements, such as program listings, are set in Adobe Letter Gothic.

WRITERS
David C. Bice, Lori E. Kaplan

DEVELOPMENTAL EDITOR
Antonio Padial

ILLUSTRATORS
Deb Dennis, Sandee Karr, Ruth Anderson, Bruce Lee

PRODUCTION EDITOR
Lorraine Findlay

LEAD WRITER
Dave Bice

Special thanks to OpenDoc recipe writers Jens Alfke, Craig Carper, Tantek Çelik, Caia Grisar, Vincent Lo, Nick Pilch, Richard Rodseth, Joshua Susser

Special thanks to human-interface designers Dave Curbow, Elizabeth Dykstra-Erickson, Kerry Ortega, Geoff Schuller

Special thanks also to Trish Eastman, Eric House, Beverly McGuire, Donald Olson, Kurt Piersol, Jon Pugh, Steve Smith

Acknowledgments to David Austin, Sue Bartalo, Kristin Bauersfeld, Jeanne Bradford, Gina Centoni, Ray Chiang, Sue Dumont, Mike Halpin, Barb Koslowski, Michael Mazour, David McCusker, Mark Minshull, Carli Scott, Eric Soldan, Alan Spragens, Dave Stafford, Mark Stern, Denise Stone, Borek Vokach-Brodsky, Thomas Weisbach

OPENDOC CLASS REFERENCE CD TEAM
Bill Harris, Liz Hujsak, Stan Kelly-Bootle, Wendy Krafft, Dan Peterson, Carli Scott, Alexandra Solinski, Alan Spragens, Denise Stone